Mathematics and Programming for Machine Learning with R

Mathematics and Programming for Machine Learning with R
From the Ground Up

William B. Claster

CRC Press
Taylor & Francis Group
Boca Raton London New York

CRC Press is an imprint of the
Taylor & Francis Group, an **informa** business

First edition published 2020
by CRC Press
6000 Broken Sound Parkway NW, Suite 300, Boca Raton, FL 33487-2742

and by CRC Press
2 Park Square, Milton Park, Abingdon, Oxon, OX14 4RN

ISBN: 978-0-367-50785-5 (pbk)
ISBN: 978-0-367-56194-9 (hbk)
ISBN: 978-1-003-05122-0 (ebk)

Typeset in Garamond
by codeMantra

This book is dedicated to my wife Shizuyo

Contents

List of Figures

List of Tables

Preface

This text came about as a compilation of various data science courses that I have taught over the past 10 years in Japan at Ritsumeikan Asia Pacific University. My students wished for a deeper look at how machine learning algorithms do their magic and how they can be implemented in code.

I teach an introductory data science course where students learn how to use data for classification and prediction. Students learn how to evaluate model performance and study pitfalls and strategies in the application of data science. We also study 6–8 algorithms in detail. However, learning the logic of an algorithm is far different than learning to code it. In this text we study the full implementation of important algorithms and thereby provide a complete understanding of algorithm logic and at the same time realize significant improvement in coding skill.

The text provides a novice programmer with step-by-step skills to understand and implement algorithms, beginning with simple implementations and fundamental computer concepts of logic, sets, and probability, then moving to powerful deep learning algorithms.

The text is provided as a complement to an introductory data science course and is meant to give the reader thorough understanding of the underlying logic of machine learning algorithms, how they are implemented, and even how they can be improved. Additionally, whether the reader is a business analyst, an engineer, or a programmer, after completing this text, the reader should feel confident in their ability to live in the world of data and converse with data scientists with a sense of assurance.

Prerequisites

The book is divided into two parts. The first eight chapters deal with probability-based machine learning algorithms. The last eight chapters deal with machine learning based on artificial neural networks. The first half of the book does not assume much in the way of mathematical sophistication, although it would be best if one has taken a course in probability and statistics. The second half assumes the reader has taken at least one semester of calculus.

Programming Skill

The book takes readers who are novices in programming with R and provides them with many real applications to test their ability to code. Upon completion, the reader will be confident in their ability to program in R and in their ability to tackle advanced R programming problems.

Practice Problems

Interspersed throughout the text are over 400 practice problems that seek to provide the reader with a more complete understanding of the material. Some of these problems provide review of material already covered, however some of the problems ask the reader to consider issues that will be covered after the problem. The point there is to attune the reader to the upcoming concept prior to reading about it.

Highlights

- Geared towards readers with a minimal amount of preparation but who aim to gain deep knowledge of R programming and machine learning.
- Over 400 exercises.
- Throughout the text, strong emphasis is placed on improving the programming skills of the reader and guiding the novice to implement full-fledged algorithms.
- The audience includes general readers, academics and researchers, graduate students, and professionals as well as university students who desire a deep understanding of the field of machine learning from the inside out.
- Beginning with fundamental computer concepts of logic, sets, and probability, the text covers these for their intrinsic value and additionally employs them as a corpus of material for improving programming skills.
- The text fills a gap in the current literature inasmuch as there are few, if any, books in R that explain in clear terms what an algorithm is in such a way that leaves the reader with a complete understanding of the mechanisms that underlie a machine learning algorithm.
- As a course, this material is a complement to a more general course on applications of algorithms (the typical first course in data science business and engineering environments). This material is used in the second course in data science providing the mathematics, computer science concepts, and programming skills to understand and fully implement machine learning algorithms from the ground up.
- Website for text at www.williamclaster.com

Acknowledgments

I am so grateful to the late Philip Sallis for his guidance, support, and friendship over the past 15 years. Without his guidance, suggestions, and generosity of spirit, this text would never have been written. I would also like to thank Monte Cassim who had the wisdom and foresight to support data science as far back as 2007 as President at Ritsumeikan Asia Pacific University. President Cassim was and is a visionary thinker and continues to push for innovation in education in Japan. I am also most grateful to Dr. Nader Ghotbi for his knowledge, support, and insights into the research we jointly pursued in this field.

In addition I would like to thank the following for their invaluable assistance in reviewing this work: Luo Xingjian, Trang Hoang Minh, Jonas Yong Siaw, and Nguyen Thi Tri An.

Author

William B. Claster is a professor of mathematics and data science at Ritsumeikan Asia Pacific University in Japan. He has been involved in data science research since 2007. He conducted pioneering research in text-mining medical records from Nagasaki Hospital in 2008. In 2011, he trained machine learning algorithms on social media to extract real-time knowledge of political unrest in Asia. Subsequently he developed methods for understanding consumer behavior in hospitality and wine consumption. The work was further advanced to produce real time dashboards for understanding sentiment on any given topic. In 2013, he collaborated with international banks to model social media for forecasting stock market movement. Additionally, Professor Claster was a founding member of the GeoInformatics Research Center in Auckland, New Zealand where his work was applied to remote sensors and viticulture. Prior to work in data science and machine learning, Professor Claster developed multi-room online conferencing software. Prof. Claster has been teaching data science at Ritsumeikan Asia Pacific University since 2010 and designed its data science curriculum. He has authored more than 20 research papers in the field of data science and received the top award for research there in 2013.

Originally from Philadelphia, Professor Claster moved to Japan where he has been a resident for over 20 years. In addition to research, his interests include Japanese architecture, Buddhism, and culture.

Chapter 1

Functions Tutorial

- Functions with and without arguments
- Defining versus running
- Arguments
- Parameter versus argument
- Argument order
- Environments
- Scope

Functions Coded in This Chapter
`myFirstFunction`
addFive
addThem
divid
outerFunction
embeddedFunction

1.1 Replicating the Results Shown Here

Note that this text uses the following version of R: version 3.4.2 (2017-09-28). Generally later versions should provide the same results, but you may also install this version at the Comprehensive R Archive Network (CRAN, https://cran.r-project.org/).

1.1.1 Knowledge of R

It is assumed that the reader has gone through the tutorial offered through an R package called Swirl. You can find out more information at https://swirlstats.com/. The tutorial can be run inside RStudio, and it gives a very good course in R. It is expected that the reader has completed the tutorial through the section on functions.

According to the website, you can run the tutorial in RStudio by following the steps given below.

Step 1: Get R. In order to run swirl, you must have R 3.1.0 or later installed on your computer. …
Step 2 (recommended): Get RStudio. …
Step 3: Install swirl. …
Step 4: Start swirl. …
Step 5: Install an interactive course. …
Step 6: Have fun!

1.1.2 Getting Set Up

To get things going, you should install R and install the free version of RStudio. Here are the steps to be followed.

1. Download and install R from https://cran.r-project.org/. On Windows, you may choose to use the "install as administrator" option since on occasion R may try to create folders; for example, when new packages are installed, and if the installation is not installed and run as administrator, Windows may block the creation of those folders.
2. Download and install the free version of RStudio from https://www.rstudio.com. The same remarks as above regarding "install as administrator".
3. Run RStudio.
4. Configure RStudio to look the way you want. You can adjust the appearance in the Global Options menu which is under Tools. When you open RStudio, it may look as shown in Figure 1.1.
5. The so-called *console* window is the large window on the left in Figure 1.1. On the right are two other windows. Each window has various tabs. The first tab on the top right-hand window is the Environment tab, and it will show any variables you have created, functions you have created, datasets that have been loaded, and so on. The bottom window currently is showing the first tab which is just a file browser for the current directory that you are

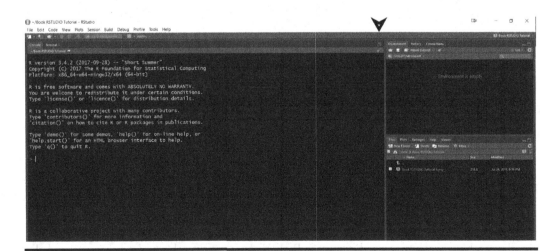

Figure 1.1   Initial configuration of RStudio.

working in. You can see that the current directory that is open is Home>Book RSTUDIO Tutorial. There is one window which is not shown now but is important. It is called the *source* window. The console allows you to type single commands into R, and when you hit the enter key, R will run that code. However, most of the time, when I am writing code, I don't want to evaluate each time I write a new line of code. I want to be able to write several lines of code first and then run it. This can't be done in the console window. The source window is used for this. To show the source window, you can either click on the icon showing two small boxes (see just below the arrow in Figure 1.1) or go to Tools<Global Options<Pane Layout. I prefer to have the console window above and the source below, but you can arrange as you wish. Also, as you can see, my background is black. This can also be adjusted in Global Options like many other options. Once you have the source window visible, you can type code in it, and then if you want to run a particular set of lines, select those lines, and then press the button on the upper right-hand side of the source window that says Run. Instead of pressing the button, you can also select the code to be run and (on Windows) press the control key and enter key simultaneously.

To run the tutorial, you need to install the Swirl package. The simplest way to install a package is to go to Tools>Install Packages. Then type in the name of the package you are looking for, in this case Swirl. Then click the install button. RStudio will download and install the package, and when it is finished, you will see the prompt symbol (looks like ">") in the console. According to the website on Swirl, next type `library("swirl")`, and hit the enter key. Then type `swirl()`, and hit the enter key. Next the website says, "the first time you start Swirl, you'll be prompted to install a course. You can either install one of the recommended courses or visit our course repository for more options. There are even more courses available from the Swirl Course Network. If you follow the instructions it will bring you to a screen where you can choose the course you want to study". The recommended course for this text is called *R Programming: The basics of programming in R*, and it is expected that you have completed up to and including the section on functions.

Note: We will often use RHS to stand for right-hand side of an equation and LHS to stand for the left-hand side of an equation.

Note: The author feels that there may be errors in the text. This is the cost of getting the text out in a reasonable period of time. He apologizes for any errors.

1.1.3 Functions Tutorial

It is assumed that you have gone through the RStudio Swirl tutorial at this point. Some of the following will be a review of the Swirl course.

Our tutorial will concentrate on building functions since this is a critical skill in the material that follows.

1.2 Functions

If you have used R at all, you have already worked with many functions. A function we often encounter is **mean(x)**.

```
x=1:5
mean(x)
## [1] 3
```

Another easy function is the function to get the date on the computer you are using, **Sys.Date**().

```
Sys.Date()
## [1] "2018-10-02"
```

There is an important difference between these two functions. They both have names, and they both have parentheses, but there is nothing inside the parentheses when we run Sys.Date(); however, there is something inside the parentheses when we run **mean(x)**. The **mean()** function requires an input. In fact, if we run it without one, we get an error message.

```
mean()
Error in mean.default() : argument "x" is missing, with no default
```

Admittedly, R has error messages that are not so easy to understand, but if you skim them, you can sometimes figure out what kind of problem has occurred.

1.2.1 Writing Our First R Function

Let's make this simple. To write a function is as simple as

```
myFirstFunction <- function(){
  print("Hi There!")
}
```

This shows the syntax of creating a function. We can divide the construction of this function into three parts. Before reading what these three parts are, look at the above statement and make a guess as to where the three parts might be. (I am not referring to the "<-" symbol as one of the parts, but of course that needs to be there.)

1. It needs a name.[1]

   ```
   myFirstFunction
   ```

2. You need to tell R that this name is the name of a function (as opposed to a text (character) variable, or a vector, or a list, or whatever else it might be).

   ```
   function()
   ```

3. You want the function to do something, and you put that inside the curly brackets {}.

   ```
   {
     print("Hi There!")
   }
   ```

This function will just print out a string: "Hi There!". Note that what is written between the curly brackets is referred to as the body of the function. The body of our function contains

```
print("Hi There!").
```

---

[1] There are cases where it is not necessary to name a function. That topic is called anonymous functions. We will not discuss it here.

1.2.2 Defining the Function versus Running It

Although we define a function, nothing happens until we run it. Running a function is done by typing its name along with the succeeding parentheses.

```
myFirstFunction()
```

Note that in RStudio, if the definition is typed into the console and the enter key is hit, then the function is defined. However, if the definition is typed into the *source* panel, it won't be defined until the *code is run* in the Source panel.

However, even after the function is defined, there will be no response from R until the function is run (this is usually referred to as "calling the function"). So, "Hi There!" will not appear in the console until myFirstFunction() is run, either by typing myFirstFunction() into the console and hitting enter or by typing myFirstFunction() into the source panel and running it. If either of these is performed, the function myFirstFunction() will be called, and then it will run the code within the curly brackets, which in this case is to print out "Hi There!"

Functions can do far more than simply print a string, but the code above is the full implementation of a function.

Practice 1.2.1
   1. Write a function named *fact* that will print the string "Tokyo is in Japan".
   Of course we will see functions that do more than just printing a string, but nevertheless we have constructed a basic function.

1.2.3 Arguments

Now try something a little more interesting. Write a function to add 5 to a given input. In this case, we need to add one more piece to the syntax of writing a function. The function needs to accept an input. That is, it needs to accept the given number. We say the function will accept an argument. The etymology of the word "argument" is fairly convoluted and comes from something in Old English. But for us, argument refers to the input that we put into the function. If we name the function addFive() and allow it to accept an input, then it would add 5 to that input to produce its output.

Ok, so now we have decided what we want addFive() to do. Now we have to write it. It needs the first three parts mentioned above plus a place to put the argument. Also of course, we have to change what is put into the curly brackets {} because we don't want the function to print out "Hi There!". We want it to add 5 to the input.

```
addFive <- function(inp){
  outp=inp+5
  return(outp)
}
```

Explanation:
We need a symbol to hold the input. We have chosen inp. Then inside the curly brackets, we add 5 to inp and assign that to the variable outp. Finally, we use the function return(). return() at the end of our code will determine what the output of the function will be. In our case, the output is contained in outp . If we run the function with an argument of 7, we should expect an output of 12.

```
addFive(7)
## [1] 12
```

1.3 Parameter versus Argument

If you want to be able to read explanations on the web about programming issues, you need to understand the difference between the two words *parameter* and *argument*. We have used the term *argument*. What is meant by *parameter*? We want to distinguish between what the user puts into our function (in the last case it was 7) and the symbol that holds that value, which is later used in the body of the function. The symbol we used to hold the argument is inp. This would be called a parameter. Thus, the argument entered into the function is 7, but the parameter is inp. It is very useful to be able to distinguish between these two when discussing our programming code, and so the concept should be well understood.

We could certainly write a function which accepts two arguments. In that case, we would use two parameters. For example, if we want to take two inputs and get their sum, we could write a function called addThem(). We hope that if we put 1 and 3 into addThem(), it will return or output 4.

```
addThem <- function(inp1,inp2){
  outp=inp1 + inp2
  return(outp)
}
addThem(1,3)
## [1] 4
```

Practice 1.3.2

1. What are the parameters in addThem()?
2. What were the arguments we used in the addThem() test above?
3. What was returned in the addThem() test above?

In the addThem() function, we said there were two parameters inp1 and inp2. We will refer to the list of all the parameters in the definition of the function as the parameter list. So here, we would say that the parameter list has two elements inp1 and inp2. A function could have any number of parameters in the parameter list.

One way to get an idea of what a function is doing is to look at the body of the function (what is inside the curly brackets). If there is a variable inside the curly brackets, then check if it is in the parameter list. If it is there, it means that this value will be supplied when the function is called and then used in the way that is written inside the curly brackets.

Another good practice for understanding what a function does is to check the output of the function. That is, check the final return() statement of the function. This will tell you what the output is and the form of the output. So far, we have had single numbers as the output of our functions, but it is possible to output other types like lists or vectors.[2] Checking the return statement is a quick way to get an idea about the function. Note also that if the function does not have a return statement, it will not show the value of the output if you simply run the function. However, even it does not contain a return statement, if the function is run, it is still assignable to a variable (see "k" in the code below).

```
addThem <- function(inp1,inp2){
  outp=inp1 + inp2
```

---

[2] Outputting a list is a convenient way to output more than one item.

```
  #Leave out the return statement
}
addThem(1,3)
k=addThem(1,3)
k
## [1] 4
```

Some readers may object to the sentence above where we wrote, "So far, we have had single numbers as the output of our functions", saying we output the text string "Hi There!". In programming, we make a distinction between what a function *prints out* and what it *returns*. It seems like an odd distinction to make, and actually in R, it may not be an important distinction, but typically in most programming languages, we cannot assign the value of the function myFirstFunction() to another variable, whereas we can certainly assign the output of addThem(1,3) to a variable. However, in R it is actually possible to assign the myFirstFunction() to a variable. This is not typical for most programming languages.

```
y=addThem(1,3)
y
## [1] 4
#What is below actually works in R. Notice that even during the
assignment, the function actually runs and outputs "Hi There!"
x=myFirstFunction()
## [1] "Hi There!"
x
## [1] "Hi There!"
```

1.4 Argument Order and Parameter Names

Sometimes the order in which we enter the arguments used when calling a function is important, and sometimes the order is not important. See the following example.

We create a function called divid() which will take two arguments and divide the first argument by the second.

```
divid <- function(numerator,denominator){
  result=numerator/denominator
  return(result)
}
#The order of the arguments clearly matters.
divid(8,2)
## [1] 4
divid(2,8)
## [1] 0.25
#On the other hand, if we specify to which parameter we want a particular
argument to be assigned, then the order does not matter. Here we are
putting 2 first and then 8, but we have specified that the 2 is for the
denominator parameter, not the numerator parameter, and the 8 is for the
numerator parameter.
divid(denominator = 2, numerator = 8)
## [1] 4
```

Practice 1.4.3

1. Write a function called *poly*, with two arguments which adds the square of one of them to the cube of the second. Use sq for the parameter that will be squared and cu for the parameter that will be cubed.
2. Run poly(4,3); then run poly(3,4).
3. Try switching the order of the arguments using the parameter names like this poly(sq = 2, cu = 3) and poly(cu = 3, sq = 2). What is your conclusion?
4. What happens if you run poly(cu = 3, 2)?

Before we go on, we briefly discuss the concept of environments in R.

1.5 Environments

When we start up R and then create a variable, for example here,

```
x <- 7
```

R needs to keep a record of the fact that a variable x has been created and that variable has been assigned the value 7. We say that the variable x has been stored in the global environment. An environment is just a place to store variables. It is like a piece of paper with the names of variables and the values of those variables. It also keeps a record of the functions that have been created. In fact, there is a command we can run to see what is currently on that "sheet of paper", i.e., what is in the global environment. It looks like the following.

```
ls(globalenv())
```

The **ls()** function will give a list of items, and so when we put **globalenv()** into it, we find out what is in **globalenv()**.

For example, if we created the function called myFirstFunction()and also created the variable x, then we would get

```
myFirstFunction <- function(){
  print("Hi There!")
}
myFirstFunction()
## [1] "Hi There!"
x <- 7
ls(globalenv())
## [1] "myFirstFunction" "x"
```

This tells us that myFirstFunction and x are in the global environment.

We can actually create separate environments. This is done with

```
my.env <- new.env()
#Now we have created a new environment. It is currently empty
ls(my.env)
## character(0)
#However, we can assign variables values in this new (separate)
environment like this:
```

```
assign("y", 100, envir=my.env)
#We can also use the $ sign to assign variables to the new environment
like this:
my.env$thursday <- "The weather is sunny"
#Now if we check the contents of the my.env environment, we will see both
these variables.
ls(my.env)
## [1] "Thursday" "y"
#So, each environment is like a separate sheet of paper, and it contains
all the variable definitions (and function names as well).
#In fact, we can have a variable x in the global environment and another
separate variable, x, in the my.env environment. They can have different
values even though they both are called x.
assign("x", 20, envir=my.env)
#We can use the name of the environment, followed by a $ sign, followed
by the name of the variable to see what the values of the variables are.
(Note: The name of the global environment is .GlobalEnv.)
.GlobalEnv$x
## [1] 7
my.env$x
## [1] 20
```

Generally, we don't create new environments for most of our programming tasks, but it is useful to see how, once created, the items in the environment can be accessed. On the other hand, R will create a new environment every time any function is called. Consider our addThem() example:

```
addThem <- function(inp1,inp2){
  outp=inp1 + inp2

}
```

If we run addThem(3, 2), then a new environment is created (a new sheet of paper) which will contain the variables inp1, inp2, and outp along with the values each variable is assigned.

> By the way, a term often used in computer science is "bindings". This usually refers to the assignment of a value to a variable. Thus, we could say that when we call addThem(3, 2), R creates a new environment with three bindings.[3]

We will see in a moment that the concept of environments is tied to the important concept of scoping.

We saw above that we can have a variable named x in two separate environments, and even though both variables are called x, they don't have the same values. That is, the fact that two variables have the same name is akin to two people having the same name. They may have the same name, but they are not the same people. With regard to our two variables, if they reside in different environments, they are different variables.

We said earlier that when a function is called, it creates its own environment, its own piece of paper, where its variables and values are stored (where its bindings are stored). Next, we consider what happens if we define a function inside another function. What do the R rules say about variables defined in the outer function? What do R rules say about variables defined in the inner

---

[3] More generally, binding refers to a mapping of one item to another.

function? If a variable is defined in the outer function, will R allow the inner function to access that variable? And vice versa, if a variable is defined in the inner function, can the outer function access it? Also, if a variable is defined in a function, can we access that variable outside the function? These are often described as properties of the scope of a variable.

What is the scope of a variable which has been defined within a function? Does it extend to functions that are defined within this function? Does the scope extend outside the function? Suppose we have a function called outerFunction(); can we define another function called embeddedFunction() inside that function? Yes, we are allowed to define functions inside other functions. What does the notion of environment imply in this situation?

```
#We define a function within another function. Then we call the outer
function. The outer function also calls the embedded function (by way of
a print statement)
outerFunction<- function(){
  myVar=2 #Where is this defined? In outerFunction, not in
embeddedFunction.
  embeddedFunction <- function(){

    myVar=5 #Where is this defined? In embeddedFunction.
    return(myVar)
  }

  print(embeddedFunction()) #We call embeddedFunction from within
outerFunction. embeddedFunction returns myVar, but which myVar?
  return(myVar) #This is the return statement for outerFunction! Which
myVar will be returned?

}
```

What will happen when we call outerFunction()? In particular, when *it* returns myVar, which myVar will it return, the myVar defined in outerFunction (and thus return a 2) or the myVar defined in the embeddedFunction (and thus return a 5). Further, what will print(embeddedFunction) do? These are decisions that the *designers* of the R programming language had to make. Let's see what they decided R should do.

```
#Call outer function, which will return its myVar value and also print
the output of the embedded function
outerFunction()
## [1] 5
## [1] 2
```

What is the explanation for the above *output* of 5 followed by 2? Note that at the end of the definition of **outerFunction**(), we have both a **print**() statement and a **return**() statement. This is why there are two lines of output when we run **outerFunction**(). Why are the outputs not the same? They both are returning (or printing) myVar. **embeddedFunction**() returns myVar and so does **outerFunction**(), so why don't they both return the same value?

First notice that the first line of the body of **outerFunction**() defines a variable called myVar. Next in the body of **outerFunction**(), there is a new function being defined: **embeddedFunction**(). That is, **embeddedFunction**() is being defined within **outerFunction**(). Now examine the body of **embeddedFunction**(). It also defines a variable called myVar. Are these two variables the same, or do they just have the same name? Remember that *when a function is called, it creates its own piece of paper to write its variables and values.*

At this point in the code, we have not called either function yet. But after defining the functions above, we do call the function **outerFunction**(). When **outerFunction**() runs, it will call **embeddedFunction**(), within its **print**() statement. When **print**(**embeddedFunction**()) is run, this causes **embeddedFunction**() to be called, and a new environment is created where the variable myVar is written with a value of 5.

At the end of the execution of **embeddedFunction**(), its return statement with myVar will give 5. However, after **embeddedFunction**() returns 5, it completes its work. We say that then "control" *passes back to* **outerFunction**(). This will mean that we are switching to the environment of **outerFunction**(). Then, finally, the last statement, **return**(myVar), in **outerFunction**() is run. Since this occurs within the environment of **outerFunction**(), myVar will be 2.

1.5.1 Nested Environments

There is one more concept associated with environments that we should discuss. Environments are said to be "nested". That is, in our example, if we changed the definition of **embeddedFunction**(), so that myVar was *only defined in* **outerFunction**() and *not defined within* **embeddedFunction**(), then we might expect an error to occur when we run our code since **embeddedFunction**() will run and try to return myVar, but myVar does not exist within **embeddedFunction**()'s environment. However, that is not what happens. What R does is search for myVar in other environments. In particular, R searches in the calling function's environment[4]. The calling function in this case is **outerFunction**(), and R will find a variable called myVar there, and this is the variable that will be used in **embeddedFunction**(). In this sense, the environments are nested.

Below is an example where we do not define myVar within the embedded function but try to access it within the embedded function anyway.

```
outerFunction<- function(){
  myVar=2
  embeddedFunction <- function(){
    #In this example, we do not create a variable called myVar within the
embedded function.
    #myVar=5
    return(myVar)
  }

  print(embeddedFunction())
  return(myVar)

}
#Call outer function, which will return its myVar value and also print
the output of the embedded function
outerFunction()
## [1] 2
## [1] 2
```

---

[4] Actually, R searches even beyond the calling functions' environment. To see all the environments that R will search in (the so-called search path), run the command **search**().

We see that the value of myVar is 2 in both cases, and in particular, it is 2 in the embedded function, even though it was not defined there. R finds myVar in the calling function **outerFunction**() and uses that binding.

1.6 Scope

Finally, we discuss one more concept related to environments, and that is the concept of the scope of a variable. The scope of a variable refers to where it "lives". We have already discussed this when we say that any variable is written into some environment. It may be written into the global environment, it may be written into a new environment which we artificially create with **new.env**(), or it may be written into the new environment that R creates whenever a function is called.

If a function defines a new variable and if that function is run, the new variable will exist in the new environment that R creates to run the function. However, once the function finishes running, it is said that the variable dies. It is no longer accessible by R. It is also said that R "forgets about it". That is, the value is still stored somewhere in the computer's memory, but R is no longer keeping track of where that piece of memory is located. In any case, the variable basically disappears. We say the scope of the variable is limited to being within the function. If we try to access that variable outside of the function, we get an error.

On the other hand, we saw above that if the variable is defined outside the function, whether it be defined in outerFunction or just defined in the global environment (not inside any particular function), then it will be accessible. Thus, it seems that accessibility goes in only one direction but not the other. That is, it goes from outer to inner but not from inner to outer. Once again, if the variable is defined "higher up on the chain" (closer to being a global variable), then it will be available to all the environments "lower down on the chain".

```
outerFunction<- function(){
#If myVar is not defined at the level of outerFunction yet it is defined
at the level of embeddedFunction, is it accessible to outerFunction? We
saw that if myVar was defined in the outer function, then we could use it
in the inner function because of what we called nested environments. We
could say the nesting "leaks down" to the embedded function. Or more
precisely, the availability of variables leaks down to nested functions.
#On the other hand, does nesting "percolate up"? Are variables defined in
embeddedFunction available to outerFunction? The answer is no, as we can
see is this example. We will get an error if we try to access myVar
within outerFunction (in the return statement) if it is not defined in
the outer function but is only defined in the inner function.  The scope
of myVar is limited.
#We will see later that there is a way to bypass this issue with the
so-called superassignment operator "<<-".
  #myVar=2
  embeddedFunction <- function(){
    #In this example, we did not create a variable called myVar in
outerFunction. (Above, we placed a # sign in front of the myVar
assignment statement so as to "commented out" myVar=2.)
    myVar=5
    return(myVar)
  }
```

```
  print(embeddedFunction())
  return(myVar)

}
#Call outer function, which will return its myVar value and also print
the output of the embedded function.
outerFunction()
## [1] 5
Error in outerFunction(): object "myVar" not found
```

Practice 1.6.4

1. Where did the error above occur? Was it in **print(embeddedFunction())**, or was it in the second **return**(myVar)?

Chapter 2

Logic and R

2.1 Logic

The logic of modern computer science has roots in Aristotle's efforts. Aristotle's central observation with regard to the study of logic was that arguments were *valid or not* based on their logical structure, independent of the non-logical words involved. The most well-known argument form he described is known as the syllogism and looks like:

1. All men are mortal.
2. Socrates is a man.
3. Therefore, Socrates is mortal.

You can replace "Socrates" with any other noun, and "mortal" with any other noun, and the argument remains valid. The validity of the argument is determined solely by its *logical structure*. The logical words "all", "is", are", and "therefore" are doing all the work.

In programming, we often see what are called "if then" statements. An "if then" statement may look like

If p then q.
If x > 5 then print "stop".

Sometimes, however, the p may not be a single simple statement but may consist of a combination of many simple statements, and it may be hard to discern under which conditions q should occur. It is useful to study concepts in logic to break down complex statements so that they can be understood more easily. That is part of our goal in this chapter.

2.2 Statements

An example of a statement is
"The number computed is greater than 100".

In logic, statements are declarative sentences that are either true or false but not both. We will primarily focus on the "either true or false but not both" part of the above sentence.

The word *declarative* is used in contrast to sentences that are interrogative – for example an interrogative sentence (basically meaning a question) is "Do I have to go to school?"

Examples of declarative sentences are "Today is Monday", "The sun is shining", and "3 + 4 = 7".

Each of the following sentences is either true or false but not both: 1 is true, 2 is true, 3 is true, and 4 is false.

1. All men are mortal.
2. Socrates is a man.
3. Socrates is mortal.
4. 10 > 12.

"Are you going home?" in addition to *not* being a declarative sentence, cannot be considered "true or false but not both", and therefore this is an additional reason it is not a statement.[1] In our exploration of mathematical and computer logic, we restrict ourselves to statements. In the rest of this text, we will often use letters like p, q, r, s, or t to represent *statements*. These are used in a way similar to the way we often use x, y, or z to represent numbers. Thus, we may say that p represents the statement "Socrates is a man" and q represents the statement "10 > 12".

Practice 2.2.1

1. Is the sentence "What is your name?" a statement? Why or why not?
2. Is the sentence "New York is the largest city in China." a statement? Why or why not?
3. Is "The mean of {1, 2, 3, 4, 5} is 700" a statement?

2.3 Boolean Data Type

In many programming languages, common datatypes are integers, decimal numbers, arrays, and lists. There is not a function in R called **datatype** which we could use to test the data type of an object, although there are various functions that serve a similar purpose. The function **is**() partially serves this purpose as does the function **class**().

In many programming languages defining something as an integer as opposed to a decimal (or double) will have unexpected consequences. For example, in Python, if you set x = 2, Python will assume x is an integer. If you set y = 2.0 it will assume it is a decimal number. If you write x/3 you will get 1 because in Python, the output of an operation on integers is an integer, and so rounding off will occur to force the output to be an integer. On the other hand, if you write y/3, you will get 0.6666… R does not behave this way. One way to get R to round the result, of course, is to use the **round**() function.

One important data type from computer logic is the Boolean (the term *logical* is also used instead of the word *Boolean*, and R uses this term).

A Boolean variable is a variable that can only take on two possible values: true or false. In R, these special values are denoted by TRUE or FALSE. (In other programming languages, the names *True* and *False* or *true* and *false* may be used.)

---

[1] Don't be confused into thinking about the answer to the question "Are you going home?" – thinking "yes" means true and "no" means false. That is not what we are referring to.

Usually we think of variables as being able to take on many values. In typical mathematical equations, we expect that variables can take an infinite number of values. For example, in the mathematical equation

$$y = 2x + 5$$

the variable x can be *any* real number. In contrast, Boolean variables can only assume *one of the two values*: true or false. Thus, Booleans are quite simple and limited. Nevertheless, they are very useful.

Consider the two statements

1. p: New York is in the United States.
2. q: 1 + 1 = 1.

First, to check our understanding, is it legitimate to use the word "statement" for each of these? Yes, because each of them is either true or false, not both.

"New York is in the United States"
is true. We say its *truth value* is TRUE.[2] On the other hand,

$$\text{"}1 + 1 = 1\text{"}$$

is false. We say its *truth value* is FALSE.

We are using this phrase "truth value" as we use the word "value" when we say that for the equation

$$x + 3 = 5$$

the value of x is 2. In other words, from all the possible values in the set of acceptable values for x (the real numbers), for *this* equation, x = 2. Remember though that for *statements*, there are only two possible truth values, true and false. Then for a particular statement, the truth value is one of these two possibilities. For example, "New York is in China" has a truth value of false.

Returning to the equation y = 2x + 5, in high school math, we might write

$$x \in \mathbf{R}$$

where ∈ means "is an element of" and R is the infinite set of all real numbers. Similarly, for a statement p, we could write

$$\text{"the truth value of p"} \in \left\{ \text{true, false} \right\}$$

to emphasize that the truth value can only come from this very limited set of values. Note, we are not saying that p can *represent* only two possible statements. p can represent any statement, for example, "Today is Monday" or "The cost of the movie was $15". We are focusing on what we call the truth value of p. The truth value of p refers to whether p is true or p is false. It is the truth value of p that is limited to the set {true, false}. Thus, symbols for statements (like the symbol p),

---

[2] Using R's symbol for true.

have two separate properties. One of these properties is the particular statement they represent. The second property is the truth value of that statement. Similarly, we may say that x can have two separate properties as well: what it stands for and what its value is. For example, the mathematical variable (not logical variable) x may *stand for* the number of oranges in the refrigerator, but its *value* may be equal to 3. Our point here though is to make clear that the truth value of a statement will only be one of two possible values: TRUE or FALSE, whereas if x is the number of oranges in the refrigerator x could be any element from the set {0, 1, 2, … }.

Practice 2.3.2

1. What are the symbols in R for the values of a Boolean variable?
2. Look up another language like Python, Java, C, or C++ and find out how the values of a Boolean in that language are denoted.
3. Let p denote a statement. How many different possible statements are there that p can denote?
4. Let p denote a statement. How many different possible truth values are there for p?
5. For the equation x + y = 5, how many different values are typically possible for x?
6. For the equation x + 6 = 10, how many different values are *possible* for x (not how many make the expression true)?

```
#First, we explore the symbols in R for "true" and "false". We can
artificially define a Boolean vector like this
B <- c(FALSE,TRUE, TRUE)
class(B) #note that R uses the word "logical" instead of "Boolean".
## [1] "logical"
#FALSE and TRUE are not strings or characters even though they seem
similar to characters. But R treats these differently.
B
## [1] FALSE  TRUE   TRUE
#One of the differences is that when R reports back the values of a
character vector, it always uses quotation marks but for Boolean vectors,
as seen in B above, it does not use quotation marks. We will see more
important differences later.
C <- c("FALSE","TRUE","TRUE")
C
## [1] "FALSE" "TRUE"  "TRUE"
class(C)
## [1] "character"
#Whenever an expression is presented to R, it will evaluate it to find
its value. This is true regardless of whether the expression is a numeric
expression or a Boolean expression. For example, if the expression is
numeric, it will evaluate the expression and then return the value of the
expression. So if we type 8, of course R will respond with 8.
8
## [1] 8
#And if we write 6+1, then R will evaluate the expression and respond
with 7.
6+1
## [1] 7
#R responds similarly if we present it with a Boolean expression, (i.e.,
a statement). It will evaluate it and return the value. However, the
```

```
value of a Boolean expression is not a number, but rather either true or
false, and thus either true or false will be returned.
5<1
## [1] FALSE
5<9
## [1] TRUE
#Simpler evaluations are like this
TRUE
## [1] TRUE
FALSE
## [1] FALSE
#These two simpler examples are similar to what happens when R evaluates
8
8
## [1] 8
```

Practice 2.3.3
1. What is the class of 5 < 1? You can use the function class() to discover an object's class.
2. If p <- 5 < 1, what does p "evaluate to"? (Note that <- is the assignment operator, but < is the less than or equal to operator.)
3. If x <- 8 + 1, what does x "evaluate to"?

Now, we return to the discussion of statements. What about an expression like x < 5? Is it a statement? The answer is no. However, once we fill in x with a value then it becomes a statement. Thus, if we have the *for loop* in R

```
 for(x in 1:5){
  if(x>3){print(x)}
}
## [1] 4
## [1] 5
```

we are generating the following five separate expressions within the loop.

```
1>3
2>3
3>3
4>3
5>3
```

Each of these is a statement because each is either true or false but not both. The *truth values* for these are

```
FALSE
FALSE
FALSE
TRUE
TRUE
```

From the R printout, we see that only when the argument in the if() function is *true* will the body of the *if* clause, print(x), be run.

2.4 Compound Statements

"6 > 4 and 6 > 9"

is called a compound statement. A compound statement is formed from two simpler statements joined by what is called a logical operator (also called a logical connective). The logical operators we will use are "and", "or", "not", and "if… then".

Examples of compound statements using "and", "or", and "if … then" are as follows:

■ 6 < 7 and 8 > 9.
■ 6 < 7 or 8 > 9.
■ If x *is divisible by 2* then x *is even.*

We next discuss each of the four connectives in detail.

2.5 Connectives

2.5.1 "and" – The Conjunction

Again p, q, and r will be used to denote statements. Any two statements can be joined by the word "and" to form a compound statement called the conjunction of the original statements. The connective "and" is called the conjunction. The conjunction of p and q is

p and q

Symbolically it is written as

p ^ q

It denotes the conjunction of the original statements and is read as "p and q".

For example, if

p: "New York is in the US"

q: "1 + 1 = 2"

then p ^ q is the compound *statement*

"New York is in the US and 1 + 1 = 2".

It is clear from these particular statements that the truth value of p is true and the truth value of q is true. What about the truth value of the statement p ^ q?

First, we should make sure that p ^ q is actually a statement. That is, can we identify it as true or false but not both? The answer is yes and of course that it is a true statement. We have combined the two statements using the conjunction operator.

This example suggests that the conjunction of two statements is itself a statement. Next we ask, under which conditions will the compound conjunctive statement be true – meaning which combination of truth values of the individual statements p and q will lead to p ^ q being true?

Given that there are two possibilities for the first element in the conjunction and two for the second element in the conjunction, there are only four possible combinations that need to be inspected. Consider the following:

i. NYC is in the US and 1 + 1 = 2
ii. NYC is in the US and 1 + 1 = 1
iii. NYC is in China and 1 + 1 = 2
iv. NYC is in China and 1 + 1 = 1.

This seems tedious and trivial, but by going through this exercise, it is possible to derive rules which help evaluating more complex statements. Which of the above compound statements are true and which are false? It is obvious using common sense that only (i) is true. The others are false. Furthermore, if we replace the statement

NYC is in the US with *Moscow is in Russia*

the true/false pattern remains the same. Only (i) would be true.

We can see that whenever the first element of the conjunction is true and the second is false, only (i) would be true. This suggests that we can build a table that shows when a compound statement that uses the conjunction connective will be true and when it will be false. Instead of using *NYC is in the US,* or *Moscow is in Russia,* or any particular statement, we just use p. We can use q for the other element of the compound statement (Table 2.1). Now we are exploring

p ^ q

Our investigation has shown that p ^ q can be tabulated as shown in Table 2.1.

In this table, T stands for true, and F stands for false, and the truth value of the compound statement is displayed in the third column. Also take note that the table shows the *truth values* for p and q, *not* the statements they represent. Notice also that in this table we have exhausted all possible combinations of the true and false values for p and q. To be clear, there is no reason we must use the order in the below table to list all these possible values. For example, we could have put F T in the first row instead of the third row. (Of course, then the third column of the first row would not be T anymore.)

Now, to put this kind of table in perspective, note that we could also make a table for the expression $x + y^2$. It might begin as shown in Table 2.2.

What is the point of bringing up this example here? In this table, we have chosen *only a few pairs of values for* x and y. If we wanted to "complete" this table, we would have to fill in every possible combination of values for x and y. This is an impossible task since there are an infinite number of possible combinations. However, for our logic table, with p and q, how many different

Table 2.1 Conjunction Truth Table

P	q	p ^ q
T	T	T
T	F	F
F	T	F
F	F	F

Table 2.2 Table of the function of x and y: $x + y^2$

x	y	$x + y^2$
1	1	2
1	2	5
1	3	10
2	5	27

possibilities do we have to fill in? Since there are only two possible truth values for p, true and false, and two possible truth values for q, true and false, there are only four possible combinations for the truth values of p and q together, and so we only need four rows! This is mentioned just to further drive home the point that we made earlier about the limits on the set of possible truth values of a Boolean statement:

$$\text{"the truth value of p"} \in \{\text{TRUE, FALSE}\}$$

and also to underscore the fact that the truth table for p ^ q is complete with the evaluation of exactly four rows.

Practice 2.5.4

1. To make a truth table for p ^ q ^ r, how many rows will be necessary?

2.6 "or" – Disjunction

Returning to the logical connectives, we can explore the connective "or". It is called the disjunction. The compound statement "p or q" is symbolized in logic by p or q. To explore the nature of "or", we can look at similar compound statements.

    i. NYC is in the US or 1 + 1 = 2
   ii. NYC is in the US or 1 + 1 = 1
  iii. NYC is in China or 1 + 1 = 2
  iv. NYC is in China or 1 + 1 = 1.

In English, the meaning of the word "or" is not necessarily clear. If you tell your child that she can have cake or she can have ice cream, but if she actually eats both, it may not be clear that she has disobeyed. Using our logic notation, when we have p or q, if both p and q are true, is p or q false? For the English word "or" the answer is not clear. This is not a good situation when programming. If we say "if x > 3 or y > 4, then … do something", it should not be ambiguous what should happen if both x > 3 and y > 4 are true. Thus, we *decide* to *adopt the convention* the statement p or q will be true even if both p and q are true. We will use the symbol 'v' to stand for this meaning of 'or' and refer to this meaning of the word 'or' and this symbol 'v' as the "inclusive or". Using the statements (i) through (iv) above as examples, we can now fill out Table 2.3 for the "inclusive or", the disjunction p or q.

Table 2.3   Disjunction Truth Table

p	q	p or q
T	T	T
T	F	T
F	T	T
F	F	F

In R, the conjunction and disjunction look like:

```
#First, we consider a conjunction of two statements in R. The symbol for
a conjunction in R is either & or &&. They are used somewhat differently.
Here we consider only &

TRUE  & TRUE
## [1] TRUE
TRUE  & FALSE
## [1] FALSE
FALSE & TRUE
## [1] FALSE
FALSE & FALSE
## [1] FALSE
#Next consider a disjunction of two statements in R. The symbol for a
conjunction in R is either | or ||. They are used somewhat differently.
Here we consider only |.

TRUE  | TRUE
## [1] TRUE
TRUE  | FALSE
## [1] TRUE
FALSE | TRUE
## [1] TRUE
FALSE | FALSE
## [1] FALSE
```

Practice 2.6.5

1. Without opening R, predict what the outcome to the following will be; then open R and
   check the answers to the following. As expected, the parenthesis indicates the order in which
   the statements need to be evaluated.
   ```
   (FALSE | FALSE) | FALSE
   (FALSE | TRUE) & TRUE
   (FALSE | TRUE) | FALSE
   (FALSE | TRUE) | (FALSE & TRUE)
   ```

2.7 Negation

The next logical operator is the negation operator. The negation of p is simply "not p".
Typical symbols for "not" in logic are "~" or "¬", so "not p" can be expressed in logic using
either of

~p or

¬p.

How do we "translate" from logical symbol to English? If p is "NYC is in the US", then ~p
is "NYC is not in the US". We could also express "not p" in English as "not NYC is in the US"
although that is not great English. The "translation" from the logical notation to English, in
general, is not necessarily straightforward. There may be numerous ways to say "not p". Perhaps
in other languages, things may be more straightforward, but generally languages will have many
ways to express the same concept. In English, some may prefer to think of "not p" as "NYC is not
in the US", and others may prefer "not NYC is in the US".

Table 2.4   Negation Truth Table

p	~p
T	F
F	T

What is the truth table for ~p? Let us first note that you may be confused because this supposedly compound statement is not even made up of two smaller statements. There is a p, but there is no q. It would be fair not to call ~p a compound statement. Nevertheless, we still want to know the relationship between p and ~p. That is, we want to know if p is true, then what about "not p"? The answer is trivial, but we still will record it in a truth table (Table 2.4).

Note: We have been using the word "connective" rather than "operator" prior to discussing negation, but they are interchangeable. But when talking about negation, since there is only a p and no q, it is more natural to use the word "operator". Further, in the case of negation, we can call it a unary operator, whereas if we are talking about conjunction or disjunction, we can say binary operator. Binary in this case means there is a statement on either side of the conjunction; unary means there is a statement on just one side of the operator.

In R, this looks like

```
#The symbol for 'not' is "!"
!TRUE
## [1] FALSE
!FALSE
## [1] TRUE
#Let's try a few more examples to make this clearer.
5<3
## [1] FALSE
!(5<3)
## [1] TRUE
#Now let's combine some of these operators.
#First just the OR operator
5<3 | 2<3
## [1] TRUE
#Now a combination of the OR operator and the NOT operator:
5<3 | !(2<3)
## [1] FALSE
#Next, since this last expression was FALSE,
what if we combine it with a TRUE statement , this time using the OR
operator? Note the parentheses.
(5<3 | !(2<3)) | 10<100
## [1] TRUE
```

Practice 2.7.6

1. Without opening R, predict what the outcome to the following will be; then open R and check your answers.
   1. ! (FALSE | FALSE) | FALSE
   2. (FALSE | TRUE) & !TRUE
   3. (FALSE | !TRUE) | FALSE
   4. ! (FALSE | TRUE) | ! (FALSE & TRUE)

2.7.1 Implication: If ... then

Our last logical connective is called implication and is expressed in English as "if ... then". The symbol we use in logic is the arrow, so that the statement "if p then q" is written symbolically as

$$p \to q$$

It can be translated into English as
    if p then q
    p implies q
    p only if q

This illustrates a point made earlier; translations from logical symbols to English are not straightforward and not necessarily unique[3].

Suppose we represent the statement "Your score on your final exam is at least 95" by p and we represent the statement "You will receive an A for the final course grade" by q, then p → q can be said in English as "If your score on your final exam is at least 95, then you will receive an A for the final course grade". Notice that both p and q are statements; i.e., they can be either true or false but not both. How about p → q, is it a statement? The answer is yes. However, this time, rather than first exploring this connective with examples, as we did for AND, OR, and NOT, it may be easier to start with the truth table (Table 2.5).

Some rows of the implication truth table may be confusing. The third and fourth rows may seem strange. Before we get confused with the puzzling parts, let's look at the parts that are easily ascertained. Consider row 2. We have T F, F.

What is this saying? It is saying that if p is true and q is false, what would you say about the statement p → q: if p then q? Again, if we have
    p: "Your score on your final exam is at least 95"
    q: "You will receive an A for the final course grade"
p → q can be translated as "If your score on your final exam is at least 95, then you will receive an A for the final course grade". Now suppose it is true that you do actually get at least 95 on your final exam *but* the instructor *does not give you an A*; then if the instructor had made the statement that "If your score on your final exam is at least 95, then you will receive an A for the final course grade", would that be true? No, you would say the instructor lied! You would say that the instructor's statement was false. So, if p is true and q is false, then p → q is a false statement, as shown in Table 2.5.

Table 2.5 Implication Truth Table

p	*q*	*p → q*
T	T	T
T	F	F
F	T	T
F	F	T

---

[3] In mathematical language, such a relation from logical expressions to English is not a function since it is one-to-many.

Considering the first row of the truth table where both p and q have truth values of T, it is clearly not false. The last two rows can be puzzling. The easiest way to understand these is not to ask if they are false but to ask if they are true. In logic, if you can't say a statement is true, then it is considered false.[4] For the fourth row, the question could be phrased as "Can you say your instructor lied if you don't get at least 95 and then the instructor does not give you an A?" In this case, the truth table says the instructor has not lied (that is, the statement is true). Similar logic applies for the third row. Nevertheless, these two rows may seem confusing. It may be possible that in English, this is not necessarily correct. However, we are running into a problem we faced with the disjunction. Whether it sounds correct in English is not exactly the point. The point is that this is how we *define* the arrow symbol. The arrow symbol may not correspond exactly to our notion of the English phrase "if then", but the truth table *is* the definition of the arrow symbol in logic.

2.8 Logical Equivalence

Two statements are said to be logically equivalent if they have the same truth tables. The symbol we will use for logical equivalence is ≡. Some seemingly obvious examples are

1. p and q ≡ q and p
2. p or q ≡ q or p
3. ~ ~p ≡ p.

   You can verify the above three examples by doing a truth table for the left-hand side and another truth table for the right-hand side and confirming that they have the same truth table. You can also get a feeling for why these are true by assigning values to p and q and seeing that the three examples above seem to be "logically equivalent". For example, if p is "today is hot" and q is "today is Monday", we would probably agree that saying p and q is the same as saying q and p. At least logically, they would be the same. Literally, they are not the same. Perhaps artistically, they may have some difference as well, but we say that logically they are the same.

   A more interesting example of logical equivalence is the logical equivalence of

4. ~ p or q ≡ p → q.

   If #4 is true, then this would mean that the implication symbol is redundant in logic and that we don't need an arrow symbol. We would call it redundant in the sense that we could always replace p → q with its logical equivalent ~ p or q, and so we would never need to use the arrow symbol. Of course, in normal conversation, being able to use a phrase like "if p then q" is most convenient; it is used all the time. However, for purposes of logic and programing, it can be replaced by "not p or q". This does not give very elegant English, but logically it is fine.

---

[4] You may not quite agree with this. That is fine. Perhaps logic, as we define things, does not quite map our actual experience and our actual world. That is, just because something is not true, perhaps it does not absolutely mean it is false. We are defining a set of rules here. They may not be a perfect fit to our actual experience. We may therefore end up proving things that don't seem to match our actual experiences, and that would be unfortunate. However, that is the price we may have to pay for making this (somewhat simple) system which we are calling computer logic or mathematical logic. Another way to look at this is that we are only considering statements; logical objects which can only be true or false but not both.

We are suggesting that the following two compound statements are logically equivalent.

- If I live in NYC, then I live in the US.
- Either I don't live in NYC, or I live in the US.

In fact, there is not even an operator in R for the implication sign.

Let us show now that the truth table for ~ p or q is the same as the truth table for p → q.

```
#Equivalence of implication and !p | q
#We already know the truth table for the implication operator. Now we
want the truth table for !p | q.
#We must use the same ordering of TRUE and FALSE that occurred in the
implication table.

#This is what the inputs to that table looked like.
#   p       q
# TRUE    TRUE
# TRUE    FALSE
# FALSE   TRUE
# FALSE   FALSE

#Next negate each p and then conjunct this with q to arrive at !p | q.
#We hope that the pattern will be the same as that we saw in the
implication table:
# TRUE
# FALSE
# TRUE
# TRUE

# !p    |   q
FALSE   | TRUE
## [1] TRUE
FALSE   | FALSE
## [1] FALSE
TRUE    | TRUE
## [1] TRUE
TRUE    | FALSE
## [1] TRUE
#Since the truth tables are the same, we have established their logical
equivalence, and p → q can be replaced with !p | q.
```

Practice 2.8.7

1. Show the following logical equivalences in R

   p ^ q ≡ q ^ p
   p or q ≡ q or p
   ~ ~p ≡ p

2.9 Implementing Logic in the Context of a Dataframe

Logical operators occur in R programming when, for example, we do subsetting and we want to select rows that satisfy the conjunction of two conditions. We will see this shortly.

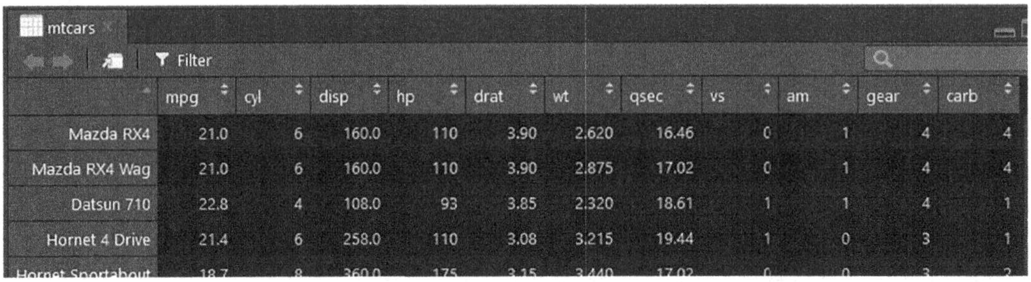

	mpg	cyl	disp	hp	drat	wt	qsec	vs	am	gear	carb
Mazda RX4	21.0	6	160.0	110	3.90	2.620	16.46	0	1	4	4
Mazda RX4 Wag	21.0	6	160.0	110	3.90	2.875	17.02	0	1	4	4
Datsun 710	22.8	4	108.0	93	3.85	2.320	18.61	1	1	4	1
Hornet 4 Drive	21.4	6	258.0	110	3.08	3.215	19.44	1	0	3	1

Figure 2.1 View of mtcars.

The primary data type in R is the vector. Scalars, in fact, are considered to be vectors of length 1.

Because some of the topics we cover in this text are originally derived from statistics, there will be occasions when we refer to *a row of a dataframe* as an *individual* or an *observational unit.* This language will be clarified in Chapter 4. For example, the preinstalled dataset in RStudio called "mtcars" has automobile data for various models of cars like the Mazda RX4, the Datsun 710, and so on. The data was extracted from the 1974 *MotorTrend* US magazine (Figure 2.1).

```
data("mtcars")
View(mtcars)
```

Each row corresponds to a model and shows various characteristics about that model such as the mpg, number of cylinders, the displacement of the engine, the horsepower, and so on. Each row is referred to as an *individual* even though this data is not about people. The word "individual" originates from the fact that many datasets are about people and each row would be a particular person and contain characteristics about that person. The word "individual" is still used in cases where the dataset does not represent people, and so we refer to each row of the mtcars dataset as an individual. Another term used sometimes instead of individual in statistics is *observational unit.*

We have studied Boolean statements like 5 > 2. We can also generate a Boolean expression within our dataset.

```
data("mtcars")
is.data.frame(mtcars) #check to see if it is a dataframe
## [1] TRUE
colnames(mtcars) #check to see what the column names are for this
dataframe
##  [1] "mpg"  "cyl"  "disp" "hp"   "drat" "wt"   "qsec" "vs"   "am"
"gear"
## [11] "carb"
df<-mtcars
#We know that the dataframe name followed by a $ operator followed by a
column name will give a vector.
head(df$mpg)
## [1] 21.0 21.0 22.8 21.4 18.7 18.1
is(df$mpg)
## [1] "numeric" "vector" #is() reveals that it is a vector and that the
elements of the vector are numeric.
is.vector(df$mpg)
## [1] TRUE
```

```
#There are various other ways to find the type of object in R. The
subject can be confusing because R has a heritage that includes the
S language and the S-Plus language. Different functions come from
different parts of the history of R. For comparison, you may want to look
into the following.

# class(df$mpg)
# str(df$mpg)
# mode(df$mpg)
# type(df$mpg)
# typeof(df$mpg)
# storage.mode(df$mpg)

#To isolate the mpg of a particular car, we can do
df$mpg[1]
## [1] 21
#or
df$mpg[2]
## [1] 21.
#Now to form a statement - a sentence that evaluates to TRUE or FALSE, we
can employ one of the numeric operators we have used above like > or <,
or we can use some of the others that we have yet to use in this chapter,
for example, <=, >=, or ==. We form a comparison like
df$mpg[1]>25
## [1] FALSE
#We see that this is a statement; i.e., it evaluates to a Boolean value.

#Next, we do something similar but with vectors. We know that R is very
comfortable with vectors and that most things that can be done with a
single number can also be done with vectors. So instead of running
something like 10<2 where we have a number on each side of the less than
sign, we can have vectors on each side of the less than sign.

a <- 1:5
b <- 5:1

#We can use cat() and the new line symbol \n, to make a nice display of
vectors a and b where they are lined up vertically.

cat(" a: ",a,"\n", "b: ",b,"\n")
##  a:  1 2 3 4 5
##  b:  5 4 3 2 1
#Show the comparison of a and b using the less than sign.
a<b
## [1]  TRUE  TRUE FALSE FALSE FALSE
#We see the result is not just one Boolean,  but rather, since we are
comparing two vectors instead of two scalars, a vector of Booleans! We
will refer to it as a Boolean vector (or logical vector). Recall that
when R compares two vectors, it compares them element by element. Thus,
in the example of a<b, it will compare 1 and 5, 2 and 4, 3 and 3, 4 and
2, and 5 and 1.

#Something very similar can be done with the vector df$mpg. We can
compare it to another vector using the less than operator.
length(df$mpg)
```

```
## [1] 32
#We will construct a vector of the same length as df$mpg with each entry
being the number 25.
x <- rep(25,length(df$mpg))
x
##  [1] 25 25 25 25 25 25 25 25 25 25 25 25 25 25 25 25 25 25 25 25 25 25 25
## [24] 25 25 25 25 25 25 25 25 25
#Now generate a Boolean vector by comparing df$mpg and x using greater
than operator.
df$mpg>x
##  [1] FALSE FALSE FALSE FALSE FALSE FALSE FALSE FALSE FALSE FALSE FALSE
## [12] FALSE FALSE FALSE FALSE FALSE FALSE  TRUE  TRUE  TRUE FALSE FALSE
## [23] FALSE FALSE FALSE  TRUE  TRUE  TRUE FALSE FALSE FALSE FALSE
#Of course, we do not actually need to create x because of R's so-called
recycling property. Note that for Python programmers this is very similar
to what is called broadcasting. Using recycling, to get the same
comparison, we can just write
df$mpg>25.
##  [1] FALSE FALSE FALSE FALSE FALSE FALSE FALSE FALSE FALSE FALSE FALSE
## [12] FALSE FALSE FALSE FALSE FALSE FALSE  TRUE  TRUE  TRUE FALSE FALSE
## [23] FALSE FALSE FALSE  TRUE  TRUE  TRUE FALSE FALSE FALSE FALSE
#Index Vectors Inside a Vector
#An index vector is a Boolean vector that is placed inside the subsetting
function []. Recall the vector "a" from above.
a
## [1] 1 2 3 4 5
#Put a Boolean vector of the same length as a inside the subsetting
function like this
u <- c(TRUE, FALSE,FALSE,FALSE,TRUE)
a[u]
## [1] 1 5
#We would call "u" the indexing vector. This will extract from "u" only
the elements of "a" that have an index of TRUE.
#We saw that df$mpg>25 is a Boolean vector, and we saw that it was the
same length as df$mpg. Therefore we can do the same thing we did with "a"
and "u", with df$mpg and df$mpg>25.
df$mpg[df$mpg>25]
## [1] 32.4 30.4 33.9 27.3 26.0 30.4
#Only the values where the Boolean vector df$mpg>25 is true appear above.
```

2.10 NA in Truth Table

When running comparisons using the arithmetic operators within the context of working with a dataframe, it is likely that some of the entries in the dataframe will be missing (those values are naturally referred to as missing values). If a compound statement occurs in such a scenario, this will generate a logical comparison between NA and either a TRUE or FALSE value. Although this is not a topic of logic, it will be worthwhile taking note of how R deals with this situation. It may be a useful exercise to ask, "How would you, if you were the designer of the R language, choose to handle the following comparisons?" There is no definitive correct answer for this.

TRUE & NA
FALSE & NA
TRUE | NA
FALSE | NA
NA | NA
NA & NA

You may choose to say that wherever there is an NA within a compound statement, the result should evaluate to NA. This is not exactly how R handles this scenario. Have a look at the printout here to see the way the R designers chose to handle NAs.

```
TRUE & NA
## [1] NA
FALSE & NA
## [1] FALSE
TRUE | NA
## [1] TRUE
FALSE | NA
## [1] NA
NA | NA
## [1] NA
NA & NA
## [1] NA
```

2.11 Conclusion

You might feel that what we have done in this chapter on logic is tedious. However, we have developed some nice machinery and skills that will boost our ability to understand programs and to think about code.

We have developed some concepts and language that will help us speak in more fluent and sophisticated terms in out next tasks in programming algorithms. As an analogy, imagine trying to learn algebra *before* knowing arithmetic. It is clearly better to learn arithmetic first and then algebra. In this chapter, we have learned the "arithmetic" of *statements* rather than the arithmetic of numbers. To continue the analogy, in elementary school, we learn about the arithmetic operations of plus, minus, multiplication, and division. Here we have developed *operations* for statements – and, or, not, if ... then – and learned how to use these operations.

What we have studied in this chapter is just one part of what is often called Discrete Mathematics, and it is highly recommended that you study this topic as a course by itself. However, for this text, this chapter and the next on sets will be enough discrete math for our purposes.

2.11.1 Extraneous Notes

There are several functions in R which are useful for orienting yourself when you are writing code or trying to follow code that is already written. It is a good practice to use these periodically to refresh your memory of what type of objects you are working with. We will briefly discuss the following useful functions.

```
mode(), str(), class(), typeof(), storage.mode(), is()
```

It is written that mode() is a mutually exclusive classification of objects according to their basic structure. The basic (also referred to as atomic) modes are *numeric, complex, character*, and *logical* (Boolean). More complex objects have modes such as *list, function, array*, and so on. To say that mode is a mutually exclusive classification simply means that if an object has one type of mode, it can't have another. For example, if something has a numeric mode, it can't have a mode of character. This is not necessarily true for the properties we cover next.

"class" is a property assigned to an object that determines how generic functions operate with it. Examples of different possible classes are: "integer", "numeric", "list", etc. What is a generic function? We explain it next. We will use the function summary() as an example here although we will not have many occasions to use this function in our coding. But this will help us to understand the concept of generic functions and therefore give insight into the meaning of the class() function.

When we apply a function to an object, for example, when we apply the summary() function to the object x as in summary(x), what R does is look for the "version" of the summary() function that will be appropriate for the class of object that x is. The version of summary() for a numeric vector would of course be different than the version for a dataframe, and therefore the code to produce a summary would need to be different. For example, suppose x is a vector but z is a dataframe. We may write summary(x), and we may also write summary(z). But obviously, the calculation and the code used to do the calculation for summary(x) and summary(z) must be different. In R, it is said that summary() is the generic function. However, since the calculations for summary(x) and summary(z) are different, R checks the class of the argument and calls different functions depending on the class of that argument. In R, there is another function called summary.dataframe() which has the specific code used to generate the summary of a dataframe. There are also functions like summary.Date(), summary.matrix(), summary.factor(), and so on. (You can see them if you type "summary." into the console in RStudio.) Each of these will consist of different code since they are meant to be applied to objects of different classes. However, as a user, we do not have to type summary.dataframe() when we want to apply summary() to the dataframe z. We only need to type summary(z). We can use summary.dataframe() if we want but we do not need to. There is also a function called summary.default(), and in fact, this is the function that is used when we write summary(x), but what this function does is to search for the form which is appropriate to the class of the argument x. Generally the function that is used is the name of the generic function followed by a dot and then followed by the class of the object. Thus, if the class of p is factor and we want its summary, the specific function that would be used is summary.factor(). Another interesting point here is that when you type the name of a function into R without using the following parentheses, that is, if you just type summary instead of summary(), we see the code for that function. If this is done with summary.dataframe, we find the code for summary.dataframe(). If this is done with summary.default, we see the code for summary.default(). However, what about if you type summary only? What should R report back? It will not show the code of summary. dataframe(), nor will it show the code for summary.default(). All we see is a reference to the useMethod() function actually. This means that all that summary does is find the right function to use based on the class of the object. Also, if we run ?summary(x), we see in the R documentation, that summary is a generic function.

Regarding the class() function, R uses the class of an object to decide which version of function to use.[5] So if you want to know which function will be used on an object X when you type

---

[5] The discussion above is for S3 functions. R relies on the S programming language, and as the S programming language progressed, there were different versions like S3, S4, and S5.

summary(X), you can check the class of X with class(X). This will tell you the class, and you can therefore determine which version of summary() will be used.

If an object has no specific class assigned to it, such as a simple numeric vector, it's class is usually the same as its mode, by convention. However, the class of an object can be changed very simply and for that matter arbitrarily. For example, suppose x is a list, say x has two elements a character vector "a" "b" and a numeric vector 1:5. That is, suppose x = list(c("a", "b"), 1:5). If we write class(x), we will see that the class is *list*. However, we can change the class of x arbitrarily to "gorilla" simply by writing class(x) = "gorilla". Now if we write class(x), we will see that the class of x is "gorilla". Thus, the class could be defined by the user. (Typically, though, we would not have a need to change an object's class.)

Whereas class can be defined by the user, *typeof* cannot. For example, define a list as follows.

```
> x<-list(c("a","b"), c(1,2))
> class(x)
[1] "list"
> # However, we can change the class.
> class(x)<-"gorilla"
> class(x)
[1] "gorilla"

> typeof(x)
[1] "list"
# This won't work however.
> typeof(x)<-"newclass"
Error in typeof(x) <- "newclass" : could not find function "typeof<-"
```

The reason that typeof cannot be changed is that typeof determines the way R stores the data on the computer. This is thus a *physical* characteristic (because it determines the way the data is physically stored on the computer).

Tip: It is a good idea to update RStudio to the latest version. On the other hand, updating R itself is not always appropriate. Some packages are written only for earlier versions of R, and so if you wish to use those packages, you would need the appropriate version of R. Additionally, as mentioned at the beginning of this text, the code in this text is based on a particular version of R. You can, however, have various versions of R installed on your computer and switch between them in RStudio (in the options menu).

Chapter 3

Sets with R: Building the Tools

- Definition
- Cardinality
- Equality
- Empty set
- Subset
- Union
- Intersection
- Complement
- Cross product
- Algebraic properties

We have covered the basics of programming in R, writing functions in R, and logic. It is time to address fundamental concepts in mathematics and see how they can be implemented in R. In this chapter, our goal is to briefly review the basic concepts relating to sets and then for each concept practice our R skill by implementing that concept with R. Although we are constructing tools that we will use to build machine learning algorithms, it may be best, at this point in your reading of the text, to treat this chapter as a set of R skill building exercises. In the text below, we will sometimes distinguish between what is done in mathematics, what is done in logic, and what is done in programming.

3.1 Sets

A set is a collection of objects, and the objects are often referred to as the elements of the set. Examples could be:

- The set of senators in the US Senate (we will be using this set frequently in our examples)
- The set of outcomes when tossing two coins simultaneously
- The set of all dogs with an IQ of more than 200 – this is most likely an example of an empty set.

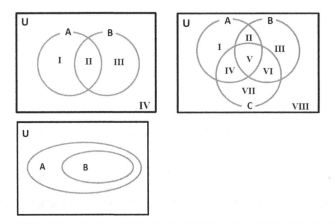

Figure 3.1   Examples of Venn diagrams.

In mathematics, we generally use brackets to denote a set and capital letters for set names. The set of all integers between −2 and 3 inclusive could be denoted like this:

$$A = \{-2, \ -1, \ 0, \ 1, \ 2, \ 3\}$$

A set does not have repeated elements. In this text, we will first consider sets as vectors. Later in the chapter on probability, in order to facilitate modeling, we will think of dataframes, the rows of a dataframe, and collections of what are called observational units (in the sense that statistics uses this phrase) as sets.

3.2 Venn Diagrams

Venn diagrams, used by John Venn (born 1834), can show various relationships between sets. Examples are shown in Figure 3.1.

Venn diagrams are used to denote relationships between sets. Note that the regions denoted by I, II, III, and IV can either be empty or contain elements. Just because an intersection is shown, it does not imply that the intersection contains elements; the intersection may in fact be empty, but the intersection is still shown.

3.3 Cardinality of a Set

In most cases, the term cardinality is just a fancy word to mean the number of elements in a set. When we are talking about infinite sets, there is more to the meaning of cardinality, but in data science, we don't typically have a need to deal with infinite sets, and so for us cardinality will simply mean the number of elements in a set.

One notation in mathematics for the **n**umber of elements of A is **n**(A). Another notation is $|A|$.

$$\text{If } A = \{-1, \ 0, \ 1\}$$

$$\text{then } n(A) = 3$$

Now we will write a function to measure the cardinality of a set. Again, for now, a set for our purposes will be represented as a vector. We will deal with the problem of repeated elements afterward. In R, we might start off like this:

```
#Create a set A with elements {1,2,3,4,5,6,7,8,cat,dog}.
***A <- c(1:8,"cat","dog")
length(A)
## [1] 10
#Next write a cardinality function. All we are really doing is making a
convenient name for the length() function.
cardinality <- function(M){length(M)}
cardinality(A)
## [1] 10
```

This is OK, but we will want to be careful in dealing with the following possible issues:

■ The set A contains NAs
■ The set A has repeated elements.

3.3.1 NAs

In R, missing values are represented by the symbol NA (NA stands for "not available"). Impossible values (e.g., values obtained by dividing by zero) are represented by the symbol NaN (*not a number*), but we won't focus on NaN here.

Try creating a dataset in Excel, leaving some cells blank. Then import it into RStudio using any method calling it testDF. Then use View(testDF), and see if there are NAs in the dataframe.

Here is a made-up dataset of pet store sales with one cell having missing data (Figures 3.2 and 3.3).

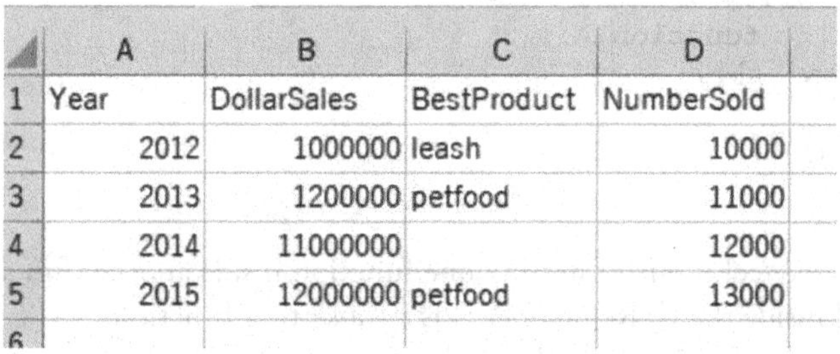

	A	B	C	D
1	Year	DollarSales	BestProduct	NumberSold
2	2012	1000000	leash	10000
3	2013	1200000	petfood	11000
4	2014	11000000		12000
5	2015	12000000	petfood	13000
6				

Figure 3.2   Missing data example.

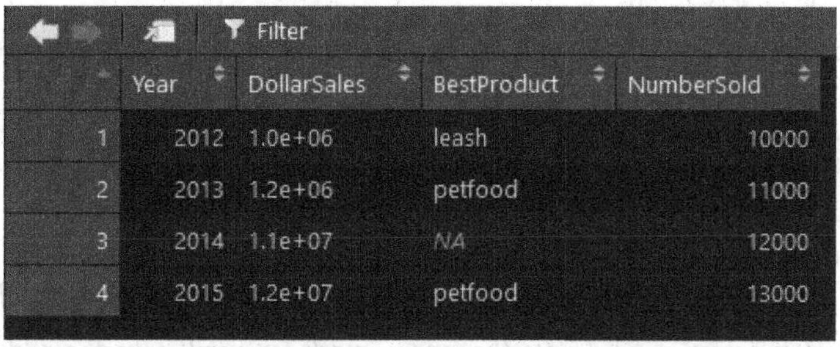

	Year	DollarSales	BestProduct	NumberSold
1	2012	1.0e+06	leash	10000
2	2013	1.2e+06	petfood	11000
3	2014	1.1e+07	NA	12000
4	2015	1.2e+07	petfood	13000

Figure 3.3   RStudio view of missing data.

To generate an NA, try creating that dataset in Excel and saving it as petStore.xlsx. Then try

```
petStore <- read.excel("petStore.xlsx")
View(petStore)
```

```
# We see above that an NA has been generated.
```

```
#It is often the case that when we read in (import) data from a csv file
or elsewhere, some of the rows will contain missing data; i.e., some
column in a row will be blank. When R reads in the data, it will usually
fill in a missing value with an NA. We say "usually" because it depends
on what technique (what function) is used to read in the data. For
example, if you use the "Import Data" button in RStudio (located in the
Environment tab), we will see NAs. Also, if you use the read.csv()
function by default, it will have respond in this way as well. Suppose we
have a set, represented by a vector, which contains NAs. How will our
cardinality() function respond?
A <- c(1:5,NA)
cardinality(A)
## [1] 6 #We see that it counts the NA as an element.
```

If we want our cardinality function to ignore NAs so as to measure the cardinality of A as 5, we must adjust the definition. We create a modification of the `cardinality()` function which will ignore NAs. With such a modification, `A<-c(1:5,NA)` will have a cardinality of 5 not 6. For emphasis, we will call this `cardinalityIGNA()` for *ignoring the NAs*.

3.3.2 R Code

```
#Adjusted cardinality()
cardinalityIGNA <- function(A){
  length(A[!is.na(A)])}
```

```
cardinalityIGNA(A)
## [1] 5
```

This definition uses the technique of nesting one function inside another function. In this example, is.na() is nested inside the []. Remember [] is a subsetting function.

`length()` like most functions in R can accept a vector as an argument. Reading from the inside out of the expression (always the best way to understand nested functions), we are applying `is.na()` to the vector A.

The output of `is.na()` is a Boolean vector, and so applying the not operator `!` gives a Boolean as well. In our `cardinalityIGNA()` function, the Boolean output of `!is.na()` is then made the argument in the subsetting function []. This has the effect of selecting only the elements which are not NAs. Then we count that with `length()`.

Math Note: This process of nesting functions when we are coding is an example of an important concept in basic mathematics called *function composition*. In mathematics, we write the composition of two functions f(x) and g(x) as f(g(x)). The mathematical notation for the composition of f(x) and g(x) is $f \circ g = f\big(g(x)\big)$. A math example would be where if f(x) = cos(x) and g(x) = (x^2 + 8), then $f \circ g = f\big(g(x)\big) = \cos\big(x^2 + 8\big)$. (*Note that many math texts will take the added step of saying* u = g(x) = (x^2 + 8) *and writing* f *as a function of* u, *not a function of* x, *like this:* f(u).)

Function	counts NAs	counts repetition
cardinality()	yes	yes
cardinalityIGNA()	no	yes
cardinalityIGNAUnique()	no	no
subset_vectors()	yes	no
subset_vectorsUnique()		no
equalSets()	yes	
equalSetsIGNA()	no	no
setequal()	yes	
intersection_of_sets()	no	no
intersect()	no	no
unionSets()		
unionSetsIGNA()	no	no
union()	yes	no
setdiff()	yes	
complementSets()	no	

Figure 3.4   Functions we build or use in this chapter and their response to NAs and repetition of elements.

Throughout this chapter, we will develop various functions and observe how they handle both NAs and repeated elements. The results are listed above in Figure 3.4. We list whether the function ignores NAs or counts them and whether each function ignores repeated elements (i.e., counts them only once) or counts them. Some of the entries are left empty as practice exercises.

3.3.3 Repeated Elements

In mathematics, by definition, a set cannot have repeated elements. If we want this to be part of our R definition of sets, we will need to make some adjustment to our cardinality function.

Next, we consider what to do if there are *repeated* elements in our vector. How should our cardinality function respond? Try to make this adjustment to the cardinality function yourself. The issue can be seen for A<-c(1:5,1:5); how many elements are in A? You could say 5, or you could say 10. Depending on the task or how you are using the function, either answer could be acceptable, but to align our definition with the mathematical definition of sets and cardinality, in this text we will choose to say there are five elements in A. However, our *current* definition of cardinality, cardinalityIGNA(), will give 10. Try to rewrite the definition of cardinality yourself to give 5. Call this function cardinalityIGNAUnique(). Hint: Consider the function **unique**(). Test it on A<-c(1:5,1:5). We will show an answer later when this becomes important in our coding problems. For now, we have

```
A <- c(1:8,"cat","dog")
D <- c(6,NA)
E <- c(1:4,1:3)
E
## [1] 1 2 3 4 1 2 3
cardinalityIGNA(A)
```

```
## [1] 10
cardinalityIGNA(D)
## [1] 1
cardinalityIGNA(E)
## [1] 7
```

Practice 3.3.1

1. As suggested above, write a cardinality function which will not count repeated elements of a set more than once.

Subset B ⊂ A

We say that the set B is a subset of the set A if every element of B is also in A (Figure 3.5).

The outer rectangle, denoted by U, is called the universal set. This U is just is a representation of the *context* of our discussion. For example, if B <- {1, 2, 3, 4} and A <- {0, 1, 2, 3, 4, 5}, U *might be* the set of digits {0, 1, 2, 3, 4, 5, 6, 7, 8, 9}. We may be talking about the set of all digits and then asking the question within that context. Later, in our discussions, the universal set will usually be the entire dataset we are working with – the entire dataframe with which we are working. From there, we will extract subsets of interest. For example, if we are working with a set of patients who are involved in the test of a new drug, U could be all the patients participating in the study, and A might be the subset of these patients that possess a particular gene. B might then be the set of patients that have this gene and are sick. Clearly, B is a subset of A, i.e., B ⊂ A.

Before we implement the subset function in R, we will look at an important function called **is.element()**.

```
#The is.element() function can take two arguments. If the first argument
is a single element and the second argument is a set, it will then check
to see if the first argument is in the second.
A <- c(1:8,"cat","dog")
D <- c(6,NA)
E <- c(1:4,1:3)
is.element(6,D) #is 6 and element of D?
## [1] TRUE
is.element(6,A) #is 6 and element of A?
## [1] TRUE
```

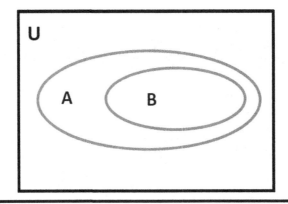

Figure 3.5   Universal set and B as a subset of A.

```
is.element(6,E) #is 6 and element of E?
## [1] FALSE
#Note: There is another way to do this. is.element(x, y) is identical to
x%in%y. To find more information about this operator, type ?`%in%` at the
prompt.
#In the next loop, we check whether each element of E is in A.
A <- c(1:8,"cat","dog")
E <- c(1:4,1:3)
D <- c(6,NA)
for(i in E){
  print(is.element(i,A))
}
## [1] TRUE
## [1] TRUE
## [1] TRUE
## [1] TRUE
## [1] TRUE
## [1] TRUE
## [1] TRUE

#now try

for(i in D){
  print(is.element(i,A))
}
## [1] TRUE
## [1] FALSE
#Note in this second loop, NA is not in A.
#Let's try
F <- c(NA,10,11)
#Now if we check to see if any of the elements of F are in D, the first
element we check in F is NA. So let's see what happens.
for(i in F){
  print(is.element(i,D))
}
## [1] TRUE
## [1] FALSE
## [1] FALSE
#So we see that is.element treats NA like a normal element, and it
reports that the NA in F is an element of D.

#Now let's try the following instead of the first loop we tried. #Instead
of
# for(i in E){
#   print(is.element(i,A))
# }
#try this:
is.element(E,A)
## [1] TRUE TRUE TRUE TRUE TRUE TRUE TRUE
#As usual, most functions in R are "vectorized", meaning you can use
vectors as arguments. This is not typical in programming languages.
Languages like Python, Java, C++, do not generally have this facility. In
general, vectorized code will run faster than a loop, but this is not
always true.
```

Practice 3.3.2

1. If G is a subset of H, describe what the result of **is.element**(G,H) would be. Explain why.

3.4 Implementing the Subset Function in R

We can implement a subset function for vectors as shown below. Later, however, we will need to implement a subset function within the context of a dataframe. That will be a different implementation.

```
#Subsets

A <- c(1:8,"cat","dog")
B<-1:5
#We will try working with an operator which is popular among programmers
but is equivalent to the is.element() function. The operator has a bit of
a peculiar appearance:

%in%

and is called the infix operator.

?`%in%` #To get help on this, use the ? and backticks.

#Returning to the previously defined sets A and B, we now use the
equivalent %in%.
A <- c(1:8,"cat","dog")
B<-1:5
B%in%A #same as is.element(B,A)
## [1] TRUE TRUE TRUE TRUE TRUE
#Now build our subset function.
subset_vectors <- function(smaller,larger){
  return(all(smaller%in%larger))
}
subset_vectors(A,B)
## [1] FALSE
subset_vectors(B,A)
## [1] TRUE
```

3.4.1 Explanation

It is clear that B ⊂ A. The statement B%in%A asks the question, Which elements in B are in A? %in% is what we call a binary operator. There are many types of operators. We have used the logical operators for "and", "or", and "not" (&, |, and ~ respectively) in the last chapter. We have also seen the statement A == B. The double equal sign is another example of an operator. Both %in% and == are called binary operators because whenever we use them, we need to have something to the left of them and something to the right. So, we need *two* elements, one on each side, and thus the word *binary*. The binary operator %in% is one of a family of operators referred to as infix operators[1]

---

[1] Note that you can even create your own operators. Suppose you want to create an operator called "ni" for "not in" instead of the "in" operator we already have. That would mean you want to negate the output of %in%. You can do this with "%ni%" <- Negate("%in%"). If this is confusing, wait until the next chapter when we discuss logic.

(see: https://cran.r-project.org/doc/manuals/r-release/R-lang.html#Infix-and-prefix-operators).
We just explained the mechanism for is.element(). To re-emphasize this, we explain it again for
B%in%A. As we said, this asks, Which elements in B are in A? Notice how many elements are
in the output of this statement. The output is TRUE TRUE TRUE TRUE TRUE. So, there are
five elements in the output, not ten. The vector A has ten elements, but the output only has five
elements. What this statement is doing is checking *each element in B* and asking whether each
is in A. So, A could have 100 elements, but the question is only about which of the elements *in*
B are in A, and thus it is only asking about the five elements in B. That is why the output is of
length 5.

Practice 3.4.3

    1. If n(A) = 10 and n(B) = 5, how many elements will be in the Boolean vector A%in%B?
       (Remember n(A) refers to the number of elements in A and is also called the cardinality
       of A.)
    2. If n(A) = 5 and n(B) = 10, how many elements will be in the Boolean vector A%in%B?

Now returning to the task of implementing a function for subset in the above code, we want to
make sure that every element in B is a member of A. In the above code, B%in%A gives TRUE
TRUE TRUE TRUE TRUE. However, if *even one* of the elements of the output had been false,
then we would not want to say that B is a subset of A. Thus, we next check if all the elements of B
are in A. This is accomplished with the function **all**(). From the R documentation, we read that
the argument to the **all**() function should be a Boolean vector. That is exactly what we have put
into **all**() when we write **all**(B%in%A). Also, from the documentation, the *output* of **all**()
is a logical vector of *length one*. (Remember, logical and Boolean mean the same thing.) So, the
output is a single TRUE or single FALSE. It will only give TRUE if every one of its arguments is
TRUE. That is exactly what we needed. Thus, we can write the **subset_vectors**() function
just by returning this:

```
all(B%in%A)
```

To emphasize the fact that the first set, in order to be a subset of the second set, should not be
bigger than the second set, we use *smaller* and *larger* for the parameter names.

```
#Next the question is whether subset_vectors ignores NA or not. What are
the possible cases to be considered? Case 1. Smaller has NA and larger
does not. Case 2. Smaller has NA and so does larger. Case 3. Smaller does
not have NA but larger does. Case 4. Neither smaller nor larger has NA.
Ana<-c(A,NA)
Bna<-c(B,NA)

A
## [1] "1"   "2"   "3"   "4"   "5"   "6"   "7"   "8"   "cat" "dog"
Ana
## [1] "1"   "2"   "3"   "4"   "5"   "6"   "7"   "8"   "cat" "dog" NA
B
## [1] 1 2 3 4 5
Bna
## [1]  1  2  3  4  5 NA
Case 3. Smaller does not have NA but larger does.
```

```
subset_vectors(B,Ana) #Actually running this does not answer the question
of "if the smaller set has an NA, will it still be considered to be a
subset of the larger?"
## [1] TRUE #The result is not surprising since B is even a subset of A.
Case 1. Smaller does not have NA but larger does.
subset_vectors(Bna,A) #Here we see it does not ignore the NA in Bna.
## [1] FALSE
Case 2. Smaller has NA and so does larger.
subset_vectors(Bna,Ana) #Actually running this is not conclusive.
## [1] TRUE
#Question: How does subset_vectors() handle repetitions?
Brep<-c(B,B)
subset_vectors(Brep,A)
## [1] TRUE #Answer: it ignores repetitions.
```

Practice 3.4.4

1. Write a function called **subset_vectorsUnique()** that does not ignore repetitions. Our current subset_vectors() will say that a = c(1:5, 1:5) is a subset of b = 1:10. This may be what we want, but as an exercise, write a function which would not allow this to be true.
2. Check the answer for case 4 above.

3.5 Equality of Sets

If two sets A and B have the same elements, we say they are *equal regardless of the order* in which they are presented. In mathematical notation we write A = B. For example, if

$$A = \{1,2,3\}, \ B = \{3,2,1\}$$

we say A equals B and write it as A = B.

This is the way mathematics handles sets. However, neither the R equality operator "==" nor the R assignment operator "=" will accomplish this for us in our journey of implementing the mathematics in R.

In mathematics, the standard way to check if two sets are equal is to show that A ⊂ B and B ⊂ A. For example, a mathematical argument to show that A = B, with A = {1, 2, 3}, B = {3, 2, 1}, would be to first show that A ⊂ B and then show that B ⊂ A.

It may seem obvious, but it is a very powerful technique in mathematical proofs. We use the idea in our R code.

```
A <- c(1:8,"cat","dog")
C <- c("cat","dog",1:8) #We want to say that these two are equal.
#We cannot use "==".
A==C #Although as sets A and C are equal, we get the following:
## [1] FALSE FALSE FALSE FALSE FALSE FALSE FALSE FALSE FALSE FALSE
#This just gives a Boolean vector resulting from checking if the sets
A and C are equal element by element. This is not at all what we want.
Instead we will build the following.
#We want to check if each element in A is also an element in C and if
each element in C is also an element of A. This is clearly related to
what subset_vectors does when it employs is.element().
is.element(A,C)
## [1] TRUE TRUE TRUE TRUE TRUE TRUE TRUE TRUE TRUE TRUE
is.element(C,A)
```

```
##  [1] TRUE TRUE TRUE TRUE TRUE TRUE TRUE TRUE TRUE TRUE

equalSets <- function(A,B){
  subset_vectors(A,B)&subset_vectors(B,A)
}
#Notice this uses the logical conjunction operator we studied in the
previous chapter.
equalSets(A,C)
## [1] TRUE
#But what about when the only difference between the two sets is an NA?
Our current version of equalSets() will say they are not the same.
Ana<-c(A,NA)
equalSets(Ana,C)
## Warning in is.element(A, B) and is.element(B, A): longer object length
is not
## a multiple of shorter object length.
## [1] FALSE  #Remember that a warning in R is not an error.
#If we want a "set equal" function which would ignore an NA, we can use
what we used earlier: A[!is.na(A)]. This filters out all the NAs from A.
equalSetsIGNA <- function(A,B){
  all((is.element(A[!is.na(A)],B[!is.na(B)]) & is.element(B[!is.
na(B)],A[!is.na(A)]))==TRUE)

}
equalSetsIGNA(Ana,C)
## [1] TRUE
#We can also use the function we wrote earlier: subset_vectors().
equalSetsIGNA <- function(A,B){
  all((subset_vectors(A[!is.na(A)],B[!is.na(B)]) & subset_vectors(B[!is.
na(B)],A[!is.na(A)]))==TRUE)

}
equalSetsIGNA(Ana,C)
## [1] TRUE
#What about sets that have repetitions? How will they be handled when
considering subsets?
Arep<-c(A,A)
Crep<-c(C,C)
Arep
##  [1] "1"   "2"   "3"   "4"   "5"   "6"   "7"   "8"   "cat" "dog" "1"
## [12] "2"   "3"   "4"   "5"   "6"   "7"   "8"   "cat" "dog"
Crep
##  [1] "cat" "dog" "1"   "2"   "3"   "4"   "5"   "6"   "7"   "8"   "cat"
## [12] "dog" "1"   "2"   "3"   "4"   "5"   "6"   "7"   "8"
equalSetsIGNA(Arep,C)
## [1] TRUE
equalSetsIGNA(Arep,Crep)
## [1] TRUE
equalSetsIGNA(A,C)
## [1] TRUE
#Thus equalSetsIGNA() will indicate two sets are equal even if there are
repeated elements in one but not the other.
```

Instead of building **equalSets**() from a conjunction of **subset_vectors**() with itself, we could have used R's setequal() function!

```
#Use setequal() to test whether two sets are equal.
A <- c(1:8,"cat","dog")
C <- c("cat","dog",1:8)

#How about setequal()?
setequal(A,C)
## [1] TRUE
#Now, what does it do in the face of an NA?
D<-c(A,NA) #Append an NA, and call this new set D.
setequal(A,D)
## [1] FALSE
```

If one of the sets has an NA and the other does not have NA, then they will not be treated as equal. This is the same as our **equalSets**().

If we are satisfied that NAs will be treated as additional elements of the set, we can use **setequal()** as our function for equality of sets. If, on the other hand, as an exercise, we want to ignore NAs when comparing two sets for equality but want to use R's **setequal**() function, we could call it **setequalIgNA()** and define it like this:

```
setequalIgNA <- function(A,B){
  A<-A[!is.na(A)]
  B<-B[!is.na(B)]
  return(setequal(A,B))
}
setequalIgNA(A,D)
## [1] TRUE
#How about repetitions? Yes, the built in function ignores repetitions.
setequalIgNA(Arep,C)
## [1] TRUE
setequalIgNA(Arep,Crep)
## [1] TRUE
setequalIgNA(A,C)
## [1] TRUE
```

Practice 3.5.5

1. Write a version of setequal() that does not ignore repetitions.

3.5.1 Fixing the Cardinality Function Discussed Earlier

```
#Recall that our cardinalityIGNA() function was not equipped to ignore
repetitions.
E <- c(1:4,1:3)
A <- c(1:4)
cardinalityIGNA(E)
## [1] 7
#To fix cardinalityIGNA(), consider
unique(E)
## [1] 1 2 3 4
cardinalityIGNAUnique <- function(A){
  length(unique(A[!is.na(A)]))}
```

Practice 3.5.6

1. Test this on E.

3.6 Empty Set: {}

A set with no elements is called an **empty set**. In mathematics, it is denoted with either of the two symbols { } or Ø. Examples would be the set of all months with 32 days or the set of integers that are both even and odd. We need to be aware of this in our code because if we make a specification on a set of variables and that specification is *overspecified*, meaning there are no elements that satisfy it, our code may fail unless we remember that this possibility may occur and deal with it in our code. In R, this could be a vector which is set to NULL.

```
J <- NULL
length(J)
## [1] 0
```

Practice 3.6.7
1. Write a function called isEmptySet() which gives TRUE if the set is set to NULL and FALSE otherwise.

3.7 Intersection: A ∩ B

The intersection of two sets, A and B, is the set of elements which are common to both and is denoted by A ∩ B (Figure 3.6).

So if A <- c(1:8, "cat", "dog") and B <- 1:5, then A ∩ B = 1:5. How do we implement this in R?

```
#Intersection of Sets A and B

A <- c(1:8,"cat","dog")
B <- 1:5
C <- c("cat","dog",1:8)
D<-c(A,NA)
E <- c(1:4,1:3)

#We can find the elements of A that are in B with the following Boolean
expression.
#This will generate a Boolean of length len(A)
#being TRUE only for the elements of A which are in B.
A%in%B
```

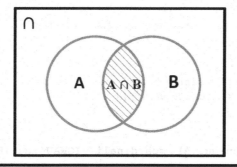

Figure 3.6   Intersection of A and B.

```
## [1]  TRUE  TRUE  TRUE  TRUE  TRUE FALSE FALSE FALSE FALSE FALSE
#Similarly we find the elements of B that are in A with
B%in%A.
## [1] TRUE TRUE TRUE TRUE TRUE
#The length of this Boolean is len(B).

#It is clear that the intersection of two sets will never have more
elements than that of the smaller of the two. Thus, if cardinalityIGNA(C)
<=cardinalityIGNA(D),
#then C%in%D will be a Boolean vector containing TRUE for every element
that is in C and also in D. Thus, we can build a conditional clause in
our intersection function based on this.
intersection_of_sets <- function(A,B){
  if(cardinalityIGNA(A)<=cardinalityIGNA(B)){
    return(A[A%in%B])
  } else
  {
    return(B[B%in%A])
  }

}
intersection_of_sets(A,B)
## [1] 1 2 3 4 5
intersection_of_sets(A,C)
##  [1] "1"   "2"   "3"   "4"   "5"   "6"   "7"   "8"   "cat" "dog"
intersection_of_sets(A,Ana)
##  [1] "1"   "2"   "3"   "4"   "5"   "6"   "7"   "8"   "cat" "dog"
intersection_of_sets(A,D)
##  [1] "1"   "2"   "3"   "4"   "5"   "6"   "7"   "8"   "cat" "dog"
intersection_of_sets(A,E)
## [1] 1 2 3 4 1 2 3
#Recall that A and E are
A
##  [1] "1"   "2"   "3"   "4"   "5"   "6"   "7"   "8"   "cat" "dog"
E
## [1] 1 2 3 4 1 2 3
#If we ask for the intersection of A and E, we get
## [1] 1 2 3 4 1 2 3
#which is not what we want. However recall our modified cardinality
function
cardinalityIGNAUnique <- function(A){
  length(unique(A[!is.na(A)]))
}
#If we use that and add in these transformations
 A=unique(A)
  B=unique(B)

#then we can correct the situation
intersection_of_sets <- function(A,B){
  A=unique(A)
  B=unique(B)

  if(cardinalityIGNAUnique(A)<=cardinalityIGNAUnique(B)){
    return(A[A%in%B])
  } else
```

```
  {
    return(B[B%in%A])
  }

}
#You may have noticed that R is treating "1" and 1 as the same here.
```

Practice 3.7.8

1. Implement **intersection_of_sets**() using **ifelse**().

Actually R has an **intersect**() function which we can also use. Let's see how it behaves on some sample sets.

```
#Recall our sample sets.
A
##  [1] "1"   "2"   "3"   "4"   "5"   "6"   "7"   "8"   "cat" "dog"
Ana
##  [1] "1"   "2"   "3"   "4"   "5"   "6"   "7"   "8"   "cat" "dog" NA
B
## [1] 1 2 3 4 5
C
##  [1] "cat" "dog" "1"   "2"   "3"   "4"   "5"   "6"   "7"   "8"
D
##  [1] "1"   "2"   "3"   "4"   "5"   "6"   "7"   "8"   "cat" "dog" NA
E
## [1] 1 2 3 4 1 2 3
intersection_of_sets(A,B)
## [1] 1 2 3 4 5
intersect(A,B)
## [1] 1 2 3 4 5
intersection_of_sets(A,C)
##  [1] "1"   "2"   "3"   "4"   "5"   "6"   "7"   "8"   "cat" "dog"
intersect(A,C)
##  [1] "1"   "2"   "3"   "4"   "5"   "6"   "7"   "8"   "cat" "dog"
intersection_of_sets(A,Ana)
##  [1] "1"   "2"   "3"   "4"   "5"   "6"   "7"   "8"   "cat" "dog"
intersect(A,Ana)
##  [1] "1"   "2"   "3"   "4"   "5"   "6"   "7"   "8"   "cat" "dog"
intersection_of_sets(A,D)
##  [1] "1"   "2"   "3"   "4"   "5"   "6"   "7"   "8"   "cat" "dog"
intersect(A,D)
##  [1] "1"   "2"   "3"   "4"   "5"   "6"   "7"   "8"   "cat" "dog"
intersection_of_sets(A,E)
## [1] 1 2 3 4
intersect(A,E)
## [1] 1 2 3 4
```

Notice how intersect() handles NAs. If both sets contain NA, then the intersection will also contain an NA. Thus, it is treating NA as an element. If both sets contain two NAs, it considers the repetition of the NAs as a single element. This aligns with our math expectations. Similarly, if H and I have repeated elements, the intersect() ignores the repetitions.

Further notice, with respect to the intersect function, that the association of the empty set with a vector defined as NULL (J = NULL) aligns with the mathematical notion that the intersection of any set A with the empty set is the empty set: $A \cap \emptyset = \emptyset$.

3.8 Union A∪B

The union of two sets, A and B, is the set of items that are in either A or B or both A and B (Figure 3.7). So if A = c(1:8) and B = 5:10, then $A \bigcup B$ = 1:10. How can we implement this in R?

```
#Union of A and B

unionSets <- function(A,B){
  unique(c(A,B))
}

unionSetsIGNA <- function(A,B){
  unique(c(A[!is.na(A)],B[!is.na(B)]))

}

unionSetsIGNA( A, B)
## [1] "1"    "2"    "3"    "4"    "5"    "6"    "7"    "8"    "cat" "dog"
unionSetsIGNA( A, C)
## [1] "1"    "2"    "3"    "4"    "5"    "6"    "7"    "8"    "cat" "dog"
unionSetsIGNA( A,Ana )
## [1] "1"    "2"    "3"    "4"    "5"    "6"    "7"    "8"    "cat" "dog"
unionSetsIGNA(A ,D )
## [1] "1"    "2"    "3"    "4"    "5"    "6"    "7"    "8"    "cat" "dog"
unionSetsIGNA( A, E)
## [1] "1"    "2"    "3"    "4"    "5"    "6"    "7"    "8"    "cat" "dog"
```

On the other hand, we don't have to implement the function. It is already there with the **union**() function.

```
A <- c(1:8,"cat","dog")
B <- 1:5
```

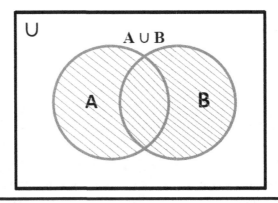

Figure 3.7   Union of A and B.

```
D <- c(B,NA)
E <- c(A,NA)
F <- c(D,NA)
F
## [1]   1   2   3   4   5 NA NA
G <- c(E,NA)
H <- c(1:8,1:8)
I <- c(1:5,1:5)
J <- NULL
#How does it handle elements that are common to both sets?
union(A,B)
##  [1] "1"   "2"   "3"   "4"   "5"   "6"   "7"   "8"   "cat" "dog"
#What does it do when one of the sets has an NA?
union(A,D) #NA is an element of the set D.
##  [1] "1"   "2"   "3"   "4"   "5"   "6"   "7"   "8"   "cat" "dog" NA
#What does it do with NA in each set?
union(D,E) #NA is an element, and just like other elements, it counts it
only once.
##  [1] "1"   "2"   "3"   "4"   "5"   NA    "6"   "7"   "8"   "cat" "dog"
F
## [1]   1   2   3   4   5 NA NA
G
##  [1] "1"   "2"   "3"   "4"   "5"   "6"   "7"   "8"   "cat" "dog" NA
## [12] NA
H
##  [1] 1 2 3 4 5 6 7 8 1 2 3 4 5 6 7 8
I
##  [1] 1 2 3 4 5 1 2 3 4 5
union(F,G)
##  [1] "1"   "2"   "3"   "4"   "5"   NA    "6"   "7"   "8"   "cat" "dog"
union(H,I)
## [1] 1 2 3 4 5 6 7 8
```

Practice 3.8.9

1. Can you find any differences between the behaviors of **unionSetsIGNA()** and **union()**?

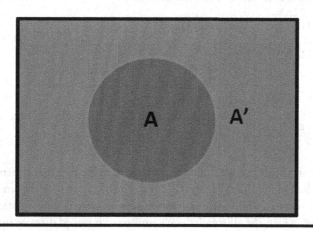

Figure 3.8   Complement of A.

3.9 Complement A′ (Absolute Complement)

The set of elements in U that are not in A is called the complement of A and is denoted as either A′, A^C, or $\overline{A}$ (Figure 3.8).

In the picture above, A is the circular set. If U = 0:9 and A = 5:9, then A^C = 0:4. In the sets package of R, we have setdiff(). We can use setdiff() here. We need to specify a U in order for the notion of complement to make sense since it is defined in terms of U.

```
U <- 1:10
even=seq(from=2,to=10,by=2)
U
## [1]  1  2  3  4  5  6  7  8  9 10
even
## [1]  2  4  6  8 10
#We can use R's setdiff() function. In mathematics, the difference of two
sets, written A - B, is the set of all elements of A that are not
elements of B. Thus, note that A - B is not the same as B - A.
L <- 1:12
setdiff(L,U)
## [1] 11 12
setdiff(U,L) #We are subtracting the right argument from the left
argument.
## integer(0)
setdiff(U,even)
## [1] 1 3 5 7 9
#What about if the right argument contains some elements not in the left
argument?
evenPlus12 <- c(even,12)
setdiff(U,evenPlus12) #setdiff() just removes the elements that are
common to the two arguments from the left argument. Thus, it is not
exactly what we want for the complement function.
## [1] 1 3 5 7 9
#Does setdiff() ignore NA?
setdiff(U_NA,even) #No, NA is treated as an element.
## [1] 1 3  5  7  9 NA
#Define complement using setdiff().
complement <- function(universal,smaller){
  if(all(smaller%in%universal)){
    return(setdiff(universal,smaller))
  }
  else(return(NULL))
}

complement(U,evenPlus12)
## NULL
complement(U,even)
## [1] 1 3 5 7 9
```

To write a complement() function, we should first check to make sure that the smaller set is actually contained in U. We have done this with an *if else* test. In the case where the smaller set is not actually a subset of U, we return NULL. Of course, we could have written this test using our subset_vector() function, and in fact, the all(smaller%in%universal) is pulled directly from the definition of subset_vector(). Also, take note of how this function deals with NA in either the smaller set or in the universal set (U_NA). If the smaller set has an NA (as is the case in M above) but U does not, then the NA is ignored. However, if U has an NA in it (U_NA) but the smaller set does not, then NA will be retained in the output. If both U and the smaller set have NA, then the complement will not have the NA. So setdiff() will behave as expected except if the smaller set has NA but U does not.

Practice 3.9.10

1. Without **sefdiff**(), can you use **is.element**() to define complement?
2. Explain why using **ifelse**() in **complement_ifelse**() as follows does not work.

```
complement_ifelse <- function(universal,smaller){
  if(all(smaller%in%universal)){
    return(setdiff(universal,smaller))
  }
  else(return(NULL))
}
```

Test it on **complement_ifelse**(U,even).

3.10 Implementation of Complement without Using setdiff()

```
#Complement of A with respect to Universal Set U

U=1:10
even=seq(from=2,to=10,by=2)
U
## [1]  1  2  3  4  5  6  7  8  9 10
even
## [1]  2  4  6  8 10
#Complement of even
U%in%even
## [1] FALSE  TRUE FALSE  TRUE FALSE  TRUE FALSE  TRUE FALSE  TRUE
!U%in%even
## [1]  TRUE FALSE  TRUE FALSE  TRUE FALSE  TRUE FALSE  TRUE FALSE
U[!U%in%even]
## [1] 1 3 5 7 9
#or we can use is.element().
is.element(U,even)
## [1] FALSE  TRUE FALSE  TRUE FALSE  TRUE FALSE  TRUE FALSE  TRUE
!is.element(U,even)
## [1]  TRUE FALSE  TRUE FALSE  TRUE FALSE  TRUE FALSE  TRUE FALSE
U[!is.element(U,even)]
## [1] 1 3 5 7 9
G=1:3
U[!is.element(U,G)]
## [1]  4  5  6  7  8  9 10
H=c(7,9,10)
U[!is.element(U,H)]
## [1] 1 2 3 4 5 6 8
Hna=c(H,NA)
U[!is.element(U,Hna)]
## [1] 1 2 3 4 5 6 8
complementSets <- function(A,U){
  if(subset_vectors(smaller=A,larger = U)&!is.element(NA,A)&!is.
element(NA,U)){
```

```
    U[!is.element(U,A)]
  } else
  {
    print("At least one of the sets has an NA or smaller set is not a
subset of U")
  }
}
complementSets(H,U)
## [1] 1 2 3 4 5 6 8
complementSets(A,U)
## [1] "At least one of the sets has an NA or smaller set is not a subset
of U"
```

3.11 Cross Product of Two Sets

The cross product of two sets is an important concept in discrete math. First let us review what is meant by an ordered pair. Examples of ordered pairs are (2,5), (u,v), ($,&), and so on. An ordered pair is a pair of elements where the order that they are written is important. The fact that the order that they are written is important means that we don't consider (2,5) to be the same ordered pair as (5,2). Also note that ordered pairs are often pictured as points in the plane. Of course, you are familiar with considering (2,5) to be a point in a plane.

Now let us consider the cross product of two sets. Given two sets A and B, the cross product, also called the Cartesian product, of A and B is denoted by A × B and is the set of all ordered pairs (a, b) where $a \in A$ and $b \in B$. For example, if $A = \{n, p\}$ and $B = \{1, 2, 3\}$, then

$$A \times B = \left\{ (n,1), (n,2), (n,3), (p,1), (p,2), (p,3) \right\}$$

Notice that A is a set, B is a set, and A × B is also a set; the elements of the set A are single letters, and the elements of B are single numbers, but the elements of A × B are ordered pairs.

Now we have a problem. R does not have a concept of a point. And similarly, it does not have a concept of an ordered pair. Actually, it does not have a concept of a set either, but we defined a set as a vector of unique elements. So how should we define a set of ordered pairs? We are kind of stuck here because we defined a set as a kind of vector. But how can we make a vector of ordered pairs in R. We can use a list to represent a set of ordered pairs of course. For example, in the above example of A × B, we could represent it as a two-element list. The first element would have the first element of each ordered pair in A × B, and the second element would have the second element of each ordered pair of A × B. It could look like the following.

First Element of List	Second Element of List
n	1
p	1
n	2
p	2
n	3
P	3

The problem with this is that the cross product of two sets is supposed to be a set, and we already defined the concept of set as a kind of vector, but this is not a vector in R. But we will use this definition anyway. (Note that we could also use the concept of matrix instead of list to define the cross product of two sets, but we will use list.) Since we won't actually use the concept of cross product in later chapters, we will leave it as an exercise for the reader to implement the cross product in R as a list.

Practice 3.11.11

1. (Optional) Implement the cross product of two sets A and B as a list. Hint: A nested set of loops should work. After implementing it, you may also check the functions **expand. grid**() and **outer**().

3.12 Handling Errors More Smoothly

```
#Printing a message like we have done may not be the best way to treat a
problem of wrong usage of the function because if the call to our
function occurs in a long sequence of code, that code may depend on the
output of this function, and so if this function is not being used
properly, we want to stop the entire sequence of code.
#This can be done by generating an actual error using stop().
complementSets <- function(A,U){
  if(subset_vectors(smaller=A,larger = U)&!is.element(NA,A)&!is.
element(NA,U)){
    U[!is.element(U,A)]
  } else
  {
    stop("At least one of the sets has an NA or the smaller set is not a
subset of U")
  }
}
complementSets(H,U)
## [1] 1 2 3 4 5 6 8
complementSets(A,U)
Error in complementSets(Hna, c(U, NA)):
  At least one of the sets has an NA or the smaller set is not a subset
of U
complementSets(Hna,U)
Error in complementSets(Hna, c(U, NA)):
  At least one of the sets has an NA or the smaller set is not a subset
of U
complementSets(Hna,c(U,NA))
Error in complementSets(Hna, c(U, NA)):
  At least one of the sets has an NA or the smaller set is not a subset
of U
#In our set union, intersection, and equality functions, we have been
treating sets with NA differently. In the current version of
complementSets(), the process stops when an NA exists, but previously we
would just remove the NA.

complementSets <- function(A,U){
if(subset_vectors(smaller=A,larger = U)){
```

```
    A=A[!is.na(A)]
    U=U[!is.na(U)]
    U[!is.element(U,A)]
  } else
  {
    stop("Smaller set is not a subset of U")
  }
}
complementSets(Hna,c(U,NA))
## [1] 1 2 3 4 5 6 8
complementSets(c(U,NA),Hna)
Error in complementSets(c(U, NA), Hna): Smaller set is not a subset of U
```

3.13 Algebraic Properties of Sets

Now that we have some simple functions, we can test them on the well-known algebraic properties of sets. There are the Commutative, Associative, Distributive, Identity, and Complement laws. We don't attempt to prove these laws. This can be done with Venn diagrams. Instead, we will just use them as an opportunity to test out our functions for cardinality, subset, intersection, union, and complement to help in confirming that our functions are working properly.

A list of these properties is given below. We will test out a few of them. It would be a good exercise for the reader to test out a few others. You can also find other laws of sets by searching them on the Internet. In addition, we will also explore a pair of statements about the cardinality of sets.

3.13.1 Commutative Laws

For any two finite sets A and B,

  i. $A \cup B = B \cup A$
  ii. $A \cap B = B \cap A$

3.13.2 Associative Laws

For any three finite sets A, B and C,

  i. $(A \cup B) \cup C = A \cup (B \cup C)$
  ii. $(A \cap B) \cap C = A \cap (B \cap C)$

3.13.3 Idempotent Laws

For any finite set A,

  i. $A \cup A = A$
  ii. $A \cap A = A$

3.13.4 Identities

  i. $A \cup \emptyset = A$
  ii. $A \cap U = A$

3.13.5 Boundedness

i. $A \cup U = U$
ii. $A \cap \varnothing = \varnothing$

3.13.6 Distributive Laws

For any three finite sets A, B and C,

i. $A \cup (B \cap C) = (A \cup B) \cap (A \cup C)$
ii. $A \cap (B \cup C) = (A \cap B) \cup (A \cap C)$

3.13.7 Cardinality for Finite Sets

i. $n(A \cup B) = n(A) + n(B) - n(A \cap B)$
ii. $n(A \cap B) = n(A) + n(B)$, if A and B are disjoint (meaning A and B have nothing in common)

3.14 Notes on the Reasoning behind These Laws

Since these are called laws, it means that they must hold true for any sets A, B, and C. Here though, we will just make up some sets and test our *functions* to see if they are working properly. None of this will prove any of the above laws. We are simply running a check to see if our functions are working. If we take three arbitrary sets A, B, and C and when using our union and intersection functions, if we find that the above Distributive Law part (i) is not true, then we would conclude that something is wrong with our functions (not with the laws).

It is seen that the above laws involve intersection and union; and they also deal with cardinality. So, we can test our functions on these laws. First though it may be useful to some readers to review a few of these (before using R).

To see how to prove these laws, the reader can search for set theory proofs and will find many fairly easy-to-understand proofs. We will not go down that route here.

3.15 Testing Some of the Properties

Testing $n(A \cup B) = n(A) + n(B) - n(A \cap B)$
    Check the left-hand side (LHS):

```
#Testing n(A∪B)=n(A)+n(B)-n(A∩B)
#Here are some sample sets.
A <- c(1:8,'dog','cat')
B <- 1:5
#First test the LHS.
unionSets(A,B)
## [1] "1"   "2"   "3"   "4"   "5"   "6"   "7"   "8"   "dog" "cat"
#Reminder: Here is our original cardinality function.
#cardinality <- function(M){length(M)}
#And here is our modified cardinality function.
```

```
#cardinalityIGNAUnique <- function(A){length(unique(A[!is.na(A)]))}

cardinalityIGNAUnique(unionSets(A,B))
## [1] 10
#Now look at the terms of the right-hand side (RHS) of
n(A∪B)=n(A)+n(B)-n(A∩B).
cardinalityIGNAUnique(A)
## [1] 10
cardinalityIGNAUnique(B)
## [1] 5
cardinalityIGNAUnique(intersection_of_sets(A,B))
## [1] 5
#Now check if the LHS is equal to the RHS.
cardinalityIGNAUnique(unionSets(A,B))==cardinalityIGNAUnique(A)+cardinal
ityIGNAUnique(B)-cardinalityIGNAUnique(intersection_of_sets(A,B))
## [1] TRUE
```

So at least in this case (for these two sets), all is working well. You can check some of the other sample sets to confirm that even if there are repeated items or NAs, the functions still perform as expected.

Practice 3.15.12

1. Choose three of the statements above and give examples. This means you should make up a few sets and see if the LHS of the statement is the same as the RHS using our set functions that we have written.
2. In question 1, you have shown that the functions seem to work as we hoped by choosing a few example sets and showing that for these sets, an algebraic property "holds". Assuming you were able to do this in question 1, does that mean you have proved the property? Why or why not?
3. Take two sets and show that the following (one of De Morgan's laws) holds, at least for the two sets and the functions we built: $(A \cup B) \cap C = (A \cup C) \cap (B \cup C)$.
4. Fill in the empty cells in the Figure 3.4.

Side note: By the way, as a point of interest, there is a relationship between *if then* statements from our logic chapter and set theory in this chapter. Recall for example the statement at the beginning of this chapter: All men are mortal. This can be thought of as a statement about sets of objects. Which sets? The set of men, and the set of mortals (things that live and die). When we say all men are mortal, we are saying that men are within the set of mortal things. That is, we are saying that the set of men is a *subset* of the set of mortals, and the same is the case with "if p then q". This can be thought of as a statement about sets as well. It says that if something is in the set of things of type p, then it must be in the set of things of type q. Again, in set language, this can be expressed as the set of things that are of type p are a subset of the set of things of type q.

Chapter 4

Probability

Probability Part 1

- Sample space
- Sampling unit/individual
- Event
- Set operations
- How to bring these concepts into our R session

This chapter will provide most of the probability concepts necessary to implement the Naïve Bayes algorithm and will show how to implement these concepts in R.

We will work with a dataset that shows the voting records of US senators on 16 issues. These votes are recorded as y (yes) and n (no). There is another variable called Class which is the senator's party affiliation (meaning which political party they belong to: Democratic or Republican). Usually we will be trying to predict the party affiliation from the voting pattern on the issues. If you are interested in what the actual issues being voted on are, you can search the web for HouseVotes84 and find these in the R documentation.

Functions Coded in This Chapter
union_event
multi_union_event
intersect_event
intersect_event 2
complement_event
prob
conditional_prob
bool2event
probArr

4.1 Dealing with Missing Values in a Dataset

The first half of this chapter focuses on basic concepts of probability. At the same time, we spend a lot of time working on how to deal with missing values in a dataframe. Although the main concern is the basic concepts of probability, it is also a good time to learn to deal with missing values, and so the issues of missing values are sprinkled throughout this chapter.

There are many approaches to dealing with NAs occurring in the dataset. Most of them revolve around interpolation. Interpolation for NAs basically means guessing what would be an appropriate value to replace the NA with. Of course, it would be nicer to say "intelligent guessing". To make the guessing intelligent, a common idea is to use regression or K Nearest Neighbor (KNN) to interpolate the values that are missing. You can search the web to find out about these approaches. We won't use any of that right now. For now, we simply delete any row that has an NA in it. The function **complete.cases**() performs this action. For datasets that have many rows, if the percentage of rows that have NAs is small and if the rows that have NAs are random (for example, they would not be random if all of the NAs only occur among the democratic senators in the current dataset), then deleting all rows that have NAs may be an acceptable course of action. In any case, we will go down this route for now.

```
#install.packages("mlbench")
library(mlbench)
## Warning: Package "mlbench" was built under R version 3.4.3.
library(dplyr)
data("HouseVotes84")
print.data.frame(head(HouseVotes84))
#In the below printout, the last column didn't fit and so is underneath.
The first number in each row is the column number and is not actually a
variable in the dataset.
##          Class V1 V2 V3    V4    V5 V6 V7 V8 V9 V10  V11    V12 V13 V14 V15
## 1   republican  n  y  n     y     y  y  n  n  n   y <NA>     y   y   y   n
## 2   republican  n  y  n     y     y  y  n  n  n   n    n     y   y   y   n
## 3     democrat <NA> y  y  <NA>     y  y  n  n  n   n    y     n   y   y   n
## 4     democrat  n  y  y     n  <NA>  y  n  n  n   n    y     n   y   n   n
## 5     democrat  y  y  y     n     y  y  n  n  n   y <NA>     y   y   y
## 6     democrat  n  y  y     n     y  y  n  n  n   n    n     n   y   y   y
##       V16
## 1     y
## 2  <NA>
## 3     n
## 4     y
## 5     y
## 6     y
#Remove NAs in the dataset
df=HouseVotes84[complete.cases(HouseVotes84),]
#Notice that the column names below are not the same as they are above.
This is because we have removed some rows.
#We add in an extra column here. We will give a reason for this later.
df$names<-rownames(df)
#View(df)  - you can run this command if you want to have a nicer view of
the data.
print.data.frame(head(df))
```

```
##          Class V1 V2 V3 V4 V5 V6 V7 V8 V9 V10 V11 V12 V13 V14 V15 V16 names
## 6    democrat  n  y  y  n  y  y  n  n  n   n   n   n   y   y   y   y     6
## 9  republican  n  y  n  y  y  y  n  n  n   n   n   y   y   y   n   y     9
## 20   democrat  y  y  y  n  n  n  y  y  y   n   y   n   n   n   y   y    20
## 24   democrat  y  y  y  n  n  n  y  y  y   n   n   n   n   n   y   y    24
## 26   democrat  y  n  y  n  n  n  y  y  y   y   n   n   n   n   y   y    26
## 27   democrat  y  n  y  n  n  n  y  y  y   n   y   n   n   n   y   y    27
```

4.2 Experiment, Outcome, Sample Space

In probability, an *experiment* is a process that when performed results in a unique observation. These observations are called either the outcomes of the experiment, the observational units, or the individuals. The collection of all the outcomes is called the *sample space*. Let's explore this a little further before we begin to code (Table 4.1).

4.3 Examples of Experiments

Simple examples of experiments involve coins, dice, or decks of cards (Figures 4.1–4.3).

Table 4.1   Examples of Experiments and Their Corresponding Outcomes and Sample Spaces

Experiment	Outcomes	Sample Space
Toss a coin once	Head, Tail	S = {Head, Tail}
Roll a die once	1, 2, 3, 4, 5, 6	S = {1, 2, 3, 4, 5, 6}
Toss a coin twice	HH, HT, TH, TT	S = {HH, HT, TH, TT}
Ask someone if they like baseball	Yes, No, Indifferent	S = {Yes, No, Indifferent}

Figure 4.1   Rolling a pair of dice.

Figure 4.2 Tossing a coin.

Figure 4.3 Minimal deck of just four cards.

4.4 Sample Space

In probability, a fundamental concept is the sample space. This is the set of all possible observations. In a simple example, consider the "experiment" of rolling a die.

We are interested in probability questions like the following:

■ What is the probability of getting an even number?
■ What is the probability of a 5?

In order to proceed methodically, we start out by considering all the different individual outcomes that *are possible* when this single die is rolled. The set of all possible individual outcomes is referred to as the sample space of the experiment and is denoted by S. (Some books use other symbols, for example, Ω.) Thus, $S = \{1, 2, 3, 4, 5, 6\}$.

What will the sample space be for our dataset, and what will this mean in R? Our dataset is the voting records of senators in the US senate on a set of 16 different issues. What should we call the sample space? Is it the set of all votes? Is it the entire dataset? We should be careful here. We will choose neither of the above to be the sample space.

4.5 Observational Units versus Outcomes

Although in the die example we called the sample space $S = \{1, 2, 3, 4, 5, 6\}$, a more careful definition would be to say that the sample space consists of the six *different faces* of the die as opposed to just the number of dots (Figure 4.4). (We will, at times, refer to these as six different observational units.)

The *number of dots* that show up on each of the faces (on each observational unit) is an *attribute* of that face (of that observational unit). This seems to be overly nitpicky and the distinction will not be essential in this text but generally leads to better machinery for doing analysis.

If we proceed like this, we could possibly come up with other attributes (also called other variables) related to the elements of the sample space besides just the *number* of dots. For example, we may be interested in

A. the maximum distance between any two dots on a face
B. the minimum distance
C. the number of straight lines that can join the dots.

The applications where we may be interested in such attributes are not the point right now; rather, this illustrates an important distinction: the distinction between outcomes of the experiment and attributes of those outcomes. The outcomes are the six faces of the die. On the other hand, there are many different attributes in which we may be interested.

As another example, we consider an experiment where we have a minimal deck of cards that consists of only these five cards (Figure 4.5).

The experiment consists of selecting one card from this minimal deck. There are five possible observational units. These are the five different cards.

However, each of these cards has various characteristics like color [red, black], suit [hearts, clubs, diamonds, spades], and face/number [8, 2, 5, Queen, Ace]. These are called attributes (or variables) of the observational units.

Figure 4.4   Standard six-sided die.

Figure 4.5 Minimal deck of cards.

When we choose to consider this distinction, the outcomes are often referred to as the *observational units*. That is to say, the elements of the sample space are called observational units. Sometimes they are referred to as the *individuals* because often the "experiment" and our data refer to people. We will try to stick with the phrase observational units here. We will keep this difference in mind: observational units versus attributes.

One more example: If we choose a student at random from the set of all students in a class, each of the different students is an observational unit (or individual). However, each student has a height, a weight, eye color, number of hours they slept in the last week, total calories consumed in the last week, etc. These are some attributes of students, i.e., some of the possible variables associated with the students (Figure 4.6).

Returning to the HouseVotes84 dataset, we will adopt the perspective of observational units and consider the different senators to be the observational units, and therefore will say that the sample space consists of the entire set of *senators*. After removing those senators who did not fully fulfill their voting obligations and thus generated NAs in our R code, we end up with 232 senators in our sample space.

```
nrow(df)
## [1] 232
```

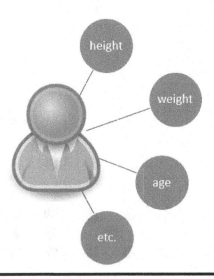

Figure 4.6 One observational unit can have many attributes.

The sample space is not the set of issues and not the party affiliation either (democrat/republican). The issues and the party affiliation are attributes or variables associated with the observational units. With any given senator, we can ask what their party affiliation is. The party affiliation of that senator would be the value of the *class* variable for that senator. We say we "measure" the class variable for each observational unit in our sample space as either democrat or republican. (The word measure is used similarly for each of the attributes, not just for the class attribute.) Each row derives from an observational unit. Each row is a set of characteristics or measurements on a particular observational unit. Again, this may seem nitpicky or subtle, but the distinction can be useful.

```
#The sample space is the set of all the 232 senators. When we run
head(df) or View(df), we don't exactly see the senators. We see a display
of the values of the variables being measured on the senators. It is a
subtle distinction but worth noting.
print.data.frame(head(df))
##         Class V1 V2 V3 V4 V5 V6 V7 V8 V9 V10 V11 V12 V13 V14 V15 V16 names
## 6    democrat  n  y  y  n  y  y  n  n  n   n   n   n   y   y   y   y     6
## 9  republican  n  y  n  y  y  y  n  n  n   n   n   y   y   y   n   y     9
## 20   democrat  y  y  y  n  n  n  y  y  y   n   y   n   n   n   y   y    20
## 24   democrat  y  y  y  n  n  n  y  y  y   n   n   n   n   n   y   y    24
## 26   democrat  y  n  y  n  n  n  y  y  y   y   n   n   n   n   y   y    26
## 27   democrat  y  n  y  n  n  n  y  y  y   n   y   n   n   n   y   y    27
```

4.6 Events

If you use the word probability in a sentence, the phrase that follows the word probability can usually be thought of as an event. For example, if we say, "The probability of sunny weather tomorrow is 80%", the event referred to is "the event of sunny weather tomorrow". Generally, when we ask about probabilities, we ask about probabilities of *events*. For example, what is the probability of the event of

- an even number
- a number greater than 4
- a senator voting yes on issue 1
- a senator voting yes on issue 1 and no on issue 5.

These are all examples of what we call events in the subject of probability. It is common in mathematics to define the word *event* as a *subset* of the sample space. For example, for the experiment of rolling a single die, we can say the sample space is the following set of outcomes.

We can denote the event of "getting a number less than 4" by the letter E and say it is *the subset of S* depicted in the following.

Returning to HouseVotes84, suppose we are interested in building an artificial intelligence (AI) model to predict whether a senator is a democrat or republican based on their voting patterns, we may ask, "In the *event* that a senator votes *yes* on issue #1 and *no* on issue #2, should we predict that they are a democrat or a republican?" Notice that this event will single out a subset of the set of all of the outcomes of the entire dataset.

```
#Events
#An example of an event: An event can be specified by a set of conditions
on the variables.
A_bool <- df$V1=='y' &    df$V2=='n'
#This may appear to be a compound statement and therefore either true or
false but not both. However, since R is vectorized, it is actually a
vector of true or false values.
head(A_bool)
## [1] FALSE FALSE FALSE FALSE  TRUE  TRUE
#Next, we put that specification in the row entry of the dataframe and
thereby extract a subset of the set of rows of the dataframe.
A <- df[A_bool,]
```

In the context of an R dataframe, we may say an event induces a subset of the rows of the dataframe. But for the sake of brevity, instead of saying an event induces a subset of the rows of the dataframe, we will just say the following (Figure 4.7):

An event is a subset of the set of rows of the dataframe.

*We will specify an event **in our R code** in a two-step process:*

```
A_bool <- df$V1=='y' &    df$V2=='n'
A <- df[A_bool,]
```

	Class	V1	V2	V3
26	democrat	y	n	y
27	democrat	y	n	y
29	republican	y	n	n
40	democrat	y	n	y
43	democrat	y	n	y

Figure 4.7 All the instances have y for V1 and n for V2.

1. Specify a Boolean vector where each entry is TRUE or FALSE depending on whether that row satisfies the event in question.
2. Insert that vector into the row specification of the dataframe. (By row specification is meant the first entry inside the square brackets: dataframeName[first entry, second entry])

To experiment with our functions, we define two more events, B and C, using the above pattern (Figure 4.8–4.10). (Note we have also redefined A to include party affiliation.)

	Class	V1	V2	V3	V4	V5	V6
26	democrat	y	n	y	n	n	n
27	democrat	y	n	y	n	n	n
40	democrat	y	n	y	n	n	n
43	democrat	y	n	y	n	n	n
44	democrat	y	n	y	n	n	n

Figure 4.8   View(A).

	Class	V1	V2	V3	V4	V5	V6	V7	V8	V9	V10	V11
26	democrat	y	n	y	n	n	n	y	y	y	y	n
33	democrat	y	y	y	n	n	n	y	y	y	y	n
40	democrat	y	n	y	n	n	n	y	y	y	y	y
75	democrat	y	n	y	n	n	y	y	y	y	y	y

Figure 4.9   View(B) where we show more columns than View(A) in Figure 4.8 because B's specification involves the variable V10.

	Class	V1	V2	V3	V4	V5
9	republican	n	y	n	y	y
31	republican	n	y	n	y	y
34	republican	n	y	n	y	y
36	republican	n	y	n	y	y
39	republican	n	y	n	y	y

Figure 4.10   View(C).

```
#We will redefine event A to: the event that a democrat would vote yes
for issue 1 and no for issue 2.

A_bool=df$Class=='democrat' & df$V1=='y' & df$V2=='n'
A=df[A_bool,]

B_bool=df$V4=='n' & df$V10=='y'
B=df[B_bool,]

C_bool=df$V1=='n' & df$V4=='y'
C=df[C_bool,]

#What type of objects are A, B, and C? Are they vectors, matrices, or
dataframes?
#If we try is(A), we will see it is a dataframe. is(A) also says it is a
list, but keep in mind that dataframes are lists, lists with some special
properties, for example, if it is a dataframe, each element in the list
(each column of the dataframe) must have the same number of elements.
#is(A) also says that the old class for C is a vector, but we won't worry
about that here, except to say that in the historical development of the
R language, objects were classified differently.
```

4.7 Compound Event Using Set Operations

4.7.1 Union, Intersection, and Negation

We will now define *set operations for events*. (These are not the set operations for vectors that we covered in the last chapter.) As we saw in the last chapter, R has set operations for vectors in the {Base} package, and we also defined our own functions for sets as well. However, we are after something different here.

4.8 Union of Two Events

The word union is used in the context of sets (union is an *operation* between sets), but since events are sets, we will take the liberty of referring to the union of two *events* (Figure 4.11).

```
#Here are our definitions of B and C in R code.
B_bool=df$V4=='n' & df$V10=='y'
```

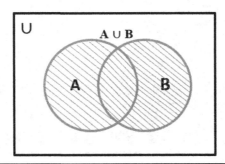

Figure 4.11 Since events can be thought of as sets, we will talk of the union of events.

```
B=df[B_bool,]
C_bool=df$V1=='n' & df$V4=='y'
C=df[C_bool,]
```

What is the union of B and C above?

It is the *set of senators* that are in either B or C or both B and C (Figure 4.12 and 4.13).

```
#Recall that rbind() can take vectors, matrices, or dataframes, for its
arguments. In the case of dataframes, which is what we are feeding it
now, rbind(B,C) forms a new dataframe that simply appends the rows of C
below the rows of B.
A simple use of rbind() to combine the rows of B and C together will
work. We should also make sure we don't duplicate rows:
B_union_C=unique(rbind(B,C))
View(B_union_C)

#We can also write this as a function
union_event <- function(E,F){
  #First make sure the two "events" E and F are both dataframes.
  if(!is.data.frame(E)|!is.data.frame(F)){
    stop("arguments must be a dataframe")
}
return(unique(rbind(E,F)))}

B_union_C=union_event(B,C)
View(B_union_C)
```

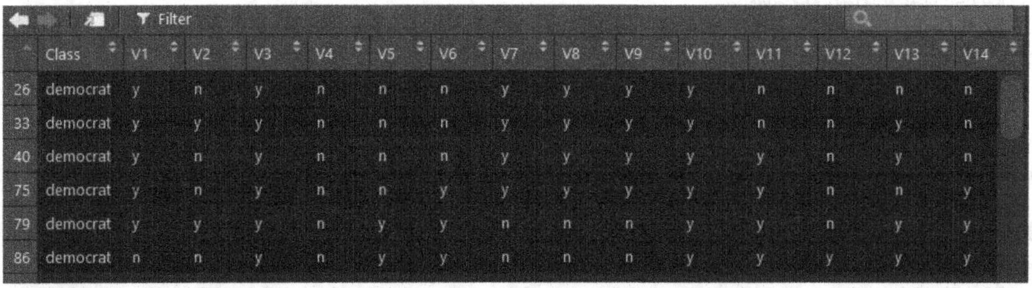

	Class	V1	V2	V3	V4	V5	V6	V7	V8	V9	V10	V11	V12	V13	V14
26	democrat	y	n	y	n	n	n	y	y	y	y	n	n	n	n
33	democrat	y	y	y	n	n	n	y	y	y	y	n	n	y	n
40	democrat	y	n	y	n	n	n	y	y	y	y	y	n	y	n
75	democrat	y	n	y	n	n	y	y	y	y	y	y	n	n	y
79	democrat	y	y	y	n	y	y	n	n	n	y	y	n	y	y
86	democrat	n	n	y	n	y	y	n	n	n	y	y	y	y	y

Figure 4.12 B_union_C. If you try the code yourself, and scroll down, you will see that they are not all "democrat".

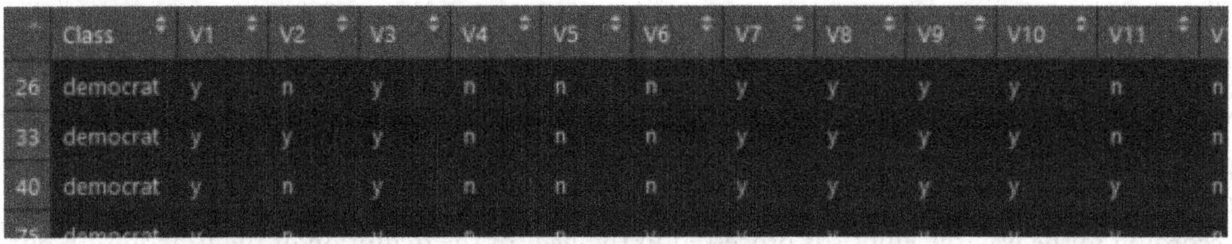

	Class	V1	V2	V3	V4	V5	V6	V7	V8	V9	V10	V11	V
26	democrat	y	n	y	n	n	n	y	y	y	y	n	n
33	democrat	y	y	y	n	n	n	y	y	y	y	n	n
40	democrat	y	n	y	n	n	n	y	y	y	y	y	n

Figure 4.13 B_union_C generated with the union_event() function gives the same result as above.

4.9 The Union of Two Events Is an Event

Recall that we defined an event as a subset of the sample space. What if we take two events A and B in the context of rolling a die. Say A is getting a number less than 4, so A = {1,2,3}, and B is the event of getting an even number, so B = {2,4,6}. Is the union of A and B also an event? Is it also a subset of the sample space? Yes. $A \bigcup B = \{1,2,3,4,6\} \subset \{1,2,3,4,5,6\} = S$. This will always be true; *the union of events is also an event.*

4.10 Union of Several Events

We also want a multi-event union function. We will introduce a new concept in R programming, the three dots ellipsis syntax.

```
multi_union_event=function(E,F,...){
  return(unique(rbind(E,F,...)))
  }
```

4.11 The Ellipsis

What if we want to have a function for the union of three events. We could easily extend our function to handle three events like the following.

```
union_event <- function(E,F,G){
  #First make sure the "events" E, F, and G
  #are each dataframes.
  if(!is.data.frame(E)|!is.data.frame(F) |!is.data.frame(G)){
    stop("arguments must be a dataframe")
  }
  return(unique(rbind(E,F,G)))}

B_union_C_union_D=union_event(B,C,D)
```

However, what if we need the union of four or more events. Instead of writing a function for each such case, there is a *three-dot ellipsis* syntax that R provides. (In R, it is a sequence of three dots like "…".) Note that this syntax is also available in other programming languages. The ellipsis is a kind of expandable parameter which allows the user to put in any number of unnamed or even named arguments, and the function will handle them all. Here we are using it to allow unnamed arguments.

```
multi_union_event=function(E,F,...){
  return(unique(rbind(E,F,...)))
  }
```

You can see that the triple dots syntax is used once in the parameter list (following the first two parameters E and F), and then it is used in the body of the function. Whatever the *user* types into the list of arguments *following the first two arguments* will be processed in the call of the function according to the way the ellipsis is processed in the *body* of the definition of the function. In our `multi_union_event()` function, the only place in the function *body* where the three dots appear is in rbind(), and so this means that any additional arguments that follow the first two arguments will be tacked onto the E and F list in **rbind**(). Now our function can handle any number of events! Many of R's native functions employ the ellipsis, and so it is good to understand it for a better general understanding of R.

```
#Of course, generally, the more the events that are included, the more
the rows we expect to have in the result. Here are some examples.
A_bool=df$Class=='democrat' & df$V1=='y' & df$V2=='n'
A=df[A_bool,]
B_bool=df$V4=='n' & df$V10=='y'
B=df[B_bool,]
C_bool=df$V1=='n' & df$V4=='y'
C=df[C_bool,]
D_bool=df$V1=='n' & df$V3=='n'
D=df[D_bool,]
E_bool=df$V1=='y' & df$V5=='n'
E=df[E_bool,]
nrow(multi_union_event(A,B,C))
## [1] 167
nrow(multi_union_event(A,B))
## [1] 78
nrow(multi_union_event(A,B,C,D))
## [1] 172
nrow(multi_union_event(A,B,C,D,E))
## [1] 193
#We see that generally the more the events that are included, the more
the rows there are.
```

4.12 Intersection

Now we write an intersection function for the intersection of two events – again in the context of dataframes. We will call it **intersect_event**(). We will take the help of the **intersection_of_sets**() function from the previous chapter. Recall that **intersection_of_sets**() was built for vectors, not for dataframes. Alternatively, we can also implement **intersect_event**() with the help of R's built-in **intersect**().

Our **intersection_of_sets()** function from the previous chapter needs *vectors* for its arguments. We cannot use our event format in this case since our events are dataframes and not vectors. If we try **intersection_of_sets(A,B)** with our previously defined A and B, we do not get the intersection of these two events. Rather, R reports (Figure 4.14)

```
"dataframe with 0 columns and 39 rows"
```

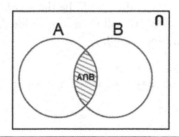

Figure 4.14   Events can be thought of as sets, and so we will speak of the intersection of events.

So how should we proceed? Recall that our dataframes have a column called "names". Recall that *we added* this column into the dataframe just after removing the NAs like this:

```
#Remove NAs in the dataset.
df=HouseVotes84[complete.cases(HouseVotes84),]
df$names<-rownames(df)
```

We did this to have an easy way to reference the row names. You may recall from your preliminary study of R that R allows you to name the elements of a vector. On the other hand, R *automatically* generates row names when a dataframe is created, and the row names are then accessible with the **rownames()** function.

> Test this out with the built-in mtcars dataset. Call **rownames(mtcars),** and you will get a vector of the row names for this dataset. (They happened to be the names of the cars.)

In our code above, we actually made an *extra column* to hold these row names. We could just reference the **rownames()** function instead, but for additional clarity, we created a column with these values.

```
colnames(A)
## [1] "Class" "V1" "V2" "V3" "V4" "V5" "V6" "V7"
## [9] "V8" "V9" "V10" "V11" "V12" "V13" "V14" "V15"
## [17] "V16" "names"
head(A$names)
## [1] "26" "27" "40" "43" "44" "75"
```

Recall that we have distinguished between observational units and attributes. We said that the observational units are not the attributes or the class. Perhaps our best stand-in for an observational unit might be the names column.[1] The names column is unique for each row and therefore for each observational unit. Thus, if we want a collection of observational units, we can point to them through the value of the names column. Now we can use the names column as a vector and input it into the **intersection_of_sets()** function. We saw that we cannot use the **intersection_of_sets()** function with events A and B; however, if we try the following, we do get the row numbers that are common to A and B.

```
intersection_of_sets(A$names,B$names)
## [1] "26" "40" "75" "91" "92" "94" "98" "170" "180" "203" "204"
## [12] "242" "245" "246" "255" "256" "261" "266" "293" "310" "318" "339"
## [23] "361" "407" "412" "427"
```

Thus, the intersection of the events A and B would be the *dataframe* that contains exactly these rows. For the intersection of A and B, we will need to mention A and B, and this time, we will include an argument for the dataframe as well.

```
intersect_event <- function(A,B,df){
  return(df[intersection_of_sets(A$names,B$names),])
}
```

---

[1] However, this is only true if each row is a distinct example. For example, if for some reason there were two rows that represented the same senator, then this would not work.

```
#As usual, we use head() so that we can look at just a few rows at the
top in order to avoid a huge printout.
head(intersect_event(A,B,df))
## Class V1 V2 V3 V4 V5 V6 V7 V8 V9 V10 V11 V12 V13 V14 V15 V16 names
## 26 democrat  y  n  y  n  n  n  y  y  y  y   n   n   n   n   y   y  26
## 40 democrat  y  n  y  n  n  n  y  y  y  y   y   n   y   n   y   y  40
## 75 democrat  y  n  y  n  n  y  y  y  y  y   y   n   n   y   y   y  75
## 91 democrat  y  n  y  n  n  n  y  y  y  y   n   n   n   n   y   y  91
## 92 democrat  y  n  y  n  n  n  y  y  y  y   y   n   n   n   y   y  92
## 94 democrat  y  n  y  n  n  n  y  n  y  y   y   n   n   n   y   y  94
#The number of rows of the intersection of A and B should not be more
than the number of rows of A and B individually and typically should be
less than either the number of rows of A or B.
nrow(A)
## [1] 39
nrow(B)
## [1] 65
nrow(intersect_event(A,B,df))
## [1] 26
```

We can also build the same **`intersect_event()`** functionality using R's built-in **`intersect()`** function.

```
intersect_event2 <- function(A,B,df){
return(df[intersect(A$names,B$names),])
}
```

Recall, earlier we said that the union of events is also an event. The same can be said for the intersection of events. The intersection of events is also an event.

Practice 4.12.1

1. If the intersection of events is also an event, what data type (what type of R object) should **`intersect_event`**(A,B,df) be?

4.13 Complement or Negation of an Event

The negation of an event A (again viewing an event as a set) is the complement of the set with respect to the universal set. In our case, the universal set is the sample space which in turn is the entire dataframe. Therefore, we seek the set of all rows in df which are not in A (Figure 4.15).

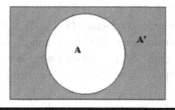

Figure 4.15   The event of A not occurring as the complement of A.

```
complement_event <- function(A,df){
  #A$names will contain the rows of df that are in A.
  #rownames(df) is the entire set of row names in df.
    #rownames(df)%in%A$names will give a logical vector of length equal
to the total number of rows of df.
    #It will be TRUE for the rows in A. Thus, to obtain the complement, we
want the negation of this logical vector.
  A_bool_complement=!(rownames(df)%in%A$names)
  return(df[A_bool_complement,])
}
```

```
head(complement_event(A,df))
##          Class V1 V2 V3 V4 V5 V6 V7 V8 V9 V10 V11 V12 V13 V14 V15 V16
names
## 6      democrat n y y n y y n n n n n y y y y 6
## 9    republican n y n y y y n n n n n y y y n y 9
## 20     democrat y y y n n n y y y y n y n n n y y 20
## 24     democrat y y y n n n y y y y n n n n n y y 24
## 28     democrat y y y n n n y y y y n y n n n y y 28
## 29   republican y n n y y y n y y y y n n y y y n y 29
#The sum of nrow(A) and nrow(complement_event(A,df)) should equal
nrow(df).
nrow(df)
## [1] 232
nrow(A)
## [1] 39
nrow(complement_event(A,df))
## [1] 193
```

As before, with union and intersection, the complement of an event is also an event.

Practice 4.13.2

1. Optional Challenge: Write the **intersect_event()** function without creating the names column.

2. In your own words, explain why we need to avoid duplicating rows when we use **rbind()** in our **union_events()** function?

3. Try the following with the mtcars dataset that is shipped with R. Show your code.
   a. After removing all the rows that contain any NAs, how many rows are left?
   b. Create an event FT which represents cars having four cylinders and three gears.
   c. Create an event GT20 which represents cars having mpg greater than 20.
   d. Run the **union_events(),** and then find out how many rows are there in this event.
   e. What is the interpretation of the union of FT and GT20? In other words, how would you describe the elements in this union?
   f. Run the **intersect_event()** function on FT and GT20, and then find out how many rows are in the intersection.

4. Build an **intersect_event_3events()** function that will accept three events as arguments and find the intersection of all three events.

5. Optional challenge (difficult): Build an **intersect_event()** function that can handle any number of events as inputs. *Hint: You may want to use the* **args()** *function and the* **unlist()** *function.*

6. The **intersect_event()** function uses a df argument. Change the definition of **multi_union_event()** so that it takes a df argument.

7. Optional challenge: Write the **complement_event()** function using **match()** instead of **%in%**. Test it to see that it mirrors the performance of the original **complement_event()**.

Probability Part 2

- Probability definition
- Rules for probability
- Conditional probability
- Independence
- Conditional independence
- Bayes theorem

4.14 Probability Definition

We will use a simple definition of probability, but it will deliver enough to provide us with the Naïve Bayes algorithm. We will assume that the sample space has a uniform distribution. This means *that each outcome* in the sample space *is equally likely*. In our previous example of rolling a die, this would mean that every face of the die is equally likely, and thus each face has probability 1/6. Such a die is usually referred to as a fair die. In the example of the minimal deck of cards that had only five cards, if each card is equally likely, then each card has a probability of 1/5. In the case of a dataframe, it would mean that each observational unit (each senator) would be equally likely to be selected.[2]

> We are assuming that each row is a senator here. That is to say, even if there are duplicate rows, they do not represent the same senator. It will only mean that two senators have the same voting pattern. Thus, we will not remove duplicate rows. On the other hand, if a dataframe contains duplicate observational units, we would want to remove those duplicates. Although we won't do this, to remove duplicate rows the **unique**() function could be used as follows.
>
> df <- **unique**(df)

With a fair die, the probability of an event E is n(E)/n(S). For example, if we want the probability of the event F of getting an odd number, we first determine F as a subset of S and see that F = {1,3,5}. Then we determine n(F) and n(S), which are 3 and 6, respectively. Thus, the probability of F, which we denote as p(F) or prob(F), is n(F)/n(S)=3/6.

In R, assuming uniform probability distribution, the probability of an event E given the sample space (dataframe) S would be as follows:

```
prob <- function(E,S){
  return(nrow(E)/nrow(S))
}
#Here is an example.
A_bool=df$Class=='democrat' & df$V1=='y' & df$V2=='n'
A=df[A_bool,]
head(A)
```

---

[2] This assumes that no senator appears in more than one row of the dataframe.

```
##         Class  V1 V2 V3 V4 V5 V6 V7 V8 V9 V10 V11 V12 V13 V14 V15 V16 names
## 26 democrat   y  n  y  n  n  n  y  y  y   y   n   n   n   n   y   y    26
## 27 democrat   y  n  y  n  n  n  y  y  y   n   y   n   n   n   y   y    27
## 40 democrat   y  n  y  n  n  n  y  y  y   y   y   n   y   n   y   y    40
## 43 democrat   y  n  y  n  n  n  y  y  y   n   n   n   n   n   n   y    43
## 44 democrat   y  n  y  n  n  n  y  y  y   n   n   n   n   n   y   y    44
## 75 democrat   y  n  y  n  n  y  y  y  y   y   y   n   n   y   y   y    75
prob(A,df)
## [1] 0.1681034
#meaning that 0.1681034 is the probability of the event A - the event
that a senator who is a democrat voted yes on issue 1 and no on issue 2.
```

It is important here to note that this is the simplest definition for a probability function and is not generally sufficient in probability theory or statistics. One clear limitation is that we have assumed all the outcomes are equally likely. In the example of rolling a die, this means that we are assuming that all the faces of the die are equally likely. This is a serious limitation and is not always acceptable. However, for what we are doing in this text, it will not present a problem. The interested reader may seek to extend the definition to a more general one and work with it instead.

Practice 4.14.3
1. Using the prob() function defined above, find out the probability of a senator being a democrat.
2. Using the prob() function defined above, find out the probability that a senator voted y on issue #1 and y on issue #2.
3. In the mtcars dataset, define the event that a car has mpg less than 20. What is the probability of such an event?
4. Write an expression to *count* how many cars have mpg less than 20.

4.15 Properties for Probability

A property of the probability function is that it will never output a negative number and it will never output a value greater than 1. This can be seen by examining the return statement in our definition above.

```
return(nrow(E)/nrow(S))
nrow(E)/nrow(S)<=1
```

Note that E is a subset of S, and since S is the entire dataframe, E is some subset of the rows of the dataframe. It is clear that the number of rows of E can never be greater than the number of rows in the entire dataframe, and so we see that the output will never be greater than 1. Thus, we see that

$nrow(E)/nrow(S) <= 1$

Next, we assert that

```
0 <= nrow(E)/nrow(S)
```

This is obvious because the number of rows is never negative, and so neither the numerator nor the denominator of this fraction is negative.

Thus, we can make this statement.

4.15.1 Property 1 for Any Probability Function p()

For any event E,

$$0 \le p(E) \le 1 \tag{4.1}$$

4.15.1.1 Mutually Exclusive Events and Disjoint Sets

The second property we assert for the probability function concerns the case where we are considering two events that have no elements (no rows) in common. Such events are referred to in probability as being *mutually exclusive*. Going back to the rolling of a single die, where S = {1,2,3,4,5,6}, we can construct events that have nothing in common easily. For example, E = {1,2} and F = {5,6}. These two events clearly have nothing in common, and therefore we would say they are mutually exclusive. Another pair of mutually exclusive events would be the event H of getting an even number when rolling the die and the event G of getting an odd number when rolling a die. H and G are also mutually exclusive, as can be seen by expressing them explicitly as sets:
H = {2,4,6} and G = {1,3,5}, and they clearly have no elements in common.

We mentioned earlier that we view events as sets. Although they are sets, they are more than sets. Events are occurrences about which we can ask probability questions. The term "mutually exclusive" is used when discussing events. However, if the events are being thought of as sets, we use the term "disjoint". Two sets that have nothing in common (their intersection is empty) are called disjoint.

Returning to the term mutually exclusive, an example which is less easily conceived of with sets would be the two events that a given person would be standing in Grand Central Station in NYC and standing in Tokyo Station at the same time and day. Mutually exclusive events cannot occur at the same time, and these two events cannot occur at the same time.

Returning to the die, provide examples of two events that would *not* be considered mutually exclusive. Take the event G of getting an odd number, and redefine the event H to that of getting a number greater than 4. Is it possible for them to occur at the same time? We can go through each possible outcome.

If a 1 occurs,	does G occur?	*Yes*	Does H occur?	*No*
If a 2 occurs,	does G occur?	*No*	Does H occur?	*No*
If a 3 occurs,	does G occur?	Yes	Does H occur?	No
If a 4 occurs,	does G occur?	*No*	Does H occur?	*No*
If a 5 occurs,	does G occur?	**Yes**	Does H occur?	**Yes***
If a 6 occurs,	does G occur?	*No*	Does H occur?	Yes

* both G and H occur

So, we see that if a 5 occurs, both G and H occur, and thus it is not impossible for them to occur at the same time, and we say they are *not* mutually exclusive. If we draw the Venn diagram, we see that they have one element in common.

Here we see the relationship between the set concept of disjoint sets and the probability concept of mutually exclusive events (Figure 4.16).

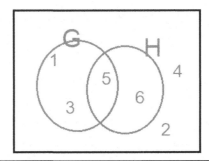

Figure 4.16 **G and H are not mutually exclusive. If a 5 is rolled, we would say that both events have occurred.**

4.16 Probability of Mutually Exclusive Events

If two events E and F are mutually exclusive and therefore the sets are disjoint, then

$$n(E \cup F) = n(E) + n(F) \tag{4.2}$$

This should be clear from Figure 4.17.

If we divide both sides of Equation (4.2) by n(S),

$$\frac{n(E \cup F)}{n(S)} = \frac{n(E)}{n(S)} + \frac{n(F)}{n(S)} \tag{4.3}$$

However, if you recall that the union of two events is an event, then you will agree that $E \cup F$ is an event, and then we can recognize that the left-hand side (LHS) is nothing but the basic definition of the probability of the *event* $E \cup F$ and the right-hand side (RHS) is $p(E) + p(F)$. This gives us a second property.

4.16.1 Property 2 for Any Probability Function p()

If E and F are mutually exclusive events, then

$$p(E \cup F) = p(E) + p(F) \tag{4.4}$$

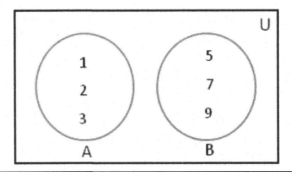

Figure 4.17 **Disjoint sets.**

Note that this argument can be generalized to more than just two events. For example, if E, F, and G are mutually exclusive, then

$$p(E \cup F \cup G) = p(E) + p(F) + p(G) \qquad (4.5)$$

Note that in our code, we will sometimes be called on to calculate the probability of *either* of two events occurring. For example, in HouseVotes84, we may be asked to calculate the probability that a senator votes *yes on issue 1* **or** *no on issue 2*. If we knew that these two events (the event of *yes on issue 1* and the event of *no on issue 2*) were mutually exclusive, then using Equation (4.4), we could calculate this as

probability(yes on issue 1) + probability(no on issue 2)

Actually though, these two events are not mutually exclusive[3], and so this calculation will not provide the correct answer.

Note: The union sign $\cup$ can be translated to the logical connective "or", and intersection sign $\cap$ can be translated to the logical connective "and". This means that p(*yes on issue 1* **or** *no on issue 2*) can be written as p(*yes on issue 1* $\cup$ *no on issue 2*).

Practice 4.16.4

1. Can you identify two events that are mutually exclusive in the context of HouseVotes84?

The next property gives a result for $p(E \cup F)$ regardless of whether E and F are disjoint or not (Figure 4.18).

If we examine the sets G and H in the Venn diagram above and apply the previous formula

$$p(E \cup F) = p(E) + p(F) \qquad (4.6)$$

to them, we will see that it does not work as we might expect since this formula is to be applied when E and F are disjoint, whereas G and H are not disjoint. We can ask, what goes wrong that prevents

$$p(G \cup H) = p(G) + p(H) \qquad (4.7)$$

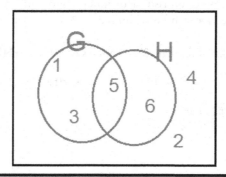

Figure 4.18   Non-disjoint sets.

---

[3] How can we check this?

from being true? This formula is essentially

$$n(G \cup H) = n(G) + n(H) \tag{4.8}$$

where the only difference between (4.7) and (4.8) is that to obtain the probability formula (4.7), we simply divide the cardinality formula (4.8) by n(S) on both sides. Therefore, we will focus on why the cardinality formula is not correct for these two events G and H.

For the LHS, we look at $G \cup H = \{1,3,5,6\}$ and see that there are four elements, and note, in particular, that *we are not counting the element 5 twice* (of course). On the other hand, on the RHS, we are counting how many elements are in G = {1,3,5} and then how many elements are in H = {5,6} and then *summing* these two amounts. For the RHS, we get 3 + 2 = 5, *but note that we have counted the element 5 twice*. Of course, if we count the element 5 only once on the LHS and then twice on the RHS, we would not expect the results to be the same and that is why

$$n(G \cup H) \neq n(G) + n(H) \tag{4.9}$$

The problem is that we counted the intersection $G \cap H = \{5\}$ only once on the LHS but twice on the RHS. Our remedy therefore would be to subtract it once from the RHS:

$$n(G \cup H) = n(G) + n(H) - n(G \cap H) \tag{4.10}$$

Now dividing each term by n(S) leads to the following:

$$p(G \cup H) = p(G) + p(H) - p(G \cap H)$$

4.16.2 Property 3 for the Probability Function p()

In general, for *any* events E and F (not necessarily mutually exclusive),

$$p(E \cup F) = p(E) + p(F) - p(E \cap F) \tag{4.11}$$

Returning to the example mentioned above regarding the HouseVotes84 dataset, to calculate the probability that a senator votes yes on issue 1 or no on issue 2, remembering that union can be rephrased as OR and intersection can be rephrased as AND, we now see that we can calculate this as

prob(yes on issue 1) + prob(no on issue 2) − prob(yes on issue 1 AND no on issue 2)

```
A_bool=df$Class=='democrat' & df$V1=='y' & df$V2=='n'
A=df[A_bool,]
B_bool=df$V4=='n' & df$V10=='y'
B=df[B_bool,]
prob(union_event(A,B),df)
## [1] 0.3362069
prob(A,df)
## [1] 0.1681034
prob(B,df)
## [1] 0.2801724
prob(union_event(A,B),df)==prob(A,df)+prob(B,df)
```

```
## [1] FALSE
prob(union_event(A,B),df)==prob(A,df)+prob(B,df)-
prob(intersect_event(A,B,df),df)
## [1] TRUE
```

Practice 4.16.5

> Tip: Our function for **union_event**() does not use a parameter to represent the dataframe but most of our other functions in this chapter do. (We often use df for this parameter.)

1. In the mtcars dataset, define any two events, and then use the appropriate functions to show that properties 1 and 3 hold.
2. Explain the double reference to df in the expression referenced above:
   prob(intersect_event(A,B,df),df)
3. In the mtcars dataset, create two events that are mutually exclusive, and use the appropriate functions to show that properties 1 and 2 hold.

4.17 Conditional Probability

Conditional probability is an important concept. We introduce it with the following example. Suppose we roll a single fair die and ask, what is the probability of the event E of getting an odd number? If we write E explicitly as a set, we get E = {1,3,5}. The answer, as we have discussed earlier, can be easily calculated as p(E) = n(E)/n(S) = 3/6. The Venn diagram looks like that shown in Figure 4.19.

Now, suppose we perform the same experiment again, but this time, the person who rolls the die looks at the result and reports to us that the number on the top face is greater than 3. Then, armed with this new information, we are now tasked with answering the question, "What is the probability of the event E of getting an odd number given this new info?" That is, we want to answer, "What is the probability of E given that the number is greater than 3?" To answer this, we first note that the new information we are given is itself an event. That is, "the number is greater

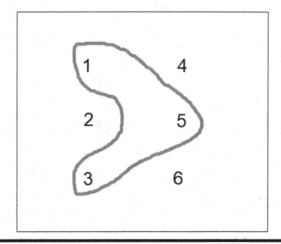

Figure 4.19   Event of getting a 1 or 3 or 5 when rolling a die.

than 3" is an event. If we denote this event as F, then we can write F = {4,5,6}, and we can show this in the Venn diagram as shown in Figure 4.20.

We can rewrite our question as "What is the probability of E given that F has occurred?" As usual, in mathematics we try to design symbols that contain as little language as possible, and so we denote the question above as p(E|F). The vertical line in this notation should be read as "given". *It does not mean divide.* It is simply a convenient symbol for the word "given".

Now that we have managed to *express* our question symbolically, how do we *get the answer for* p(E|F), the probability of E given F? The analysis proceeds as follows. We are given that F has occurred, and so it is no longer possible to get a 1, 2, or 3. The only possible outcomes are 4, 5, and 6. That is to say, the new set of possible outcomes is F, which means that F is our new sample space! Thus, our new sample space only has three elements in it. Further, we argue that none of the elements in this new sample space F are more (or less) likely than any other element in F. That is, all the elements in F are equally likely. Since our new sample space is F, we can replace S by F in the formula for the calculation of the probability of E. Thus, we had n(S) in the denominator before, whereas now we will have n(F). Furthermore, since we have been told that F has occurred, not all the elements of E are now possible. Neither 1 nor 3 is possible. The only part of E that is possible is the part of E that is in F. That is, the outcomes that are possible are

$$E \cap F$$

So, the answer to p(E|F) becomes

$$p(E|F) = \frac{n(E \cap F)}{n(F)} \tag{4.12}$$

If we divide the numerator and denominator by n(S), we get

$$p(E|F) = \frac{n(E \cap F)/n(S)}{n(F)/n(S)} = \frac{p(E \cap F)}{p(F)} \tag{4.13}$$

We will consider Equation (4.13) as the definition of p(E|F).

Using the above definition, if you work out the details for the probability of getting an odd number, given that the outcome is greater than 3, you will find that the answer is 1/3 (Figure 4.21). Recall that although the probability of odd (without anything given) is 1/2, now we get 1/3!

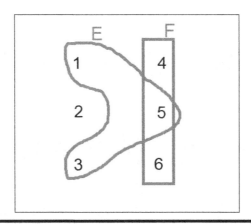

Figure 4.20   Illustration of the events E and F.

```
#Conditional Probability
#Now we can define our conditional probability function.
conditional_prob <- function(A,B,df){
prob(intersect_event(A,B,df),df)/prob(B,df)
}

A_bool=df$Class=='democrat' & df$V1=='y' & df$V2=='n'
A=df[A_bool,]
B_bool=df$toss2=='H'
B=bool2event(B_bool,df)
conditional_prob(A,B,df)
## [1] 0.4
```
#Construct a dataframe to simulate the tossing of a single die. Then
check the probability of getting an even number. Compare this result with
probability of "even given that the number is greater than 3".

#To simulate a die with a dataframe, we simply need one row for each
outcome. In this way, each outcome is equally likely.
```
die <- as.data.frame(1:6)
str(die)
## 'data.frame': 6 obs. of 1 variable:
## $ 1:6: int 1 2 3 4 5 6
View(die)
```

#Note that the column name is `1:6`, and so if you want to refer to the
first column, it would be die$`1:6`, and in R you must use the backticks.
These are often located on the upper LHS of the keyboard. Instead we can
rename it as
```
colnames(die) <- c("roll1")
```
#To create an event like "the event of getting an even number", we **cannot**
use
#even<-die[c(2,4,6),].
#Even for a simple experiment, we will follow the two-step process.
#First we need a **logical** vector. Here are two ways to achieve it:

Figure 4.21   RStudio view of the sample space for rolling a fair die.

```
one way is die$roll1==c(7,2,7,4,7,6). #The 7 is arbitrary and is just
used to obtain the TRUE FALSE pattern below.
## [1] FALSE TRUE FALSE TRUE FALSE TRUE
#The following would also work.
die$roll1%%2==0
## [1] FALSE TRUE FALSE TRUE FALSE TRUE
#Or we could just define the Boolean vector manually.
even_bool=c(FALSE,TRUE,FALSE,TRUE,FALSE,TRUE)
#Any of these is fine, so let's do it the second way.
even_bool <- die$roll1%%2==0 #This is vector comparison (a comparison of
two vectors).

#To define our event, unfortunately (and unexpectedly), this does not
work.
even <- die[even_bool,]
#If you test the structure of "even" with str(even), you will see that
this does not produce a dataframe! However we need our event, "even", to
be a dataframe.
str(even)
## int [1:3] 2 4 6
even <- die[even_bool,,drop=F] #It turns out that if we don't add the
"drop" argument and set it equal to F, because there is only 1 column,
R will (unexpectedly) convert the result to a vector. Again, this is a
choice the designers of R make, and so we need to be aware of it. You can
think of this as a somewhat arbitrary grammatical rule in a spoken
language that you simply have to learn and memorize.

even
## roll1
## 2 2
## 4 4
## 6 6
#The first column of numbers above are just the row names.
str(even)
## 'data.frame': 3 obs. of 1 variable:
## $ roll1: int 2 4 6
over3_bool <- die$roll1>3
over3=die[over3_bool,,drop=F]
prob(even,die)
## [1] 0.5
prob(over3,die)
## [1] 0.5
conditional_prob(even,over3,die)
## [1] 0.4
```

Practice 4.17.6

1. What is the result of **conditional_prob**(even,over3,die)==**intersect _ event**(even,over3,die)/**prob**(B,die) and why?

4.18 Additional Terminology

In a theory of statistics called Bayesian statistics, the following terms are used frequently: prior probability, posterior probability, and likelihood. The prior probability in terms of p(E|F) is p(E).

This is the probability of E *prior to being given any information* (for example, prior to knowing that F has occurred). The word "posterior" comes from the Latin word "post" which means after. The p(E|F) is called the posterior probability since it is calculating the probability of E *after* being given that F has occurred. The likelihood is p(F|E).

4.19 Independent Events

Two events are called independent events if the fact of one of the events having occurred does not affect the probability of the other event. An example of independent events occurs when we consider an experiment of first tossing a coin and then rolling a die. The fact that a head occurred when tossing the coin will not affect the probability of getting an even number when rolling the die. Therefore, we say that the event of "getting and even number" is independent of the event of "a head occurring".

Generally, when working with real data, it is rarely obvious that two events are independent. For example, it is not obvious whether the event of a senator voting yes on issue 1 is independent of the event where they vote yes on issue 2. And this is not simply because we have not explored clearly what issue 1 and issue 2 are. Even if we know what they are, the independence of these two events would not be obvious. The concept of independence is of fundamental importance in our upcoming discussion of the Naïve Bayes algorithm.

Can we derive a formula for independence? Let us consider the example of the experiment of tossing a coin and then rolling a die. Define F as the event that a head occurred when tossing the coin. Define E as the event of getting a 5 when rolling the die. We said above that these two were independent, and the reason we gave is that the probability of getting a 5 did not depend on whether a head was obtained when tossing the coin. How can we write this with the notation from the previous section on conditional probability? The idea is to say that the probability of E given F is no different than simply the probability of E. That is to say, knowing that F occurred has no bearing on our calculation of the probability of E. This is expressed by saying

$$p(E|F) = p(E) \qquad (4.14)$$

We take this to be the definition of the independence of the events E and F. This is the intuitive version of the expression of independence. There is a simple algebraic manipulation that leads to another form of the equation which is more often used when doing calculations. We show that next.

Recall the *definition of the conditional probability* (4.12)

$$p(E|F) = \frac{p(E \cap F)}{p(F)}$$

If we replace p(E|F) in Equation (4.14) by its definition, we get

$$\frac{p(E \cap F)}{p(F)} = p(E) \qquad (4.15)$$

Then multiplying the left and right sides by p(F) gives

$$p(E \cap F) = p(E) * p(F) \qquad (4.16)$$

Although less intuitive, this is an alternate form of the definition of the independence of events E and F that we will frequently use in calculations.

From this second form, it is easy to see that if E is independent of F, then F is independent of E, and that is why we have been using the phrase "E and F are independent" rather than saying E is independent of F or vice versa.

If we compare independence with property 2 of probability functions (4.4) which was true when two events are mutually exclusive, we can see a nice way to remember both the formula for independence and the probability formula for mutually exclusive events.

Mutually exclusive events E and F obey property 2 (4.12):

$$p(E \cup F) = p(E) + p(F)$$

Independent events E and F obey (4.14):

$$p(E \cap F) = p(E) * p(F)$$

To help remember these two, we can say that if E and F are mutually exclusive, then union "translates" to addition, and if E and F are independent, intersection "translates" to multiplication.

4.20 Examples

We can ask whether the events A and B as defined earlier are independent.

```
A_bool=df$Class=='democrat' & df$V1=='y' & df$V2=='n'
A=df[A_bool,]
B_bool=df$toss2=='H'
B=bool2event(B_bool,df)
#Independence of two events

prob(intersect_event(A,B,df),df)
## [1] 0.112069
prob(A,df)*prob(B,df)
## [1] 0.04709795
```

We can see that they are *not* independent. As mentioned earlier, it is hard to come up with real-life examples that show truly independent events. Next, we will construct an artificially simple example that does provide us with an example of independent events. Let us try to construct a dataframe that represents the tossing of two fair coins (Figure 4.22).

names	toss1	toss2
R1	H	H
R2	H	T
R3	T	H
R4	T	T

Figure 4.22 **Representation of tossing two fair coins.**

	names	toss1	toss2
1	R1	H	H
2	R2	H	T
3	R3	T	H
4	R4	T	T

Figure 4.23 RStudio view of representation of tossing two fair coins.

If all the rows are equally likely, as we have been assuming, then each of R1, R2, R3, and R4 are equally likely, and so this does represent the tossing of two *fair* coins. We can construct each column as a vector and then bind them together with **cbind**(). Recall the **cbind**() outputs a dataframe (Figure 4.23).

```
names=c("R1","R2","R3","R4")
toss1=c("H","H","T","T")
toss2=c("H","T","H","T")
df=cbind(names,toss1,toss2)
df=as.data.frame(df)
is.data.frame(df)
## [1] TRUE

#Although it is not necessary, to practice our function defining skills,
we can define a function bool2event() to output the dataframe.
bool2event<-function(E_bool,df){return(df[E_bool,])}
A_bool=df$toss1=='H'
A=bool2event(A_bool,df)
B_bool=df$toss2=='H'
B=bool2event(B_bool,df)

prob(intersect_event(A,B,df),df)
## [1] 0.25
prob(A,df)*prob(B,df)
## [1] 0.25
```

In this case, event A and event B, getting heads on the first toss and getting heads on the second toss, are independent as we would expect since the following is true:

$$p(E \cap F) = p(E) * p(F) \tag{4.17}$$

4.21 Conditional Independence

Suppose we select two people and test to see if they have a specific genetic disease. Suppose that the prevalence of the disease in the population is 0.005. Define

E to be that the first person has the disease
F to be that the second person has the disease.

Thus, $p(E) = 0.005 = p(F)$. If the two people are selected at random, then the two events should be independent, meaning whether one has the disease or not should not affect whether the second has the disease, and therefore $p(E|F) = p(E) = 0.005$. On the other hand, what if we define

G to be the event that the two people (the first and second) are siblings.

Now it would seem that given that they are siblings and if one of them has the disease, then the probability that the other has the disease will go up since it is a genetic disease. This is the idea of *conditional* independence (or in this case conditional dependence). The probability of E given *both* G and F will not be the same as the probability of E given F. We can express this in notation as

$$p(E|(F \text{ and } G)) \neq p(E|F) \tag{4.18}$$

Recall that intersection is translated as AND, and so we usually write this as

$$p(E|E \cap F) \neq p(E|F) \tag{4.19}$$

This is called conditional *dependence*. Conditional *independence* is

$$p(E|F \cap G) = p(E|F) \tag{4.20}$$

An alternate expression for conditional independence is

$$p(E \cap F|G) = p(E|G) * p(F|G) \tag{4.21}$$

Notice how it resembles the second form of (non-conditional) independence (4.17)

$$p(E \cap F) = p(E) * p(F)$$

The equivalence of (4.20) and (4.21) can be seen by

$$
\begin{aligned}
p(E \cap F|G) &= p(E \cap F \cap G)/p(G) \\
&= \frac{p(E \cap F \cap G)}{p(F \cap G)} * \frac{p(F \cap G)}{p(G)} \\
&= p(E|F \cap G) * p(F|G)
\end{aligned}
\tag{4.22}
$$

Now if we use the assumption of conditional independence from Equation (4.20), we get

$$= p(E|F) * p(F|G)$$

We have shown that (4.20) implies (4.21).

Practice 4.21.7
   1. Show that (4.21) implies (4.20).

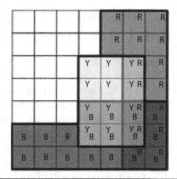

Figure 4.24 Graphic representation of the three events which we will call event Red, event Blue, and event Yellow. Squares with Y are yellow, squares with B are blue, and squares with R are red.

Let's look at a visual example of conditional independence.

Consider the diagram in Figure 4.24.[4]

There are $7 \times 7 = 49$ squares here. Some blocks contain multiple colors. The bottom two rows are blue. The two right-most columns are red. The third row from the bottom has blue in the last four columns. There is a set of 12 yellow blocks. The experiment here is to select a square at random, and we define three events: R: getting a red square, B: getting a blue square, and Y: getting a yellow square. We can see that $p(Y) = 12/49$, $p(B) = 18/49$, and $p(R) = 16/49$.

Before asking about *conditional* independence, we first ask whether R and B are independent. We need to check that R and B satisfy Equation (4.14):

$$p(R \cap B) = p(R) * p(B)$$

We already calculated the probabilities on the RHS. For the LHS, we can see that

$$p(R \cap B) = \frac{6}{49} \neq \frac{16}{49} = p(R) * p(B)$$

Thus, it turns out the RHS and LHS are not equal, and so R and B are not independent. This does not, however, mean that R and B are not *conditionally* independent given Y. So, let's check to see if these are conditionally independent *on Y*.

We use the second version of the definition of conditional independence from Equation (4.21):

$$p(R \cap B|Y) = p(R|Y) * p(B|Y)$$

The LHS is $2/12 = 1/6$.

The RHS is $4/12 * 6/12 = 1/3 * 1/2 = 1/6$.

Thus, even though they are not independent, R and B are *conditionally* independent on Y. Let's see how we could implement this in R.

---

[4] From Wikipedia.

4.22 An Illustration of Conditional Independence with R Using Arrays

#We DO NOT use dataframes here! We can say that dataframes are two-dimensional, in the sense that they have rows and columns. We want to construct something that has, in effect, three dimensions.
*#This is a bit of a digression from our dataframe discussion but does allow us to explore the concept of conditional independence. Let's try to construct the 7 by 7 figure of the diagram above. Even though it is a two-dimensional object, it will turn out to be easier to represent it with three dimensions. (A Rubik's cube is three dimensional, for example.) We will construct it as an array. Note that a matrix is a two-dimensional array. A vector is a one-dimensional array. In this example, we will construct a three-dimensional array. This will allow us to have three dimensions. The first two dimensions will be 7 and 7 as we saw in the figure. However, the array will also have a third "depth" dimension. The depth will be 3 units, and thus this will provide us with three layers in the array. Then we can use each layer to represent one of the colors. You will see how we do this in a moment. One layer will be for designating whether a square has red **or not**. One layer will be for designating whether a square has blue **or not**. One layer will be for designating whether a square has yellow **or not**.*
#We begin by filling the array with numbers, but this is arbitrary, and the numbers are just acting as meaningless placeholders.
ci=**array**(1:(49*3),dim=**c**(7,7,3)) *#named ci for conditional independence because we are constructing this array to represent an example which will allow us to test for conditional independence.*

#Next, we set dimension names. This is optional, and we are only giving names for the depth layer.

dimnames(ci)=**list**(NULL,NULL,**c**("R","B","Y"))
head(ci)
[1] 1 2 3 4 5 6
#Layer 2 is the blue layer. We will replace the numeric placeholders with the symbol "b" wherever we want a blue square (as shown in Figure 4.24). Elsewhere in layer 2, we leave the numeric placeholders.
#Note: To point to an element in our three-dimensional array, we must give the "address" of the row, column, and depth. Thus, for example, we could use ci[4,5,2] to point to the element in row 4, column 5, and layer 2.
#For the assignment of blue, first we enter "b" in rows 6 and 7, columns 1 to 7.
ci[6:7,1:7,2]=**c**("b")
#Then we enter "b" into the third row but only in the last four cells.
ci[5,4:7,2]=**c**("b")
#Layer 1 is the red layer. We will replace
#the numeric placeholders with the symbol "r"
#wherever we want a red square.
ci[1:7,6:7,1]=**c**("r")
ci[1:2,5,1]=**c**("r")
#Layer 3 is the yellow layer. We will replace
#the numeric placeholders with the symbol "y"
#wherever we want a yellow square.
ci[3:6,4:6,3]=**c**("y")

#Here is an example layer. Layer 1 is the red layer, and we can see which cells are assigned "r". (Remember that the numbers in the other locations have no meaning other than being placeholders.)

```
ci[,,1] #By putting 1 in the third entry, we are only seeing what is in
layer 1.
##      [,1]  [,2]  [,3]  [,4]  [,5]  [,6]  [,7]
## [1,]  "1"   "8"  "15"  "22"   "r"   "r"   "r"
## [2,]  "2"   "9"  "16"  "23"   "r"   "r"   "r"
## [3,]  "3"  "10"  "17"  "24"  "31"   "r"   "r"
## [4,]  "4"  "11"  "18"  "25"  "32"   "r"   "r"
## [5,]  "5"  "12"  "19"  "26"  "33"   "r"   "r"
## [6,]  "6"  "13"  "20"  "27"  "34"   "r"   "r"
## [7,]  "7"  "14"  "21"  "28"  "35"   "r"   "r"
```

#The following is a Boolean matrix that is TRUE when there is a "b" in the third layer. However the third layer is for yellow, so there should not be any "b".

```
ci[,,3]=="b"
##        [,1]  [,2]  [,3]  [,4]  [,5]  [,6]  [,7]
## [1,]  FALSE FALSE FALSE FALSE FALSE FALSE FALSE
## [2,]  FALSE FALSE FALSE FALSE FALSE FALSE FALSE
## [3,]  FALSE FALSE FALSE FALSE FALSE FALSE FALSE
## [4,]  FALSE FALSE FALSE FALSE FALSE FALSE FALSE
## [5,]  FALSE FALSE FALSE FALSE FALSE FALSE FALSE
## [6,]  FALSE FALSE FALSE FALSE FALSE FALSE FALSE
## [7,]  FALSE FALSE FALSE FALSE FALSE FALSE FALSE
```
#On the other hand, there is "y" in the third layer.
```
ci[,,3]=="y"
##        [,1]  [,2]  [,3]  [,4]  [,5]  [,6]  [,7]
## [1,]  FALSE FALSE FALSE FALSE  FALSE FALSE FALSE
## [2,]  FALSE FALSE FALSE FALSE  FALSE FALSE FALSE
## [3,]  FALSE FALSE FALSE TRUE   TRUE  TRUE  FALSE
## [4,]  FALSE FALSE FALSE TRUE   TRUE  TRUE  FALSE
## [5,]  FALSE FALSE FALSE TRUE   TRUE  TRUE  FALSE
## [6,]  FALSE FALSE FALSE TRUE   TRUE  TRUE  FALSE
## [7,]  FALSE FALSE FALSE FALSE  FALSE FALSE FALSE
```
```
which("y"==ci) #This will tell us which entries have y, but first it
stretches out the array into a giant vector.
## [1] 122 123 124 125 129 130 131 132 136 137 138 139
length(which("y"==ci)) #How many y's are there?
## [1] 12
```
#To see the actual location of each y, the arr.ind must be set to TRUE. Then we can see, for example, by reading the first line of the output below that there is a y at position ci[3,4,3].
```
which("y"==ci, arr.ind = TRUE)
##       dim1 dim2 dim3
## [1,]    3    4    3
## [2,]    4    4    3
## [3,]    5    4    3
## [4,]    6    4    3
## [5,]    3    5    3
## [6,]    4    5    3
## [7,]    5    5    3
## [8,]    6    5    3
## [9,]    3    6    3
```

```
## [10,]   4   6   3
## [11,]   5   6   3
## [12,]   6   6   3
#Below, we assign the results of which() to y, r, and b. Note we are
using y and "y", r and "r", b and "b" in our notation here.
#By specifying the layer in the last index of the array, we limit the set
of possible entries to 49 (=7x7). Furthermore, which() returns a vector.
Each of the 49 possible entries is associated with a cell in Figure 4-24.
y=which(ci[,,3]=="y")
r=which(ci[,,1]=="r")
b=which(ci[,,2]=="b")
y
## [1] 24 25 26 27 31 32 33 34 38 39 40 41
r
## [1] 29 30 36 37 38 39 40 41 42 43 44 45 46 47 48 49
b
## [1] 6 7 13 14 20 21 26 27 28 33 34 35 40 41 42 47 48 49
#The first element of the vector y is associated with the first yellow
cell in Figure 4-24. (Remember matrices in R are populated column by
column, not row by row.)
If the entries of y, r, or b above have any elements in common, it means
that the corresponding cell in Figure 4.24 contains both of those colors.

#Find the intersection of y and r and so on.
#We can use intersect() or intersection_of_sets() to get
intersYR=intersect(y,r).
intersYR
## [1] 38 39 40 41
intersBR=intersect(b,r)
intersBR
## [1] 40 41 42 47 48 49
intersYB=intersect(y,b)
intersYB
## [1] 26 27 33 34 40 41
#Is P(R,B)=P(R)*P(B)? That is, are R (red squares) and B (blue squares)
independent?
#We saw earlier that they are not independent.
#We confirm it here as well.
#First, we define a new probability function since the version we had
before was for dataframes, but now we have an array not a dataframe.
#An example of the first argument of the probArr() function defined below
could be:
which(ci[,,3]=="y").
This means that it will be a vector and specifically a subset of the
vector 1:49 as we saw above. We may view the first argument as indicating
which cells are included in the matrix of cells in Figure 4.24.

probArr=function(a,ar){
length(a)/length(ar[,,1])
}
#Now try a test of regular independence. We will test with Y and R.
probArr(intersYR,ci)
## [1] 0.08163265
probArr(y,ci)*probArr(r,ci)
## [1] 0.07996668
```

```
#We see that these are not equal, and so we don't have independence.
#Conditional Independence
#Now we will try a test of conditional independence. We just tested
regular independence of Y and R above. It doesn't make sense to ask if Y
and R are conditionally independent because we need three events to talk
about conditional independence. In this sense, conditional independence
and regular independence are not even related. In other words, you would
not say conditional independence implies regular independence, for
example, because one deals with three events and one deals with two
events. So they are not even dealing with the same set of events.
#OK, we will test if B and R are conditionally independent given Y.
#That is, from equation (4-20), is P(intersBR|Y)=P(R|Y)*P(B|Y)?
#Let's look at LHS.
```

Mathematically we are checking

$$p(B \cap R|Y) = p(B|Y) * p(R|Y)$$

But since $B \cap R$ is an event in and of itself, by the definition of conditional probability, we can write the LHS as

$$p(B \cap R|Y) = \frac{p((B \cap R) \cap Y)}{p(Y)}$$

```
#In R, that would be
#P(intersBRY)/P(y).
#What is intersBRY?
#This is not a dataframe question. It started as an array question but
now is a vector question. Since these are vectors and not dataframes, we
don't need intersect_event(). We are using the built-in intersect() from
the {base} R package.
intersBRY=intersect(intersect(y,r),b)
#so P(intersBRY)/P(y) is:
probArr(intersBRY,ci)/probArr(y,ci)
## [1] 0.1666667
#RHS has two factors:
#P(R|Y)=probArr(intersYR,ci)/probArr(y,ci)
#P(B|Y)=probArr(intersYB,ci)/probArr(y,ci)
(probArr(intersYR,ci)/probArr(y,ci))*(probArr(intersYB,ci)/probArr(y,ci))
## [1] 0.1666667
#The LHS and RHS are equal; thus, we have established conditional
independence!
```

Note that the above representation of ci is similar to the way image data is stored. That is, in image recognition tasks, the image has to be stored (and then fed into the model). An image is actually a collection of pixels (short for pixel elements). Each pixel consists of a blend of red (R), green (G), and blue (B). The data is often stored in an array with the layers containing the amount of red, green, and blue. For example, in the red layer, instead of storing either r or "not r", a number from 0 to 255 is entered in the cell, with 0 indicating no red and 255 being the largest possible amount of red.

Practice 4.22.8

1. Try the above to show that blue and red are conditionally independent using our **intersection_of_sets**() function instead of the built-in **intersect**() function. Is it possible? Are there any noticeable differences?
2. Change the cells in layer 3, row 7, columns 4, 5, and 6 to yellow. Will this change whether R and B are independent? Are they still conditionally independent?

4.23 Bayes Theorem

4.23.1 Introductory Problem

Suppose we have two boxes. Box 1 is green and has four blue balls and eight yellow balls. Box 2 is purple and has 2 blue balls and 10 yellow balls. Suppose we select a box at random and then select a ball at random. Then we can ask questions like the following (Figure 4.25):

What is the probability of getting a blue ball, given that we selected Box 1?

This can be written as

P(BlueBall|Box1)

A more confusing question might be the following:

What is the probability that we selected Box 1, given that the ball is blue?

How do we write this second question?

P(Box1 | BlueBall)

This question is difficult to even think about because the order of the events is mixed up. What is actually done in the experiment is as follows:

First the box is selected; then the ball is selected. But here we are asking a question where it seems that the order is opposite to what is actually done in the experiment.

Bayes theorem will allow us to reverse the order, if we want, and only confront questions in the original order.

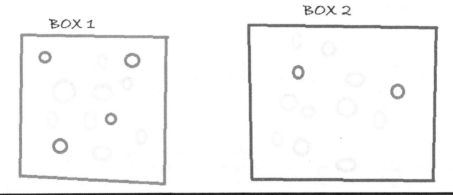

Figure 4.25 Two boxes with blue and yellow balls. The box on the left is Green. The box on the right is Purple. The balls that appear as dark gray are blue. The balls that appear as light gray are yellow. Since the box is selected at random, each box has a 50–50 chance of being selected.

4.24 Statement of Bayes Theorem

The following is a statement of Bayes theorem. Notice how the expression on the LHS has the order of A|B, but this is reversed to B|A in the expression on the RHS.

$$P(A|B) = \frac{p(B|A) * p(A)}{p(B)} \tag{4.23}$$

For our purposes, the point of Bayes theorem is that it allows us to reverse the order of the two parts of a conditional probability expression. Before proving Bayes theorem, let us explore it a little more. Going back to the question about the green box, Box 1, and the purple box, Box 2, how does it make the difficult question easier? The difficult question we asked was

P(Box1 | BlueBall).

Now, using Bayes theorem, it can be answered with

$$\frac{p(BlueBall|Box1) * p(Box1)}{p(BlueBall)} \tag{4.24}$$

If we examine each of these RHS calculations, they seem to be easier than the original difficult question. Of course, there are three calculations on the RHS, whereas there was only one on the left, and so we can think of this as the price of facing easier calculations – we have to do more of them.

Let us see what the calculations for the three pieces are.

$p(BlueBall|Box1) = \dfrac{4}{12}$ because there are four blue balls in box 1.

$p(Box1) = \dfrac{1}{2}$ since the box is selected at random and there are only two boxes.

The last calculation, p(BlueBall), is not so straightforward. It seems that the answer to this is simply the total number of blue balls divided by the total number of balls. This is correct, but we will want a more general answer. We will postpone the answer to this and first prove Bayes theorem.

4.25 Partition of a Set

We introduce the idea of a partition of a set. A partition of a set is a grouping of the set's elements into non-empty subsets, in such a way that no two sets have any elements in common; that is to say, each pair of sets is disjoint. A simple example is illustrated with Figure 4.26.

Here we have a set U which is partitioned into two sets A and $\bar{A}$, where $\bar{A}$ is the complement of A. One feature of a partition of a set that may not have been clear in the above definition is that the union of all the sets in the partition must give the entire set. This is true in Figure 4.26 since

$$A \cup \bar{A} = U \tag{4.25}$$

The fact that the sets must be disjoint shows up in this example as

$$A \cap \bar{A} = \varnothing \tag{4.26}$$

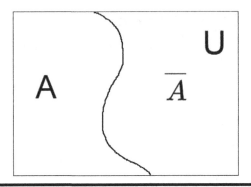

Figure 4.26   A partition of U into two sets.

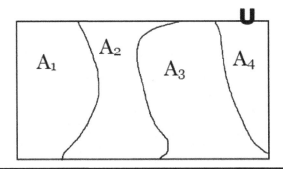

Figure 4.27   A partition of U into four sets.

Partitions are not limited to two sets. Here is a partition of U consisting of four sets A_1, A_2, A_3, and A_4 (Figure 4.27)

This partition is sometimes denoted by $\{A_i\}$ which emphasizes that it is a set of sets. Suppose we have a set of n sets $\{A_i\}$ which partition

a set U. Then $U = A_1 \cup A_2 \cup A_3 \cdots \cup A_n$, and this is sometimes written as

$$U = \bigcup_1^n A_i \tag{4.27}$$

and of course, each of the A_i is a subset of U. The fact that the sets must be disjoint can be expressed as follows.

$$A_i \cap A_j = \varnothing \quad \text{for any i and j as long as } i \neq j$$

Now suppose we have another set B which is a subset of U. B is an additional set, *not part of the original partition*. The diagram may look like that in Figure 4.28.

It is interesting to note that we can write B as a union of sets as follows:

$$B = (B \cap A_1) \cup (B \cap A_2) \cup (B \cap A_3) \cup (B \cap A_4) \tag{4.28}$$

which can be seen from Figure 4.29.

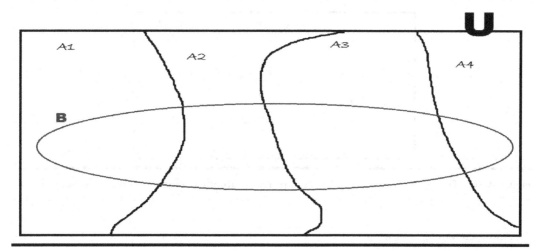

Figure 4.28 A partition of U into four sets and another subset of U called B.

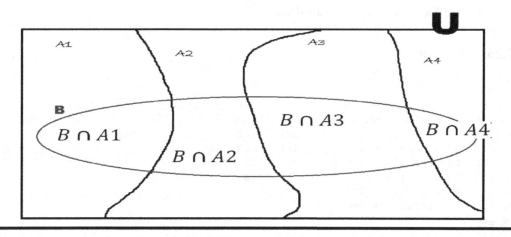

Figure 4.29 B can be written as the disjoint union of the four sets indicated.

Furthermore, each of these $B \cap A_i$ is disjoint!

Now let us switch our point of view from sets to events. If we view the above as a diagram about events, we can write

$$p(B) = p\big((B \cap A_1) \cup (B \cap A_2) \cup (B \cap A_3) \cup (B \cap A_4)\big) \tag{4.29}$$

And now apply property 2 for probability functions (which concerns disjoint sets) and write

$$= p(B \cap A_1) + p(B \cap A_2) + p(B \cap A_3) + p(B \cap A_4) \tag{4.30}$$

We will need this result shortly to write Bayes theorem.

Let us consider one more example before we show the proof of Bayes theorem. We can view A together with its complement $\overline{A}$ as a partition of U as shown in Figure 4.30.

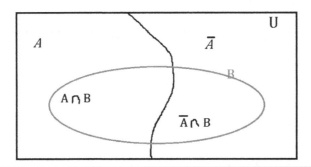

Figure 4.30 **The event B written as the sum of two mutually exclusive events as indicated.**

And therefore, we can write

$$p(B) = p(A \cap B) + p(\overline{A} \cap B) \tag{4.31}$$

again because A and its complement are disjoint.

4.25.1 R Code

```
#Partitions

#We have said earlier that we will treat our dataframe as a sample space
and therefore as a set of outcomes. Since it is a set, we can apply our
concept of partition to it. In our first example of a partition of a
dataframe, we will break it up into sets, randomly, just as an
illustration of the concept of partition.
#By taking a sample of the list of rows of the dataframe, df, we
basically reorder the set of rows.
randomrows=sample(1:nrow(df))
length(randomrows)
## [1] 232
#We haven't removed any rows. There are still as many rows as there were
in df.
length(randomrows)==nrow(df)
## [1] TRUE
#We can see that the order of the rows is now random.
head(randomrows)
## [1] 53 133 156 203 186 79
#Now we partition our sample space into five sets A1, … , A5.
A1=df[randomrows[1:50],]
A2=df[randomrows[51:60],]
A3=df[randomrows[61:90],]
A4=df[randomrows[91:150],]
A5=df[randomrows[151:nrow(df)],]
#Make sure that you agree that the above five sets A1, …, A5 form a
partition of df.
#Create some set B as in Figure 4.30. Here we use two conditions on the
variables to get a set B.
B_bool=df$V4=='n' & df$V10=='y'
```

```
B=df[B_bool,]
#Show that prob(B) is the sum of prob(A1 intersect B) + … + prob(A5
intersect B). This should hold from property 2 of probability because we
have partitioned S into disjoint sets.

prob(B,df)
## [1] 0.2801724
prob(intersect_event(A1,B,df),df)+prob(intersect_event(A2,B,df),df)+prob
(intersect_event(A3,B,df),df)+prob(intersect_event(A4,B,df),df)+prob
(intersect_event(A5,B,df),df)
## [1] 0.2801724
```

Practice 4.25.9

1. Rather than a random partition of the dataframe, partition it more meaningfully using conditions on one or more variables, and then run the same set of steps as above. For example, it could be partitioned into democrats and republicans, or it could be partitioned into senators who voted in one of the four patterns:

    y on issue #1 and y on issue #2
    y on #1 and n on #2
    n on #1 and y on #2
    n on #1 and n on #2

    In your answer, note how many sets you have partitioned the dataframe into (how many sets are there in your {A_i}).

2. Repeat the previous practice problem for the mtcars dataset.

4.26 Proof of Bayes Theorem

See if you can follow the proof of Bayes theorem given below.

$$p(A|B) = \frac{p(B|A)p(A)}{p(B)} \tag{4.32}$$

We start out with the definition of $p(A|B)$.

$$p(A|B) = \frac{p(A \cap B)}{p(B)} = \frac{p(B \cap A)}{p(B)} \tag{4.33}$$

But we also note that

$$p(B|A) = \frac{p(B \cap A)}{p(A)} \tag{4.34}$$

which implies that

$$p(B \cap A) = p(B|A)p(A) \tag{4.35}$$

We take this expression and replace $p(B \cap A)$ with $p(B|A)p(A)$ in the previous equation to get

$$p(A|B) = \frac{p(B \cap A)}{p(B)} = \frac{p(B|A)p(A)}{p(B)} \tag{4.36}$$

This is the expression of Bayes theorem we wanted to prove!

Now we will rewrite the denominator in two ways to give two alternative expressions.

If we partition the sample space S by just two sets, A and its complement $\bar{A}$, then, as we mentioned in Equation (4.31), we can express the denominator as
$p(B) = p(A \cap B) + p(\bar{A} \cap B)$, and so, we can write

$$p(A|B) = \frac{p(B|A)p(A)}{p(A \cap B) + p(\bar{A} \cap B)} \tag{4.37}$$

But now notice that

$$p(A \cap B) = p(B \cap A) = p(B|A)p(A) \tag{4.38}$$

and

$$p(\bar{A} \cap B) = p(B \cap \bar{A}) = p(B|\bar{A})p(\bar{A}) \tag{4.39}$$

which provides us with a **second version** of Bayes theorem as

$$p(A|B) = \frac{p(B|A)p(A)}{p(B|A)p(A) + p(B|\bar{A})p(\bar{A})} \tag{4.40}$$

4.27 Another Version of Bayes Theorem

We leave it to the reader to verify that if $\{A_i\}$ is a partition of S into n sets, then we can write a third version of Bayes theorem

$$p(A_j|B) = \frac{p(B|A_j)p(A_j)}{\sum_{1}^{n} p(B|A_i)p(A_i)} \tag{4.41}$$

Practice 4.27.10

1. Define an event B to denote that the senator voted y on the last two issues. Use the partition that you created in the last practice problem to generate the different events $\{A_i\}$ referred to in the third version of Bayes theorem, and then using R, show that Bayes theorem is true for this partition. (Choose one of the sets in $\{A_i\}$ to be the A_j on the LHS.) The purpose of this exercise is to show that the conditional probability function is working correctly and to make sure the reader has a clear understanding of Bayes theorem.
2. Explain in words what the LHS of the calculation in part 1 is asking?
3. Repeat parts 1 and 2 of this practice set for the mtcars dataset. Define your own event B.

Note on additional terminology

In the language of statistics, it is sometimes said that Bayes theorem deals with a hypothesis and evidence for that hypothesis. Whereas we presented Bayes theorem for p(E|F) where E and F are *any* events, sometimes Bayes theorem is presented as p(some *hypothesis* | some *evidence*). An example which bridges both statistics and machine learning could be the problem of classifying what kind of chocolate someone likes (white, dark, or milk). We may encounter something like p(milk chocolate | **X**) where X may be that the person is between 5 and 10 years old. In the language of statistics, we could refer to milk chocolate (the preference for milk chocolate) as a hypothesis – the hypothesis that a person prefers milk chocolate. And we could refer to X as the evidence. In the framework of a machine learning problem we would call milk chocolate the class value and X the input data.

As second example from the study of statistics, in discussions of what is referred to as *hypothesis testing*, we find questions like the following.

> A company that sells tires makes the claim that the lifetime of their tires is at least 100,000 kilometers. A test is conducted to determine whether the claim is fair or misleading. The test consists of drawing a sample of 500 previously sold tires and calculating their average lifetime. The result of this calculation is used to decide whether the company's claim should be rejected or not. In statistics, the claim that the tires last at least 100,000 kilometers is referred to as a hypothesis. The results of the test are referred to as the evidence. As part of the decision, we calculate *p(hypothesis | evidence)* If this probability is very low, we may have reason to reject the tire company's claim.

The above two examples illustrate where the terms *hypothesis* and *evidence* appear as a conditional probability question.

Chapter 5

Naïve Rule

- A sample dataset
- Notation
- Estimation, prediction, classification
- R implementation of the Naïve Rule

We have covered the basics of programming and writing functions in R, sets, logic, and probability. It is time to use these tools to construct machine learning algorithms that can classify and predict. We will see exactly what this means below.

Functions Coded in This Chapter
`NaiveRule`

5.1 A Sample Dataset

Typically, we have one or more predictors (input variables) as well as a target variable (output variable). There are various terms for predictors and the target. Sometimes we say *input* and *output*. In statistics, the terms *explanatory* and *response* variables are often used. Let us consider a well-known example, the Iris dataset. If the output variable is *class* (the variable we are trying to predict), then the input variables we use to make the prediction are sepal length, sepal width, petal length, and petal width. The Iris dataset has 150 rows which we refer to as either specimens, instances, or examples (Figures 5.1–5.3).

5.2 Labeled Data

This data is referred to as "labeled" data. The label is the class and is the entity we are hoping to predict. In this Iris flower example, typically the class is the species name, but we could choose any of the fields to be the output field or label. If we are using the species as the class, then when we

sepallength	sepalwidth	petallength	petalwidth	class
5	2	3.5	1	Iris-versicolor
6	2.2	4	1	Iris-versicolor
6	2.2	5	1.5	Iris-virginica
6.2	2.2	4.5	1.5	Iris-versicolor
4.5	2.3	1.3	0.3	Iris-setosa

Figure 5.1   Snapshot of the Iris dataset.

Figure 5.2   Three species of Iris flowers are identified in the class variable.

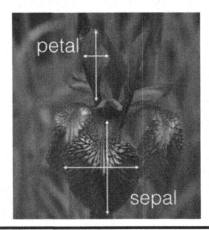

Figure 5.3   We measure the petal length and width and sepal length and width for each of the 150 specimens. Thus, we have five measurements on each specimen.

say it is labeled, we mean that we know the *class* of each specimen. Of course, the point in build-ing a model would be to be able to predict the label of a new specimen for which we do not know the label. That is to say, if we have a specimen where we know the sepal length, sepal width, petal length, and petal width, we would like to put it into our model and have the model tell us (hope-fully correctly) the class of this specimen. Typically we randomly select part of our dataset and use it for training our model. For example, in the Iris dataset, we may take 100 rows and use them as the *training data*. The machine learning algorithm is tasked with learning the labeling from the training data. The rest of the data, the 50 rows that were not in the training data, are then used to test how well the machine learning algorithm has learned the labeling process. These 50 rows are collectively referred to as the test data. We feed these instances (with the exception of the class variable) into the algorithm and ask it to provide a label, that is, ask it to provide the class. We then check to see how many times the algorithm got the label right and how many times it got the label wrong. We can do this because, even though we don't tell the algorithm the correct label, we do actually know the correct labels for these 50 items in our test set. For example, if the algorithm got 30 out of the 50 correct, then we would assign the number 60% to the accuracy of the model.

Practice 5.2.1

  1. Why do we leave out the class variable when feeding the test data into our model?

5.3 Notation for a Model

In our discussion, we will want to refer to the predictor variables (the inputs) and the target variable (the output). We can use X_i for the inputs and C for the class or target variable. It is also common to use y for the class variable, and we will use that notation in later chapters when we study neural networks. Often when the output variable is *numeric*, it is denoted by Y, but sometimes even when it is categorical, it is denoted by Y. With regard to the inputs, if there are n inputs, we may denote them with $X_1, X_2, X_3, ..., X_n$. The class or output variable will be denoted by C in this chapter. We build a model with our training data which will take a set of values for the $X_1, X_2, X_3, ..., X_n$ and generate a prediction of the class C. In the Iris dataset, we have four input variables X_i and then the class variable C. For example, we could assign X_1 to sepal length, X_2 to sepal width, X_3 to petal length, X_4 to petal width, and C to the type of Iris (Setosa, Versicolor, Virginica). Our expectation is that the class C depends on the input variables X_i, and we could express this as

$$C = f(X_1, X_2, X_3, X_4)$$

or more specifically, for the Iris dataset,

$$\text{species} = f(\text{sepal length, sepal width, petal length, petal width})$$

Mathematically we construct a vector which consists of all the X_i, that is, which consists of $X_1, X_2, X_3, ..., X_n$. This is usually denoted by either an X with an arrow above it like $\vec{X}$ or as a bold uppercase X like **X**. When writing on a board, it is easier to write $\vec{X}$, whereas when typing, the bold **X** is easier. **X** refers to the vector of all the input variables. Note that in R, when we speak of vectors, more often than not, we are referring to a specific set of values. For example, if we write

$$x = c(1, 25, 9, 2, 1)$$

we are saying not only that we have a vector with five elements but also that we have specified exactly which values each of the five elements assumes. Some mathematics texts use different notations for vectors, such as

$$\mathbf{X} = <1, 25, 9, 2, 1>$$

$$\mathbf{X} = [1, 25, 9, 2, 1].$$

The angle brackets are more common in physics. In either case, we say that $\mathbf{X}$ is a five-dimensional vector and that $\mathbf{X}$ is an element of $\mathbf{R}^5$, which is usually written as $\mathbf{X} \in \mathbf{R}^5$. If you are not familiar with the notation $\mathbf{R}^5$ (read "R 5"); it simply means that $\mathbf{X}$ is a vector with five components and each of those components is a real number.

5.4 Estimation, Prediction and Classification

Estimation and prediction are often used interchangeably, and we will follow this practice. However some writers distinguish between the terms saying that estimation, as used in Statistics, is used in the context of estimating a parameter, whereas prediction is used for predicting values. We should also mention the difference between classification and estimation or prediction. Data science is a relatively new field and does not have a set of standard notations or terminologies. Different practitioners develop their own vocabularies. This is true for the terms "classify" and "predict". It does seem though that an agreement has been reached that classification will refer to the case where the output variable is categorical and estimation (or prediction) will refer to the case where the output variable is numeric. Thus, if we are trying to classify an individual as to whether they prefer Mercedes, Lexus, or Jaguar, this would be a classification task since the output variable is not a number. If we are trying to predict *how much* money a person will spend on their next car, we would refer to this as estimation or prediction. Another word that is used instead of numeric is quantitative. Other terms for non-numeric variables are "qualitative" or "categorical" variables. In spite of the above terminology conventions, the word "predicting" is so common in the English language that sometimes, even though the output is categorical, it is clearer or more convenient to use the word "prediction". Another set of terms to refer to this distinction is "classification" and "regression". Regression can refer to a particular modeling technique (called Regression), but it may also be used to mean an algorithm or model where the output variable is numeric.

Practice 5.4.2

1. Give two terms that indicate a numeric output variable.

5.5 Naïve Rule – the Most Rudimentary Model

Our first classifier is called the Naïve Rule. Note this is not the Naïve Bayes classifier. This is just the first step in building up to the Naïve Bayes classifier. The Naïve Rule is probably the simplest possible algorithm. It is so simple that you may not even consider it an algorithm. Here is an example of the thinking behind it.

Suppose there are 50 people riding in a train car. Our job is to build a model to predict whether the next person who enters the car believes in ghosts or not. We are allowed to ask each person currently in the car to fill out a survey, and we will assume they are all willing to fill it out. The survey asks the following five questions.

1. Do you believe in ghosts (yes or no)?
2. Do you earn more than $60,000?
3. What was the population of the city or town you grew up in?
4. Do you believe in evolution?
5. Have you ever been to a fortune teller?

Each question can be represented by a variable. Some of the variables are going to be yes/no variables, and some will be numeric.

G: ghost y/n
I: income (y/n)
P: population (numeric)
E: evolution (y/n)
T: fortune teller (y/n)

It would seem plausible that

$$G = f(I, P, E, T)$$

That is, it is plausible that belief in ghosts is a function of these variables and that some or all of the variables I, P, E, and T could assist us in predicting whether a person will believe in ghosts or not. After collecting the results of this survey, if a *new* person enters the train, and if we are permitted to ask them the questions involving the input variables I, P, E, and T, we would expect that using their answers may help us to make an "educated" guess about whether they believe in ghosts. *However*, the Naïve Rule would not allow you to give the survey to the *new* person. You would simply have to make a guess as to whether or not the new person believes in ghosts with no knowledge of the values of the input variables for this new person. In such a case, what should we predict for this new person? Although we will not have access to the input variables, we will have access to the percentage of people who believe in ghosts in the train. Suppose that among the people currently in the car, 20% believe in ghosts and 80% don't. What should we guess about the new person? If we have no knowledge of the values for any of our input variables for this new person, then arguably our best guess would be to say the new person doesn't believe in ghosts. Why? Because that is the most prevalent class in the train (in our training set). This is the mechanism for how the Naïve Rule classifies new instances. It uses the "majority" class from the training set and will classify *every* new instance as that class. It ignores all the input variables. The Naïve Rule ignores all the predictor information X_1, X_2, X_3, …, X_n and simply predicts a class for the new person, based on whatever the majority value is for the class variable. This is just about as simple a prediction rule as we can imagine. As it ignores all the input variable information, we would hope that any other algorithm should perform at least as well as this model. Thus, it is often said that the Naïve Rule is the *benchmark* by which all other models are measured, and it is said to provide a baseline performance level.

The Naïve Rule goes by other names as well. For example, in the open source project Weka, it is referred to as ZeroR. The "Zero" in ZeroR is there because it uses zero input variable information to predict the output class.

Practice 5.5.3

1. Is the Naïve Rule a classifier or an estimator? That is, is the output variable numeric or categorical?
2. Given your answer to the previous question, would it make sense to try to make a version of the Naïve Rule for the other type of variable? Why or why not?

Also, note that in many texts, algorithms: classifiers and estimators, are described as *empirical* rules. The word "empirical" is there to indicate that the rule is derived from data and not from theoretical insight into the specific phenomena. In contrast, in physics, we try to "understand" the way physical phenomena behave. Of course, physics uses data, but it usually is used to confirm or reject a theory – a theory has been developed through an understanding of the underlying mechanism of the phenomena. If we were to use a "data science approach" in the field of physics, for example, in explaining the trajectory of a rocket, we would collect data on many rocket trajectories and then use that data to build a model that would predict the path of a rocket. This would be an interesting task, but it is different than the traditional study of physics. In fact, there are some data scientists who are trying to generate the laws of physics using a machine learning approach.

Next, we will implement the Naïve Rule in R.

5.6 R Implementation of the Naïve Rule

We will make use of an R function called **table**(). This function takes an argument and then generates some sort of *count* based on the argument. Let's see some examples (Figure 5.4).

```
#install.packages("mlbench")
library(mlbench)
data("HouseVotes84")

#We use the table() function on the first column of HouseVotes84, the
class variable: democrat/republican. As we said, table() tries to count
something.
table(HouseVotes84[,1])
##
##    democrat republican
##       267        168
#Here, in the output of the table() function, we see two columns. If
HouseVotes84[,1] had more than two possible values (levels), we would see
more columns - a column for each level. The numbers represent the number
of senators in each level - there are 267 democrats and 168 republicans
in the first column of HouseVotes84.
#If we try table(HouseVotes84[,1:2]), that is, if we try putting two
variables into the table function, it will put the values of the first
variable vertically on the left side of the table and the values of the
second variable across the top of the table. Here we will see democrat/
republican on the side and y/n on the top. We will clarify this in a
moment.
table(HouseVotes84[,1:2])
```

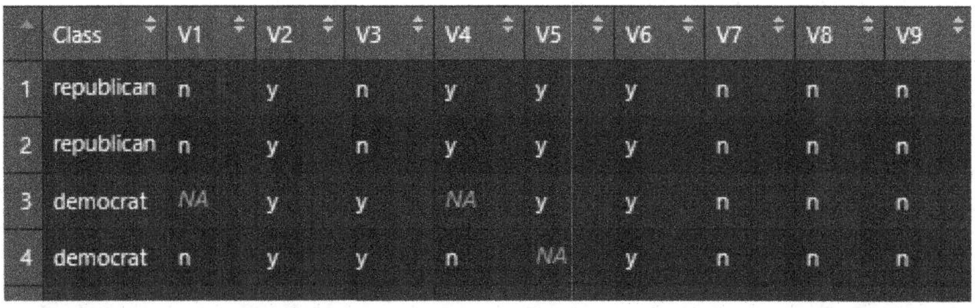

	Class	V1	V2	V3	V4	V5	V6	V7	V8	V9
1	republican	n	y	n	y	y	y	n	n	n
2	republican	n	y	n	y	y	y	n	n	n
3	democrat	NA	y	y	NA	y	y	n	n	n
4	democrat	n	y	y	n	NA	y	n	n	n

Figure 5.4   View(HouseVotes84).

```
##                 V1
## Class           n   y
##    democrat    102 156
##    republican  134  31
```

```
#This is an alternate means of generating the same table.
table(HouseVotes84[,1],HouseVotes84[,2])
##
##                n   y
##    democrat   102 156
##    republican 134  31
```

What does the 102 mean here? It means that there were 102 "no" votes by democrats. What does the 134 mean? It means that there were 134 "no" votes by republicans. Note that this is for issue #1 because we have HouseVotes84[,2], which extracts the second column of our dataframe which is issue#1 (Figure 5.5).

Practice 5.6.4
1. What is the sum of all the entries in the above table, and what does it refer to?
2. What is the sum and interpretation of the first column of numbers in the above table?
3. What is the sum and interpretation of the second column of numbers in the above table?
4. What is the sum and interpretation of the first row of numbers in the above table?
5. Suppose we took each element in the above table and divided it by the sum of all the entries like this:

```
table(HouseVotes84[,1:2])/sum(table(HouseVotes84[,1:2]))
```

The result will be a table with five entries. Can you give any interpretation to the meaning of these entries?

```
#The following example is not very useful, but just for a full
understanding of the table() function, we put the same variables on top
and along the side.
table(HouseVotes84[,1],HouseVotes84[,1])
##
##                democrat republican
##    democrat       267          0
##    republican       0        168
```

Practice 5.6.5
1. What do the zeros mean?

	mpg	cyl	disp	hp	drat	wt	qsec	vs	am	gear	carb
Mazda RX4	21.0	6	160.0	110	3.90	2.620	16.46	0	1	4	4
Mazda RX4 Wag	21.0	6	160.0	110	3.90	2.875	17.02	0	1	4	4
Datsun 710	22.8	4	108.0	93	3.85	2.320	18.61	1	1	4	1
Hornet 4 Drive	21.4	6	258.0	110	3.08	3.215	19.44	1	0	3	1

Figure 5.5 mtcars.

```
#Note that it will make more sense to use the table() function, as we
have done above, when the variable we are trying to count is categorical.
If the data is numeric, the table function is not usually of much use.
However, we will try using table on a numeric variable as an experiment.
data(mtcars)
colnames(mtcars)
## [1] "mpg" "cyl" "disp" "hp"  "drat" "wt"  "qsec" "vs" "am" "gear"
## [11] "carb"
View(head(mtcars))#See Figure 5.6
```

```
#It is not terribly enlightening, but we do see some numbers other than
1. For example, the first 2 is for 10.4 which means there were two
occurrences of cars that got exactly 10.4 mpg.
table(mtcars[,1])
##
## 10.4 13.3 14.3 14.7 15 15.2 15.5 15.8 16.4 17.3 17.8 18.1 18.7 19.2 19.7
##    2    1    1    1 15    2    1    1    1    1    1    1    1    2    1
##   21 21.4 21.5 22.8 24.4 26 27.3 30.4 32.4 33.9
##    2    2    1    2    1  1    1    2    1    1
```

Practice 5.6.6

1. What appears across the top of the table in the previous example?
2. Why are we likely to see many 1s if table() is used with numeric variables?

```
#This example of mtcars is a bit more interesting since we are analyzing
cycles which are numeric, but there are only three possible values for
cycles: 4, 6, and 8.
table(mtcars[,2])
##
##  4  6  8
## 11  7 14
```

5.7 Levels

This is a good time to introduce another piece of terminology. When dealing with categorical variables, the most typical R datatype that we will encounter is the factor. In the HouseVotes84 database, all the variables are categorical. (In the mtcars database, none are categorical). If either **read.csv**() is used to import a csv file or if the import data function in RStudio is used (the import data function's default option for importing uses read.csv()), R will treat categorical variables as factors. If we examine the structure of HouseVotes84, we see factors.

```
str(HouseVotes84)
## 'data.frame':    435 obs. of   17 variables:
## $ Class: Factor w/ 2 levels "democrat","republican": 2 2 1 1 1 1 1 2
2 1 ...
## $ V1   : Factor w/ 2 levels "n","y": 1 1 NA 1 2 1 1 1 1 2 ...
## $ V2   : Factor w/ 2 levels "n","y": 2 2 2 2 2 2 2 2 2 2 ...
## $ V3   : Factor w/ 2 levels "n","y": 1 1 2 2 2 2 1 1 1 2 ...
## $ V4   : Factor w/ 2 levels "n","y": 2 2 NA 1 1 1 2 2 2 1 ...
## $ V5   : Factor w/ 2 levels "n","y": 2 2 2 NA 2 2 2 2 2 1 ...
## $ V6   : Factor w/ 2 levels "n","y": 2 2 2 2 2 2 2 2 2 1 ...
## $ V7   : Factor w/ 2 levels "n","y": 1 1 1 1 1 1 1 1 1 2 ...
## $ V8   : Factor w/ 2 levels "n","y": 1 1 1 1 1 1 1 1 1 2 ...
```

```
## $ V9   : Factor w/ 2 levels "n","y": 1 1 1 1 1 1 1 1 1 2 ...
## $ V10  : Factor w/ 2 levels "n","y": 2 1 1 1 1 1 1 1 1 1 ...
## $ V11  : Factor w/ 2 levels "n","y": NA 1 2 2 2 1 1 1 1 1 ...
## $ V12  : Factor w/ 2 levels "n","y": 2 2 1 1 NA 1 1 1 2 1 ...
## $ V13  : Factor w/ 2 levels "n","y": 2 2 2 2 2 2 NA 2 2 1 ...
## $ V14  : Factor w/ 2 levels "n","y": 2 2 2 1 2 2 2 2 2 1 ...
## $ V15  : Factor w/ 2 levels "n","y": 1 1 1 1 2 2 2 NA 1 NA ...
## $ V16  : Factor w/ 2 levels "n","y": 2 NA 1 2 2 2 2 2 NA ...
```

What are the two possible values for the class variable? Democrat and republican. These are referred to as the levels of this factor. What are the possible values of V1? "n" and "y". These are referred to as the levels of this factor. The levels of a factor are the set of possible values that the categorical variable can take. You can prevent the read.csv() function from reading in string/text data as factors by setting the parameter `stringsAsFactors=` FALSE.

5.8 Naïve Rule Implementation and Explanation

Now we can implement the Naïve Rule.

```
NaiveRule<-function(output="Class" ,df=df){
  #Replace "class" with the name of the class variable.
  classTable=table(df$Class)
  return(names(classTable[which.max(classTable)]))
}
```

Note that the **NaiveRule**() function requires the user to specify the output variable in the dataframe, which is Class in HouseVotes84. It also requires the name of the dataframe.

How does **NaiveRule**() employ the **table**()? As we said, the Naïve Rule chooses the majority class. Thus, we need to only count up each of the levels of the class variable and choose the one with the maximum count. The **table**() function together with a function called **which.max**() will handle this. **which.max**() accepts a numeric vector[1] and returns the *index* of the element that has the maximum value. For example, **which.max**(c(4,10,4,6,9,8)) will return the *index* number of the element in the vector that is largest which in this case is 10, and since 10 has index 2, it will return 2.

```
which.max(c(4,10,4,6,9,8))
## [1] 2
```

For the **NaiveRule**(), we then simply feed this index into the classTable to extract the level with the largest count.

To run our code and also make sure it gives the correct output, we can run the following.

```
NaiveRule(Class,HouseVotes84)
## [1] "democrat"
table(HouseVotes84[,1])
##
##    democrat republican
##         267        168
```

---

[1] Although technically **table**() does not output a vector, **which.max**() will accept the output of **table**() as input.

Ok, we have implemented our first model! It is simple, but it is the first step in moving toward the Naïve Bayes implementation. What sorts of precautionary procedures might be good to include in this implementation? For example, what if the dataset has not been imported into the R session yet? What if it is not a dataframe? What if the dataframe contains **NAs** or **NANs**? What if …? You might try to implement a more robust version of this before moving on to our next model – the Complete Bayes classifier.

Practice 5.8.7

1. Add in an **ifelse**() or **if … else** statement that will check to make sure that the argument for df in the **NaiveRule**() is actually a dataframe. Use stop() to generate an error if it is not a dataframe. Test it with a matrix as the df input.
2. Test the **NaïveRule**() on a dataframe that has NAs. How does it work? If there is a problem, can you change **NaiveRule**() to avoid the error?
3. Does our current implementation of the **NaiveRule**() work for numeric output variables? Why or why not?
4. Is the implementation of the **NaiveRule**() robust enough to work on other datasets? There are quite a few datasets that are included in the R base package. You can do a search for "The R Datasets Package" or follow this link: https://stat.ethz.ch/R-manual/R-devel/library/datasets/html/00Index.html. The **NaiveRule**() supposedly allows the user to specify the class variable and the name of a dataframe. Does it work on dataframes that have a categorical class variable other than HouseVotes84? Test it and see. You can choose any categorical variable in the dataset and let that be the class variable for your test.
5. Can you write the Naïve Bayes without the **table**() function but rather using a loop? Generally, using loops will take longer. See if you can check the time it takes to run the loop and compare it with that taken to run it using the **table**() function. You can use the following idea to measure how long it takes to run the loop.
   ```
   start_time <- Sys.time()
   Place your code here.
   end_time <- Sys.time()
   end_time - start_time
   ```

Chapter 6

Complete Bayes

- A sample dataset
- Notation
- R implementation of the Complete Bayes

We discussed and implemented the Naïve Rule – a rudimentary model that can be used as a benchmark to compare other more sophisticated algorithms. Before discussing the Naïve Bayes classifier, we need to discuss the Complete Bayes (also known as the Exact Bayes or just the Bayes classifier). After writing our Complete Bayes code, the Naïve Bayes will make a simplifying assumption on the Complete Bayes which will both improve its ability to classify and the speed of the classification process.

Functions Coded in This Chapter
CompleteBayes_singlesClass
predCompleteBayes
CompleteBayes_singleClassEllipsis

6.1 Classification Task in Data Science

The primary task in data science is to understand data, and most of the time, our goal is to classify or estimate data, i.e., to determine what class a particular record belongs to or estimate a value. There are other ways data scientists spend their time as well, for example, visualizing data and preprocessing, but their main task is as mentioned above.

Here is another example. Suppose an online chocolate store wants to classify its customers based on their preference for dark, milk, or white chocolate or dislike for any of these. This is clearly a classification task as the output variable is "type of chocolate", a categorical variable. If we denote this variable with C, and code it in R as a factor, we would say that C has four *levels*: dark, milk, white, and none. Let's further suppose that the visitors to a website have been asked to fill out a questionaire. The following information about the customers is collected.

A: age (young *(<18)*, mid *(18 to 35)*, older *(>35)*)
G: gender (F/M)
S: likes spicy food (Y/N)
I: likes ice cream (Y/N)
W: kg over- or underweight (numeric)
D: dieting (Y/N)

These are the input variables. Notice that all but W are categorical variables. The Bayes type algorithms we are building will not handle a numeric variable like W, and so for the time being, we won't use this part of our dataset.[1]

We are looking for a way to predict the value of our class variable C (the type of chocolate preferred) given a set of values for our input variables $[A, G, S, I, D]$. For example, suppose a customer looks like this:

$$\left[A = young, G = F, S = N, I = Y, D = N \right]$$

Should we classify them with a dark, milk, or white chocolate preference?

We are assuming there is a relationship between the inputs and the output. Typically we would express this as follows.

$$C = f(A, G, S, I, D) \tag{6.1}$$

In an earlier discussion, we used the notation $\mathbf{R}^5$. This was used to represent the set of all vectors with five entries where each of the entries is a real number (a numeric value). If the entries are categorical (nominal) rather than numeric, we will use $\mathbb{N}^5$. *This is not a standard notation.* In fact, this would much more typically mean a vector of natural numbers. But we will stick with our interpretation here.

In Section 6.1, we covered various concepts in probability, including events and conditional probability. This has prepared the way for a discussion of the Complete Bayes classifier. We also talked about observational units and records. The observational units here would be the customers. We will also call the observational units as instances.[2] The records (observational units/instances) are the *rows* of our dataset.

Going back to the mathematical context, we would say each record is a vector or element of $\mathbb{N}^6$. If we ignore the class variable and focus just on the data minus the label column, then our vectors are in $\mathbb{N}^5$.

Recall that labeled data refers to the fact that we know the class of the instance (the record), whereas unlabeled refers to data where the label is unknown. So if it is unlabeled, we don't have the class variable C. We will denote the unlabeled instance with a bold $\mathbf{X}$, and we can write

$$\mathbf{X} \in \mathbb{N}^5 \tag{6.2}$$

---

[1] We could bin the W variable, but we won't bother about that here. Binning, in this case, would simply mean breaking up the weight into intervals which we could call something like "low weight", "medium weight", and "high weight". The names of these intervals and the number of them would be up to the data scientist.

[2] In a much later chapter of this text, when we discuss the object-oriented programming (OOP) concept of classes, the word "instance" will be used in an unrelated way.

6.2 Complete Bayes Classifier

The Complete Bayes was mentioned in a paper by Hand et al. in 2001.[3] It answers the question "Which class should I assign to instance **X**?" in a natural way. Take the example mentioned above, where

$$\mathbf{X} = \left[A = young, G = F, S = N, I = Y, D = N \right] \tag{6.3}$$

Then our question is, "Given that we have an **X** like this, what is the value of the class variable C? Which chocolate does this person prefer?" (*The fact that the word "given" appears in the question suggests that conditional probability may be involved.*) The idea behind the Complete Bayes classifier is as follows:

1. Find all the records in our dataframe that are exactly like **X**, i.e., all the records that look like this: $\left[A = young, G = F, S = N, I = Y, D = N \right]$.
2. Some people who look like

$$\left[A = young, G = F, S = N, I = Y, D = N \right]$$

may have a class value of dark chocolate (i.e., preference for dark chocolate). Some may have a class value of milk chocolate, and some may have white chocolate, and some may be in the *none* category. Count how many prefer dark, how many milk, how many white, and how many *none*.

3. Then, for the new record **X**:

$$\left[A = young, G = F, S = N, I = Y, D = N \right]$$

assign it to the class in step #2 with the highest count.

Note the following:

i. In step 1, instead of counting the people who look like X, we can compute the probability of X within the sample space (the dataframe). This simply means that instead of computing n(**X**) we compute n(**X**)/n(**S**).

ii. In step 2 above, instead of counting the people who prefer a particular level of the class variable (for example, dark chocolate) from within the set of people who look like **X**, that is, instead of calculating

$$n\left(\mathbf{X} \cap Dark\ Chocolate \right)$$

we can count those and then divide by n(**S**), thus calculating again a (conditional) probability.

Notice that in the steps above, we *do* use the input data to help us predict a class for our new instance. Recall that in the Naïve Rule, we *did not* use any of the input data to make the prediction.

Note further that in step (ii), we are actually calculating conditional probabilities. When we select only the records that match **X** and then count how many have a class of, for example, dark chocolate, this is calculating

$$p(C = Dark\ Chocolate \mid \mathbf{X}) \tag{6.3}$$

[3] Hand, D. J., & Yu, K. (2001). Idiot's Bayes—Not so stupid after all?. *International Statistical Review*, 69(3), 385–398.

Step (ii) says that this must be done for each of the classes. So we end up calculating

$$p(C = \text{Dark Chocolate} \mid \mathbf{X}) \tag{6.4}$$

$$p(C = \text{White Chocolate} \mid \mathbf{X}) \tag{6.5}$$

$$p(C = \text{Milk Chocolate} \mid \mathbf{X}) \tag{6.6}$$

$$p(C = \text{none} \mid \mathbf{X}) \tag{6.7}$$

Once we have these calculations, the answer to our question "Which class should **X** be assigned to?" seems natural. We will classify **X** with the label that has the highest probability within these four calculations. This is the Complete Bayes classifier! We will develop the code for it below. First let's discuss why the Complete Bayes is problematic and why we have to go beyond the Complete Bayes to develop the Naïve Bayes. Why isn't the Complete Bayes good enough?

6.3 Weakness in the Complete Bayes

Let's review what is involved in doing this calculation:

$$p\big(C = \text{dark chocolate} \mid \mathbf{X}\big)$$

Remember that **X** is a vector. In our particular example, where **X** was initially $\big[A = \text{young}, G = F, S = N, I = Y, D = N\big]$ and[4] so $\mathbf{X} \in \mathbb{N}^5$, we are interested in calculating

$$p\big(C = \text{dark chocolate} \mid \big[A = \text{young}, G = F, S = N, I = Y, D = N\big]\big)$$

which is more typically written without the square brackets like this:

$$p\big(C = \text{dark chocolate} \mid A = \text{young}, G = F, S = N, I = Y, D = N\big)$$

In part 1 of this text, we saw that

$$\mathbf{X} = \big[A = \text{young}, G = F, S = N, I = Y, D = N\big]$$

is the intersection of the five events: $A = \text{young}$, $G = F$, $S = N$, $I = Y$, and $D = N$. We also saw that the intersection of events is itself an event. Therefore **X** is a particular event. So a probability expression like

$$p\big(C = \text{dark chocolate} \mid A = \text{young}, G = F, S = N, I = Y, D = N\big)$$

can be thought of as $p(C = \text{dark chocolate} \mid \mathbf{X})$ where both $C(= \text{dark chocolate})$ and **X** are events.

Thus, all we are doing is calculating a simple conditional probability. But in doing this calculation, we need to find all the records that match **X**. Now if our *dataframe* is really huge, say if it

---

[4] Earlier we defined nominal data with $\mathbb{N}$.

contains 10 million records, then the chances are high that we will find a good number of records that match **X**. *However*, if the dataframe only contains a small number of records, say 50, then the chances of finding even one record that matches **X** may be small. We may not find any records that match **X**. In that case, none of these

$$p\big(C = \text{dark chocolate} \,|\, A = \text{young}, \; G = F, \; S = N, \; I = Y, \; D = N\big)$$

$$p\big(C = \text{milk chocolate} \,|\, A = \text{young}, \; G = F, \; S = N, \; I = Y, \; D = N\big)$$

$$p\big(C = \text{white chocolate} \,|\, A = \text{young}, \; G = F, \; S = N, \; I = Y, \; D = N\big)$$

$$p\big(C = \text{none} \,|\, A = \text{young}, \; G = F, \; S = N, \; I = Y, \; D = N\big)$$

can be calculated.

In this case, the algorithm fails. It fails in the sense that it won't tell us which of the four classes is the best label for **X**. This is an example of the weakness of the Complete Bayes.

Practice 6.3.1

1. Explain in terms of sets and subsets in what sense is C = dark chocolate an event. What is the sample space?

Let's dive into this a bit more. In the above example, we have five input variables. This is a relatively small number. Many times we will have to handle 20, 50, 100 or even several thousand variables. Look at Kaggle.com competitions to see examples of this. Suppose that there are just 20 categorical input variables (as factors) and that each has five levels (not a particularly large number of levels). How many possible combinations of the values of these 20 variables are possible? There are 5^{20} different possible combinations. That is about 10^{14} possible combinations.

Even if our dataframe has 1 million rows, the chances are still very high that *we will not find any records* that match **X** (the new instance we want to classify), and the Complete Bayes classifier will fail, and there will be no estimate of the class for this **X**.

Now, with an understanding of the weakness of the Complete Bayes algorithm, let's try our hand at implementing it.

6.4 Complete Bayes Implementation in R

We will implement a simple version of the Complete Bayes classifier and then a bit more robust version.

We start out with the HouseVotes84 dataset and classify a senator as republican or democrat based on the pattern of their votes. In the second implementation of the Complete Bayes classifier, we extend it to function on datasets other than the HouseVotes84 dataset. In the first version, we limit the number of input variables to four. One reason for this is that in the dataframe with which we have been experimenting, HouseVotes84, there are 16 inputs, whereas the number of records in the dataframe is under 500. With 16 binary (yes/no) inputs, we have 2^{16} possible permutations of voting patterns. That is 65,536 different possibilities. The chances are good that for any combination of the 16 votes that is choosen, there will be zero records that match this input variable specification, and thus we again will not be able to obtain probability estimates for the various classes. That would mean we would not be able to decide on democrat or republican. This is not a satisfying result. If we limit the input to our function to only four votes, then it is more likely we will be able to get a nonzero probability of democrat and republican. Of course, there is a price to pay in terms of accuracy of the prediction, but at least, we will get a prediction.

```
#install.packages("mlbench", "mice")
library(mlbench)
library(mice)
data("HouseVotes84")
intersect_event <- function(A,B,df){
  return(df[intersect(A$names,B$names),])
}
prob <- function(E,S){
  return(nrow(E)/nrow(S))


}
#In our last example, we used complete.cases() to weed out the rows that
contained NAs. Here we will try an alternative approach. We use a package
called mice which stands for Multivariate Imputation by Chained
Equations. We won't go into the details here. Suffice to say that this is
a way of "guessing" what a good value to replace the NA with would be.
There are a number of other choices for imputing values, for example,
Amelia, missForest, Hmsic, and mi. By guessing the values of NA, it won't
be necessary to delete rows.

imputeddf=mice(HouseVotes84,m=1,maxit=50,meth='pmm',seed=500)
#The output for imputedf is long and will not be displayed here.
completedData <- complete(imputeddf,1)
df=completedData
df$names<-rownames(df)
#We have not discussed default values for arguments and briefly mention
it now. It is possible to construct a function with default values for
the inputs. That is what is done in this example. The default value for
class is 'republican', the default value for V1 is 'y', and so on.
CompleteBayes_singleClass <- function(class='republican',v1='y',v2='y',v3
='y',v4='y',dfparam=df){
# A sample call of the function:
  #CompleteBayes_singleClass('democrat','y','y','y','y')
  #This function will accept the first four input variables - the first
four votes on the first four issues only. Also, note that the parameter
called "class" uses a lowercase c, whereas the party affiliation variable
in HouseVotes84 is 'Class' with a capital C. Note further that all the
parameter names start with small (not capital) letters, e.g., v1, whereas
the all the attribute names in the dataframe start with capital letters,
e.g., V1. Next is the familiar step of creating a Boolean. Note that we
are writing this function for the HouseVotes84 dataframe. It uses the
names of the attributes of that particular dataframe, i.e., V1, V2, V3,
V4, and Class, and therefore it won't work as it is for other datasets.
Note also that the name dfparam is used to keep the parameter name
distinct from the name of the dataframe which is denoted by df.

  X_bool=df$V1==v1 & df$V2==v2 & df$V3==v3 & df$V4==v4
```

```
#Create the event that is generated from the specification of X - the
specification of the input variables.
#Call this event X.
X=df[X_bool,]
```

#classE, in the HouseVotes84 example, is one of the two events: the
senator being a democrat or the senator being a republican. In general, it
is the event in which one particular level of the class variable occurs.

```
class_bool=df$Class==class
classE=df[class_bool,]
```

#As mentioned, given a particular set of input variables, denoted by the
vector X, the Complete Bayes algorithm will calculate the probability of
each level of the class variable. In the function we are currently
constructing (CompleteBayes_singleClass), we specify a level and calculate
its probability. After we finish writing this function, we will place it
in a loop that will iterate through each value of the class variable so
that we can calculate the probability for each of the levels. Finally, we
select the level with the highest probability as the predicted class.

Practice 6.4.2

1. Write down the mathematical version (not the R code) of conditional probability.

   #In the process of calculating the probability of a particular level,
   we will bump into a conditional probability calculation. One way to do
   this is to calculate the intersection of X and classE. This requires
   the intersect_event() function we built earlier.
   ```
   ClassIntsX=intersect_event(X,classE,dfparam)
   ```

   #Now calculate the probability of this intersection.
   ```
   numeratorProb=prob(ClassIntsX,dfparam)
   ```

   #Now we have the numerator of the conditional probability calculation.
   The denominator is just the probability of X.
   ```
   denominatorProb=prob(X,dfparam)
   return(numeratorProb/denominatorProb)
   }
   ```

Practice 6.4.3

1. What would you say is the difference between using a print() statement to print
   out the numeratorProb/denominatorProb and using the return statement
   return(numeratorProb/denominatorProb)?

   #Test the implementation. Below, it should produce a conditional
   probability of the specified level of the class ('democrat') given X
   ('y','y','y','y'). We call it singleClass because we are calculating the
   Complete Bayes for just one level of the class variable.
   ```
   CompleteBayes_singleClass('democrat','y','y','y','y',df)
   ## [1] 0.2
   ```
   #Test it again. We get a surprising result.
   ```
   CompleteBayes_singleClass('democrat','y','y','y','n',df)
   ## [1] 1
   ```

```
#It says that any senator that votes yyyn on the first four issues
must be a democrat. You can export the dataframe to a csv file with
write.csv(df, file = "ImputedwithMICEHouseVote84.csv") and open it as
a spreadsheet or use View(df) to visually check if this is correct.
#Note that since we defined default values for the arguments, the
function can also be run without specifying arguments.
```

Practice 6.4.4

1. What is the probability of republican yyyn?
2. What is the probability of republican yynn?

```
CompleteBayes_singleClass()
## [1] 0.8
#Alternatively, some arguments can be specified and some left unspecified.
The unspecified arguments will assume the default values, like this
CompleteBayes_singleClass("democrat",,"y",,"n",df)
## [1] 1
```

TIPS

1. To avoid headaches, in the function signature, don't let parameter names and default values be identical. By function signature, we will mean the first line of the function definition, where the parameters and the function name are given. We will mean everything up to the first curly bracket. Either of the following will be referred to as a function signature.
   - `CompleteBayes _ singleClass <- function(class='republican',v1='y',v2='y',v3='y',v4='y',dfparam=df)`
   - `CompleteBayes _ singleClass("democrat",,"y",,"n",df)`
2. Install packages using the menu under Tools. In the author's experience, sometimes typing install.packages() does not install all the dependencies.
3. When the ellipis in used in the function signature, then in the function call, all arguments must be supplied in succession and none left out.

Practice 6.4.5

1. Redo the implementation of this function using the **conditional _ prob**() function defined in the previous chapter. Test your implementation with the same set of inputs as we have done above to make sure everything is correct.

6.5 Which Level Is Most Likely?

Next we need to decide which value of the class variable (which level), democrat or republican, is the "best" category to classify our instance **X**, where by "best", we mean most likely. We do this by checking which level achieves the highest probability. This can be accomplished by running the **completeBayes _ singleClass**() function through a loop with each iteration checking one of the possible levels of the class variable and keeping a record of which one has the highest probability.

6.6 *Side Note* on the Use of $ Sign

We have been using the $ sign to access columns of a dataframe. For example, in the HouseVotes84 dataframe, we can access the first variable (the class variable) using df$Class or HouseVotes84$Class. The underlying mechanism for the dollar sign is a special case of the double square brackets that are used for extraction. For example, using the double square brackets, we can write HouseVotes84[["Class"]]. This gives the same result as HouseVotes84$Class. Many programmers prefer to use the $ sign notation. However it is important to note that the dollar sign is a shorthand for the double brackets. Furthermore, whereas you can put a variable into the double bracket notation, R does not allow us to do that with the dollar sign notation. To see this, consider the following.

```
x="Class" #Assign a string to a variable.
#The first two work fine, but the last one does not work as hoped - it
just gives NULL.
head(HouseVotes84[[x]])
## [1] republican republican democrat    democrat    democrat    democrat
## Levels: democrat republican
head(HouseVotes84[,x])
## [1] republican republican democrat    democrat    democrat    democrat
## Levels: democrat republican
head(HouseVotes84$x)
## NULL
```

The fact that the variable cannot be processed after the dollar sign is explained as "variables' names cannot be interpolated". Other limitations of the dollar sign are as follows:

■ You cannot use integer indices.
■ If the name of the variable (or column) contains special characters, the name must be enclosed in backticks.

We are mentioning these issues regarding the dollar sign because it would be tempting to use them in the following code, but for the reasons mentioned, it would not work.

End of side note on the $ sign.

We are returning to the task at hand – predicting the most probable class. We call the function to accomplish this **predCompleteBayes()**. It uses **CompleteBayes _ singleClass()** and runs it for each possible level of the class variable to determine which level is most likely.

```
predCompleteBayes=function(class="Class",v1='y',v2='y',v3='y',v4='y',dfpa
ram=df){

    #Sample call:
#predCompleteBayes(class="Class",v1='n',v2='n',v3='n',v4='n',dfparam=df)
#First, we will create something to store our results. We won't actually
use it until the end of the code, but we set it up now. Most algorithms
that we can access in the many R packages store their results in a list.
This is convenient because lists can store text, vectors, other lists,
and just about anything else, and so they are a convenient storage
container. We will try this ourselves.
#All our list will do is store the name of the predicted class and its
probability. Even though it will not contain much information, we are
following the convention in R of storing results of algorithms in a list.
```

```
forecast=list()
```

#The above list is set up for later use. Now we proceed with the main task. Next we want to know all the levels of the class variable in order to loop through these levels so as to determine which the most likely level is, given our instance X. Of course, for HouseVotes84, we know the levels - democrat and republican, and so we don't need to go to all this trouble, but we will write our code so that it will go through all the levels of the class variable regardless of how many levels the class has.
 #As mentioned above, it is tempting to use the next line, but R won't accept a variable following the dollar sign.

 #lev=levels(dfparam$class)
#Instead access the column with dfparam[,class]). (Note the lowercase "c".) In fact, either dfparam[[class]] or dfparam[,class] will work. R will look for a column whose name is class.
 lev=**levels**(dfparam[,class]) *#lev is now a vector containing the strings "democrat" and "republican".*
#Next, loop through all the levels of the class variable, and in each iteration of the loop, calculate the probability of that level. If it is higher than the levels of the previous iterations, we record the probability and also record the level associated with this probability. Thus, here we define a variable to keep track of the highest probability tested at any point in the loop. It starts out as 0.

 classprob=0
 #Next, we store the level with the highest probability. This will be updated in the loop if we come across a level that has a higher probability. We start out by storing the first level in lev and then commence with looping.
 predictedclass=lev[1]
 for(i **in** lev){
 #As we said, predCompleteBayes() will call CompleteBayes_singleClass(). CompleteBayes_singleClass() requires arguments. It requires the votes on the first four issues, the class, and the dataframe. How do we fill these in? Remember CompleteBayes_singleClass() is being called from within predCompleteBayes().
 #Here is the call of predCompleteBayes.
 predCompleteBayes(class="Class",v1='n',v2='n',v3='n',v4='n',dfparam=df)
 #Then within the body of predCompleteBayes, we have the call to CompleteBayes_singleClass. What arguments will it require? Here is a typical call when it is not being called from inside another function.
 CompleteBayes_singleClass('democrat','y','y','y','n',df)
 #We will see that any of these arguments that are required by CompleteBayes_singleClass() can be "transferred" from the arguments passed into predCompleteBayes(). Specifically, v1, v2, …, v4 are obtained as arguments from predCompleteBayes() and are copied from the arguments of predCompleteBayes and fed as arguments into CompleteBayes_singleClass. Where are these arguments stored in predCompleteBayes()? Answer: In predCompleteBayes()'s parameters. Thus, we place these parameters in the signature of CompleteBayes_singleClass().
 #The same is true for dfparam. However, for the class variable, CompleteBayes_singleClass will need to test each level, and so we need to loop through all the class levels. To accomplish this, we put "i" in the slot for the class parameter in CompleteBayes_singleClass. Note that we

use small case "v" not capital "V" for the arguments. Why is that?
Because "v" is the parameter.
#To explain this in a slightly different way, when predCompleteBayes() is
run, all its arguments are then available inside the body of
predCompleteBayes(). They can be used in any way inside the body. In
particular, they can be used as arguments for CompleteBayes_singleClass()
as long as it is called within the body of predCompleteBayes().

```
    p=CompleteBayes_singleClass(i,v1,v2,v3,v4,dfparam)
```

#p was assigned just above. It is the probability computed by
CompleteBayes_singleClass() for the current class level. Next, we check
if it is larger than the probability for the current highest level. If it
is, both classprob and predicted class are updated. Otherwise we move on
to the next value of "i" in the loop. In this way, we only update when we
reach a larger probability, and thus at the end of the loop, we will have
stored the highest probability and the corresponding class in classprob
and predicted class, respectively.

```
    if(classprob<p){ #only edit classprob and predictedclass if p>classprob
      classprob=p
      predictedclass=i
```

#Use the list we defined earlier to store the results. We will add two
elements to the list. One is called predicted class, and the other is
called probability. The value of these elements will contain the results
of our algorithm up to now.

```
      forecast[["predicted class"]]=predictedclass
      forecast[["probability"]]=classprob


    }


  }
  return(forecast)

}
```

Practice 6.6.6

1. Try rewriting the code above but using lev=**levels**(dfparam$class) instead of lev=**levels**(dfparam[,class]). What error do you get? What does it mean?

6.7 Testing the Function with Various Instances

Testing the function with various instances.
#We will test with various voting patterns.
```
predCompleteBayes(class="Class",v1='y',v2='y',v3='y',v4='y',dfparam=df)
## $`predicted class`
## [1] "republican"
##
## $probability
## [1] 0.8
predCompleteBayes(class="Class",v1='n',v2='n',v3='n',v4='n',dfparam=df)
## $`predicted class`
## [1] "democrat"
##
## $probability
```

```
## [1] 0.8888889
predCompleteBayes(class="Class",v1='y',v2='n',v3='y',v4='n',dfparam=df)
## $`predicted class`
## [1] "democrat"
##
## $probability
## [1] 1
```

We have our first implementation of the Complete Bayes algorithm! It tells us, for example, that given an instance where the votes are yyyy (meaning yes on the first vote, yes on the second, yes on the third, and yes on the fourth), the predicted class is "democrat". The output of our modeling function is a list, and this is a standard convention in R.

Practice 6.7.7

1. Why did we "initialize" `classprob` as 0? Why not choose some other value greater than 0? What if we initialized it as a negative number? Do you think it would work?

6.8 Complete Bayes Implementation 2 – *A More Robust Version*

One limitation of the current implementation is that it uses exactly 4 of the 15 votes in the HouseVotes84 dataset. If the user of the function wanted to use a different number of input variables or a different set of input variables, they would be out of luck. A second limitation is that this code currently works only for this one dataset: HouseVotes84. In this section, we will explore a more robust implementation. You may also consider your own implementation of the function.

Currently the function signature looks like this:

```
CompleteBayes_singleClass=function(class,v1='y',v2='y',v3='y',v4='y'dfpar
am=df)
```

We will use R's ellipsis feature again.

```
CompleteBayes_singleClassEllipsis=function(className="Class",classValue="
democrat",dfparam=df, …)
```

Notice the difference between the two signatures. In the new signature, we allow the user to specify the class variable and the class value. Furthermore, we do not name the input variables in the new signature, rather they will be held in the ellipsis. Although we are using the ellipsis, we still specify some parameters *explicitly*, namely, className, classValue, and dfparam. No other parameters are mentioned explicitly in the signature. This version allows the user to enter the name of the *class* variable. In the HouseVotes84 dataset, that was "Class" (with an uppercase C). In our first version of Complete Bayes, we hard-coded this and did not provide the option for the user to specify a class variable. In a database for predicting cancer, the class variable might be called PatientStatus; in the Iris dataset we saw before, it was also called Class (with levels Virginica, Setosa, and Versacolor).

Practice 6.8.8

1. Where was the name of the class variable (not the level but the name) hard-coded into the code and therefore not specifiable by the user? Hint: It is in **CompleteBayes _ singleClass**.

	ID	Treatment	Sex	Age	Improved
1	57	Treated	Male	27	Some
2	46	Treated	Male	29	None
3	77	Treated	Male	30	None
4	17	Treated	Male	32	Marked
5	36	Treated	Male	46	Marked
6	23	Treated	Male	58	Marked
7	75	Treated	Male	59	None

Figure 6.1 **Arthritis dataset from the vcd package with attributes ID, Treatment, Sex, Age, and Improved.**

The next explicitly mentioned parameter *classValue* is the value of the class variable we are trying to predict. (Remember that this is the "singleClass" part of the implementation and that this part will subsequently be run through a loop.) For example in the HouseVotes84, it has been either "republican" or "democrat". *dfparam* is the name of the dataset.

In this second version, the user should be able to specify the class variable and the dataset. Further, we want to allow the user to specify the input variable names and values for the input variables. In other words, if the dataset is not HouseVotes84, then the variables will most likely not be V1, V2, V3, and V4 (the first four votes). In the next example, we will use a dataset called Arthritis. It comes from an R package named "vcd". It looks like Figure 6.1.

```
colnames(Arthritis)
## [1] "ID"        "Treatment" "Sex"        "Age"        "Improved"
```

Our first version of Complete Bayes would not allow for such variables because the specific names V1, V2, etc. were mentioned in the code here.

```
X_bool=df$V1==v1 & df$V2==v2 & df$V3==v3 & df$V4==v4
```

The ellipsis will help us to implement the ability to allow for variables that can be decided at the time the function is called and not explicitly defined within the code.

6.9 Manual Preprocessing of the Dataset

Before doing anything else, however, let's clean up the Arthritis dataframe. It would be better if we could do this cleanup within the body of our function, but for now, we will just do it manually outside of the function definition. The ID column is not needed because it is not useful in making forecasts. In general, if the value of a variable is unique for each row of the dataframe, it cannot contribute any information to the prediction process (this is not true if the value contains textual information that can be analyzed).

Thus, we should remove the ID column with something like this:

```
Arthritis=Arthritis[,-c(1)]
```

Furthermore, the Age variable is numeric. We will not use numeric data. Thus, we should remove the Age column as well with something like this:

```
Arthritis=Arthritis[,-c(3)]
```

Note that we could have done this in one step with

```
Arthritis=Arthritis[,-c(1,4)]
```

Now, if **View**(Arthritis) is run, we obtain the results shown in Figure 6.2.

Returning to HouseVotes84 again for a moment, of course whatever parameters we write into the signature of the function will be operated on in some manner within the body of the function – that is the point of using parameters. As we saw before, the ellipsis can be thought of as a variable to hold all the other arguments entered into the function call that are not specified explicitly in the function signature. For example, here if we design the signature to be

```
CompleteBayes_singleClassEllipsis=function(className="Class",classValue="
democrat",dfparam=df, ...)
```

the user could call this function like this:

```
CompleteBayes_singleClassEllipsis("Class","democrat", df, v1='y',v2='y',v
3='y',v4='y',v5='y', v6='y',v7='y')
```

and hopefully the function will know how to process all the parameters after the df. On the other hand, later the user may want to specify just the first six votes like this:

```
CompleteBayes_singleClassEllipsis("Class","democrat", df, v1='y',v2='y',v
3='y',v4='y',v5='y', v6='y')
```

and again hopefully our implementation will also be able to handle this call as well.

As mentioned, the ellipis will hold any number of arguments entered by the user. Thus, we need some means to "unravel" these arguments. This is typically handled by beginning with a statement like this:

	Treatment	Sex	Improved
1	Treated	Male	Some
2	Treated	Male	None
3	Treated	Male	None
4	Treated	Male	Marked
5	Treated	Male	Marked

Figure 6.2 Arthritis dataset with some attributes removed.

```
args<-list(...)
```

(Please note that `args` is just a variable name. There is also an R function called **args**(). This variable has nothing to do with that function.)

Notice where the ellipsis is – inside the **list**() function.This creates a *list* from the arguments entered by the user. Each element of the list contains the value of a parameter, and the name of each element is the name of the parameter. Returning to the Arthritis dataset, it will be assumed in the code below that the class variable is in the first column of the dataframe. If we call the function as

```
CompleteBayes_singleClassEllipsis("Treatment","Treated",Arthritis,
Sex='Male',Improved='Marked')
```

and if the body of this function includes the code

```
args<-list(...)
```

then `args` would be a *named* list, where the *names* are "Sex" and "Improved", and the "Sex" element of the list would consist of the entry "Male", and the "Improved" element would consist of the element "Marked".

Note that you could use this instead:

```
args<-c(...)
```

This would produce a named vector. (Recall that a vector can also have names for its elements.) This is ok to do if all the arguments that the ellipsis will represent are of the same type (for example, if they are all numeric), but if they are not of the same type, this may cause problems. That is why, when unraveling the contents of the ellipsis, the list() function is often used. We use it here just to maintain greater generality.

This args variable is *constructed within the body of the function* **CompleteBayes _ singleClassEllipsis**(), and thus we can see it only within the function.[5] We will discuss a method to view it from within the function in a moment, but let us artificially construct a "replica" of what it would look like. There is a nice function called **setNames**() which we can use with an existing list to create (or rewrite) the names for the list. You will see that the second argument to the **setNames**() function consists of the names of the elements in the list and that the list is specified in the first argument. We will create a list with

```
as.list(c("Male","Marked"))
which will look like this
## [[1]]
## [1] "Male"
##
## [[2]]
## [1] "Marked"
```

You will see that when we call

```
CompleteBayes_singleClassEllipsis("Treatment","Treated",Arthritis,
Sex='Male',Improved='Marked')
```

---

[5] This has to do with the concept of scope, and we will talk about that much later when we deal with OOP and classes near the end of this text.

our `args` variable will contain exactly this list, but it will be a named list. It will look like this:

```
## $Sex
## [1] "Male"
##
## $Improved
## [1] "Marked"
```

Our artificial construction, however, is missing the names of the elements – names of "Sex" and "Improved". The following is an artificial construction of the named list above.

```
args <- setNames(as.list(c("Male","Marked")),c("Sex","Improved"))
args
## $Sex
## [1] "Male"
##
## $Improved
## [1] "Marked"
```

6.10 A Short Tutorial on paste0() and eval(parse())

paste0()

paste0() is a convenient function which is a variation of paste(). Both of these allow us to concatenate strings. In other words, they allow us to combine strings.

```
paste("many", "strings", "to","one", "string")
## [1] "many strings to one string"
#paste() has a "sep" parameter which allows us to choose what separates
the pieces. The default value for "sep" is " " (in other words, a space).
However, we can set it to a different character or characters.
paste("many", "strings", "to","one", "string", sep="__")
## [1] "many__strings__to__one__string"
#Note that each of the strings to be concatenated in paste are separated
by a comma in the function call.
#In fact, we can enter in as many strings (separated by commas) as we
want. Does this remind you of something? How does paste do this? Answer:
In its definition, it uses the ellipsis!
#Note that paste will behave a bit unexpectedly if the entries between
the commas are vectors. But we will not consider that here.

#paste() can include the use of variables. If you include a variable as
an argument, paste() will evaluate that variable (sometimes called
interpolating) and output the value.
#Define a variable.
v="and a variable"
paste("many", "strings",v, "to","one", "string")
## [1] "many strings and a variable to one string"
```

Practice 6.10.9

1. Create a new variable, add it to the above print statement, and show the results.

```
#We can even put paste() into a loop and have the loop variable be one
of the arguments in paste(). Here we use "i" as the loop variable and
include it as an argument in paste().

for(i in 1:2){
  #Inside a loop, we have to use print() to actually see the results.
  print(paste("many", "strings",i, "to","one", "string"))
}
## [1] "many strings 1 to one string"
## [1] "many strings 2 to one string"

#What about paste0? Whereas the default value for the "sep" argument
in paste is " ", the default argument for "sep" in paste0 is ""(mean-
ing no space). That is the only difference between paste and paste0.
Probably the 0 in the name refers to zero space.
paste0("many", "strings", "to","one", "string")
## [1] "manystringstoonestring"
```

6.11 eval(parse())

Suppose we have a **string** like "1:10". If we type that into the R console *including* the quotation marks, R will *not* treat it as the vector. It will *not* show this:

```
## [1]  1  2  3  4  5  6  7  8  9 10
```

Rather, R will just treat "1:10" as a string.

```
"1:10"
## [1] "1:10"
```

The combination of **eval(parse())** will allow this string to be evaluated as though it were an expression. There is a parameter in **parse()** called *text*, and we set that equal to "1:10" like this:

```
#eval(parse())
eval(parse(text="1:10"))
## [1]  1  2  3  4  5  6  7  8  9 10
```

This seems like unnecessary trouble to go through, but our code will require us to use a loop to build a string. We will then want to evaluate the string as though it were an expression, as we just showed with "1:10".

In fact, in the second version of our Complete Bayes algorithm, since we are allowing any number of attributes to be entered into the function call, the length of the boolean statement will not be known until the function is actually called (known as "at runtime"). Recall, for example, that in the first version of the Complete Bayes algorithm, we had a line of code like this:

```
X_bool<-df$V1==v1 & df$V2==v2 & df$V3==v3 & df$V4==v4
```

There are four "parts" here (and correspondingly three conjunctions). This is hard-coded into the function definition. But the second version of the algorithm will be constructed to allow the user to choose which attributes and how many to enter at the time of the call. Thus, we don't want to hard-code the definition of X_bool.

Furthermore, we don't know the names of the variables (or the levels for those variables) before runtime. So we have to refer to the parameters (for example, class) for the unknown attribute names when writing our code. This means that we cannot use the dollar sign like this df$class. We have to use the double bracket notation instead, as mentioned earlier in this chapter.

Here is an example of the kind of *string* we will need to build. (Notice it is encased in quotation marks.)

```
"dfparam[,names(args)[1]]==args[[1]]&dfparam[,names(args)[2]]==args[[2]]"
```

The reason we need to "build" it and not just write it is that, as we said, we may want it to be longer (or shorter) than what is written above. On inspecting this string, we see that it repeats itself before and after the & conjunction but with the number 1 being changed to the number 2. We may require another &, and then the same pattern would be repeated but with the number 3. Thus, this string will have to be constructed with a loop, but it will have to be created *after* the arguments have been entered (in other words, at runtime). The loop will then iterate 1, 2, 3, or more times.

Let's look at the first part of the string, the part before the & conjunction.

```
dfparam[,names(args)[1]]==args[[1]]
```

You will notice the Boolean operator == here. This part of the expression is testing whether the left-hand side (LHS), dfparam[,names(args)[1]], is equal to the right-hand side (RHS), args[[1]]. Recall that args will be a list. If the function call for **CompleteBayes _ singleClassEllipsis**() has these arguments

"Treatment","Treated",Arthritis, Sex='Male',Improved='Marked'

then we saw that the contents of args will be

```
args
## $Sex
## [1] "Male"
##
## $Improved
## [1] "Marked"
#Now, focusing on the LHS of the statement, if we check the names of this
list with names(), we see this:
names(args) #this is a vector
## [1] "Sex"        "Improved"
#We can access the elements of the vector like this:
names(args)[1]
## [1] "Sex"
names(args)[2]
## [1] "Improved"
#Continuing with the analysis of the LHS of dfparam[,names(args)
[1]]==args[[1]]
#next we extract the "Sex" column of our dataframe (as a vector).
dfparam[,names(args)[1]]
##  [1] Male    Male    Male    Male    Male    Male    Male    Male    Male    Male
## [11] Male    Male    Male    Male    Female  Female  Female  Female  Female  Female
## [21] Female  Female  Female  Female  Female  Female  Female  Female  Female  Female
## [31] Female  Female  Female  Female  Female  Female  Female  Female  Female  Female
## [41] Female  Male    Male    Male    Male    Male    Male    Male    Male    Male
## [51] Male    Male    Female  Female  Female  Female  Female  Female  Female  Female
```

```
## [61] Female Female Female Female Female Female Female Female Female Female
## [71] Female Female Female Female Female Female Female Female Female Female
## [81] Female Female Female Female
## Levels: Female Male
```
#We can also extract the "Improved" column of our dataframe (as a vector).
```
dfparam[,names(args)[2]]
##  [1] Some   None   None   Marked Marked Marked None   Marked None   None
## [11] None   Some   None   Marked None   None   Some   None   Marked None
## [21] Marked Marked Marked Marked Marked Marked Marked None   Marked Marked
## [31] Marked Marked Some   Marked Marked Marked Some   Marked None   Some
## [41] Some   None   None   None   None   None   None   None   None   None
## [51] None   Marked None   None   None   Some   None   Marked None   None
## [61] None   None   None   None   None   None   None   None   Marked Marked
## [71] None   Some   Some   Some   Marked None   Some   None   Marked None
## [81] None   Some   Some   Marked
## Levels: None < Some < Marked
```

Now we examine the RHS of the == sign. We see

```
args[[1]]
```

Recall that by using the extraction, *double* brackets returns the value of the first element of the args list, which is "Male". (This is not returned as a list but rather as a string.[6]) Thus, this part of our string

```
dfparam[,names(args)[1]]==args[[1]]
```

is testing to see which rows in the "Sex" column are "Male". The result of this will be a Boolean vector which will be TRUE whenever the "Sex" variable is "Male" and FALSE otherwise. The string then continues after the conjunction "&".

Practice 6.11.10

1. If we call the function like

   ```
   CompleteBayes _ singleClassEllipsis("Treatment","Treated",Arthritis,
   Sex='Male',Improved='Marked'),
       what is the second part
   dfparam[,names(args)[2]]==args[[2]]
       of the string testing for?
   ```

---

[6] args[[1]]
 [1] "Male"
 args[1]
 $Sex
 [1] "Male"
 str(args[[1]])
  chr "Male"
 str(args[1])
 List of 1
  $ Sex: chr "Male"

As mentioned above, the whole string could have 1 conjunction, 2 conjunctions, or more, and this will have to be built up in the loop.[7] Once the string is built, we will need to use **eval(parse**()) to get it to run because remember it is a string, not an expression.

6.12 Debugging in R

If we want to see what is actually created by calling **CompleteBayes _ singleClassElli psis**("Treatment","Treated",Arthritis, Sex='Male',Improved='Marked')

we can use a simple debugging technique in R to see the contents of args within the program. If we add

```
browser()
```

as one line of code just before the args<-**list**(...) like this

```
browser()
args<-list(...)
```

and then try running the code like this

```
CompleteBayes_singleClassEllipsis("Treatment","Treated",Arthritis,
Sex='Male',Improved='Marked')
```

the program will halt at the **browser**() line. (Also, RStudio will switch to different file in the Source panel, so don't get confused by that.) Then we can run the rest of the code in the function line by line by typing "n" (without the quotation marks) and pressing the enter key. This is a good way to figure out what is going on in your code and is a simple part of a fairly extensive set of debugging tools that R has. If "n" is typed and the enter key is pressed, then the next line of code will run. In this case, that would mean the line

```
args<-list(…)
```

would run and args would now be assigned **list**(…). This is great because now we can check to see what args looks like. Just type *args* at the prompt, and we see (the prompt has changed to Browse[2] to remind us we are in debugging mode)

```
Browse[2]> args
$Sex
[1] "Male"

$Improved
[1] "Marked"
```

And as expected (and similar to the artificial creation of args we ran earlier), args is a list that contains two elements whose names are "Sex" and "Improved". The "Sex" element has the character

---

[7] We are not accounting for the possibility that there are no arguments entered into the ellipsis. This should be accounted for if we want the code to be robust and not confuse the user.

value "Male", and the "Improved" element has the character value "Marked". We could have tried typing str(args) at the Browse[2]> prompt and would have gotten similar information.

```
Browse[2]> str(args)
List of 2
 $ Sex     : chr "Male"
 $ Improved: chr "Marked"
```

Note that you can also put expressions in the browser() function. For example, in a loop, if you want the loop to continue until the iteration where k = 3, you can write **browser**(expr = {k == 3}).

To exit debugging mode, hit the escape key several times.

Now we exit our discussion of debugging and return to the discussion of **CompleteBayes _ singleClassEllipsis()**.With the ellipsis feature, we can *catch* all the arguments the user wants to enter. To make use of the arguments individually, we have to *unravel* this list. We can usually do this with a loop. We show that next. There will be several functions we will use, and so we will first explain those.

Practice 6.12.11

1. Try the same debugging technique but using HouseVotes84. Show a screenshot of the results when you run str(args).

Practice 6.12.12

1. Before going on, try R's debugging tool **browser**(). Use it in the first version of Complete Bayes. Type the **browser**() function just above this line in the definition of the **CompleteBayes _ singleClass**() function.

   ```
   X _ bool=df$V1==v1 & df$V2==v2 & df$V3==v3 & df$V4==v4
   ```

   Then call the function with something like this:

   ```
   CompleteBayes _ singleClass("democrat",'y','y','y','y')
   ```

   The program should stop at the **browser**() line (and RStudio will switch the source pane as well). If you type "n" into the *console* window and then press enter, the next line of code will run. That is the X _ bool line. Now if you type X _ bool into the *console* window, you can see what has been assigned to X _ bool. What did you get for X _ bool?

   If you type "n" again and then press the enter key, this line will run.

   ```
   X=df[X _ bool,]
   ```

   Now if you type X into the console, you can see what X has been assigned. (Note, if you had typed X before typing the "n" and entering, then you would get an error message about X not existing yet.)
2. What is the problem that **eval(parse())** solves for us in the second version of our Complete Bayes algorithm?

Note of caution: Although we are using the **eval(parse())** construction, there is a debate in the R community as to whether this kind of code should be used where the code could be publicly accessed.

6.13 Returning to Complete Bayes

Ok, that is the end of our short tutorial on **paste0()** and **eval(parse())**. Now we will return to our second version of the implementation of the Complete Bayes algorithm. We show the entire code below.

```r
#install.packages("vcd","mlbench")
library(vcd)
library(mlbench)
library(mice)
data("Arthritis")
data("HouseVotes84")
intersect_event <- function(A,B,df){
  return(df[intersect(A$names,B$names),])
}
prob <- function(E,S){
  return(nrow(E)/nrow(S))

}
#In our last example, we used complete.cases() to weed out the rows that
contained NA.
#Here we will try an alternative approach.
#We use a package called "mice" which stands for Multivariate Imputation
by Chained Equations.
#We won't go into the details here. Suffice to say that this is a way of
"guessing" what the best value to replace the NA with would be.
imputeddf=mice(Arthritis,m=1,maxit=50,meth='pmm',seed=500)
#Output of mice is long and not shown.
completedData <- complete(imputeddf,1)
df=completedData
#df$names<-rownames(df)

CompleteBayes_singleClassEllipsis=function(className="Class",classValue="
democrat",dfparam=df, ...){
  #className is the name of the attribute to classify.
  #classValue is the particular level of the class variable of which to
calculate the probability.
  #Remember that this function needs to be put into a loop. This will be
done in predCompleteBayes().
#Make sure the dfparam is a dataframe.

  dfparam=as.data.frame(dfparam)
#As before, we add in the names variable.
  dfparam$names<-rownames(dfparam)
  args<-list(...)

#First take account of the number of arguments in the ellipsis (which has
just been assigned to a list called args). This will determine how many
times the loop should be run to construct the Boolean string.

  count <- length(args)
#As we have done many times before, we will create a Boolean of the
conditions we are trying to match for each of the input variables. A
possible example of what we may want is a Boolean like this:
```

```
#Sex=="Male" & Improved=="Marked"
#This is a compound statement which will result in a Boolean value
(or vector).
#This is inserted into the dataframe, in the row specification position,
to extract the rows that satisfy this compound condition. What is new
here is that we don't know how many input variables the user of the
function will enter in the call of the function. Thus, this has to be
constructed at runtime. Our function must read the list of arguments the
user enters and then build the statement in the row specification
position - dfparam[here,]. Since we need to add in an unknown number of
conditions to create our compound statement, and since this is being
created in a loop, we will build our compound statement as a string
using paste0(), and then ask R to evaluate it after it is fully
constructed. This step is new. In the past, we just wrote X_bool
ourselves like this:
#X_bool=df$V1==v1 & df$V2==v2 & df$V3==v3 & df$V4==v4
#But in the above statement, we knew that the user was going to enter
four input arguments (v1, v2, v3, v4).
#Now, however, we are creating our compound Boolean statement using a
loop since we are trying to handle the case where the number of arguments
is unknown prior to the function being actually called. We build the
string first, but then this string will need to be evaluated. This is
also new. We will use the special construction, eval(parse()), to
evaluate it. We use xb1 to hold the string. After evaluating the string,
the result will be assigned to X_bool.

  xb1 <- ""
  for(i in 1:count){

     if(i==1){ # We need to treat i=1 as a special case, simply because
the first component of our Boolean string does not begin with an "&", but
all the following components do begin with an "&".
        xb1=paste0(xb1,"dfparam[,names(args)[",i,"]]==args[[",i,"]]")}
     else #If it is not the first element of the string then preface it
with &.
        xb1 <- paste0(xb1,"&","dfparam[,names(args)[",i,"]]==args[[",i,"]]")

  }

  #Now xb1 is the string that needs to be "evaluated".
   X_bool<- eval(parse(text=xb1))

   #X_bool is now the Boolean vector we sought.

Browse[2]> X_bool
 [1] FALSE FALSE FALSE  TRUE  TRUE  TRUE
 [7] FALSE  TRUE FALSE FALSE FALSE FALSE
[13] FALSE  TRUE FALSE FALSE FALSE FALSE
[19] FALSE FALSE FALSE FALSE FALSE FALSE
[25] FALSE FALSE FALSE FALSE FALSE FALSE
[31] FALSE FALSE FALSE FALSE FALSE FALSE
[37] FALSE FALSE FALSE FALSE FALSE FALSE
[43] FALSE FALSE FALSE FALSE FALSE FALSE
[49] FALSE FALSE FALSE  TRUE FALSE FALSE
```

```
[55] FALSE FALSE FALSE FALSE FALSE FALSE
[61] FALSE FALSE FALSE FALSE FALSE FALSE
[67] FALSE FALSE FALSE FALSE FALSE FALSE
[73] FALSE FALSE FALSE FALSE FALSE FALSE
[79] FALSE FALSE FALSE FALSE FALSE FALSE
```

```
  X=dfparam[X_bool,]
#The creation of the class event is a familiar step.
  class_bool=dfparam[,className]==classValue
  classE=dfparam[class_bool,]
```

```
 #As mentioned prior to the coding of the algorithm, given a particular
set of input variables which has been denoted by the vector X, the
Complete Bayes algorithm calculates the probability of each class. In
the function we are currently engaged in writing, we specify one class in
the call. After we finish writing this function, it is run in a loop
thereby iterating through all the classes, keeping track of the class
with the highest probability and also the name of that class. In this
process, it is necessary to calculate conditional probabilities, and we
employ the intersect_event() function built earlier for this purpose.
```

```
  ClassIntsX=intersect_event(X,classE,dfparam)
```

```
 #Next calculate the probability of this intersection. This will be the
numerator.
  numeratorProb=prob(ClassIntsX,dfparam)
```

```
 #The denominator is just the probability of X.
  denominatorProb=prob(X,dfparam)
#Return the ratio.
  return(numeratorProb/denominatorProb)
```

```
 #sample call
 #CompleteBayes_singleClassEllipsis("Treatment","Treated",Arthritis,
Sex='Male',Improved='Marked')
```

```
}
#Test the code.
CompleteBayes_singleClassEllipsis("Treatment","Treated",Arthritis,
Sex='Male',Improved='Marked')
## [1] 0.8333333
#Next, as in version 1, run CompleteBayes_singleClassEllipsis() through a
loop. This is done in the following modification of predCompleteBayes().
predCompleteBayes=function(class="Class",dfparam=df, ...){
  #sample call
  #predCompleteBayes("Treatment",Arthritis, Sex='Female',Improved='Some')
  forecast=list()
  argsPred=list(...) #This is a list form of the arguments. For example,
#argsPred
#$Sex
#[1] "Female"
#$Improved
```

```
#[1] "Marked"

  #lev is a vector containing the levels of the class variable.
  lev=levels(dfparam[,class])

  classprob=0
  predictedclass=lev[1] #Set predictedclass to the first level, but
update it if any other level will give a higher probability.
  for(i in lev){

    p=CompleteBayes_singleClassEllipsis(class,i,dfparam,...)
    if(classprob<p){
      classprob=p
      predictedclass=i
      forecast[["Instance"]]=argsPred
      forecast[["predicted class"]]=predictedclass
      forecast[["probability of predicted class"]]=classprob

    }


  }

  return(forecast)
  #sample calls
  #predCompleteBayes("Treatment",Arthritis, Sex='Female',Improved='Some')
  #predCompleteBayes(who,agaricus_lepiota,var1='x',var2='s')
}
#Now test the code.
predCompleteBayes("Treatment",Arthritis, Sex='Female',Improved='Marked')
## $Instance
## $Instance$Sex
## [1] "Female"
##
## $Instance$Improved
## [1] "Marked"
##
##
## $`predicted class`
## [1] "Treated"
##
## $`probability of predicted class`
## [1] 0.7272727
predCompleteBayes("Class",HouseVotes84, V1='y',V2='y')
## $Instance
## $Instance$V1
## [1] "y"
##
## $Instance$V2
## [1] "y"
##
##
## $`predicted class`
## [1] "democrat"
##
```

```
## $`probability of predicted class`
## [1] 0.626087
predCompleteBayes("Class",HouseVotes84, V1='y',V2='y',V3='n')
## $Instance
## $Instance$V1
## [1] "y"
##
## $Instance$V2
## [1] "y"
##
## $Instance$V3
## [1] "n"
##
##
## $`predicted class`
## [1] "republican"
##
## $`probability of predicted class`
## [1] 0.375
```

Practice 6.13.12: Challenge

1. Can you figure out how to clean up a general dataframe within the body of **CompleteBayes _ singleClassEllipsis**()? In the above code, we removed a numeric variable. Could we have run this inside the code and have it search for any numeric variables and remove them?

Practice 6.13.13

1. Can you implement the Complete Bayes algorithm without using a loop? *Try running the following lines of code as a hint.* Call your new Complete Bayes algorithm **predCompleteBayesLoopFree**().

```
instance _ Bool <- dfparam$V1=='y'& dfparam$V2=='y'& dfparam$V3=='y'&
dfparam$V4=='y'
instance= dfparam[instance _ Bool,]
table(instance[,1])
sum(table(instance[,1]))
table(instance[,1])/sum(table(instance[,1]))
which.max(table(instance[,1]))
names(which.max(table(instance[,1])))
model _ complete <- list()
model _ complete[["Predicted      Class"]]      <-      names(which.
max(table(instance[,1])))
model _ complete[["Probabilities"]]      <-      table(instance[,1])/
sum(table(instance[,1]))
model _ complete
```

Note that if you are able to accomplish this, you will have avoided having to write two separate functions: the single class function and then the **predCompleteBayes**() which had the loop in it. Everything will be easily accomplished with just one (much simpler) function!

2. Can you improve upon the code in the previous practice? In that exercise, it was assumed that the class variable was in column 1. However, that is not always the case. Can you make the code more robust so that the signature for **predCompleteBayesLoopFree**() has a parameter for the name of the class variable and then determines the correct column for that name. Call this parameter className. For example, the user could enter "Treatment" as that argument to indicate that the class variable is called "Treatment". Then the code should be able to identify which column is the "Treatment" column. Hint: Play around with the following snippets of code.

```
colnames(dfparam)=="Treatment"
which(colnames(dfparam)=="Treatment")
```

Test it with HouseVotes84 and then with another dataset.

Chapter 7

Naïve Bayes Classifier

- Introduction
- Notation
- Trying out the Naïve Bayes classifier
- R implementation of the Complete Bayes

Functions Coded in This Chapter
probBxconditional_prob
conditional_prob_bool
prob_per_class_NaiveBayes
NaiveBayes_singleClassEllipsis
predNaiveBayes

7.1 Introduction

We have now implemented the Complete Bayes algorithm and are ready to take the last step and cover the Naïve Bayes classifier. In the previous chapter, we discussed the problems entailed when there are either a large number of inputs or when a variable can take on a large number of values. We showed that for a classification task involving just 20 categorical input variables, each with five possible levels, the number of possible input vectors would be about 10^{14}. We said that if our dataset was even as large as 1 million records, the likelihood of finding a match within our dataset for a given input vector (the essential step in the Complete Bayes algorithm) will often be zero. This will mean we cannot classify our given input vector, and thus our algorithm will be useless. (We said it will fail.) Data Science is a practical exercise, and if we cannot use an algorithm in the real world, we must push on to find something else that will work. This does not suggest that the Complete Bayes algorithm is incorrect in any way but only suggests that it won't be very useful in predicting stock price movements or classifying a cancer treatment as effective.

This problem was faced by various researchers in the 1970s and 1980s and also before that. Various approaches were developed. The paper mentioned earlier by Hand et al.[1] discusses some of these. The approach known as Naïve Bayes roughly makes the "naïve" assumption that the input variables are independent of each other. It is not quite that they are independent. Recall our discussion of conditional independence. Actually Naïve Bayes makes the assumption that the input variables are *conditionally independent* of each other. Recall what the concept of independence means. When we toss a coin twice (in succession), we usually say that what happens on the second toss is independent of what happens on the first toss. On the other hand, if we select two students at random from a classroom of 50 students, you might say that the chance that the second one is sick with a cold is not independent of whether the first one is sick with a cold (the event that one has a cold takes the roll of the yellow colored square in our previous example). This is because colds are contagious, and so if one student is sick, the other students also have a higher chance of being sick. These two examples illustrate the concept of independent events and conditional independent events. Naïve Bayes works with *conditional* independence.

One obvious question or objection here is, "Who said that these input variables are independent (conditionally)?" If this question jumped out at you, you are correct in questioning it. The paper referenced earlier by Hand et al. discusses why this assumption may be justified. However, it is possible that the history of the development of the Naïve Bayes algorithm was somewhat more practically based. It may be that a researcher tried Complete Bayes, but realizing that Complete Bayes will fail often, the researcher may have considered how to overcome this issue – the issue that the *possible* number of inputs is much greater than the size of the dataset. The question we are trying to work with expressed mathematically is

$$P(C \mid \mathbf{X})$$

or more explicitly

$$P(C \mid X_1 = x_1, X_2 = x_2, \ldots, X_n = x_n) \tag{7.1}$$

or with slightly more brevity

$$P(C \mid x_1, x_2, \ldots, x_n).$$

Recall that these are all just differences in notation for the same thing. (In mathematical notation, when lowercase x is used as opposed to upper case X, we are referring to a *value* for variable X, rather than the variable itself.)

In order for such a calculation to result in a non-zero value for at least one value of the class variable C, there must be at least one record in our dataset that matches the vector $[x_1, x_2, x_3, \ldots, x_n]$.

But often we won't find a match. This would mean that for all four values of the *class variable* (dark, milk, white, and none), we may end up with zero for the above probability. Although the calculation would be correct in this case, we will not be able to choose a class. As a classical scientist, this should be acceptable, but a data scientist researcher may not be willing to stop here. The researcher may suggest that it may be considerably more likely to find a match just for $X_i = x_i$ for each i individually.

[1] Hand, D. J., & Yu, K. (2001). Idiot's Bayes—Not So Stupid After All? *International Statistical Review*, 69(3), 385–398.

To make this concrete, going back to our chocolate example, it may be difficult to find

$$\left[A = young, \ G = F, \ S = N, \ I = Y, \ W = -2, \ D = N \right]$$

that is, a *young female* who *does not like spicy food* and *does like ice cream* and who is *2 lbs underweight* and is *not dieting*. But it should be considerably easier to find A = young: a young person. The first condition is very strongly specified. The second one is much less specific, and so it will be easier to locate such an example in our dataset. Consequently it should be fairly easy to find examples of A = young and preferring dark chocolate or A = young and preferring milk chocolate, or A = young and preferring white chocolate and so it should be fairly easy to calculate the following as non-zero probabilities.

p(dark|young)[2]
p(milk|young)
p(white|young)
p(none|young)

The same goes for the second variable G = F: gender is female. These should also be relatively easy to obtain:

p (dark|female)
p (milk|female)
p (white|female)
p (none|female)

and so on for all the *individual* input variables A, G, S, I, W, D.

So to review, we are seeking

$P(C|x_1, x_2, x_3, \ldots, x_n)$

But it seems unlikely we will find a match for a compound specification like $X_1 = x_1$, $X_2 = x_2$, $X_3 = x_3, \ldots, X_n = x_n$.

However, we see that is considerably more likely to find matches for individual specifications like $X_1 = x_1$ (or $X_2 = x_2$, and so on). That is to say, the following are more likely to be non-zero:

$P(C|x_1), P(C|x_2), P(C|x_3), \ldots P(C|x_n)$.

Unfortunately, these are *not* what we are looking for. Still, the data science researcher may *test* replacing

$$P\left(C|x_1, x_2, \ldots, x_n\right) \tag{7.2}$$

with

$$P\left(C|x_1\right) * P\left(C|x_2\right) \cdots P\left(C|x_n\right) \tag{7.3}$$

---

[2] Actually because of Bayes Theorem we are seeking the "reverse" type of question, e.g. P(young|dark) instead of P(dark|young), but the argument is similar and to remove some complexity from the explanation we state it this way. However, in the next section when we show the calculation more formally we will work with expressions of this form: P(young|dark).

without any theoretical justification. And if it turns out that the predictions made by this approach are accurate in the test data, then *the approach may be employed* inspite of the fact that there may not be any theoretical justification for its use.

Recall that testing this model just involves selecting people for whom we know their chocolate preferences and comparing that with the type of chocolate the researcher *predicts* would be preferred and then comparing that with the type they *actually* like. We may expect that since the researcher made this purely self-serving assumption, with no theoretical support, her predictions will be wildly off the mark. Remarkably though, the predictions turn out to be pretty close to the mark for many data sets!

This author speculates that the above scenario may in fact be a description of the historical development of this classifier. If you read Hand's paper, he describes various possible justifications for why the replacement of Equation 7.2 with Equation 7.3 is justified. But in fact, these justifications *may* have come "after the fact". This process may be different from what we expect typcally in science. Nevertheless it has value.

In addition, regarding the general development of machine learning algorithms, it is also being suggested that the development of an algorithm is, to some degree, based on "playfulness". There may not necessarily have been a solid theoretical reason for making the switch from Equation 7.2 to Equation 7.3. The researcher was stuck, could not get a prediction, and just started experimenting to see what may help. Perhaps this is an example of Voltaire's maxim "don't let the perfect be an enemy of the good" or "adversity is the mother of invention". In any case, if this is in fact the correct historical description of Naïve Bayes, it seems that this experimentation led to a good result.

In the above discussion, where did conditional independence come in? If you go back and review our discussion of conditional independence, you will see that replacing Equation 7.2 with Equation 7.3 is equivalent to asserting conditional independence. We will show that clearly next.

7.2 Developing the Naïve Bayes Classifier

Early in the text, we covered probability and in particular both Bayes Theorem and conditional independence. If you understand these two concepts, the steps from the Complete Bayes to the Naïve Bayes are not difficult.

In Complete Bayes, we had a formula for calculating $P(C_i| x_1 \ldots x_p)$. To review this, C is the class variable, and x_i are input variables. We also will use the notation that $\mathbf{X} = [x_1 \ldots x_p]$. Also, since there are various levels for C, we use $C_1, C_2, \ldots, C_n$ and in general C_i for the different levels. Again, to make this concrete, C_1 may stand for dark chocolate, C_2 may stand for milk chocolate, and so on. There is a lack of consistency in this notation that may confuse the reader. The subscripts on the class variable denote different levels of the *same* (class) variable. The subscripts on the x variables denote *different* variables! Please take note of this.

Now Bayes *theorem* will give us the following expression for $P(C_i|x_1 \ldots x_p)$.

$$P(C_i|x_1,\ldots, x_n) = \frac{P(x_1,\ldots, x_n|C_i)P(C_i)}{P(x_1,\ldots, x_n|C_1)P(C_1)+\cdots P(x_1,\ldots, x_n|C_m)P(C_m)} \quad (7.4)$$

Note: You may be confused by the fact that we have $x_1, x_2, \ldots, x_p$. Remember that comma means intersection and the intersection of events is an event.

Now recall we had two expressions for the meaning of *conditional* independence, Equations (4.20) and (4.21).

$$p(R|B \cap Y) = p(R|Y)$$

or equivalently

$$p(R \cap B|Y) = p(R|Y) * p(B|Y)$$

If we assume conditional indepedence, then we are free to use either of these equations. It is not hard to generalize either of them for more than R and B. For example, to generalize to three events; R, B, and G, the second equation will be

$$p(R \cap B \cap G|Y) = p(R|Y) * p(B|Y) * p(G|Y) \tag{7.5}$$

With the assumption of conditional independence, Equation 7.4 can be rewritten as follows. We use a new symbol, P_{nb}, which will be explained below.

$$P_{nb}\left(C_i|x_1,\ldots,x_n\right)$$

$$= \frac{p(C_i)\left[p(x_1|C_i)p(x_2|C_i)\cdots p(x_n|C_i)\right]}{\left(p(C_1)\left[p(x_1|C_1)p(x_2|C_1)\cdots p(x_n|C_1)\right] + \cdots + p(C_m)\left[p(x_1|C_m)p(x_2|C_m)\cdots p(x_n|C_m)\right]\right)} \tag{7.6}$$

The next three expressions are often used but are not necessary. We present them here in case you come across these in the literature.

Since the denominator will be the same for any C_i, it is sometimes thought of as a constant. Considering the denominator as a constant we may write that the left side is proportional to the right (with the constant of proportionality being the denominator of equation 7.6).

$$P_{nb}\left(C_i|x_1,\ldots,x_n\right) \propto p(C_i)\left[p(x_1|C_i)p(x_2|C_i)\cdots p(x_n|C_i)\right] \tag{7.7}$$

Equation 7.7 can be rewritten using the capital Greek letter Π below (the Greek letter for the English P). Here Π is used to indicate the product of all the factors (over each possible value of j). It is just a convenient notation, and is not necessary to write our equation this way.

$$P_{nb}\left(C_i|x_1,\ldots,x_n\right) \propto p(C_i)\prod_{j=1}^{n} p(x_j|C_i) \tag{7.8}$$

Next, the following equation means that we are seeking the C_i that leads to the largest probability as calculated in equation 7.8.

$$C = \text{argmax}_i p(C_i)\prod_{j=1}^{n} p(x_j|C_i) \tag{7.9}$$

Argmax here means interate over all the values of i and choose the the largest value of $p(C_i) \prod_{j=1}^{n} p(x_j|C_i)$. Finally we assign that value to C, where C is the *predicted* class.

We used the new notation $P_{nb}(C_i|x_1,\ldots,x_n)$ to indicate that this is the Naïve Bayes estimation of the probability of class C_i where our calculation includes the *assumption* of conditional independence. "nb" stands for Naïve Bayes.

The calculation in 7.6 (or 7.7 or 7.8) results in a number.[3] As in the Complete Bayes[4], we do such a calculation for each level of the class variable and then assign the record **X** to the level that is highest. That is it! We now have the Naïve Bayes classifier. Let's do the calculations with actual data and see what we get.

Practice 7.2.1
1. In the mathematical expression for P_{nb}, what is the first term of the denominator?
2. In the mathematical expression for P_{nb}, what is the numerator of P_{nb}?
3. Suppose the class variable has five levels, how many terms would the denominator have?
4. Suppose there were eight input variables. How many factors would there be in an individual term of the denominator?
5. Consider Equation 7.4 in light of our derivation of Bayes theorem beginning in Section 4.25 where we talked about the partitioning of the set and an arbitrary set B.
   a. What is the sample space for 7.4?
   b. Where do the partitions show up in 7.4?
   c. What is the evidence (also referred to as inputs) in the discussion of partitions and the arbitrary set B? Here you are being asked to draw the connection between the discussion of partitions and the discussion of the input variables and the class variable.

7.3 Trying Out the Naïve Bayes Classifier

We will use the well-known Golf dataset, which has 14 rows, for this example. This dataset is available on the Internet. It consists of only nominal data. If you find a copy on the web and import it, make sure to set stringsAsFactors = TRUE like this: Golf <- read.csv(file = "Golf.csv", stringsAsFactors = TRUE). Otherwise you can copy the set from the table below and paste it into an Excel spreadsheet and save it as a .csv file (Figure 7.1).

To make our calculations simpler, we will use only the *humidity* and *windy* columns to classify *play*.

Shading the cells will make it easier to follow along (Figure 7.2).

7.4 Independence and Conditional Independence

First, to bring everything back to basics, note that in the language of probability, *windy = TRUE, humidity = high,* and *play = yes* are each separate events. Recall that our sample space is the set

---

[3] Often texts will explain that the denominator in our calculation will be the same across all levels, C_i, of the class variable, and so if we want to reduce the number of calculations (and thereby increase the speed of the code), we can calculate only the numerator. In our code, we don't take this route, but that is just for the sake of clarity.

[4] And as argmax indicates in equation 7.9.

outlook	temperature	humidity	windy	play
sunny	hot	high	FALSE	no
sunny	hot	high	TRUE	no
overcast	hot	high	FALSE	yes
rainy	mild	high	FALSE	yes
rainy	cool	normal	FALSE	yes
rainy	cool	normal	TRUE	no
overcast	cool	normal	TRUE	yes
sunny	mild	high	FALSE	no
sunny	cool	normal	FALSE	yes
rainy	mild	normal	FALSE	yes
sunny	mild	normal	TRUE	yes
overcast	mild	high	TRUE	yes
overcast	hot	normal	FALSE	yes
rainy	mild	high	TRUE	no

Figure 7.1   Golf dataset.

humidity	windy	play
high	FALSE	no
high	TRUE	no
high	FALSE	yes
high	FALSE	yes
normal	FALSE	yes
normal	TRUE	no
normal	TRUE	yes
high	FALSE	no
normal	FALSE	yes
normal	FALSE	yes
normal	TRUE	yes
high	TRUE	yes
normal	FALSE	yes
high	TRUE	no

Figure 7.2   Golf dataset with just two input variables.

of all rows. Then the statement *windy = TRUE* selects a subset of the set of all rows. So windy = TRUE selects a subset of the sample space and is thus an event. The same reasoning holds true for *humidity = high* and *play = yes*.

Now we review the concept of independent events with this dataset. In general, it is rare that two events are actually independent, but as an example, we will go through a calculation to check if, say, *windy = TRUE* and *humidity = high* are independent. Letting W be the event that it is windy and H be the event that humidity is high, we investigate whether

$$P(W \cap H) = P(W) * P(H)$$

$W \cap H$ refers to rows 2, 12, 14, and so $n(W \cap H) = 3$ and $p(W \cap H) = \dfrac{3}{14}$. It will be left to the reader to do the calculation on the RHS and to show that the LHS and the RHS are not equal, thus showing that W and H are not independent.

Practice 7.4.2
1. What is p(W) and what is p(H)?

Next, test conditional independence. As an example, we will check to see if the events W and H are independent given the event Play = YES. Denoting Play = YES by G ("go golfing"), we will check to see if the following is true. It is the first equation for conditional independence (Equation 4.20).

$$p(W|H \cap G) = p(W|G)$$

For the LHS, we need to identify the rows that have both H and G. These are rows 3, 4, and 12. Next, we check which of these rows are W? Just row 12. Thus, $P(W|H \cap G) = \dfrac{1}{3}$. Now for the RHS, we first identify which rows are G. These are rows 3, 4, 5, 7, 9, 10, 11, 12, and 13. From within these, we identify which rows are W? These are 7, 11, and 12. So the RHS is 3/9. It seems that the LHS is equal to the RHS, and thus W and H are conditionally independent given G. This is surprising since arbitrary pairs of events are not generally either independent or conditionally independent.

Practice 7.4.3
1. Recall that in Section 4.18 ("Additional Terminology"), we discussed the terms "prior probability" and "posterior probability". Is p(W|G) a prior or posterior probability?
2. Is p(W) a prior or posterior probability?

7.5 Naïve Bayes Example Using the Golf Dataset

Ok, we have practiced some calculations on the golf dataset. Now we proceed to a Naïve Bayes classifier calculation. Which should we choose as the class variable? Any of them would be fine, but usually most texts use the *play* variable as the class variable, so we will stick with that. In this case, the input variables will be "humidity" and "windy". Thus, we want to take a new record (a new instance) of particular values for the input variables and see how the Naïve Bayes classifier will classify it. Since both of these variables are binary (have only two possibilities), together there are just the following four possible combinations. We could use any of them for our example.

Humidity	Windy
High	TRUE
High	FALSE
Normal	TRUE
Normal	FALSE

Suppose "humidity" is high (we denoted this as H) and "windy" is TRUE (we denoted this as W), will Naïve Bayes classify such an instance as play = yes or play = no? Recall the concept of training set versus testing set. Usually, the dataset will be divided into two subsets of records. One subset is called the training set, and the second is called the testing set. However, here, for the sake of simplicity, in this example, we use the entire dataset as our training set and our testing set.

We will use the notation ~G for "not play". We are interested in whether G or ~G is more "likely"[5] given H and W. Writing our question in the notation we have developed, we need to calculate both

$$P_{nb}(G|H,W)$$

and

$$P_{nb}(\sim G|H,W)$$

Each of these will give a numeric result. More explicitly, the first will give the probability of G given H and W *assuming conditional independence*, and the second will give the probability of ~G given H and W *assuming conditional independence*. Then, we will just choose the class (either G or ~G) that has the larger result.

Again, the general formulation for this calculation from Equation 7.6 is

$$P_{nb}(C_i|x_1,\ldots,x_n)$$

$$= \frac{p(C_i)\big[p(x_1|C_i)p(x_2|C_i)\cdots p(x_n|C_i)\big]}{\big(p(C_1)\big[p(x_1|C_1)p(x_2|C_1)\cdots p(x_n|C_1)\big]+\cdots+p(C_m)\big[p(x_1|C_m)p(x_2|C_m)\cdots p(x_n|C_m)\big]\big)}$$

In our case, since there are only two possible C_i, only two possible classes – play and not play – the denominator will have just two terms. Further, since there are two possible classes, we will do the entire calculation above twice, once when C_i is "play golf", G, and once when C_i is "not play", ~G. To relate this to our earlier discussion of partitions and Bayes theorem, note here that it is the class variable that is playing the role of the partition, and so the number of levels of the class variable determines the number of sets in the partition.

Practice 7.5.4

1. In the Probability chapter, how many partitions were shown in the drawing of the partitions? (See Figures 4.28 and 4.29)
2. Suppose there were three levels for the class variable *play*. How many terms would there be in the denominator of P_{nb}?
3. Compare the RHS of Bayes theorem in the Probability chapter with the RHS of P_{nb} here. In the conditional probability calculations, what is the "condition" event (as opposed to the "prior" event) in Bayes theorem, and what is it here in P_{nb}? Why are they different?
4. Optional challenge: Try to implement the intersection function as an operator with the name %inSec%.

---

[5] I am using likely with quotation marks because we are measuring how likely something is with the Naïve Bayes measure P_{nb} and not just the straightforward probability function P. P_{nb} has the embedded assumption of conditional independence.

7.6 Naïve Bayes Classification for Class G

For the above formula, we need the following calculations:

$$P(G) = \frac{9}{14}$$

$$P(H|G) = \frac{2}{9}$$

$$P(W|G) = \frac{3}{9}$$

$$P(\sim G) = \frac{5}{14}$$

$$P(H|\sim G) = \frac{4}{5}$$

$$P(W|\sim G) = \frac{3}{5}$$

Now we can calculate the following:

$$P_{nb}(G|H,W) = \frac{\left(\frac{9}{14} * \frac{2}{9} * \frac{3}{9}\right)}{\left[\left(\frac{9}{14} * \frac{2}{9} * \frac{3}{9}\right) + \left(\frac{5}{14} * \frac{4}{5} * \frac{3}{5}\right)\right]} = 0.22$$

$$P_{nb}(\sim G|H,W) = \frac{\left(\frac{5}{14} * \frac{4}{5} * \frac{3}{5}\right)}{\left[\left(\frac{9}{14} * \frac{2}{9} * \frac{3}{9}\right) + \left(\frac{5}{14} * \frac{4}{5} * \frac{3}{5}\right)\right]} = 0.78$$

Since ~G has a higher value for P_{nb} when "humidity" is high and it is "windy", then the Naïve Bayes classifier would classify this instance, (H, W), as ~G, not playing golf!

If you wanted to compare this with a different classifier, you could try to compare it with the Complete Bayes classifier. If you check this, the Complete Bayes will give the same answer for this data. This is assured because, as shown earlier, it so happens that W and H are conditionally independent given G, and thus $P_{nb}(C_i |W,H) = P(C_i|W,H)$.

Practice 7.6.5

1. From the above paragraph, can you state a general condition where Complete Bayes and Naïve Bayes will result in the same predictions?

Next, we will implement the Naïve Bayes classifier in R.

7.7 R Implementation of the Naïve Bayes: Version 1

The first version is built specifically for the HouseVotes84 dataset. It assumes that there are three input variables named V1, V2, and V3 and that the class variable is called Class.

```
#install.packages("mlbench","mice")
library(mlbench)
library(mice)
data("HouseVotes84")
imputeddf=mice(HouseVotes84,m=1,maxit=50,meth='pmm',seed=500)
#Results of "mice" are not shown.
completedData <- complete(imputeddf,1)
df=completedData
df$names<-rownames(df)


intersect_event=function(a,b,df=df){
  return(df[intersect(a$names,b$names),])}

union_event=function(E,F){
  if(!is.data.frame(E)|!is.data.frame(F)){
    stop("arguments must be a dataframe")
  }
  return(unique(rbind(E,F)))}

multi_union_event=function(E,F,...){return(unique(rbind(E,F,...)))}

complement=function(a,df){
  df[!a,]
}

probBxconditional_prob= function(a,b,s){
  return(prob(intersect_event(a,b,s),s))}

prob<-function( e,  s) {
  return(nrow(e)/nrow(s))}

conditional_prob=function(a,b,s){
  return(prob(intersect_event(a,b,s),s)/prob(b,s))

}
```

```
#The following is an example of another version of a function to
calculate conditional probabilities of one event given another event.
In the previous version, we had to construct events first before putting
them into the function conditional_prob(). Recall that we needed to have
the events A and B already constructed and then we ran the function as
conditional_prob(A,B,df).
#In this version, all that is needed is the names of the variables and
their levels. For example, if we want the conditional probability that
the class is "democrat" given that the senator voted y on the first issue
p(Class='democrat'|V1='yes'), we denote Class as the prior variable and
V1 as the conditional variable. Then substitute Class for varPrior,
democrat for varPriorLevel, V1 for varCondition, and y for
varConditionalLevel. (df also needs to be specified.)
```

That is, if we wanted this calculation

$$p(\text{varPrior} = \text{varPriorLevel}|\text{varCondition} = \text{varConditionalLevel})$$

we could call it with the below function like this:

```
#Sample call for function defined below
#conditional_prob_bool(varPrior, varPriorLevel, varCondition,
varConditionLevel, df)
conditional_prob_bool <- function(varPrior, varPriorLevel, varCondition,
varConditionLevel, df){
  #sample call
  # conditional_prob_bool('Class', 'democrat', 'V1', 'y', df)

  prior_bool <- df[,varPrior] == varPriorLevel
  prior_event <- df[prior_bool,]
#
  condition_bool <- df[,varCondition] == varConditionLevel
  condition_event=df[condition_bool,]
#

  return(prob(intersect_event(prior_event,condition_event,df),df)/
prob(condition_event,df))
}
```

Test the following conditional probability: $p\big(\text{democrat}|V1 = y\big)$.

```
conditional_prob_bool('Class', 'democrat', 'V1', 'y', df)
## [1] 0.8376963
#Build the function to calculate Pnb for one level of the class variable.
prob_per_class_NaiveBayes=function(class, v1='y',v2='y',v3='y',df){
  df=as.data.frame(df)
  df$names<-rownames(df)

  A_bool=df$V1==v1 & df$V2==v2& df$V3==v3
  A=df[A_bool,]

  class_bool=df$Class==class
  classE=df[class_bool,]
```

Recall Equation 7.6.

$$P_{nb}\big(C_i|x_1,\ldots, x_n\big)$$

$$= \frac{p(C_i)\big[p(x_1|C_i)p(x_2|C_i)\cdots p(x_n|C_i)\big]}{\big(p(C_1)\big[p(x_1|C_1)p(x_2|C_1)\cdots p(x_n|C_1)\big]+\cdots+p(C_m)\big[p(x_1|C_m)p(x_2|C_m)\cdots p(x_n|C_m)\big]\big)}$$

```
#We needed the intersect_event() function before, but now, by the
assumption of independence, we won't need to make as much use of it.
(It is actually employed when calling our conditional_prob function.)
The denominator must be "responsive" to the number of levels that exist.
```

In other words, the denominator will have multiple terms - one for each level of the class variable.

```
numerator=prob(classE,df)*conditional_prob_bool('V1', v1,'Class',class,
df)*conditional_prob_bool('V2', v2,'Class',class,df)*conditional_prob_
bool('V3', v3,'Class',class,df)

lev=levels(df$Class)
denominator=0

for(i in lev){
  class_bool=df$Class==i
  classE=df[class_bool,]
  class=i
  denominator= denominator+(prob(classE,df)*conditional_prob_bool('V1',
v1,'Class',class,df)* conditional_prob_bool('V2', v2,'Class',class,df)*
conditional_prob_bool('V3', v3,'Class',class,df))

}

return(numerator/denominator)
#sample call
#prob_per_class_NaiveBayes("democrat", v1='y',v2='y',v3='y',HouseVo
tes84)
}
#Test our function
prob_per_class_NaiveBayes("democrat", v1='y',v2='y',v3='y',df)
## [1] 0.9684853
```

Practice 7.7.6

1. For the HouseVotes84 dataframe, in the calculation of P_{nb}, what is the first term of the denominator?
2. For the HouseVotes84 dataframe, in the calculation of P_{nb}, what is the numerator of P_{nb}?
3. For the Arthritis dataframe, how many terms are there in the denominator?
4. Write **prob_per_class_NaiveBayes**() using the original conditional probability function we had: **conditional_prob**().
5. Write the **predNaiveBayes**() function which will loop through all the levels of the class variable and will show the predicted class and its "probability". Use the **predComplete-Bayes** from the last chapter as the model.

7.8 Version 2 of Naïve Bayes in R

Following is the second version of the Naïve Bayes algorithm. Again, it has two parts: **NaiveBayes_singleClassEllipsis**() and **predNaiveBayes**(). It is not constrained to a single dataframe but rather is flexible enough to handle various dataframes and also can handle many input variables.

```
#install.packages("mlbench","mice")
library(mlbench)
library(mice)
```

```
data("HouseVotes84")
imputeddf=mice(HouseVotes84,m=1,maxit=50,meth='pmm',seed=500)
#"mice" calculations are not shown here.
completedData <- complete(imputeddf,1)
dfHouse=completedData
df$names<-rownames(df) #If this is left out, errors show up later.

intersect_event=function(a,b,df=df){
  return(df[intersect(a$names,b$names),])}

union_event=function(E,F){
  if(!is.data.frame(E)|!is.data.frame(F)){
    stop("arguments must be a dataframe")
  }
  return(unique(rbind(E,F)))}

multi_union_event=function(E,F,...){return(unique(rbind(E,F,...)))}


complement=function(a,df){
  df[!a,]
}

#A function which is not actually used in this version of Naïve Bayes:
probBxconditional_prob= function(a,b,s){
  return(prob(intersect_event(a,b,s),s))}

prob<-function( e,  s) {
  return(nrow(e)/nrow(s))}

bool2event<-function(E_bool,df){return(df[E_bool,])}

conditional_prob=function(a,b,s){
  return(prob(intersect_event(a,b,s),s)/prob(b,s))
}

conditional_prob_bool <- function(varPrior, varPriorLevel, varCondition,
varConditionLevel, df){

  prior_bool <- df[,varPrior] == varPriorLevel
  prior_event <- df[prior_bool,]
  #
  condition_bool <- df[,varCondition] == varConditionLevel
  condition_event=df[condition_bool,]
  #
  return(prob(intersect_event(prior_event,condition_event,df),df)/
prob(condition_event,df))
}
conditional_prob_bool('Class', 'democrat', 'V1', 'y', dfHouse)
## [1] 0
#install.packages("vcd")
library(vcd)
data("Arthritis")
data("HouseVotes84")
imputeddf=mice(Arthritis,m=1,maxit=50,meth='pmm',seed=500)
```

```
#"mice" calculations are not shown here.
completedData <- complete(imputeddf,1)
dfArthritis=completedData
df$names<-rownames(df)


NaiveBayes_singleClassEllipsis=function(className="Class",classValue="dem
ocrat",dfparam=df, ...){
  #Sample call:
 #NaiveBayes_singleClassEllipsis("Treatment","Treated",Arthritis,
Sex='Male',Improved='Marked')
  #className is the name of the attribute you want to classify.
  #classValue is the particular level of the class variable you want to
calculate the probability of.
  #Remember that this function needs to be put into a loop which is done
in predCompleteBayes()

  dfparam=as.data.frame(dfparam)
  dfparam$names<-rownames(dfparam)

  args<-list(...)


  count <- length(args)


  class_bool=dfparam[,className]==classValue
  classE=dfparam[class_bool,]
#Note that the above step could be done in one line and that we will have
occasion to do that later, but putting it in one line makes it more
challenging to read.
# classE=dfparam[dfparam[,className]==classValue,]


#Start the loop with numerator set as the probability of the level of the
class variable being considered. (For example, for the HouseVotes84,
classValue= "democrat", or for the Arthritis dataframe,
classValue= "Placebo".)
  numerator=prob(classE,dfparam)

  for(i in 1:count){
    # Recall that this is how we call conditional_prob_bool:
    #conditional_prob_bool('Class', 'democrat', 'V1', 'y', df)
    #The numerator in the Naïve Bayes calculation is calculated as
numerator=numerator*conditional_prob_bool(names(args)[i],args[[i]],classN
ame,classValue,dfparam)
  }
```

#It is important to note that the first term in the denominator is the
same as the entire numerator.
#Then the subsequent terms in the numerator mirror this first term with
only the class level being different for each subsequent term.
#Thus, to get the terms in the denominator, use the loop that generated
the numerator, and run it multiple times – once for each level of the
class variable. Thus, we have a loop of a loop, otherwise called a nested
loop. The loop that generated the numerator is run multiple times, but
each time, the level of the class variable is changed.

```
#Recall from basic math the difference between the words "term" and
"product". These terms are separated by a plus sign. So, a+b+c has three
terms. A product consists of factors separated by multiplication signs.
So, abcd is the product of four factors.
#The denominator is calculated as a sum of terms, and each term is the
product of factors. And so, we can set the denominator initially equal to
zero prior to the looping. If it were a product, then setting it equal to
zero prior to the looping would force it to always be zero since the
product of 0 times anything is 0.
  denominator=0

#As mentioned above, the denominator will need a term for each level of
the class variable, and so we first create a vector of all the levels.
classLevels will be the vector of all the levels of the class variable.
  classLevels=levels(dfparam[,className])

#We need to add a term for each level. We achieve this with a loop, and
so we need to know how many times to iterate through the loop. This is
the length of the previously defined classLevels vector.
  countOfClassLevels=length(classLevels)

  #Start the looping.
  for(j in 1:countOfClassLevels){

  #Class_bool will be the Boolean for this particular iteration's class
level. The iteration variable is j.
    class_bool=dfparam[,className]==classLevels[j]
    #The value for the current level of the class is
    classE=dfparam[class_bool,]

  #As mentioned above, the denominator is a bunch of terms, and each
term is a product of factors. So, abcd + efgh has two terms, and the
first term consists of the factors a, b, c, and d. We are building the
denominator terms using the denominatorFactor variable. The first factor
of each term will be the probability of the current level of the class
variable.
    denominatorFactor=prob(classE,dfparam)
  for(i in 1:count){
    #Recall the arguments needed for conditional_prob_bool('Class',
'democrat', 'V1', 'y', df).
    denominatorFactor=denominatorFactor*conditional_prob_bool(className,
classLevels[j],names(args)[i],args[[i]],dfparam)
    }
    denominator=denominator+denominatorFactor
  }

  return(numerator/denominator)

  #As mentioned, given a particular set of input variables and their
values, which we denote with the vector X, the Complete Bayes
  #will need to calculate the P_nb of each class.
  #In the function we are currently writing (NaiveBayes_
singleClassEllipsis), we specify one level of the class variable.
  #After we finish writing this function, we will run it in a loop
  #to allow it to loop through all the classes,
```

```
#and then following that, it will select the class with the highest
#probability.
#Don't be confused. You may complain that we are running through all
the levels even in this current function (NaiveBayes_
singleClassEllipsis). Yes, we are using all the levels, but all the
levels are required in the denominator even for this "singleClass".

#Sample call:
 #NaiveBayes_singleClassEllipsis("Treatment","Treated",Arthritis,
Sex='Male',Improved='Marked')

}
  NaiveBayes_singleClassEllipsis("Treatment","Treated",Arthritis,
  Sex='Male',Improved='Marked')
## [1] 0.4880952
```

Practice 7.8.7

1. What is the first term in the denominator of P_{nb} in the above code?
2. What is the value of first term in the denominator of P_{nb} in the above code? One way to find out is to insert the **browser**() function nearby.
3. What is the value of the numerator of P_{nb} in the above code? One way to find out is to insert the **browser**() function nearby.
4. For Arthritis, how many terms are there in the denominator?
5. Suppose the class variable has five levels, how many terms would the denominator have?
6. Suppose there were eight input variables. How many factors would there be in an individual term of the denominator?
7. Challenge: Rewrite **NaiveBayes_singleClassEllipsis**() using our original **conditional_prob**() function.

```
#Now we build the function predNaiveBayes() which runs NaiveBayes_
singleClassEllipsis() multiple times to select the best level for our
instance X.
 predNaiveBayes=function(class="Class",dfparam=df, ...){
  #Sample call:
  #predNaiveBayes("Treatment",Arthritis, Sex='Female',Improved='Some')
  forecast=list()
  argsPred=list(...)

  #It is tempting to use the next line
  #lev=levels(dfparam$class)
  #but recall that R won't accept a variable following the dollar sign
 here.

  #So, we access the column with the following alternative.
  #R will look for a column whose name is class.

  lev=levels(dfparam[,class]) #Alternatively, either dfparam[[class]] or
 dfparam[,class] will work here.


  classprob=0
  predictedclass=lev[1]
```

```
for(i in lev){
  #Recall the sample call:
  #NaiveBayes_singleClassEllipsis("Treatment","Treated",Arthritis,
  Sex='Male',Improved='Marked')

  p=NaiveBayes_singleClassEllipsis(class,i,dfparam,...)
  if(classprob<p){
    classprob=p
    predictedclass=i
    forecast[["Instance"]]=argsPred
    forecast[["predicted class"]]=predictedclass
    forecast[["probability of predicted class (if independence
assumption is true)"]]=classprob


  }


}

  return(forecast)
  #sample call
  #predNaiveBayes("Treatment",Arthritis, Sex='Female',Improved='Some')

  #predNaiveBayes(who,agaricus_lepiota,var1='x',var2='s')
}
#predNaiveBayes("Treatment",Arthritis, Sex='Female',Improved='Marked')
 predNaiveBayes("Treatment",Arthritis, Sex='Female',Improved='Some')
## $Instance
## $Instance$Sex
## [1] "Female"
##
## $Instance$Improved
## [1] "Some"
##
##
## $`predicted class`
## [1] "Placebo"
##
## $`probability of predicted class (if independence assumption is
true)`
## [1] 0.5119048
```

Practice 7.8.8

1. Why might it be that dfArthritis and Arthritis result in the same "probability"?

```
predNaiveBayes("Class",HouseVotes84, V1='y',V2='y')
## $Instance
## $Instance$V1
## [1] "y"
##
## $Instance$V2
## [1] "y"
##
```

```
##
## $`predicted class`
## [1] "democrat"
##
## $`probability of predicted class (if independence assumption is
true)`
## [1] 0.6137931
predNaiveBayes("Class",dfHouse, V1='y',V2='y',V3='n')
## $Instance
## $Instance$V1
## [1] "y"
##
## $Instance$V2
## [1] "y"
##
## $Instance$V3
## [1] "n"
##
##
## $`predicted class`
## [1] "democrat"
##
## $`probability of predicted class (if independence assumption is
true)`
## [1] 0.6137931
```

Practice 7.8.9

1. Can you write a test to show that conditional independence of the input variables *for a particular set of values* does *not* hold by using functions we wrote for this chapter and the last chapter? Note that showing that the variables, as opposed to the *values*, are independent would require testing every possible set of inputs, and that would require additional steps, and so this question does not ask us to show that the variables are independent. It asks only for a test to show particular values are independent. Hint: The two functions to use will be **prob _ per_class_NaiveBayes()** and **prob _ per_class_CompleteBayes()**.

2. Explain what the note "if independence assumption is true" in the output of **predNaiveBayes()** means and why it is important.

3. Challenge: Use the **bin()** function in the OneR package to bin all the numeric variables in mtcars. For simplicity, strive for two, three, or four bins for each numeric variable (as you wish). Make sure to convert each resulting variable to a factor if it is not already one. After binning each variable, test the result in Naïve Bayes. Use the binned versions of cyl, disp, and hp to predict the binned version of mpg. Our Naïve Bayes prediction function requires that we specify a set of inputs (an input vector **X**), in order to get a class prediction. Therefore, try something like **predNaiveBayes("newMpg",newMtcars, newCyl="", newDisp="", newHp="")** assuming you named your new variables as above. (You will fill in what should go between the quotation marks with elements from the labels you created.)

    Here is an example of binning a vector x into just two bins.

```
install.packages("OneR")
library(OneR)
#Data to bin
```

```
x <- 1:6
x
## [1] 1 2 3 4 5 6
#Just two bins
newX=bin(x,nbins = 2, labels=c("small","big"))
newX
## [1] small small small big   big   big
## Levels: small big
```

7.9 Conclusion

We have studied in a great deal of detail the Naïve Bayes machine learning algorithm. We spent a good deal of effort learning concepts in probability. Why? Naïve Bayes is clearly based on the concepts of probability. There are other algorithms that are also based on probability. However, there are many that are not. Although the reader has hopefully gained a good amount through this detailed study, it would be misleading to think that the way we constructed programs so far will make sense for other algorithms. For example, the concept of an event is part of probability theory and may have nothing to do with other algorithms. In fact, when we study neural networks, there is no necessity of discussing events. Therefore, it is hoped that the reader has developed programming skills and a good understanding of the Naïve Bayes algorithm, but it would lead to confusion if the reader tried to carry the concept of probability into algorithms where it is not the main approach to the classification process.

## Chapter 8

Stored Model for Naïve Bayes Classifier

- Introduction
- Building the Learned Model
- Matrices to Hold the Model Parameter
- Building the Matrices
- apply() Family of Functions
- Training and Testing

Functions Coded in This Chapter
prob_from_params
probAdj

8.1 Introduction

Often, this step in developing a classifier may be left out from an explanation of its mechanics. However for completeness and for the programming steps that it requires, we will discuss the difference between how the algorithm classifies (or predicts) outcomes and how the learning that it does on the training set is stored so that it can be applied to new unlabeled data. In machine learning, in so-called parametric based learning, what is learned through training on the training data, is stored in parameters (on the other hand, there are so-called non-parametric algorithms as well, for example KNN). This is an entirely different meaning from the term "parameter" that we have been using for certain elements of the function signature. *These two uses of the word "parameter" have nothing to do with each other* -one is a computer science term, the other is a statistics term.

A simple illustration of this would be in the case of a numeric input variable X_1 and a numeric output Y with the model $Y = a X_1 + b$. The training data will determine the coefficients a and b. So, we can say that the coefficients contain the learned information. Once they have been obtained, the training data is no longer necessary to hold onto. The model can now be used on new data.

Thus, we can say that we are using the parameters learned in the training set to make predictions on the test set. Additionally, this will allow us to test the accuracy of the algorithm realistically by testing it on unseen data.

For the Naïve Bayes algorithm we implemented in the last chapter, the additional programming task now is that of building a structure to hold the learned parameters and then writing a function that can read that structure dynamically (at runtime).

8.1.1 Matrices to Hold the Learned Conditional Probabilities

The changes to our code in this chapter will primarily be in adding a structure to hold the parameters. These will be a bunch of matrices that store the conditional probabilities learned in the training of the model. We will create one matrix for each input variable. The rows of these matrices will be the levels of the class variable, and the columns will be the levels of the associated input variable. *The cells of the matrix will hold the conditional probabilities.*

Here is an example of one of the matrices that we may construct (Figure 8.1).

For example, for the nominal.weather dataframe, one matrix we will construct is for the input variable *humidity*. Recall that the *humidity* variable has only two levels: high and normal. Therefore, there will be two *columns* for this matrix, and the column names will be labeled "high" and "normal". There will be two rows for this matrix because the class variable, play, has just two levels "yes" and "no". The labels for the row names will therefore be "yes" and "no". The name of this matrix will be *cond_params_Humidity*.

We say the conditional probabilities are "learned" because they are created during training. The above matrix in Figure 8.1 contains entries for p(humidity=high|play=yes), p(humidity=high|play=no), p(humidity=normal|play=no), and p(humidity=normal|play=yes). How do we get these values? They are calculated based on the contents of the *training* data.

For our predictions on the test data, we retrieve the information in these newly created matrices.

We will also have to adjust the function that calculates the Naïve Bayes estimate of a class given a set of values for the input variable. Whereas the training and testing data were the same and we used conditional probability calculated from the full dataset to calculate the Naïve Bayes estimates before, now we will retrieve the conditional probabilities from the above-mentioned matrices.

	high ⬍	normal ⬍
no	0.8000000	0.2000000
yes	0.3333333	0.6666667

Figure 8.1 This matrix holds conditional probabilities in its entries. This would be constructed if the data were from the nominal.weather dataset. This matrix would be associated with the *humidity* variable in that dataset. For example, the first entry, 0.8000000, is p(humidity=high|play=no). The matrix would be named as cond_params_Humidity.

8.2 Building the Learned Model

As before, we will need functions for the following tasks.

1. A function to calculate the Naïve Bayes "probability" estimate of a class level given a set of values for the input arguments. In this chapter, this function will be named NaiveBayes_singleClassEllipsis().
2. A function to apply NaiveBayes_singleClassEllipsis() to each possible level of the class variable and select the one with the highest NaiveBayes_singleClassEllipsis() to be the estimated class for this set of inputs. This function will be named predNaiveBayes().
3. A function that can read these arrays. This function needs to accept inputs dynamically (during runtime) because the user will input a particular set of inputs and their values and which inputs and which values will not be known until that point (until the user calls the function).
4. We will adjust our probability function. The issue that motivates this is that in Naïve Bayes calculations, the numerator will be a product of probabilities. The adjustment will be *to add 1 to the numerator* of a probability calculation *if the numerator is equal to zero*. We want to avoid getting zero in the numerator. This is a choice we make; it is not part of the theory. It does not have to be done this way, but it is not an uncommon choice. If the numerator is zero, of course the probability for the corresponding class level will be zero. If several class levels give zero for their Naïve Bayes estimate, then our classifier may become less useful.

   The justification here, if there is one, is that we view the data from which we are constructing our algorithm as just a *sample* from the much larger set of all possible relevant data (referred to as the population in statistics). Thus, although we may not have found an instance to make a factor non-zero within our sample of data, if we collected a larger sample from the population, we may find one.

   One task you may want to try is changing this choice and allow zeros in the numerator and test both versions on various datasets to see which method leads to greater accuracy.

8.3 Matrices to Hold the Model Parameters

First, we build the structure to hold the model parameters, and then we construct a function to read parameters from that structure. The rest of the tasks in making the Naïve Bayes estimates are nearly the same as those in the previous chapter.

As mentioned, we construct one matrix for each input variable. For example, for the weather. nominal dataset, since the inputs are usually *outlook*, *humidity*, *windy*, and *temperature*, there would be four matrices created. We assign names like this to the matrices: cond_params_Outlook, cond_params_Humidity, cond_params_Windy, and cond_params_Temperature. Figure 8.1 shows how the cond_params_Humidity matrix may look.

The columns are the levels of the input variable (*humidity*) and the rows are the levels of the class variable (Play). The entries are the conditional probabilities. Recall that in Naïve Bayes, we need to do calculations like this: p(Humidity=high | Play=yes). In other words, the input variable comes *first*, and the class variables comes *second*. This is a bit counterintuitive, but we explained this in our initial discussion of Naïve Bayes in Chapter 4. Although we are trying to make classifications based on p(Play=yes|X), as a result of our use of Bayes theorem, the two events inside the parentheses switch places. Thus, the 0.800 in the first cell here is p(Humidity=high | Play=no), the 0.200 is p(Humidity=normal | Play=no), and so on.

8.4 Building the Matrices

In the following code, the dataframe will be referred to as either df or dfparam. If we are using the weather.nominal data, we would have a statement like this at the top of the code:

```
df=weather.nominal
```

As before, we also need an extra column called names which gives a unique identifier for each row.

```
df$names<-rownames(df)
```

The column names of the dataframe contain the vector of all the variables names. We will use the **colnames**() function to get these and then store them in a vector called "colname" like this:

```
colname <- colnames(df)
```

Next, we employ the well-known, convenient, and powerful function **lapply**(). Before using it in our code, it is worth taking a (long) digression here to discuss this function.

8.5 Digression on the apply() Functions

lapply() is part of a group of similar functions: lapply, mapply, sapply, vapply, tapply, and apply. The letter preceding *apply* may indicate whether the output of the function will be a list, matrix, or a vector. We discuss lapply and sapply below.

Here is an example of when **lapply**() may be useful. Suppose we want to convert every column of a dataframe to factors. How could we do that? We could write a loop: for each column x, do something like x= **as.factor**(x). **lapply**() can accomplish the same thing. The first argument for **lapply**() will be the object we want to change. In this example, it is the dataframe (not just a column but the entire set of columns). The second argument of **lapply**() will be a function that we want to apply to this dataframe. In this example, we want to apply the function **as.factor**(), and we want to apply it to each column separately. That is exactly what **lapply**() will do if we write df=**lapply**(df,as.factor).

Facts about **lapply**() are as follows:

1. lapply returns a list.
2. lapply returns a list of the same size as the first argument of lapply(). In our use of lapply(), the first argument will be df, which refers to our dataframe, and so we will get a list as the output. The list will be the same size as df. That means, in the case of a list or dataframe, the output will have the same number of elements as the number of elements of the input list and in our case the same number of columns as the input dataframe. On the other hand, if the input is a vector, then the same size would mean the number of elements in the vector. The function we are applying appears as the second argument of lapply.

3. The second argument of lapply() is is.factor(). Note that when a function is used as an argument in lapply, we don't include the brackets and so we don't write lapply(df, as.factor()) but rather lapply(df, as.factor).

4. The function that is applied is applied to each element. In our case, we will apply as.factor() to each element of df. What does that mean? Since df is essentially a list, as.factor() will be applied to each element of that list – meaning it will be applied to each column of our dataframe. It will convert each column to a factor.

5. Typically we can assure this is done when the dataframe is created, with the "as.factor" argument set to TRUE, but we are using lapply just to assure that everything is a factor.

6. Another example of using lapply() is as follows:

Define x as a list as follows:

```
x <- list(a = 1:10, y = exp(-3:3), z = c(TRUE,FALSE,FALSE,TRUE))
```

Compute the mean for each element of the list.

```
x <- list(a = 1:10, y = exp(-3:3), z = c(TRUE,FALSE,FALSE,TRUE))
lapply(x, mean)
## $a
## [1] 5.5
##
## $y
## [1] 4.535125
##
## $z
## [1] 0.5
```

8.5.1 Explanation

You can see that x starts out as a list with three elements. (You may be confused by y = exp(−3:3), but if you run it in R, you will see that y is just a vector of the values e^{-3}, e^{-2}, e^{-1}, e^0, e^1, e^2, and e^3, and so it is a vector of numbers). By using lapply(), we apply the mean() function to this list of three elements. This means we will apply mean() separately to each element of the list. Since x contains three elements (a, y, and z), we will attempt to calculate the mean of each of these. It seems peculiar to speak of the mean of the last element of our list, z. But remember that the mean() function treats an occurrence of TRUE as a 1 and an occurrence of a FALSE as a 0. Whether we like this or not, this is what the creators of the R language decided to do with the mean() function. Thus the mean of z is 2/4 = 0.5. The fact that we are using lapply, instead of one of the other apply functions, means that we obtain a *list* as the output. If a vector is preferred as the output, another of the functions in this group could be used.

8.5.2 lapply versus sapply

Let's look at the difference between using lapply(x,mean) and sapply(x,mean). The difference between these two will be in the form of the output. The sapply() function works like lapply(), but it tries to simplify the output to the most elementary data structure that is possible. So, whereas lapply(x,mean) returns a list, sapply(x,mean) will try to return the same values but as a vector. Oftentimes this is what you would want, and that is why sapply() was created. The "s" in sapply() stands for "simplify". Let's see both of these in action.

```
x <- list(a = 1:10, y = exp(-3:3), z = c(TRUE,FALSE,FALSE,TRUE))
lapply(x, mean)
## $a
## [1] 5.5
##
## $y
## [1] 4.535125
##
## $z
## [1] 0.5
sapply(x, mean)
##        a        y        z
## 5.500000 4.535125 0.500000
```

Another way to achieve the effect of returning a vector is to use the unlist() function together with lapply(). We will use this function in our code, and thus a brief introduction may be useful. We might say that unlist() tries to "tear down" the structure of the list. It will usually convert a list to a vector – often a named vector. Here is an example. Suppose we have this list:

```
x <- list(a = 1:3, y = exp(0:3))
#We see that it is a list.
x
## $a
## [1] 1 2 3
##
## $y
## [1]  1.000000  2.718282  7.389056 20.085537
```

But if we apply unlist() to it, it breaks up the list.

```
#Note that it is not just a vector but a named vector.
unlist(x)
##        a1        a2        a3        y1        y2        y3        y4
##  1.000000  2.000000  3.000000  1.000000  2.718282  7.389056 20.085537
```

How can we use unlist and lapply to achieve the effect of sapply? We see that the following both give the same result.

```
#Both give the same result
sapply(x, mean)
##        a        y
## 2.000000 7.798219
unlist(lapply(x,mean))
##        a        y
## 2.000000 7.798219
```

To put the above discussion into perspective, let us achieve the same results using loops. R aficionados try to avoid loops because functions like lapply and sapply() are considerably faster than loops[1]. We will create loops to achieve same results obtained for the two statements: lapply(x, mean) and sapply(x, mean).

---

[1] This is not generally true of the apply() function though.

```
#The following generates a list but without the element names.
count=0
l=list() #to get a list output

for(i in x){
  count=count+1
  l[count]=mean(i)
}
print(l)
## [[1]]
## [1] 2
##
## [[2]]
## [1] 7.798219
#To get the names as well,
count=0
l=list() #to get a list output

for(i in x){
  count=count+1

  l[count]=mean(i)
}
names(l)=names(x)
print(l) #a list output
## $a
## [1] 2
##
## $y
## [1] 7.798219
```

Now to get the same result as sapply(x,mean),

```
count=0
v=vector() #to get a list output

for(i in x){

  count=count+1

  v[count]=mean(i)

}
names(v)=names(x) #without this
#We would not have a named vector.
print(v) #a vector output
##        a         y
## 2.000000 7.798219
```

We will leave it to the reader to explore other variants in the apply() family of functions. Now, we exit our digression on the "apply" family of functions and return to the Naïve Bayes model.

We have our dataframe stored in the variable df. To assure that all columns are imported as factors (so that we can use the **levels**() function on them later), we use lapply() to apply the as.factor() function to the dataframe df.

```
df=data.frame(lapply(df, factor))
```

Next, we discuss an adjustment to the probability function that was mentioned earlier.

8.6 Avoiding Probabilities of Zero

In the Naïve Bayes algorithm, recall that the numerator is a term with many factors. Of course, if any of those factors were equal to zero, this would cause the numerator to be zero, and thus the entire calculation (numerator/denominator) would also be zero. Since there may be many factors in the numerator (as many as the number of input variables), this may result in P_{nb} equaling zero frequently. As discussed earlier this would be undesirable. Therefore, we will make the following adjustment.

Recall our probability function:

```
prob<-function( e,  s) {
  if (nrow(e)==0){
    return(nrow(e)/nrow(s))
  } else {
    return(nrow(e)/nrow(s))}
}
```

To prevent the numerator from equaling zero, we define an adjusted probability function as follows.

```
probAdj<-function( e,  s) {
  if (nrow(e)==0){
    return((nrow(e)+1)/nrow(s))
  } else {
  return(nrow(e)/nrow(s))}
}
```

Now use this adjusted probability function in the calculation of conditional probabilities. (Remember that df$names<−rownames(df) is required in order for intersect_event() to work).

```
conditional_prob_bool <- function(varPrior, varPriorLevel, varCondition,
varConditionLevel, df){
  #Sample call:
  ##conditional_prob_bool('Class', 'democrat', 'V1', 'y', HouseVotes84)
  df$names<-rownames(df)
  prior_bool <- df[,varPrior] == varPriorLevel
  prior_event <- df[prior_bool,]
  condition_bool <- df[,varCondition] == varConditionLevel
  condition_event=df[condition_bool,]

  return(probAdj(intersect_event(prior_event,condition_event,df),df)/
probAdj(condition_event,df))
  df=subset(df, select=-c(names))
}
```

8.7 Other Helper Functions

```
#We will make use of functions from two packages: mlbench and mice. We
will use the Arthritis data set from the vcd package. The Arthritis data
set investigates whether a new treatment for rheumatoid arthritis
improves the patient condition.
#install.packages("mlbench","mice")
library(mlbench)
library(mice)

#install.packages("vcd")
library(vcd)
data("Arthritis")
colnames(Arthritis)
[1] "ID"        "Treatment" "Sex"        "Age"        "Improved"
#In our analysis "Treatment" will be the class variable and we use Sex,
Age, and Improved as inputs.

intersect_event=function(a,b,df=df){
  return(df[intersect(a$names,b$names),])}

union_event=function(E,F){
  if(!is.data.frame(E)|!is.data.frame(F)){
    stop("arguments must be a dataframe")
  }
  return(unique(rbind(E,F)))}

multi_union_event=function(E,F,...){return(unique(rbind(E,F,...)))}

complement=function(a,df){
  df[!a,]
}

prob<-function( e,  s) {
  return(nrow(e)/nrow(s))}
probAdj<-function( e,  s) {
  if (nrow(e)==0){
    return(nrow(e)+1/nrow(s))
  } else {
    return(nrow(e)/nrow(s))}
}
```

8.8 Split Data into Training and Testing

Next, we split the dataset into two parts. Seventy percent of the dataset will be allocated to the training set and the rest to the test data. We will use R's sample() function to randomly assign which data goes to the training set and which to the testing set.

The following section of code occurs within the body of predNaiveBayes(), but we show it here. percentSplit is a parameter of predNaiveBayes(), but it is assigned a value here just to show as an example of what it could look like inside predNaiveBayes().

```
#Use Arthritis data for this example:
  percentSplit=0.7
  dfparam=Arthritis
  smp_size <- floor(percentSplit * nrow(dfparam))
  train_ind <- sample(seq_len(nrow(dfparam)), size = smp_size)
  train <- dfparam[train_ind, ]
  test <- dfparam[-train_ind, ]
  intersect_event<-function(a, b, df){

      return(df[intersect(a$names, b$names),])
  }
```

Quick review of arrays and matrices

Before moving onto the next section, let us review arrays and matrices in R.

```
#Show that an array is a matrix.
a2 <- array(1:8, dim=c(2,4))
a2
##      [,1] [,2] [,3] [,4]
## [1,]    1    3    5    7
## [2,]    2    4    6    8
is.matrix(a2)
## [1] TRUE
#Note that the second argument in array() is dim. It gives the dimensions
of the array. Our array above was 2x4.
#Note: the terminology 'dimensions' and 'dimensional' may be a bit
confusing. We say that the above array is 2-dimensional, but we also say
that the dimensions of this 2-dimensional array are 2 and 4.

#As an example of a 3-dimensional array try the following (of course we
cannot show a 3-dimensional object on a flat page and so we need some
other way to display it):

a3 <- array(1:12, dim=c(2,3,2))
a3
## , , 1
##
##      [,1] [,2] [,3]
## [1,]    1    3    5
## [2,]    2    4    6
##
## , , 2
##
##      [,1] [,2] [,3]
## [1,]    7    9   11
## [2,]    8   10   12
#a3 is a three-dimensional array. (That is, it is something like a cube.)
It has two 2x3 layers.

#Of course, a3 is not a matrix.
is.matrix(a3)
## [1] FALSE
#The number of entries in "dim" indicates the dimension of the array.
For a2, with dim=c(2,4), the number of entries is 2 and it was a
```

two-dimensional array (i.e., a matrix). For a3, with dim=c(2,3,2), the number of entries in dim is 3, and so it is a three-dimensional array (something like a cube). Note that we can get this information by checking length(dim).

```
#We next add in column names and row names. The array() function has a
parameter called dimnames for this purpose. It must be a list. Each
element of the list will handle one of the dimensions. The first element
of the list will give the row names; the second element of the list will
give the column names. If there were a third dimension (for example, as
there would be in a cube), the third element would give the names for the
layers. a2 is a matrix. We will add in row and column names for it with a
list which we call a2Dimnames.
a2Dimnames <- list(c("Hello","Goodbye"),c("morning","afternoon",
"evening","asleep"))

a2Dimnames
## [[1]]
## [1] "Hello"    "Goodbye"
##
## [[2]]
## [1] "morning"   "afternoon" "evening"   "asleep"
#Now we will redefine a2 this time including dimnames=a2Dimnames.
a2 <- array(1:8, dim=c(2,4), dimnames=a2Dimnames)

a2
##          morning afternoon evening asleep
## Hello          1         3       5      7
## Goodbye        2         4       6      8
```

Practice 8.8.1

 1. Create a list which will give names to the rows, columns, and layers of a3, and then use it to redefine a3.

End of quick review of arrays and matrices

8.9 Build Conditional Parameter Matrices

Although we *refer* to the parameter matrices as matrices, the **array**() function will be used to construct them. Remember that a matrix is a 2-dimensional array.

The number of rows and the number of columns of these matrices will equal

- the number of levels of the class variable
- the number of levels of the input variable

respectively.

For example, in Figure 8.1 for cond_params_Humidity, we saw that the dimensions were 2×2 because the class variable Play has two levels, and the *humidity* variable also has two levels.

Now we return to the Arthritis data set from the vcd package.

```
colnames(Arthritis)
[1] "ID"        "Treatment" "Sex"        "Age"        "Improved"
#In our analysis "Treatment" will be the class variable.
```

*#We create a vector to store the dimensions and call it dim1 and create a
list to store the dimension names and call it dimnames1. dimnames1 is
required to be a list since it will be the dimname argument in the
array() function.*

*#We use dfparam in the code to denote the dataframe. Since the
conditional probability parameter matrices are being built from the
training data, we assign "train" to dfparam.*

```
dfparam=train
dim1 <- vector()
dimnames1 <- list()
class <- c("Treatment")
colname <- colnames(dfparam)

colname
## [1] "ID"        "Treatment" "Sex"        "Age"        "Improved"
length(colname)
## [1] 5
```

*#colname will hold the set of input variables. We will not include Age as
an input variable since it is numeric and we will also remove ID.*

```
colname <- colname[!is.element(colname, c(class,"names","ID","Age"))] #H
```
*ere we assume that the only non-input variables in the dataset are "class"
and "names". Matrices will be constructed for all input variables.*

```
for (i in 1:length(colname)) { #Loop through all the input variables
and create a matrix of conditional probabilities for each.
    dim1 <- vector()
    dimnames1 <- list()

    dim1 <- length(levels(as.factor(dfparam[, class])))  #at this point,
dim1 is a vector with a single element which is the number of levels of
the class variable.
    dim1 <- append(dim1, length(levels(as.factor(dfparam[,
colname[i]]))))# dim1 now has two elements; the second element is the
number of levels of the ith input variable in colname.
```
*#dimnames1 will be used to store the column names and row names of the
matrices that hold the (conditional) probabilities. It is a list. The
first element of this list will be the levels of the class variable and
the row names of our matrix. The second element of dimnames1 will be the
levels of the input variable (specified by colname[i]) and will give the
column names for our matrix.*
```
    dimnames1[length(dimnames1) + 1] <- list(c(levels(as.factor(dfparam[,
class]))))
    dimnames1[length(dimnames1) + 1] <-list(c(levels(as.factor(dfparam[,
colname[i]]))))
```
*#Store the levels of the class variables and the levels of the input
variable in classnames and varnames, respectively.*
```
    classnames <- c(levels(as.factor(dfparam[, class])))
    varnames <- c(levels(as.factor(dfparam[, colname[i]])))
```

```
#Set up a temporary array which will be repopulated. For now, we just
fill it with 0s.

    x <- array(0, dim = c(dim1), dimnames = dimnames1)
```

Practice 8.9.2

1. What are the three parameters in the array() function above used for?

```
#Shortly, we will create a nested loop. Remember, however, that these are
embedded in the loop above.
#Continuing to use the example of the weather.nominal data as an example,
note that below we will be performing calculations like
#P(Outlook="Cloudy" |  class="yes").
#This may seem to be the reverse of what we want since ultimately we are
seeking conditional probabilities like
P(class="yes" | Outlook="Cloudy").  But remember that, as a result of
having used Bayes Theorem, such conditional probabilities are reversed.
#For example, suppose our conditional probability matrix is called x.
Continuing with the nominal weather data set, suppose that the classnames
are listed in the order "no" "yes", and varnames are listed in the order
"cool" "hot" "mild".  If we are in the first iteration of the nested
loops that fill in the entries of the matrix x, what should we find in
x[classnames[1], varnames[1]]?
That is, what would we find in our matrix x in the location
x["no","cool"]?
#We would want to fill this with p("cool"|"no") (not the reverse)!.
#Using the conditional probability function conditional_prob_bool(), we
would calculate
    #conditional_prob_bool(colname[i], varnames[k],class,classnames[j],df)
which, after the arguments are evaluated would be
    #conditional_prob_bool("temperature", "cool", class, "no", df)
#After the above explanation, we proceed to fill in each entry in our
matrix x. We loop through all the classnames and all the varnames.
    for (j in 1:length(classnames)) {
      for (k in 1:length(varnames)) {

        x[classnames[j],varnames[k]] <- conditional_prob_bool(colname[i],
                            varnames[k],class,classnames[j],dfparam)

      }

    }
        #Finally we need to assign a name like cond_params_Humidity to
the matrix x. We are creating the name dynamically  -  meaning inside the
loop and where the name depends on the index i. We construct the name
with the paste() function like this: paste('cond_params', colname[i], sep
= "_"). However, we need to assign that name to the current matrix, whose
name is currently x. You may like to try
#x <- paste('cond_params', colname[i], sep = "_")
but this will wrongly rewrite the value of x with something like cond_
params_Humidity. It will not change the name of x. To change the name of
x, we use a new function that we have not encountered before: assign().
```

The first parameter in assign() is the new name. The second parameter is the name of the object for which you want to change the name, which in our case is x.

```
  assign(paste('cond_params', colname[i], sep = "_"), x)

}

#End of section for creating conditional probability matrices
```

What do our conditional parameter matrices look like?

```
cond_params_Improved
##               None      Some      Marked
## Placebo 0.6333333 0.1666667 0.2000000
## Treated 0.2857143 0.1785714 0.5357143
cond_params_Sex
##               Female      Male
## Placebo 0.7000000 0.3000000
## Treated 0.8214286 0.1785714
```

Practice 8.9.3

1. Explain the interpretation of the number 0.1785714 in the matrix cond_params_Improved.
2. Are these matrices created with data from the training set or the testing set?
3. Why are we building these matrices, and when will they be used?

We need one more function. When performing the Naïve Bayes calculations, once we have the conditional parameter matrices, we need to be able to read the probabilities from them. In earlier chapters, when calculating the numerator and denominator, the conditional probability function conditional_prob_bool() was used. However in our test–train scheme, this is not appropriate since this would mean using the current data, the test data, for the conditional probabilities, whereas the conditional probabilities should come from the training set. The conditional probabilities are stored in the conditional parameter matrices, and so it is necessary to read these matrices. We construct a function prob_from_params() to do that.

Recall that our matrices are used for calculations of the RHS of P_{nb}, and they answer questions like "p(humidity=high|play=no)=?" That is, they answer questions like p(A|B), where A is an event derived from the input variable and B is an event derived from the class variable. The args variable in **NaiveBayes _ singleClassEllipsis**() will hold the input variable name and value. Our new prob_from_params() will be called like this.

```
prob_from_params(names(args)[i],args[[i]],className,classValue)
```

Here is the definition.

```
prob_from_params <- function(inputVarName, inputVarLevel, className,
classLevel){

  #condMatrix will hold the name of the matrix. For example, it could
hold the name cond_params_Humidity.
  condMatrix=paste("cond_params",inputVarName,sep="_")
```

```
#We want to read the contents of the matrix. For example, if the matrix
is cond_params_Humidity, we may want cond_params_Humidity[No,High]. We
will use eval(parse()) for this.
return(eval(parse(text=paste(condMatrix,'[classLevel,inputVarLevel]',
sep = ""))))
}
```

Now we have all the necessary elements to run the new versions of predNaiveBayes() and
NaiveBayes_singleClassEllipsis(). The matrix-building code will be placed in predNaiveBayes(),
and the prob_from_params() function that reads the contents of the matrices will be placed in
NaiveBayes_singleClassEllipsis() where we need to compute the numerator and denominator with
conditional probabilities.

```
#install.packages("mlbench","mice","mlbench","vcd")
library(mice)
library(vcd)
#library(mlbench)
data("Arthritis")
#data("HouseVotes84")
imputeddf=mice(Arthritis,m=1,maxit=50,meth='pmm',seed=500)
## Long output is not shown here.

completedData <- complete(imputeddf,1)
df=completedData
df$names<-rownames(df)#Including this is very easy to forget. Without
this, intersect_event() will not work.
predNaiveBayes=function(class="Class",dfparam=df, percentTrain=0.7, ...){
  #Sample call:
  #predNaiveBayes("Treatment",Arthritis, Sex='Female',Improved='Some')

  #Split the data into training and testing sets.
  set.seed(123)
  smp_size <- floor(percentTrain * nrow(df))
  train_ind <- sample(seq_len(nrow(df)), size = smp_size)
  train <- df[train_ind, ]
  test <- df[-train_ind, ]

  #First we train. We will build the conditional parameter matrices on
the training set.
  df=train
  dim1 <- list()
  dimnames1 <- list()
  colname <- colnames(df)
  colname <- colname[!is.element(colname, c(class,"names"))]#This assumes
that the only non-input variables in the dataset are "class" and "names".
Matrices will be constructed for all other variables.
#We are going to loop through all the input variables. In each iteration,
we will create a dim1 variable to hold the dimensions for that input
variable and dimnames1 for the names of the levels for that input
variable. Once we have dim1 and dimnames1 for this variable, we will
construct the conditional parameter matrix for this input variable.
Then we iterate to the next input variable until we have built all the
conditional parameter matrices.
```

```r
  for (i in 1:length(colname)) {
    dim1 <- list() #This is being reset to empty within the loop.
    dimnames1 <- list() #This is being reset to empty within the loop.
    dim1 <- length(levels(as.factor(df[, class])))  #dim1 is a vector
with the single element 2.
    dim1 <- append(dim1, length(levels(as.factor(df[, colname[i]]))))#
dim1 now has two elements: 2 and 3.
    dimnames1[length(dimnames1) + 1] <- list(c(levels(as.factor(df[,
class]))))
    dimnames1[length(dimnames1) + 1] <-
      list(c(levels(as.factor(df[, colname[i]]))))
    classnames <- c(levels(as.factor(df[, class])))
    varnames <- c(levels(as.factor(df[, colname[i]])))

#Build the conditional probability matrices.

    x <- array(0,dim = c(dim1),dimnames = dimnames1)
    for (j in 1:length(classnames)) {
      for (k in 1:length(varnames)) {

        x[classnames[j],varnames[k]] <- conditional_prob_bool(colname[i],
                                 varnames[k],class,classnames[j],df)

      }

    }
    assign(paste('cond_params', colname[i], sep = "_"), x, pos =
".GlobalEnv")

  }

#End of section for creating conditional probability matrices

  #Now we switch from the training data to the testing data.
  dfparam=test

  forecast=list()
  argsPred=list(...)

  #Remember we cannot use $ sign construction like this:
  #lev=levels(dfparam$class)
  #So instead we access the column with the following alternative.
  #Instead of dfparam[,class], you can also use dfparam[[class]].
  lev=levels(dfparam[,class])  #lev will contain all the levels of the
class variable.


  classprob=0
  predictedclass=lev[1]
  for(i in lev){
    #Recall the sample call.
    #NaiveBayes_singleClassEllipsis("Treatment","Treated",Arthritis,
Sex='Male',Improved='Marked')

    p=NaiveBayes_singleClassEllipsis(class,i,dfparam,...)
```

```
    if(classprob<p){
      classprob=p
      predictedclass=i
      forecast[["Instance"]]=argsPred
      forecast[["predicted class"]]=predictedclass
      forecast[["probability of predicted class (if independence
assumption is true)"]]=classprob

    }


  }

  return(forecast)
  #sample call
  #predNaiveBayes("Treatment",Arthritis, Sex='Female',Improved='Some')
}

NaiveBayes_singleClassEllipsis=function(className="Class",classValue="dem
ocrat",dfparam=df, ...){
  #Sample call:
  #NaiveBayes_singleClassEllipsis("Treatment","Treated",Arthritis,
Sex='Male',Improved='Marked')

  #className is the name of the attribute you want to classify.
  #classValue is the particular level of the class variable you want to
calculate the probability of.
  #Remember that this function needs to be put into a loop which is done
in predCompleteBayes().
  dfparam=as.data.frame(dfparam)
  dfparam$names<-rownames(dfparam)
  args<-list(...)
  count <- length(args)
  class_bool=dfparam[,className]==classValue
  classE=dfparam[class_bool,]
  numerator=probAdj(classE,dfparam)
  for(i in 1:count){
    #We use the prob_from_params() function instead of
conditional_prob_bool()

    numerator=numerator*prob_from_params(names(args)[i],args[[i]],class
Name,classValue)
  }
  denominator=0
  classLevels=levels(dfparam[,className])
  countOfClassLevels=length(classLevels)

  for(j in 1:countOfClassLevels){
    class_bool=dfparam[,className]==classLevels[j]
    classE=dfparam[class_bool,]
    denominatorFactor=prob(classE,dfparam)
    for(i in 1:count){
      denominatorFactor=denominatorFactor*prob_from_params(names(args)
[i],args[[i]],className,classValue)
```

```
    }
    denominator=denominator+denominatorFactor
  }
  return(numerator/denominator)
}


predNaiveBayes("Treatment",Arthritis, Sex='Female',Improved='Some')
## $Instance
## $Instance$Sex
## [1] "Female"
##
## $Instance$Improved
## [1] "Some"
##
##
## $`predicted class`
## [1] "Treated"
##
## $`probability of predicted class (if independence assumption is true)`
## [1] 0.5384615


predNaiveBayes("Treatment",Arthritis, Sex='Male',Improved='Some')

## $Instance
## $Instance$Sex
## [1] "Male"
##
## $Instance$Improved
## [1] "Some"
##
##
## $`predicted class`
## [1] "Treated"
##
## $`probability of predicted class (if independence assumption is true)`
## [1] 0.6153846
```

Practice 8.9.4

1. Why don't the two predictions above for predNaiveBayes("Treatment",Arthritis,Sex= 'Female',Improved='Some') and predNaiveBayes("Treatment",Arthritis,Sex=Male, Improved='Some') add up to 1.0?
2. Why do we use "probability" in quotes when talking about the Naïve Bayes classifier estimate? Why not say the Naïve Bayes estimates the probability of a level of the class variable given the set of inputs?
3. Write a loop that accomplishes the same thing as lapply(x,mean) where x is x <- list(a = 1:10, y = exp(-3:3), and z = c(TRUE,FALSE,FALSE,TRUE)).
4. Challenge. Can you bring the splitting of the data into train and test sets outside of the definition of predNaiveBayes()? You may consider changing the function signature to something like predNaiveBayes=function(class="Class",dfparam="train",testParam="test", ...) and then changing the line that says: `dfparam=test` to `dfparam=testParam`.
5. Challenge: In order to run the model on the *test* data, we must generate the p_array matrices and have them available. Can you rewrite the code so that the "model" is stored on disk and

then can be imported later without having to generate them anew? This will require some ingenuity on your part.

6. Try changing the algorithm by replacing "probAdj" with "prob" wherever it occurs. Try both ways on various datasets – first building a model on the training set and then testing it on the test set. Which version of the algorithm performs better? You may want to consider your own additional tweaks of this Naïve Bayes code to obtain improved performance.

7. Challenge. Add code to predNaiveBayes() that will output the accuracy (=number of correctly classified instances/total number of instances in test data set).

8. Challenge. Add code to predNaiveBayes() that will output the confusion matrix (based on its performance on the test data).

Chapter 9

Review of Mathematics for Neural Networks

9.1 Mathematical Review of Vectors

We start out with vectors. A vector for our purposes is a string of values. For instance, we can have a string of 5 values like this (9,2,6,4,8). It can also be a string of variables, like (x,y,z) or (m,p,r). We say that the first vector is five dimensional. We say the last two vectors are three dimensional. Different books use different notations. Sometimes you will see <m,r,p>, for example. Here we will sometimes use (x,y,z) and sometimes use [x,y,z]. Do not be confused, and consider the second of these as an R list. Often, names are assigned to vectors names using either a capital bold letter, for example, $\mathbf{X}$, or a letter with an arrow above it, for example, $\vec{X}$. When writing on a whiteboard, it is difficult to make something bold, and so the arrow notation is more convenient. Here we will use the bold capital letter notation. So we may write $\mathbf{X} = $ [m,r,p]. Regardless of whether we are referring to a vector of variables, e.g., $\mathbf{X} = $ [m,r,p], or a vector of values, e.g., $\mathbf{X} = $ [1200, 6, 2], we will refer to the m, r, and p or the 1200, 6, and 2 as the elements of the vector. We would say that m or 1200 is the first element of the vector, r or 6 is the second element, and so on.

Recall that in earlier chapters, we used notation like this: s = f($\mathbf{X}$), instead of s = f(m, r, p). We will also say that X is a three-dimensional vector.

Usually the elements of our vectors will be from the set of real numbers. The set of real numbers is denoted by $\mathbf{R}$. In this text, we won't need to consider vectors whose elements are from the set of imaginary numbers, but the set of imaginary numbers is denoted by $\mathbb{C}$. If our vectors consist of two elements, each from the set of real numbers, we say the vector is in $\mathbf{R}^2$ (which is read as R two). If there are three elements, each of which is a real number, we say the vector is in $\mathbf{R}^3$. If there are n elements, each of which is a real number, we say the vector is in $\mathbf{R}^n$. The symbol for "is an element of" is $\in$. So if $\mathbf{X} = $ [1200, 6, 2], then we can write $\mathbf{X} \in \mathbf{R}^3$.

9.2 Another Perspective on R²

Recall the meaning of the term *ordered pair* in mathematics. (3,8) is referred to as an ordered pair since it is clearly a pair and it is ordered in the sense that we distinguish it from (8,3). For an ordered pair, the order in which the elements are expressed matters. We say that 3 is the first element of the ordered pair (3,8) and 8 is the second element. Now, take two sets $A = \{2,9,4\}$ and $B = \{q,r\}$. Let us think of something new. Let us consider the set of ordered pairs where the first element of each ordered pair comes from A and the second element of each ordered pair comes from B. For example, (9,q) is such an ordered pair and so is (2,r). The entire set of all such ordered pairs is denoted as A x B and is read as A "cross" B. Thus,

$$A \times B = \{(2,q),(2,r),(9,q),(9,r),(4,q),(4,r)\} \tag{9.1}$$

In set builder notation, this is $A \times B = \{(x,y) \mid x \in A \text{ and } y \in B\}$ where the vertical bar | is read as "such that" and $\in$ is read as "is an element of". This is called the cross product of A and B or the Cartesian cross product of A and B. We can extend this idea to a cross product of *three* sets. That is, if we have a third set $C = \{w,p\}$, then we can speak of the cross product of all three: $A \times B \times C$. In that case, we are talking about ordered triples, for example, one element of this cross product would be (4,q,w). In fact, we can extend this idea to any finite number of sets.

With the definition of cross product in mind, what is the meaning of $\mathbf{R} \times \mathbf{R}$? It is

$$\{(x,y) \mid x \in \mathbf{R} \text{ and } y \in \mathbf{R}\}$$

This is the set of all possible ordered pairs where each element is a real number. We denote $\mathbf{R} \times \mathbf{R}$ as $\mathbf{R}^2$. Note that there is a one-to-one correspondence between $\mathbf{R} \times \mathbf{R}$ and the xy-plane. One-to-one correspondence here means that for each element in $\mathbf{R} \times \mathbf{R}$, there is a point in the plane, and for each point in the plane, there is an element of $\mathbf{R} \times \mathbf{R}$. Thus, because of this one-to-one correspondence, we often equate the xy-plane with $\mathbf{R}^2$. Next, we can ask about $\mathbf{R} \times \mathbf{R} \times \mathbf{R}$. There we have ordered triples like (3,5,1). There is a one-to-one correspondence between this set of ordered tirples and the points in three-dimensional space (xyz-space). This set of ordered triples is referred to as $\mathbf{R}^3$. We can also consider $\mathbf{R}^4$, although there is no physical space with which to make a one-to-one correspondence. In fact, we can do this for any number n. $\mathbf{R}^n$ is the cross product of $\mathbf{R}$ with itself n times. We refer to these as ordered n-tuples. We easily make a correspondence between the notation for an ordered n-tuple and vector of dimension n. That is, without much confusion, we can associate the notation (3,5,1) with the notation for a vector [3,5,1].

Practice 9.2.1

1. What is the cross product of {2,3,4} and {a,b}?
2. What is the cross product of {2,3,4}, {a,b}, and {u,v}?
3. There is a cross product function in the base installation[1] of R called crossprod(). Try it on question 1 above and show the results.

---

[1] *Base* installation means the set of packages and functions that are installed when you download and install R as opposed to functions and packages that you can install with install.packages().

9.3 Vectors as Arrows

There is another way to think of vectors, and that is to view vectors as arrows in the plane or possibly in three-dimensional space (Figure 9.1).

We will not use this often, but it is worthwhile reviewing it. If we have a two-dimensional vector [1,3], we can think of it as a point in the plane. (The plane can be referred to as $\mathbf{R}^2$.) That is, we can think of it as the point (1,3). Then we can draw an arrow originating at the origin (0,0) and extending to that point. Often, we say that this arrow is the vector [1,3]. We can do something similar when we have a three-dimensional vector, say [2,3,1] in three-dimensional space (also referred to as $\mathbf{R}^3$). We can draw an arrow from the origin to the point (2,3,1) and call this arrow the vector (Figure 9.2).

Once we switch from thinking of a vector as an ordered pair or ordered triple to thinking of it as an arrow, we can say that a vector is an object that has both a magnitude and a direction. For example, the vector [1,3] located in $\mathbf{R}^2$, by the Pythagorean theorem, has a length of

$$\sqrt{(1-0)^2 + (3-0)^2} = \sqrt{10}$$

It also has an angle θ, where $\tan\theta = \dfrac{3}{1} = 3$, which, according to Google, gives $\theta = 1.24904577$ rad or about 71 degrees. Similarly, any vector in either $\mathbf{R}^2$ or $\mathbf{R}^3$ can be uniquely located by its magnitude and its angle just as surely as by its coordinates. Thus, it is alternatively said that a vector is an object with direction and magnitude.

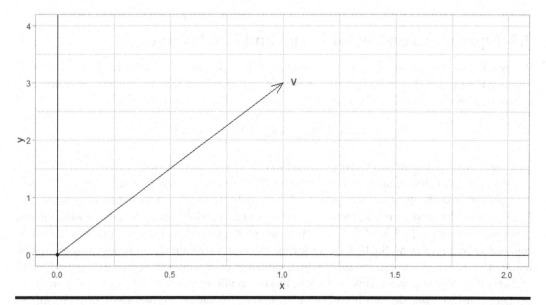

Figure 9.1   Vector v pictured as an arrow in the plane. This vector is associated with the ordered pair (1,3).

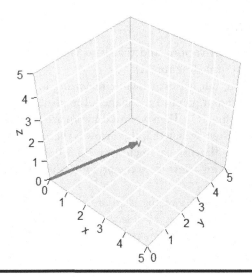

Figure 9.2 **(2,3,1) visualized as an arrow in 3D.**

9.4 Dimension

The concept of dimension originates in the three dimensions of physical space that we live in but as we have said, we may be interested in functions of 10, 100, 1000 or more variables, and so we want to allow for **X** to have many elements. For example, if **X** has 10 components, we will say that **X** is a 10-dimensional vector.

9.5 Operations on Vectors: Sum and Dot Product

We now define the notion of addition and subtraction of vectors. For example, for the two vectors [2,3,1] and [3,2,7], define the sum as what is obtained when the first elements are added, the second elements are added, and the third elements are added. In this case, we get

$$[2,3,1]+[3,2,7]=[2+3,3+2,1+7]=[5,5,8]$$

Take note that the sum of two vectors, defined in this way, is also a vector.

Next, we will define another operation. It is called dot product, and in some ways, it is a product although it probably is not what we would naturally think of as the product of two vectors. If asked what the product of the vectors [1,2,3] and [0,2,7] should be, many people would guess that what is meant is $\left[2*3,3*2,1*7\right]$. In other words, to get the product, multiply elements component by component. Such an operation exists, but it turns out that it is not that commonly required. It is called the Hadamard product, probably after someone named Hadamard, who probably had some reason to define and use it. But this is not what is referred to as the dot product.

Let's consider a practical business example. Suppose we have three factories that make shirts. Suppose **n** = [2,3,1] represents the number (in hundreds) of shirts produced per day at the three factories. Suppose **c** = [3,2,7] represents the cost (in dollars) of producing a single shirt at each of these three factories. For example, by examing c, we see that for some reason, the cost of producing a shirt is relatively high at factory number 3. We may like to know the *total* cost per day in our *three* factories. Doing the "natural" product that was suggested above would give us the *vector* $[2 \times 3, 3 \times 2, 1 \times 7] = [6,6,7]$ which does not seem to be what we were looking for. We wanted the total cost over all the factories. That is a number, but what we just arrived at above was a vector, and so it clearly is not exactly what we are seeking. A better answer is obtained by saying that factory #1 makes 200 shirts per day and the cost is $3 per shirt. The contribution to the overall cost via factory #1 is $200 \times \$3$ or $600 per day. For factory #2, there are 300 shirts produced per day, and the cost per shirt is $2, so that gives a cost of $600 per day. Finally, in factory #3, we have 100 shirts per day and $7 per shirt for a cost of $700 per day. Summing these up, we get $600 + $600 + $700 = $1900. Thus, we are not really interested in a vector [6,6,7] but rather interested in a number, the number $1900. This sequence of multiplications and sums turns out to be useful in a wide variety of problems (not just manufacturing shirts), and thus it will be beneficial for us to define an operation that generates this answer. The new operation will take two vectors **n** and **c** and return a *number* as their "product". This product is called the dot product. (It is also called the inner product, but the inner product is a more general concept.) The notation for this dot product of n and c is **n** · **c**. Using the dot notation, we can see the calculation as

$$[2,3,1] \cdot [3,2,7] = (2 * 3) + (3 * 2) + (1 * 7) = 6 + 6 + 7 = 19(\text{hundred})$$

In R, we can use any of the following.

```
A=c(2,3,1)
B=c(3,2,7)
A%*%B #Note that this gives a matrix as the result, but the numeric value
is correct.
##      [,1]
## [1,]   19
A*B #This results in the element by element multiplication, but the
result is a vector not a number.
## [1] 6 6 7
sum(A*B) #Note that this gives a vector as the result. As we have seen
before, a vector with just one numeric element is the closest we can come
in R to a scalar.
## [1] 19
#Another option is to use the R package pracma to perform a dot product.
install.packages("pracma")
library(pracma)
dot(A,B) #Note this gives a vector.
## [1] 19
```

The general definition of the dot product of two vectors $\mathbf{a} \in \mathbf{R}^n$ and $\mathbf{b} \in \mathbf{R}^n$ where $\mathbf{a} = [a_1, a_2, ..., a_n]$ and $\mathbf{b} = [b_1, b_2, ..., b_n]$ is

$$\mathbf{a} \cdot \mathbf{b} = a_1 b_1 + a_2 b_2 + \cdots + a_n b_n = \sum_{i=1}^{n} a_i b_i \tag{9.2}$$

Practice 9.5.2

1. Find the dot product of $[2,1,1] \cdot [1,2,7]$ by hand and then with each of the R methods shown above.

9.6 Matrices

We saw matrices in the previous chapter. Let us review by saying that a matrix is a rectangular array of numbers or other elements. For example, here are five matrices A, B, C, D, and E.

$$A = \begin{bmatrix} 1 & 2 & 4 \\ 4 & 2 & 2 \\ 7 & 3 & 3 \end{bmatrix} \quad B = \begin{bmatrix} 2 & -5 & 3 \end{bmatrix} \quad C = \begin{bmatrix} 5 \\ 4 \end{bmatrix} \quad D = \begin{bmatrix} 6 & 1 & 5 \\ 2 & 2 & 1 \end{bmatrix} \quad E = \begin{bmatrix} x & z \\ y & w \end{bmatrix}$$

(9.3)

We count the number of rows in a matrix and the number of columns, and so we will say A has three rows and three columns, and we also use the term "dimension" of the matrix and say that A has dimension 3×3, B has dimension 1×3, C has dimension 2×1, and D has dimension 2×3. Matrix B is referred to as a row matrix, and matrix C is referred to as a column matrix. The following matrix would have dimension m × n.

$$E = \begin{bmatrix} a_{11} & a_{12} & \cdots & a_{1n} \\ a_{21} & a_{22} & \cdots & a_{2n} \\ \vdots & \vdots & \ddots & \vdots \\ a_{m1} & a_{m2} & \cdots & a_{mn} \end{bmatrix}$$

Sometimes we may denote matrix E with either of the following notations.

$$\left(e_{i,j} \right)$$

$$\{E\}_{i,j}$$

9.7 Matrix as a Vector of Vectors

It may be convenient to think of a matrix as a vector of vectors. The following shows A expressed as n column vectors with each vector having m elements. We can say that A is a row vector but its elements are themselves vectors (column vectors).

$$A = \begin{bmatrix} \begin{bmatrix} a_{11} \\ a_{21} \\ \vdots \\ a_{m1} \end{bmatrix} & \begin{bmatrix} a_{12} \\ a_{22} \\ \vdots \\ a_{m2} \end{bmatrix} & \cdots & \begin{bmatrix} a_{1n} \\ a_{2n} \\ \vdots \\ a_{mn} \end{bmatrix} \end{bmatrix}$$

Alternatively, we could just as easily express A as a vector of row vectors.

9.8 Matrix Addition

Matrix addition is defined as element-by-element addition. Thus, if D and G are defined as

$$D = \begin{bmatrix} 6 & 1 & 5 \\ 2 & 2 & 1 \end{bmatrix} \quad G = \begin{bmatrix} 1 & 0 & 1 \\ 0 & 2 & 2 \end{bmatrix}$$

then the sum of D and G is

$$D + G = \begin{bmatrix} 6+1 & 1+0 & 5+1 \\ 2+0 & 2+2 & 1+2 \end{bmatrix} = \begin{bmatrix} 7 & 1 & 6 \\ 2 & 4 & 3 \end{bmatrix}$$

Note that D and G must have the *same dimensions* in order for this addition to be defined. Here both D and G have dimensions 2×3. Sometimes we may write $\dim(D) = 2 \times 3$, but remember that in R, $\dim(D)$ will give a vector: (2,3).

Practice 9.8.3

1. Find the sum of D and G above using R. Matrix addition in R is obtained by using the plus operator: D + G.

9.9 Matrix Multiplication

Next, we define matrix multiplication, denoted as AB. It is somewhat non-intuitive. We provide some motivation for this unexpected definition of matrix multiplication after discussing its definition.

First, note that matrix multiplication between two matrices A and B is only allowed when the number of columns of A is the same as the number of rows of B. So, if, for example, A is a 5×4 matrix and we want to consider AB with some other matrix B, then B must have four rows. That is, B must have dimension $4 \times p$. (p can be anything, but B must have four rows in order for this so-called matrix multiplication to be allowed.) Next, we ask, what will be the *dimensions of the product* of A and B; that is, what are the dimensions of AB? In the above example, the dimension of AB will be $5 \times p$.

In general, let A be an **m × n** matrix, and let B be the **n × p** matrix. The *matrix product* AB will be an m × p matrix, and therefore it will have m × p entries. Let us denote the result of the product of A and B, by the matrix C. That is

$$AB = C$$

C will therefore have m rows and p columns. The m will come from the number of rows of A, and the p will come from the number of columns of B. Next, we need to say what each of the elements in C will be. Let us denote the entries of C with the notation $c_{i,j}$. That is, $c_{i,j}$ is the entry in the ith row and jth column of C. The $c_{i,j}$ entry is calculated as the *dot product* of the ith row of A and the jth column of B. Wow, that sounds complicated. It is a bit complicated. To get just a single entry $c_{i,j}$ of C, we need to do a dot product! That means we are going to have to do a lot of dot products.

Do these dot products even make sense? In order to do a dot product between two vectors, they both have to have the same number of elements. Well, notice that both the ith row of A and the jth column of B each have n entries, and so it is ok to consider their dot product.

$$
\begin{bmatrix}
a_{11} & a_{12} & \cdots & a_{1n} \\
\vdots & & & \vdots \\
[a_{i1} & a_{i2} & \cdots & a_{in}] \\
\vdots & & & \vdots \\
a_{m1} & a_{m2} & \cdots & a_{mn}
\end{bmatrix}
\begin{bmatrix}
b_{11} & \cdots & \mathbf{b_{1j}} & \cdots & b_{1p} \\
b_{21} & & \mathbf{b_{2j}} & & b_{2p} \\
\vdots & & \vdots & & \vdots \\
b_{n1} & \cdots & \mathbf{b_{nj}} & \cdots & b_{np}
\end{bmatrix}
$$

Notice that in the above matrices, the ith row of the first matrix and the jth column of the second matrix are shown in bold face font and highlighted with their own pair of square brackets.

Thus the i,jth entry of the product of A and B, being the dot product of the two highlighted vectors, will be calculated as

$$
c_{ij} = a_{i1}b_{1j} + a_{i2}b_{2j} + \cdots + a_{in}b_{nj} = \sum_{k=1}^{n} a_{ik}b_{kj}. \tag{9.4}
$$

Practice 9.9.4

1. Which of the two matrix multiplications below are possible for the previously defined matrices A and B from (9.3)? If the operation is defined, what is the product? If the product is defined, show the calculation of the first and second elements of the resulting matrix by hand.
   a. AB
   b. BA

9.10 Matrix Multiplication in R

```
A <- matrix(1:9, nrow = 3)
A
##      [,1] [,2] [,3]
## [1,]    1    4    7
## [2,]    2    5    8
## [3,]    3    6    9
B <- matrix(1:3, nrow = 1)
B
##      [,1] [,2] [,3]
## [1,]    1    2    3
A%*%B
Error in A %*% B : non-conformable arguments
#The above error arises from the fact that A is 3 × 3 and B is 1 × 3.
We explained that for matrix multiplication of any two matrices A and B,
the number of columns of A must equal the number of rows of B. This is
not the case for the two matrices A and B defined above.

B%*%A
##      [,1] [,2] [,3]
## [1,]   14   32   50
```

Practice 9.10.5

1. Find the product of m1 = matrix(1:24,3,8) and m2 = matrix(1,8,2).
2. What are the entries of m2?
3. If a n × p matrix m is multiplied by a p × r matrix q, where all the elements of q are 1s, is the result of mq = m?
4. If m1 and m2 are defined with the array function (you have to adjust some of the arguments), does m1%*%m2 still work and give the same result?
5. If m3 = matrix(1:4,2,2) and m4 = matrix(4:7,2,2), are both m3 × m4 and m4 × m3 defined?
6. With m3 and m4 defined above, find m3 × m4 and m4 × m3 if possible. Are they equal? Is matrix multiplication commutative (meaning does the order of the operands matter – does it matter which one is on the right and which is on the left)?

9.11 Transpose of a Matrix

One simple operation on matrices is the **transpose**. The transpose of an m × n matrix A is the n × m matrix, and it is denoted by A^T.

A^T is obtained by writing the rows of A as columns. For example, if

$$A = \begin{bmatrix} 1 & 2 & 3 \\ 4 & 5 & 6 \end{bmatrix}, \text{then } A^T = \begin{bmatrix} 1 & 4 \\ 2 & 5 \\ 3 & 6 \end{bmatrix}$$

More abstractly, the ijth entry of A^T is a_{ji}, the jith entry of A. For example, $\{A\}_{2,3} = 6$ and $\{A^T\}_{3,2} = 6$ as well.

The transpose operation turns row vectors into column vectors and vice versa. We also have the following results (both of which are not difficult to prove mathematically):

$$\left(A^T\right)^T = A \tag{9.5}$$

If A is m × n and B is n × p, then

$$(AB)^T = B^T A^T \tag{9.6}$$

```
A <- matrix(1:9, nrow = 3)
A
##      [,1] [,2] [,3]
## [1,]    1    4    7
## [2,]    2    5    8
## [3,]    3    6    9
t(A) #transpose of A
##      [,1] [,2] [,3]
## [1,]    1    2    3
## [2,]    4    5    6
## [3,]    7    8    9
B <- matrix(1:3, nrow = 1)
```

```
B
##       [,1] [,2] [,3]
## [1,]    1    2    3
t(B) #transpose of B
##       [,1]
## [1,]    1
## [2,]    2
## [3,]    3
```

Practice 9.11.6

1. For the matrices $D = \begin{bmatrix} 6 & 1 & 5 \\ 2 & 2 & 1 \end{bmatrix}$ and $G = \begin{bmatrix} 1 & 0 & 1 \\ 0 & 2 & 2 \end{bmatrix}$, do the following:

   a. Find D^T.
   b. Find the dot product of the first row of D^T with the first column of G.
   c. Find the dot product of the second row of D^T with the second column of G.
   d. Find the dot product of the third row of D^T with the third column of G.

2. Using R, show that Equation (9.6) is true for A and B given above.

3. Optional challenge: Try to prove Equation (9.6) or look up its proof.

The transpose will largely operate as a notational convenience for us. For example, consider $\mathbf{a}, \mathbf{b} \in \mathbf{R}^n$ to be *column vectors*.

$$\mathbf{a} = \begin{bmatrix} a_1 \\ a_2 \\ \vdots \\ a_n \end{bmatrix} \quad \mathbf{b} = \begin{bmatrix} b_1 \\ b_2 \\ \vdots \\ b_n \end{bmatrix}$$

Then the dot product $\mathbf{a} \cdot \mathbf{b}$ is

$$\mathbf{a} \cdot \mathbf{b} = a_1 b_1 + a_2 b_2 + \cdots + a_n b_n. \tag{9.7}$$

However, we can write an equivalent expression but *in matrix form* if we define
A as an $n \times 1$ *matrix*
and
B as an $n \times 1$ *matrix*.
(It is unfortunate and a little confusing that we are using the same square brackets to denote vectors and matrices in this example)

$$A = \begin{bmatrix} a_1 \\ a_2 \\ \vdots \\ a_n \end{bmatrix} \quad \text{and} \quad B = \begin{bmatrix} b_1 \\ b_2 \\ \vdots \\ b_n \end{bmatrix}$$

Note that, A^T is $1 \times n$.

$$A^T = \begin{bmatrix} a_1 & a_2 & \cdots & a_n \end{bmatrix}$$

And so, if we calculate $A^T B$, we get

$$A^T B = \begin{bmatrix} a_1 & a_2 & \cdots & a_n \end{bmatrix} \begin{bmatrix} b_1 \\ b_2 \\ \vdots \\ b_n \end{bmatrix} = \begin{bmatrix} a_1 b_1 + a_2 b_2 + \cdots + a_n b_n \end{bmatrix} \tag{9.8}$$

The above *matrix* multiplication results in a 1×1 matrix which contains the same value as would the result of the dot product of the *vectors* **a** and **b**. Take note that in most math texts, vectors are assumed to be column vectors. If that is the case, then AB does not make sense, and we need A^T to multiply to the left of B like this: $A^T B$. However, some texts may just write AB. This can be confusing. Technically, if vectors are assumed to be columns, then we need the transpose.

All we have shown here is that we can take two column vectors, *view them as matrices*, and by using the transpose of one of them, use matrix multiplication to obtain the same result as the dot product of the vectors. There will be times when we want to deal with matrices instead of vectors, and this shows how we can accomplish that, and it shows the relationship between dot product and matrix multiplication.

Practice 9.11.7

1. In R, show that $(BA)^T = A^T B^T$ for A and B defined as

```
A <- matrix(1:9, nrow = 3)
B <- matrix(1:3, nrow = 1)
```

2. In R, show that AB is not the same as BA. What do you get when you try AB?

Note: In the following discussion, we will sometimes consider a 1×1 matrix to be equivalent to a scalar. Also, vectors are generally written with commas between components but matrices are not.

9.12 Functions of a Single Input Variable

When we first learn about functions, we learn about a single-valued function of a single variable. What does that mean? Take, for example, the following function:

$$y = f(x) = 3x^2$$

We say that the input variable is x and the output variable is y. Other terminologies that may also be used are: x is the independent variable and y is the dependent variable. However, in this text, we will usually use the words "input" and "output". So, for this example, x is the only input, and y is the only output. If our variables are both elements of the set of real numbers and if our function is called f, we would express the fact that there is one (real number) input and one (real number) output by writing

$$f : \mathbf{R} \rightarrow \mathbf{R}$$

The arrow here means that f takes a real number as its input and "sends it" or "maps it" to a real number. As a practical example, suppose we are trying to predict the selling price of a home. To express the fact that the selling price s depends on size m of the house, we can write

$$s = f(m)$$

And for the sake of comparison with non-numeric variables, suppose we have a data science problem where we are going to predict someone's favorite beer from among three Japanese beers {Asahi, Sapporo, Kirin} and we are going to do that based on the continent they live in {Europe, Africa, America}. If we denote the set of beers by B and the set of continents by C, then this is not a function from real numbers to real numbers but rather a function from C to B and can be written as

$$f : C \rightarrow B$$

For example, we may have that

$$Asahi = f(Europe)$$

and this would mean that for a European, the prediction of the preferred beer is Asahi.

The terms domain and range of a function are also useful when discussing functions. The *domain* is the set of inputs for the function, and the *range* is the set of outputs. Thus, in this example, the domain is C, the set of continents, and the range is B, the set of beers.

9.13 Multivariate Functions

Returning to the selling price of a house, it is normal to expect that only knowing the size won't allow for a very accurate estimate of the selling price. There are so many other factors that will influence the selling price: the number of rooms, how many swimming pools it has, how old it is, and so on. That is, we may believe that the selling price is a function of not a single variable but rather many variables. In data science, often we encounter functions of 10, 100, 1000, or more variables. In this case, where there is more than one ***input*** variable, the function is said to be multivariate.

The above discussion is meant to motivate our study of multivariate scenarios. If there are three input (independent) variables, size: m, number of rooms: r, and number of swimming pools: p, we write

$$s = f(m, r, p)$$

In general, we will denote the output variable with y and the input variables with x_1, x_2, and x_3 and write

$$y = f(x_1, x_2, x_3)$$

or more generally

$$y = f(x_1, x_2, \ldots, x_n)$$

and we write

$$f : \mathbf{R}^3 \to \mathbf{R}$$

or more generally

$$f : \mathbf{R}^n \to \mathbf{R}$$

Practice 9.13.8

1. The **mean**() function in R can take a vector of any length. In the case of a vector input, what is the domain of the **mean**() function and what is the range?

9.14 Vector-Valued Functions

Suppose we want to model the path of a football player as she runs around the football field over time (as a function of time t). At the beginning of the game, which we could call time t = 0, the player is standing somewhere on the field. We can label one of the corners of the field the origin and then measure the x and y coordinates of the player at the beginning of the game. Suppose we use units of meters, and suppose that the player starts out at x equals 7 and y equals 10. As the game continues, the player's position will change, and so her position coordinates are a function of time. More specifically we can say that her x coordinate is a function of time and separately her y coordinate is a function of time, and we could express this as

$$\left[x(t), y(t) \right]$$

or we can write it like this: $\mathbf{f}(t) = \left[x(t), y(t) \right]$.

When we write x(t), we are saying that there is some function that will give the x coordinate of the football player's position given a time t. This just means that at any time t, there is a corresponding value for x. The same applies when we write y(t): at any time t, there is a corresponding value for y.

From either of these expressions, you can see that any given value of t will generate an x coordinate and a y coordinate. Thus, the input variable is t, and there are two separate outputs, x and y.

As an example, suppose

$$x(t) = 2t$$

$$y(t) = t^2$$

and so

$$\mathbf{f}(t) = \left[x(t), y(t) \right] = \left[2t, t^2 \right]$$

For example, if t = 1, we can determine both the x and y coordinates to be (2,1). If t = 2, we can determine them to be (4,4). If t = 3, we can determine the x and y coordinates to be (6,9).

It is clear that given any time t, the above expression will determine the x and y coordinates and thus the location in the plane.[2]

We have constructed a function of a *single input* variable but **two output variables**. We saw earlier that $\mathbf{R}^2$ stands for a vector with two elements. Thus, we can identify our function $\mathbf{f}(t) = [x(t), y(t)]$ with this property:

$$\mathbf{f} : \mathbf{R}^1 \to \mathbf{R}^2$$

which says that if you put in a (single) value for the input t, the output will be a vector with two components x and y (therefore the output will be in $\mathbf{R}^2$).

If you want to know the graph of this function, you can substitute various values for t and generate corresponding values for (x,y). Another way to figure out what the graph is would be to solve x(t) = 2t for t and then substitute that t into y(t). This will allow us to see the problem in a more familiar setting. This gives

$$t = \frac{1}{2}x$$

$$y = \left(\frac{1}{2}x\right)^2 = \frac{1}{4}x^2$$

We are quite familiar with this and recognize easily that it is a parabola in the xy-plane. Thus, we can conclude that the path of the football player is along a parabola. Knowing that the path is a parabola does not tell us how quickly they are running along this path. In this algebraic manipulation, we have eliminated the t variable, and so we cannot know the speed from this analysis. We won't worry about that here, but of course, it would be of interest to a physicist or engineer. Also, note that x(t) = 4t and y(t) = 4t² would also give the same parabola. Clearly in this second example, the football player is moving more quickly but still following the same path.

When the output of a function is a vector, as it is here with **f**, the function is said to be *vector-valued*. When the output of a function is a vector, we will use boldfaced font to write the name of the function as we did here. Of course, we are not limited to outputs in $\mathbf{R}^2$; we can have outputs in $\mathbf{R}^3$. For example, if we are tracking the path of a bird in the sky instead of a football player running on a field, then we would say the *position in space* is a function of t like [x(t),y(t),z(t)], and we see that given a particular time t, we will get a particular position. That is to say, given a particular time, we get a particular value for the three-dimensional vector.

More generally, we can construct functions with input t and output in $\mathbf{R}^n$.

$$\mathbf{f} : \mathbf{R}^1 \to \mathbf{R}^n$$

Again, as an example with non-numeric data, suppose we have a data science problem where we are going to predict someone's favorite beer from among three Japanese beers {Asahi, Sapporo, Kirin} *and* their favorite Japanese snack from among these two {senbei, Pocky}. Suppose we are going to do that based on the continent in which they live {Europe, Africa, America}. If we denote

---

[2] Of course, the field is not the entire plane, and so we have to put some kind of restriction on t to keep the location of the player within the field, but we won't worry about that here.

the set of beers by B, the set of snacks by S, and the set of continents by C, then we have a function from C to B × S and write this as

$$\mathbf{f} : C \rightarrow B \times S$$

where by B × S, we mean the cross product of B and S, which is the set of all possible ordered pairs where the first element of the ordered pair is an element of B and the second element of the ordered pair is an element of S. That is, B × S = {(Asahi,senbei), (Asahi,Pocky), (Sapporo,senbei), (Sapporo,Pocky), (Kirin,senbei), (Kirin,Pocky)}. Notice again that we have used a boldfaced $\mathbf{f}$ to denote our function because its *output* is a vector.

9.15 Multivariate Vector-Valued Functions

Combining the two concepts of *multivariate* and *vector-valued*, we can construct a function of many input variables and also many output variables. In this case, we could describe the function as a multivariate vector-valued function. Take the following example:

$$\mathbf{f}(x, y, z, t) = \left[yzt, \left(x^2 + y^2\right), (7 + t) \right] \tag{9.9}$$

This function has four inputs and three outputs. (*Notice there are two commas in the output vector which means it has three elements.*) We can therefore describe it as

$$\mathbf{f} : \mathbf{R}^4 \rightarrow \mathbf{R}^3$$

Again, notice that f is boldfaced.

Here we have not given any real-world meaning to this function; it is just a mathematical possibility but nonetheless an example of a multivariate vector-valued function.

9.16 Explicit versus Implicit Formula for a Function

By the way, we would call Equation (9.9) an explicit form of the relationship between the inputs and outputs of $\mathbf{f}$ because it tells exactly (explicitly) the way the outputs are calculated from the inputs. On the other hand, the implicit representation of this function could be

$$\mathbf{f}(x, y, z, t) = \left[u_1(x, y, z, t), u_2(x, y, z, t), u_3(x, y, z, t) \right] \tag{9.10}$$

Here, we don't know the explicit way to calculate the functions u_i. We just know that each of them depend on x, y, z, and t. The implicit representation, just as does the explicit representation, tells us that $\mathbf{f}$ is vector-valued and has three components.

Practice 9.16.9

1. For the multivariate vector-valued function defined in (9.9), given an input of [2,0,1,2], what is the output?
2. For the implicitly defined multivariate vector-valued function defined in (9.10), given an input of [2,0,1,2], what is the output? (Express it as a vector using the square bracket notation.)

3. Using R, define a function called **myMultiVV()** which mimics the function **f** defined in Equation (9.9).

4. Suppose we want to use the four input variables sepal length, sepal width, petal length, petal width to predict the probability that a flower is either a rose or a tulip. Suppose also that our prediction will come in the form of a probability that the flower is a rose and also the probability that the flower is a tulip. Thus, the output of the function is a vector. Write an *implicit* function to express this situation.

5. Optional: Referring to the football field example, suppose the origin of the coordinate system is at the lower left-hand side of the football field. Imagine that the football player starts at the origin and traces out a parabolic curve as the path that they run. Can you write an R function that describes the path of the football player as a function of the single variable t? Call it **playerPath()**. There are many different parabolas that the player could traverse, and so there is not just one answer. Also, the player could be running slowly or running fast, and so this is another reason why there could be many possible answers.

Chapter 10

Calculus

10.1 Single-Variable Derivatives

In this text, it is assumed that the reader is familiar with the concept of the derivative. This is covered in the first half of a Calculus course. Here we will provide a quick review of its meaning and some of the notation used for the derivative.

The notion of rate of change is the fundamental concept to which the derivative relates. Rates of change are everywhere and of interest throughout every scientific study, be it hard sciences or soft sciences. *Speed* is the rate of change of distance per unit of time (for example, mph). *Return on investment* is a rate of change. Social scientists may study how happiness depends on income and would be interested perhaps in the rate of change of *happiness per increase in income*. Many scientific questions involve rates of change. Mathematics abstracts the common notion from all these examples and just identifies them all as rates of change. We study rates of change early in our mathematical education as the slope of a line. The slope, usually denoted by m, is the change of y divided by the change of x. We sometimes use the Greek letter delta, Δ to denote "change in", and write m = $\Delta y/\Delta x$. If the graph of the relationship between two variables y and x is linear and y = mx + b, then the rate of change is the slope of the line. Calculus becomes important when the relationship is not linear.

When the relationship between x and y is not linear, what is the rate of change? The question itself is wrong because there is no single rate of change in this case, and so there is no single numeric answer. But Calculus can guide us to the right questions and their answers. It allows us to suggest a rate of change if exactly one point on the graph is specified (Figure 10.1).

It imagines that we draw a tangent line to our curve at that point and answers the question, what is the slope of that tangent line. This is referred to as the "instantaneous" slope at the point, and the method for obtaining this slope is called calculating the derivative. We sometimes will speak inaccurately and say the slope of f.

Although we won't use it in our discussions, the mathematical definition is given below.

$$f'(a) = \lim_{h \to 0} \frac{f(a+h) - f(a)}{h} \tag{10.1}$$

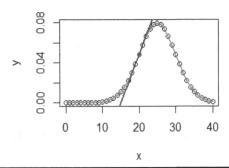

Figure 10.1 Tangent line to the curve at a point.

There are various notations for the derivative as it was developed by different mathematicians and used in various fields over the last 300 years. Here are a few:

$$\frac{dy}{dx}$$

$$f'(x)$$

$$y' \tag{10.2}$$

$$D_x[f]$$

$$D_x(f(x))$$

The first one is called the Leibnitz notation. They all can be read as "the derivative of y with respect to the variable x" or just "the derivative of y with respect to x". Sometimes you will hear $\frac{dy}{dx}$ read as "d y d x".

The reader is most likely familiar with derivatives of some of the simpler functions. For example, if $y = x^2$, then $y' = 2x$. Or if $y = x^3$, then $y' = 3x^2$. Later we will have to deal with the function $y = e^x$ and its derivative.

10.2 Sum and Difference Rules

A rule, covered in Calculus, is the rule for the derivatives of sums and differences.

Sum Rule

$$D_x\big[f(x)\pm g(x)\big]=\big[f(x)+g(x)\big]'=D_x\big[f(x)\big]\pm D_x\big[g(x)\big] \tag{10.3}$$

Practice 10.2.1
   1. Use the sum rule to find the derivative of $x^5 + x^3$.

10.3 Product Rule

The product rule is used when we want the derivative of a product of two functions. It says

$$\text{if } f(x) = g(x)h(x), \text{ then}$$
$$f'(x) = g'(x)h(x) + g(x)h'(x) \tag{10.4}$$

Practice 10.3.2

1. Given that the derivative of sin(x) is cos(x), use the product rule to find the derivative of $x^2\sin(x)$.

10.4 Chain Rule

The chain rule is essential to our study of neural networks. Whereas the product rule asks if there is a way to express the derivative of the *product* of two functions in terms of the derivatives of the individual functions, the chain rule asks if there is a way to express the derivative of the *composition* of two functions in terms of the derivatives of the individual functions.

Recall that if

$$h(x) = (f \circ g)(x) = f(g(x))$$

then we say that h is the composition of f with g. Notice that we are putting g(x) into f. If we want to take this a bit more slowly, we can say that g gives an output which we can call something, say call it u, and then we put that output, that u, into f and arrive at an output; we can call the output of f something, say call it h. That is, the whole process of starting with x, putting it into g, and then putting that result into f is called h. Being a little more explicit, we are saying that u = g(x) and then y = f(u). And altogether h(x) = f(g(x)). Now our question is, what is h′(x) or more precisely *can we write it* in terms of g′(x) and f′(x)? The answer is here:

$$h'(x) = \left[f'(g(x))\right] * \left[g'(x)\right] \tag{10.5}$$

Although the following requires a bit of an explanation which we will not provide, if everything is expressed in Leibnitz notation, the same chain rule looks like this:

$$\frac{dy}{dx} = \frac{dy}{du}\frac{du}{dx} \tag{10.6}$$

An intuitive example of the 10.6 version of the chain rule is the following.

Suppose machines A, B, and C each produce shirts, and we are given the following information:

■ Machine A produces shirts two times faster than machine B.
■ Machine B produces shirts three times faster than machine C.

How many times faster is machine A producing shirts compared with machine C. The answer is of course, six times faster. However, this can be expressed as an example of the chain rule.

We write the question as, what is $\dfrac{dA}{dC}$, that is, what is the ratio of how many shirts are produced by machine A compared to machine C? The chain rule allows us to write

$$\frac{dA}{dC} = \frac{dA}{dB}\frac{dB}{dC} = 2 * 3 = 6$$

10.5 Derivative of e^x

One function that often shows up in neural networks is the exponential function e^x. It can be shown that when you differentiate a function, if you get that exact function back again, then the original function *must* be e^x. That is, e^x is the only function whose derivative is itself.[1]

In mathematical notation (using the third notation in our list of derivative notations above),

$$D_x\left[e^x\right] = e^x \qquad (10.7)$$

This fact is important in discussions of neural networks.

10.6 Sigmoid Function and Its Derivative

The S-curve or sigmoid curve is so named because its graph looks something like an S. There are a variety of functions that could be said to look like an S and thus may be called S-curves, but the one that most texts are referring to has the equation

$$\sigma(x) = 1/\left(1 + e^{-x}\right)$$

It is also called a logistic curve. Its graph is shown in Figure 10.2.

An important feature of such a curve, at least for our purposes, is that it is bounded (in this case by the line $y = 0$ and $y = 1$). The word "bounded" refers to the height of the function (and therefore the y variable). "Bounded" means that it never gets higher than a certain value and never gets lower than a certain value. In the case of the above curve, it never gets higher than 1, and it never gets

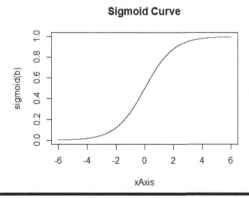

Figure 10.2 Sigmoid curve as an example of the general family of curves referred to as S-curves.

---

[1] Actually $y = ke^x$ for any constant k, also has this property and so we should say that any member of this family of functions has this property.

lower than 0. We can use the phrases "bounded from above" and "bounded from below" to say that the sigmoid curve is bounded from below by 0 and bounded from above by 1. The fact that the sigmoid curve is bounded is important for us because it means that no matter the input (the x variable), the output, the y variable, will be "squished" between two values (in this case 0 and 1).

Additionally, there is another property of this curve that is attractive for many applications. We can ask, how much difference will there be in the height if we move from say x = 1,000,000 to x = 2,000,000? The answer, by looking at the graph, should be clear – almost none. There is much more of a reaction (a change in the height) by moving from x = 1 to x = 2 than from x = 1,000,000 to x = 2,000,000. For some applications, this is a desirable property. That is, it could be desirable that a function is really only sensitive to changes when x is near zero. One possible example of where an S curve could be useful is in modeling the learning of some task. At the beginning, it may be true that a little effort goes a long way, but once the subject is nearly mastered, it may require a lot of effort to make a small improvement.

The answer to "what is the derivative of this sigmoid function?" turns out to have a simple expression, although arriving at the answer is not as simple.

$$\frac{d\sigma}{dx} = \sigma(x) \cdot (1 - \sigma(x)) \tag{10.8}$$

Although we won't need the proof of this fact, it may be of interest to the reader since it uses the chain rule a few times.

$$\frac{d}{dx}\sigma(x) = \frac{d}{dx}\left[\frac{1}{1+e^{-x}}\right]$$

$$= \frac{d}{dx}\left(1+e^{-x}\right)^{-1}$$

$$= -\left(1+e^{-x}\right)^{-2}\left(-e^{-x}\right)$$

$$= \frac{e^{-x}}{\left(1+e^{-x}\right)^2}$$

$$= \frac{1}{1+e^{-x}} \cdot \frac{e^{-x}}{1+e^{-x}}$$

$$= \frac{1}{1+e^{-x}} \cdot \frac{\left(1+e^{-x}\right)-1}{1+e^{-x}}$$

$$= \frac{1}{1+e^{-x}} \cdot \left(\frac{1+e^{-x}}{1+e^{-x}} - \frac{1}{1+e^{-x}}\right)$$

$$= \frac{1}{1+e^{-x}} \cdot \left(1 - \frac{1}{1+e^{-x}}\right)$$

$$= \sigma(x) \cdot (1 - \sigma(x))$$

This is a rather "clean" result in the sense that the derivative of σ is a fairly simple function of σ.[2]

---

[2] This is unusual. For example, we don't usually think of the *derivative* of $f(x)=x^2$ as being a simple function of $f(x)$.

Practice 10.6.3

1. Optional: Give the reasoning for each step above.

10.7 Derivatives for Multivariate and Vector-Valued Functions

As we said earlier, the derivative tells us about the slope of a curve. It is often used to find the minimum of a function. For example, suppose we have a relationship between the *average cost of producing a product* and the *number of products made*. Just as an artificial mathematical construction of this relationship, suppose y is the average dollar cost of producing the product and x is the number of products produced, and suppose for simplicity (not realistically) the relationship is as follows.

$$y = f(x) = (x - 1000)^2 + 20 \tag{10.9}$$

A common question in finance, business, or economics may be, "Is there a number of goods produced, x, that will give a *minimum average cost per product*, y"? If we see the graph of this function, we may be able to estimate the lowest point of the graph (Figure 10.3).

In the figure above, the x-axis is the number of products produced. The y-axis is the average cost per good. Here we can guess that the lowest point occurs when x = 1000, meaning that if 1000 goods are produced, the *average cost per good* would be least. (We can also see that this lowest price per good will be $20.) However, it may not always be so easy to visually identify the answer, and furthermore, the derivative can give us the exact answer without resorting to a visual representation. As we said, the derivative gives the slope of the (tangent line to the) curve. The derivative technique takes advantage of the observation that *the slope of the tangent line to the curve is zero at the lowest point*. (In the graph in Figure 10.3, that is (1000, 20).) Thus, if we can find the derivative and set it equal to zero and then solve that equation, we may have located the minimum *or* at least a candidate for the lowest or minimum point.

Practice 10.7.4

1. What is the derivative of $f(x) = x^3 - x^2$?
2. When is the slope of the above f(x) equal to zero?

10.8 Minimums and Maximums of a Function

Sometimes the equation for the derivative may be complicated. In the above example, where $y = f(x) = (x - 1000)^2 + 20$, the equation for the derivative is $f' = 2x - 2000$. $2x - 2000$ is quite a simple expression, and solving it for zero is trivial. However, if we had a formula whose derivative was

$$f'(x) = x^5 - x - 1 \tag{10.10}$$

then it would turn out that it is not possible to solve it for zero. (Yes, even this seemingly relatively simple equation, $x^5 - x - 1 = 0$, is not solvable.)

Thus, mathematicians have sought other ways to find the minimum of a function. The method we will use in neural networks is called *gradient descent*. It is an iterative process. That means it

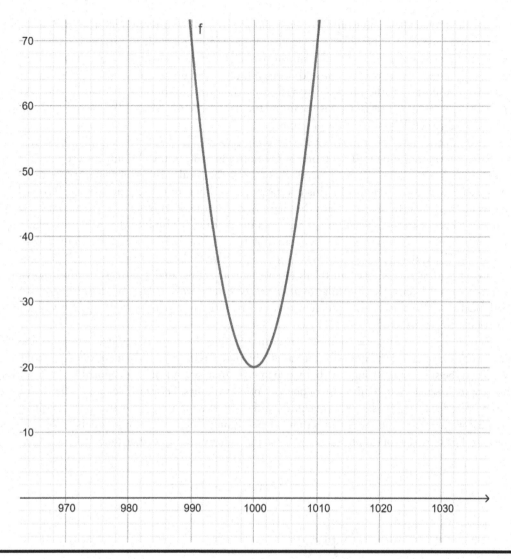

Figure 10.3 **Average cost as a function of the number of goods produced. We may want to find the lowest average cost.**

will not be done in one step, but rather, we repeat something many times, hopefully each time getting closer and closer to the lowest (or highest) point on the graph.[3] In such an iterative process, we may not expect to find the lowest point exactly but rather hope to just get real close to it. (Just like we don't expect automatic language translation from Japanese to English to be perfect, we will be happy if it is close to perfect.) The idea is something like this. Imagine you are on either a 2D curve or a 3D surface. You may imagine it as a huge valley, and you are seeking the bottom of the valley. Imagine it is night-time and you cannot see the bottom. The question is, which direction should you walk? Actually, in the 2D parabola example pictured earlier, there are only two possible directions, but in the physical 3D valley, there are an infinite number of directions.

---

[3] This is called a numeric solution instead of an analytic solution to the problem.

In the case of the valley, you would *feel with your feet* to find the direction of greatest slope downward. In the case of the parabola, you would just have to decide which of the two possible directions (to the right or to the left) will result in the height of the curve decreasing. Then you would take a step in that direction. That would bring you to a new spot in the valley or on the parabola. Then you would repeat the process again, finding the direction of greatest descent and taking a step in that direction. This is what is meant by the process being iterative. We keep repeating this process, and hopefully it will lead to the bottom.

On the other hand, if the valley has several "bottoms" as shown in Figure 10.4, then this iterative process may only lead us to one of the bottoms and not the absolute lowest point. In the figure, if we start at point B, the process may lead to the local minimum at point C rather than the absolute minimum at point E. This is a potential weakness of this method. We will come back to this method later. It, together with the chain rule, is at the heart of learning in neural networks and many deep learning algorithms. It serves as the method for finding the minimum of a curve when we cannot solve the equation generated by setting the derivative equal to zero. Solving by setting the derivative equal to zero is referred to as solving the problem analytically as opposed to solving it numerically. We can think of solving something analytically as meaning solving it with our calculus derivative formulas to *arrive at the exact solution*. (Another definition of "solving analytically" is "a solution to a problem that can be written in 'closed form' in terms of known functions, constants, etc."[4])

Returning to the analytic solution – meaning setting the derivative equal to zero to find the minimum, let us bring the question into a multivariate environment. As mentioned previously, it would not be surprising to suggest that y depends on more than just x. It is possible that the average cost to produce an item may also depend on other variables. For example, it may depend on the cost of electricity, labor costs, exchange rates, and so on. We can imagine many such dependencies. Suppose we propose a model that says that y depends on x: the number of products *and* on the *cost of labor*. For purposes of graphing, we will rename our variables, so that the output variable, the

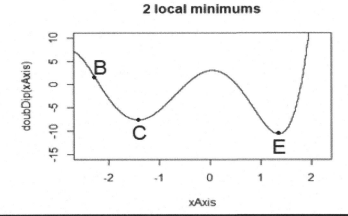

Figure 10.4   A cost curve that has two local minima. Starting at B, if we use the process of "taking a step in the direction that leads downward", we may only locate C rather than the absolute minimum at E.

---

[4] http://mathworld.wolfram.com/Analytic.html.

average cost of producing an item, is labeled z instead of y. We will say that y is the *cost of labor per item*. Now we can write

$$z = f(x, y)$$

and to make up an artificially simple example,

$$z = (x - 10)^2 + (y - 15)^2 \qquad (10.11)$$

Now we again may be interested in finding the lowest average cost z, and this now will involve finding the x and y that will lead to this lowest cost. Again, a picture may help, but this time it may not be as easy to see the answer visually. That is, it may not be easy to see at what xy coordinates, the height z will be lowest (Figure 10.5).

If we move to a model which has three input variables (this time, let us denote them as x_1, x_2, and x_3), we won't even be able to do a standard 3D visualization. Thus, it would be great if we had a technique, similar to the technique we described previously – setting derivatives equal to zero to find the minimum. For some functions, using multivariate calculus, we may be able to find an analytic solution, but for other functions, we may not find an analytic solution. (We saw that even in the case of a single input variable, the fifth-degree equation could not be solved for zero.) However, we may be able to use an iterative process (also called a numerical solution). This is not a course in multivariate calculus, however, and so here we will describe only some of the important concepts and do so as briefly as possible. There are several excellent texts on multivariate or vector calculus. One that is recommended is by Colley. The reason we delve into multivariate calculus is because the iterative process does actually depend on "multivariate" derivatives.

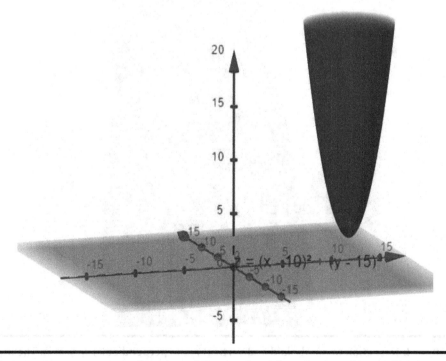

Figure 10.5   Average cost as a function of the number of products and cost of labor.

10.9 Partial Derivatives

When dealing with multivariate functions, the notion of partial derivatives is important for finding a minimum or maximum for both the analytical approach and the (iterative) gradient descent approach. The idea behind what we call a partial derivative may be most easily understood in the 3D scenario.

We imagine taking our 3D graph and slicing it with a vertical plane as shown in Figure 10.6.

It hopefully is clear in this picture that the intersection of the (inverted) paraboloid and the vertical plane is a 2D curve. (In fact, it is an inverted parabola.) Recall that we are using an xyz-coordinate system and z is the vertical axis. In the above figure, the vertical plane is green, the x-axis is red, and the y-axis is green. The 2D curve we are referring to lives in the plane. Since this is a 2D curve, we can call on our original concept of derivative – that is we can use the derivative from single-value calculus! We said that the derivative would tell us the slope of tangent lines. Thus, if we could find the derivative for this inverted 2D parabola, it would tell us the slope lines tangent to this parabola. It turns out to be very easy to calculate the derivative if we use a vertical

Figure 10.6 **Intersection of paraboloid and vertical plane perpendicular to y-axis. The intersection of these two is a parabola.**

plane that is *perpendicular to the y-axis*. Note that such a parabola (that lives in this plane) will have a fixed y! Thus, as we traverse the parabola, y will remain fixed, but x and z will change. To find the derivative, the trick is to treat y as a constant in the formula. Let's suppose that the formula for the *paraboloid* is

$$z = -x^2 - y^2 + 10 \qquad (10.12)$$

Practice 10.9.5
1. Given the equation above, if we fix y = 3, what is the resulting equation?
2. Given that y is set to y = 3 and we are living in the 2D xz-plane with the two variable functions referred to in part 1 of this practice set, find the derivative of z with respect to x: $\dfrac{dz}{dx}$.

To say that we are treating y as a constant means that you could think of it as say just a 100 (we are just using 100 arbitrarily here to hopefully make this concept more concrete). In that case, how do you do the derivative with respect to x, $\dfrac{dz}{dx}$? In other words, if the equation looked like

$$z = -x^2 - 100 + 10$$

would you have trouble finding $\dfrac{dz}{dx}$? No. In this case, it would be easy, and it would be

$$\frac{dz}{dx} = -2x$$

This is how the partial derivative with respect to x is done. Treat y as though it were a constant. To help us remember that this is a partial derivative, we use a different notation. The notation is

$$\frac{\partial z}{\partial x} = -2x$$

We can do something similar in order to find the derivative of z with respect to y. We treat x as a constant. Then we will get

$$\frac{\partial z}{\partial y} = -2y$$

Just to make this a bit clearer, let us explore the meaning of these partial derivatives. $\dfrac{\partial z}{\partial x} = -2x$ implies that as x increases, the height of the paraboloid decreases.

Practice 10.9.6
1. What is the height of the paraboloid when x = 2 and y = 2?
2. If we cut the paraboloid with the plane y = 2, what is the shape of the curve that forms the intersection of the plane and the paraboloid?
3. If we cut the paraboloid with the plane y = 2, what is the formula of the curve that forms the intersection of the plane and the paraboloid?

4. If we cut the paraboloid with the plane y = 2, what is the slope of the line which is tangent to the curve that forms the intersection of the plane and the paraboloid when x = 2?

To extend this process of finding partial derivatives to functions of more than two independent variables, we proceed similarly. For example, if

$$z = f(x_1, x_2, x_3, x_4, x_5) = x_1 x_3 + x_1^2 x_4 + x_5 \qquad (10.13)$$

and we want to find $\frac{\partial z}{\partial x_1}$, we simply treat all the input (independent) variables other than x_1 as constant and then do the derivative. We end up with this:

$$\frac{\partial z}{\partial x_1} = x_3 + 2x_4 x_1$$

Practice 10.9.7

1. Find $\frac{\partial z}{\partial x_2}$.

2. Find $\frac{\partial z}{\partial x_3}$.

Standard notations for the partial derivative of f with respect to x_i are

$$\frac{\partial f}{\partial x_i}, D_{x_i}\left[f(x_1,\ldots,x_n)\right], \text{ and } f_{x_i}(x_1,\ldots,x_n)$$

Although we will not use this, the mathematical definition of a partial derivative is

$$\frac{\partial f}{\partial x_i} = \lim_{h \to 0} \frac{f(x_1,\ldots,x_i+h,\ldots,x_n) - f(x_1,\ldots,x_n)}{h}$$

Returning to the paraboloid above, we calculated

$$\frac{\partial z}{\partial x} = -2x$$

This gives us the slope of the tangent line on the parabola which was the intersection of the paraboloid and the plane y = 2. Thus, if we want focus on a particular point on the curve, say (2, 2, 2) (verify that this is a point on the curve and on the paraboloid), we can talk about the slope in the y = 2 plane, and say it is −4. We are in the y = 2 plane because y is fixed at y = 2. We can also talk about the slope in x = 2 plane because we calculated

$$\frac{\partial z}{\partial y} = -2y$$

and we can say it is also −4 (at the point (2, 2, 2)).

Going further, you may guess that with the information on partial derivatives, we may be able to do something similar to what is done with single-variable derivatives, that is, to find the maximum or minimum of a function. That is, we may be able to find out where the peak of the paraboloid is. This is what is done in multivariate calculus courses. We will not go down that route here, however. The reason is that, as stated earlier, there are many functions for which it may be difficult or possibly even impossible to get an analytic solution. In fact, most of the functions that we would need to work with in neural networks will have this problem.

Thus, we will skip this part of multivariate calculus and return to the technique of gradient descent armed with our understanding of partial derivatives. First we consider the chain rule for multivariate functions.

10.10 Multivariate Version of the Chain Rule

Recall the chain rule in the context of a single input variable Equation 10.5. Given functions

$$h\!:\!R \to R, \quad f\!:\!R \to R, \quad g\!:\!R \to R$$

$$\text{if } h(x) = (f \circ g)(x) = f(g(x)), \text{ then}$$

$$h'(x) = \left[f'(g(x)) \right] * \left[g(x) \right]$$

(as long as the domains and ranges match).

We also wrote the chain rule like this:

$$\frac{dy}{dx} = \frac{dy}{du}\frac{du}{dx}$$

We have this chain rule for a function of a single variable. When dealing with neural networks, we will need a chain rule for functions of more than one variable.

Again, we won't spend the time necessary to cover this topic rigorously.

As usual, we want to be able to deal with situations where our functions are multivariate (i.e., they have more than one input variable).

As in the single input variable scenario before, in the case of the chain rule, we are dealing with two functions (say f and g, as above). Perhaps we would like to be able to handle cases where both are multivariate functions. But it will be easier to understand if we go step by step and first consider the case where just one is multivariate and the other is just a function of one variable.

We will begin with the case where f is a multivariate function of x and y, i.e., f(x,y). **g** will be a function of a single variable t, i.e., **g**(t). Note, however, that if we want to write f(**g**(t)), then g must have two outputs because f requires two inputs x and y. Thus, **g** *must be a vector-valued function* meaning that it outputs a vector. That is, **g**(t) = [x(t), y(t)] – the output of g is a vector.

$$\mathbf{g}\!:\!R \to R^2, \quad f\!:\!R^2 \to R, \quad h\!:\!R \to R$$

Now, for reasons that will become clear later, we will name the output of **g** with the letter x, but we need to use a bold **x** since it is a vector:

$$\mathbf{x}(t) = \left[x(t), \, y(t) \right]$$

This is admittedly confusing since one of its components is called x and now we are calling the entire vector **x**. (The reason we call the entire vector **x** now is because it is standard to use the letter x as the input and we are inputting the entire vector into f.) Now we can write h(t) = f(**x**) or h(t) = f(**x**(t)) or even h(t) = f([x(t), y(t)]). (Take note of when bold font is used and when it is not.) Since we are delving into the chain rule, the kind of question we are wondering about is, how does h change when t changes? We see when h is written as

$$h(t) = f\left(\left[x(t),\ y(t)\right]\right)$$

that when t changes, both components of **x** change; that is, both x(t) and y(t) change, and then as **x** changes, it causes h to change.

10.11 Example of Multivariate Chain Rule

Suppose

$$z = f(x,y) = 2x + y^2$$

$$x(t) = [6t,\ t+2]$$

f(x, y) is multivariate, and **x** is vector-valued. We want to know how z = f(x,y) changes when t changes. But currently z = f(x, y) is given in terms of x and y and not t. Thus, it appears that a chain rule would be called for. However, it is not difficult to see that we can write z = f(x, y) strictly as a function of t. Thus, we will do that and figure out the derivative $\dfrac{df}{dt}\left(=\dfrac{dz}{dt}\right)$ directly. Then, we develop a multivariate chain rule and try it with this new more general chain rule, of course, hoping that the result will be the same using either approach.

10.12 $\dfrac{df}{dt}$ without the Chain Rule

Without the chain rule, we need to express f directly as a function of t first. This is easy since we know that x = 6t (that is not a bold x) and y = t + 2. Thus,

$$f(x,y) = 2x + y^2$$

$$= 2(6t) + (t+2)^2$$

$$= 12t + t^2 + 4t + 4$$

$$= 16t + t^2 + 4$$

Now it is a simple matter to see how f changes as t changes. In other words, it is a simple matter to find the derivative $\dfrac{df}{dt}$. (Notice this is not a partial derivative because we have managed to express f in terms of the single variable t.) We see that

$$\frac{df}{dt} = 16 + 2t$$

We did this without any use of a chain rule.

It should be noted that we are abusing our notation a little here. We are using f technically for two different functions. One is a function of x and y. The other is a function of t. Technically they are different, and this could be a source of some confusion later.

Also, make sure you agree that we should write $\frac{df}{dt}$ *and not* $\frac{\partial f}{\partial t}$.

10.13 Multivariate Version of the Chain Rule Version 1 (f Is Multivariate but x and y Are Univariate)

Now we discuss a chain rule for this situation: f is a multivariate function of x and y and both x and y are functions of t. Recall that we have both x and y being functions of t. You will sometimes see this written a bit confusingly as

$$x = x(t)$$

$$y = y(t)$$

A possible point of confusion here is that x is the output and also x is the name of the function. Nevertheless, it is fairly common to see this notation. And we have seen the following notation before.

$$\mathbf{x} = \mathbf{x}(t) = \big[x(t), y(t)\big]$$

where $\mathbf{x} = \mathbf{x}(t)$ will be a vector-valued function of a single variable t. (We have switched from using **g** to using **x** for our notation to emphasize that this is an input vector.)

Now we ask, as mentioned above how does f change as t changes? This is written again as $\frac{df}{dt}$. The chain rule for this scenario will be

$$\frac{df}{dt} = \frac{\partial f}{\partial x}\frac{dx}{dt} + \frac{\partial f}{\partial y}\frac{dy}{dt} \qquad (10.15)$$

The diagram for this looks like that in Figure 10.7.

How are the edges labeled? Each edge is labeled with a derivative. It is labeled as the derivative of the quantity to the left of the edge with respect to the quantity to the right of the edge. The derivative will be either a partial derivative or a normal derivative (non-partial) depending on whether the quantity on the left is being considered as a function of a single quantity or a function of more than one quantity. Thus, for example, we write $\frac{dy}{dt}$ because y is being thought of as a function of only t.

Before discussing (10.15), a multivariate form of the chain rule, let us orient ourselves by checking where we see partial derivatives and where we see full (normal) derivatives and also where

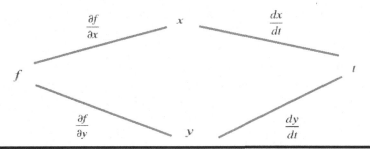

Figure 10.7 **The chain rule for $f \circ x$ where $f : R^2 \to R$ and $x : R^1 \to R^2$.**

we see vectors and where we see scalars (non-vector quantities) and see that equation (10.15) agrees with our expectations.

First, we see $\frac{df}{dt}$. Should this be a partial derivative or a normal derivative? It is a normal derivative, not a partial derivative. Does this make sense? Yes, if we are thinking of f as a function of t, then we are not thinking of it as a multivariate function. We saw this in the example above when we wrote $f = 16t + t^2 + 4$. In this case, it is proper to use a full derivative. Of course, f is a multivariate function of x and y, and so if we were to ask about how f changes with respect to a change in x, we should use a partial derivative, but here we are asking how f changes with respect to a change in t. How about the next derivative $\frac{\partial f}{\partial x}$? Is it correct for this to be a partial derivative? Yes, in this case, we know that f depends on both x and y, and so it is a multivariate function of x and y, and thus if we are only asking about how f changes when x changes, this is a partial derivative. We can see this when we wrote $f(x, y) = 2x + y^2$ in the previous example. The last two terms in the chain rule can be checked in a similar way.

Now in the current form of the chain rule (Equation 10.15), we do not see any vectors. Where would we expect vectors? The input to f should be a vector quantity. Previously we have denoted that by **x**. But we also have another quantity called x. Recall we made the (somewhat confusing) choice of symbols **x** = [x, y]. The x we see in the chain rule is not the vector and similarly for the y. If we want to emphasize that vectors are involved, we can rewrite our chain rule like this:

$$\frac{df(t)}{dt} = \frac{\partial f(\mathbf{x})}{\partial x}\frac{dx(t)}{dt} + \frac{\partial f(\mathbf{x})}{\partial y}\frac{dy(t)}{dt} \tag{10.16}$$

Make sure you agree with the boldfaced and non-boldfaced choices of fonts above.

10.14 $\frac{df}{dt}$ Using the Chain Rule

Next, we use this chain rule from equation (10.16) on our previous example and see if it gives the same answer we calculated earlier.

With $f(x, y) = 2x + y^2$ and $\mathbf{x}(t) = [x(t), y(t)] = [6t, t + 2]$, we get the following:

$$\frac{\partial f}{\partial x}\frac{dx}{dt} = 2 * 6$$

$$\frac{\partial f}{\partial y}\frac{dy}{dt}=2y*1$$

$$\frac{df}{dt}=\frac{\partial f}{\partial x}\frac{dx}{dt}+\frac{\partial f}{\partial y}\frac{dy}{dt}=2*6+2y*1$$

$$=12+2(t+2)=16+2t$$

which agrees with the calculation done without the use of the chain rule.

Practice 10.14.8

1. Suppose we have the following:

$$z=f(x,y)=x^3+y^2$$

$$\mathbf{x}(t)=\left[t^2,\ t+2\right]$$

Find $\frac{dz}{dt}$ both with and without the chain rule.

2. Which is the correct notation in part 1 and why?

   a. $\dfrac{\partial y}{\partial t}$

   b. $\dfrac{dy}{dt}$

3. Which is the correct notation in part 1 and why?

   c. $\dfrac{\partial f}{\partial y}$

   d. $\dfrac{df}{dy}$

4. Which is the correct notation in part 1 and why?

   e. $\dfrac{\partial z}{\partial t}$

   f. $\dfrac{dz}{dt}$

Our chain rule can be generalized to the case where f is a function of n variables and thus $\mathbf{x}\in\mathbf{R}^n$ as follows. In this case, we could write $\mathbf{x}=[x_1, x_2, \ldots, x_n]$, and the chain rule becomes

$$\frac{df(t)}{dt}=\frac{\partial f(\mathbf{x})}{\partial x_1}\frac{dx_1(t)}{dt}+\frac{\partial f(\mathbf{x})}{\partial x_2}\frac{dx_2(t)}{dt}+\cdots+\frac{\partial f(\mathbf{x})}{\partial x_n}\frac{dx_n(t)}{dt} \qquad (10.17)$$

10.15 Chain Rule as Matrix Multiplication

Note that chain rule can also be written as a *matrix multiplication*! Pay attention to the subscripts here. We are assuming $\mathbf{x}(t_0) = \mathbf{x}_0 = (x_0, y_0)$.

$$\frac{df}{dt}(t_0) = \left[\frac{\partial f}{\partial x_1}(\mathbf{x}_0) \cdots \frac{\partial f}{\partial x_n}(\mathbf{x}_0) \right] \begin{bmatrix} \dfrac{dx_1}{dt}(t_0) \\ \vdots \\ \dfrac{dx_n}{dt}(t_0) \end{bmatrix} \tag{10.18}$$

Note the dimensions of the two matrices: $1 \times n$ and $n \times 1$. This results in a 1×1 matrix, which for our purposes can be considered as a scalar.

10.16 Multivariate Version of the Chain Rule Version 2 (f Is Multivariate, and x and y Are Each Multivariate)

Suppose that f is multivariate as before (this time depending on three variables: x, y, and z, instead of just two), and now assume that each of these three variables are also multivariate. (They will each depend on not just t but also s now). Without going into the particulars of this more general version of the chain rule, we present it as

$$\frac{df}{ds} = \frac{\partial f}{\partial x}\frac{\partial x}{\partial s} + \frac{\partial f}{\partial y}\frac{\partial y}{\partial s} + \frac{\partial f}{\partial z}\frac{\partial z}{\partial s}$$

and

$$\frac{df}{dt} = \frac{\partial f}{\partial x}\frac{\partial x}{\partial t} + \frac{\partial f}{\partial y}\frac{\partial y}{\partial t} + \frac{\partial f}{\partial z}\frac{\partial z}{\partial t}$$

Note that if we denote $x = u_1$, $y = u_2$, and $z = u_3$, then we can express these more generally as

$$\frac{\partial f}{\partial t} = \sum_i \frac{\partial f}{\partial u_i}\frac{\partial u_i}{\partial t}$$

and

$$\frac{\partial f}{\partial s} = \sum_i \frac{\partial f}{\partial u_i}\frac{\partial u_i}{\partial s}$$

Practice 10.16.9

1. Again, let us orient ourselves by checking where we see partial derivatives and where we see full (normal) derivatives in Figure 10.8. In Figure 10.7, we saw some normal derivatives (non-partial derivatives). Why are they gone in this diagram?

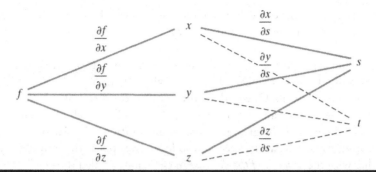

Figure 10.8   The chain rule for f ∘ x where f : R³ → R and x : R² → R³.

10.17 Gradient Descent with Partial Derivatives

We will return to the first example of a paraboloid from above

$$z = (x - 10)^2 + (y - 15)^2 \tag{10.19}$$

which has the graph in Figure 10.9.

First verify that (9, 14, 2) is a point on this graph.

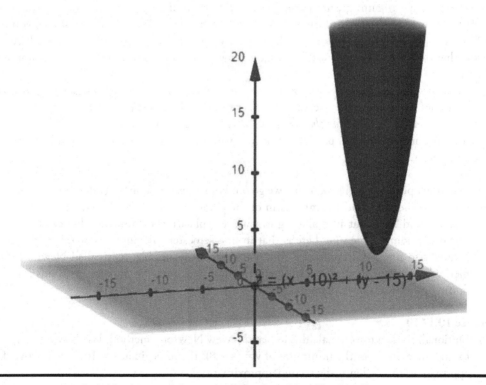

Figure 10.9   Paraboloid whose minimum is difficult to identify visually.

Recall the idea of gradient descent. It attempts to answer the question, "Suppose we are at some point on the surface and want to find our way to the lowest point on the graph, what set of steps can we take?"

As we said before, since it is a surface, we imagine that we are standing somewhere on this surface. We can walk 30° to our right, 40° to our right, 30° to our left, etc. There are so many directions in which we can walk. One of these directions is the direction which would lead to the greatest descent. By that, we mean that there is one *direction* for which, if we take a single step in that direction, we will achieve the greatest decrease in elevation. The size of the step will be relevant when we study neural networks later, and so for now, suppose that our step size is 1 m. The *direction* together with the *amount of the decrease* in elevation is called the *gradient* of the function *at our current point* on the surface. So, for example, maybe walking 20° from due north will give us the greatest decrease in elevation, and perhaps that decrease in elevation is 0.5 m for a single (unit) step. Then the gradient is that direction together with the magnitude of 0.5. From this, we see the gradient can be thought of as a vector since it has direction and magnitude.

The question is, how do we find that direction? If you are physically *walking* on the surface, you can feel with your feet and try to determine the direction. But how can we do it analytically? That is, if we have an equation for the surface, can we figure out, given that equation, what the gradient will be at any specified location on the surface?

By the way, one point which has confused the author is the following. The gradient is a direction *in the* xy-*plane*. Even though we are talking about a 3D surface (the paraboloid), the gradient is a vector in the xy-plane. It indicates a direction. If we move in *any* direction in the xy-plane, of course we expect the z value (the height of the surface) typically to change. However, if we move in *the direction of the gradient*, then the z-value (the height of the surface) of our function z = f(x,y) will increase by an amount greater than if we were to move in any other direction in the plane. You may see some misleading information on the Internet regarding this. For example, you may see "Think about hiking, the gradient points directly up the steepest part of the slope". It should be clear that this is not quite correct. The gradient lays in the xy-plane and therefore cannot point "directly up".

Once again, the gradient is a vector in R^2, not in R^3, even though our surface is in R^3. This may seem confusing. However, we can say the gradient tells the direction of movement *in the* xy-*plane* in order for the *height of the surface* to increase most dramatically.

With our understanding of partial derivatives, we can clarify our concept of gradient, and we will do that next.

> Two other points to mention before we go on: For the example above (Equation 10.19), it is not difficult to find the minimum of the paraboloid analytically. We don't study that method here, but it is a straightforward application of multivariable calculus. The other point to mention here is that in first semester calculus, a *numeric* method is taught to find minimums of a function of a single variable. It is called Newton's method. Gradient descent is a different method, but both are numeric methods for finding minimums or maximums.

Practice 10.17.10

1. Optional: Return to your calculus text and review Newton's method. Use Newton's method to find an estimate of the minimum of y = (x − 8)² if you begin at x = 16. What is the "first approximation"? What is the second approximation?

10.18 Gradient Example

Ok, so when we give the gradient, it had better come in the form of a vector because just above, we said that it is a vector. So, don't be confused if we state it as a vector. It turns out that the gradient is just the *vector of partial derivatives*. What does that mean? If we are talking about z = f(x, y), then the gradient is the vector containing $\frac{\partial z}{\partial x}$ and $\frac{\partial z}{\partial y}$. That is, the gradient is $\left[\frac{\partial z}{\partial x}, \frac{\partial z}{\partial y}\right]$. So, in the case of z = x² + y², the gradient will be [2x, 2y].

This is a vector, and it contains the partial derivatives, and so it is the vector of partial derivatives. One point of confusion may be that we expect vectors to have numbers as their components, but [2x, 2y] has functions as its components. But that is because we have not yet specified where on the surface of z = x² + y² we are. Once we specify that we are at (1, 1, 2), then we can say that the gradient is [2, 2].

What is the interpretation of this? Well, as we said, this can be viewed as an arrow. This arrow points in the direction of greatest ascent. But we are looking for the direction of greatest descent. To get the direction of greatest descent, we take the negative of the gradient, that is, −[2, 2] which is [−2, −2].

> One more possible point of confusion: When we introduced the concept of a *vector as arrow*, we said that the arrow must be drawn to start at the origin and end at the specified coordinates. Thus, you may think that the vector [−2, −2] must be drawn that way. However, what we have said up to now is that the gradient vector will give the direction of greatest ascent. First of all, it should be noted that we have not proved that fact (and we won't do that in this text). Second of all, the meaning of this statement "the gradient vector will give the direction of greatest ascent" is that given the point on the surface of the function at which we are "standing", the direction we should move to achieve greatest ascent is [2, 2]. This means that we should draw an arrow starting from the point *where we are* and extending two units in the x direction and two units in the y direction. Thus, we should draw the arrow [2, 2] *starting from the point where we are* and not from the origin.

Practice 10.18.11

1. If z = x³ + y³, what is $\frac{\partial z}{\partial x}$?

2. If z = x³ + y³, what is $\frac{\partial z}{\partial y}$?

3. What is the gradient of z?

4. What is the gradient at the point (1, 1)? It should be a vector.

At any particular point (x, y), if we can calculate the partial derivatives, we can now know what is the direction of greatest ascent for z! As we just showed for of z = x² + y², the direction of greatest ascent at the point on the paraboloid where x = 1 and y = 1 is [2, 2]. However, for this relatively simple function, perhaps it is easy to have guessed that this is so. We are talking about a paraboloid. If we are standing at the point (1, 1, 2), which direction should we go to get the greatest increase in height of the surface (Figure 10.10)?

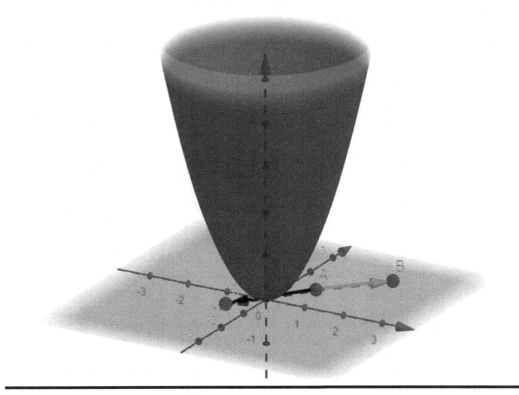

Figure 10.10 Two candidates for the gradient originating at the point A.

It should be clear that we should walk "away from" the origin. (Remember we are talking about directions as indicated by vectors in the xy-plane.) [2, 2] is a vector which points precisely away from the origin – it points radially outwards, away from the origin. This is as we predicted. Let's try it again. Suppose we check what the result would be if we are starting at (0, 0, 0) – that is, starting at the origin. What is the direction of greatest ascent from there? Putting this into [2x, 2y], we get [0, 0]. Oops, that is not such a great result. The direction of the greatest ascent is the vector [0, 0]. Actually, the vector [0, 0] is called the $\vec{0}$ vector and, as you may expect, is the only vector which does not have a direction! So what is going on here? At (0, 0, 0), which is the direction of greatest ascent? Every direction gives equal increase from the point (0, 0), and so our answer of $\vec{0}$ may actually be acceptable! We return to the previous example where we said we are located at (1, 1, 2). There, according to the gradient, the direction of greatest ascent is indicated by [2, 2]. What does this mean? Perhaps comparing it to another direction may be insightful. For example, suppose the gradient had turned out to be [–2, –2]. How do the directions [2,2] and [–2,–2] compare?

In the figure above, we can see two vectors *in the* xy-*plane*. Both begin at the point A(1, 1). One extends from the point A to the point B. The other extends from the point A to the point C. Starting at A, the vector AB originates at the point (1, 1) and extends to the point B whose coordinates are $\left(1+\sqrt{2},1+\sqrt{2}\right)$. The vector AC also begins at A and extends to the point C whose coordinates are $\left(1-\sqrt{2},1-\sqrt{2}\right)$. We can use R to calculate the heights of the paraboloid at both B and C. We will find that the height is considerably higher at the point B.

```
x=1+sqrt(2)
x
## [1] 2.414214
z=x^2+x^2
z
## [1] 11.65685
x=1-sqrt(2)
x
## [1] -0.4142136
z=x^2+x^2
z
## [1] 0.3431458
```

The height of the paraboloid at B is 11.7 and but at C it is 0.34. Thus, as the gradient predicted, moving in the direction from A(1,1) to B $(1+\sqrt{2},1+\sqrt{2})$ causes z to increase more than in the direction from A(1,1) to C$(1-\sqrt{2},1-\sqrt{2})$. In fact, the direction from A to B produces a greater increase in the height of the paraboloid than any other direction (when starting from point (1, 1)). And this is not a coincidence. As we asserted before, the gradient always gives the direction of the greatest ascent.

Practice 10.18.12
1. What is the height of the function (the z-value) at the point?
2. What is the gradient of the function?
3. What is the value of the gradient at (0,1)?
4. If we move in the *direction* of the gradient and the *distance* moved is the magnitude of the gradient, where do we end up and what is the height of the paraboloid there?

What if, instead of two inputs, we have n input variables like this: $z = f(x_1, x_2, \dots x_n)$? Then what is the definition of the gradient? The generalization of the gradient for an input vector in $\mathbf{R}^n$ is, as may be expected,

$$\left[\frac{\partial z}{\partial x_1}, \frac{\partial z}{\partial x_2}, \frac{\partial z}{\partial x_3}, \dots, \frac{\partial z}{\partial x_n} \right]$$

It is said that the gradient is a multivariable generalization of the derivative. While a derivative can be defined on functions of a single (input) variable, for functions of several (input) variables, the gradient is the replacement for the derivative. Note that the gradient is actually a vector-valued function, as opposed to the basic derivative, which is scalar-valued.

10.19 Possible Point of Confusion – The Gradient Has the Same Number of Elements as the Number of Input Variables

We mentioned that the gradient for $z = x^2 + y^2$ was [2x, 2y]. You can see that to graph $z = x^2 + y^2$, we need three dimensions. But the gradient is specified with just two dimensions. Is there something wrong with this? Let's go back to the simplest gradient – the derivative for a single-valued function. The derivative of $y = f(x)$ has just one component $\left(\dfrac{dy}{dx} \right)$, but the graph of the function needs two dimensions. The gradient extends this pattern. There is one element in the gradient for each *input* dimension.

10.20 Notation

The notation for the gradient of a function of several variables, say a function f(x_1, x_2, x_3), is usually written with the upside down delta, ∇ (the nabla symbol), followed by the function, and so it would look like this: ∇f(x_1, x_2, x_3). Another notation is grad f. Either of these is read as "the gradient of f".

We can use vector or matrix notation to express the notion of gradient of a scalar-valued multivariate function f: $R^n \rightarrow R$ to be the *vector*

$$\nabla f = \left[\frac{\partial f}{\partial x_1}, \frac{\partial f}{\partial x_2}, \ldots, \frac{\partial f}{\partial x_n} \right]$$

As we said earlier, this expresses that the gradient is the vector of partial derivatives. It is important to note, however, that the above is really an operator. It does not have a numeric value yet. In the same way, $\frac{dy}{dx}$ does not have a numeric value until it is applied to a specific function and at a specific value of x! For example, the derivative of x^2 is 2x, but 2x is not a number. If we ask what the value is at x = 5, then we get a number, 10. Similarly for the gradient, if we add in a *specific* vector **a**, then we get a particular value.

$$\nabla f(\mathbf{a}) = \left[\frac{\partial f(\mathbf{a})}{\partial x_1}, \frac{\partial f(\mathbf{a})}{\partial x_2}, \ldots, \frac{\partial f(\mathbf{a})}{\partial x_n} \right]$$

In addition, we can also use matrix notation. Many texts define the *derivative* of a multivariate function f *at* **a**! We have not done this yet, but we do it now. We use the D notation, and the derivative of a multivariate function will be defined as a row matrix whose entries are the components of $\nabla f(\mathbf{a})$. This will be useful and interesting because since it is a matrix, we can use matrix multiplication later.

$$D_x f(a) = \left[\frac{\partial f(\mathbf{a})}{\partial x_1} \quad \frac{\partial f(\mathbf{a})}{\partial x_2} \quad \cdots \quad \frac{\partial f(\mathbf{a})}{\partial x_n} \right]$$

The only difference between this and the gradient is that the gradient is given in vector form, whereas we purposely defined the derivative as a matrix. Other than that, they are the same thing.

We will use the gradient to train our neural network. Note, however, that actually we will be looking for the direction of greatest *descent* instead of greatest *ascent* and this will just be the negative of the gradient.

Practice 10.20.13

1. Have we defined ∇f when f is a vector-valued function?
2. Find ∇f, if f = $t^3 s^2 + t^7 s$.
3. Given f as in #1, what is ∇f(2,1)?

10.21 Conclusion

This is the end of our mathematical discussion of the gradient. In neural networks and in our programming of them, we will apply the gradient to a particular function called the error function. We will be using an example where the output variable in our machine learning algorithm is numeric and not categorical. Recall that in Naïve Bayes, we only worked with datasets where the output variable was categorical (play/not play, democrat/republican, etc.). For our neural network study, we will use datasets where the output is numeric. (In our deep learning chapter, we will use a non-numeric output variable.) In the case of a numeric output, the error is the difference between the predicted numeric output and the true numeric output. We will write a formula (a function) for the error. Of course, we want to minimize the error if we can. This is a calculus problem – minimizing a function. We use gradient descent to achieve this, which of course will require the gradient. We calculate partial derivatives of the error function. (Perhaps our error function could look like the upward facing paraboloid we looked at earlier.) Then we move in the direction of the (negative of the) gradient in order to reduce the error. We repeat this process over and over, hoping to arrive at the minimum of the error function. We will see this more clearly in the next chapters.

Chapter 11

Neural Networks – Feedforward Process and Backpropagation Process

---

We will study three simple neural networks as pictured in Figures 11.1–11.3 in order of complexity. Neural networks were originally designed to attempt to mimic (in an extremely simplified way) the way neurons in the human brain interact to produce intelligence. We will not go into that aspect of neural networks and rather will concentrate on the structure of these artificial neural networks (ANNs). We say "artificial" because they are not the same, obviously, as the complex neurons in the human brain.

We begin with what is called the feedforward process for these networks. This is the simpler part of the process. Then we will study the backpropagation process.

Functions Coded in This Chapter
sigmoid
jCostScalar
jCost2Inputs
sigmoidPrime
averageJCost
updateWeights
normal.5
predNNSingleValue
fullUpdateWeights
Jcost
predNNEpoch

11.1 1–1–1 Architecture of Feedforward Process

First, we will cover some terminology. All three of the Figures 11.1–11.3 can be referred to as graphs. The word "graph" is not used with its typical mathematical meaning here. This is a specialized use of the word in a field of mathematics called Graph Theory. There, a graph is defined as a set of vertices (also referred to as points or nodes) and a set of edges (also referred to as lines or connections) that connect the nodes. The circles above can be seen as the nodes, and the lines can be seen as the connections (or edges).

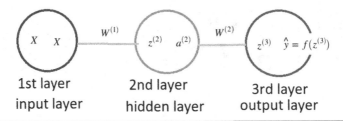

Figure 11.1 **Simplest neural network architecture: 1–1–1.**

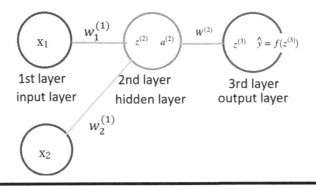

Figure 11.2 **Two-input-node architecture: 2–1–1.**

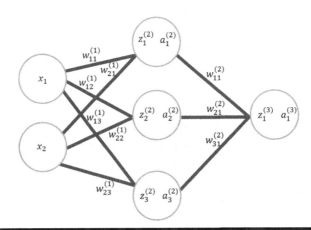

Figure 11.3 **2–3–1 neural network architecture.**

We also refer to layers of the network. The node with the x in it is called the first layer. It is also called the input layer. The node with the $z^{(2)}$ (and the $a^{(2)}$) is called the second layer. It is also called the hidden layer. The node with the $z^{(3)}$ (and the $\hat{y}$) is referred to as the third layer. It is also called the output layer.

In all three graphs above, there are three layers. Generally, a neural network will have an input layer, an output layer, and then any number of hidden layers.

Thus, a neural network is represented as a graph since it has nodes and edges. You may notice in the diagrams above that edges are labeled with w's. These are called the weights. In the Figure 11.1, we see weights for $w^{(1)}$ and $w^{(2)}$ and also a function at the end labeled with an f. The superscript notation is somewhat atypical in math, but the reason for the use of this notation, superscripts in parentheses, is because shortly two *subscripts* will be necessary for other items in the w notation and three subscripts may be overly confusing. Further, if we were to use a superscript without parentheses, it would quickly be mistaken for a power of w. The superscript in parentheses is the common way to indicate the layer to the left of the w, so that the layer to the left of $w^{(1)}$ is layer 1. Another way to read the (1) superscript is that $w^{(1)}$ is the first set of weights and $w^{(2)}$ is the second set of weights. The word "set" is used because shortly there will be several weights in the first layer and several weights in the next layer. In this text, we will use the sigmoid function for f, but there are a number of other functions that can be used instead. These functions, within the subject of neural networks, are typically referred to as either threshold functions or activation functions.

Once the two w's and the function are specified, the following indicates how the initial *input* value x gets processed and the network finally outputs what we usually denote as $\hat{y}$.

$$z^{(2)} = xw^{(1)}$$
$$a^{(2)} = f\left(z^{(2)}\right)'$$

where f is either the sigmoid function or some other threshold function. *This f is not shown in Figure 1.1 to avoid overly heavy notation.*

$$z^{(3)} = a^{(2)}w^{(2)}$$
$$\hat{y} = f\left(z^{(3)}\right) = f\left(f\left(xw^{(1)}\right)w^{(2)}\right)$$

We also refer to $\hat{y}$ as $a^{(3)}$ or as the prediction, and so

$$\text{prediction} = \hat{y} = a^{(3)}$$

We will also define a function J as follows which will be explained shortly.

$$J = 1/2\,(y - \hat{y})^2$$

We can do some simple replacements to get

$$J = 1/2\left(y - f\left(f\left(xw^{(1)}\right)w^{(2)}\right)\right)$$

Because it is not convenient to use a symbol like $\hat{y}$ in RStudio, we will often use "yhat" instead of $\hat{y}$. Note that in the subject of statistics, it is typical to use a hat above a symbol to indicate that it is an estimate of the quantity without the symbol. So, just from its notation, $\hat{y}$ would be expected to be an estimate of y. Here y is what we referred to in chapter 5 as the label and $\hat{y}$ is the predicted value for the label. However from this chapter forward y and its label will both be numeric, not categorical.

As a quick example, suppose x = 0.2, w$^{(1)}$ = 0.3, w$^{(2)}$ = 0.4, and f is the sigmoid function. What is ŷ? We simply need to fill in these values into our network equation $\hat{y} = f\left(f\left(xw^{(1)}\right)w^{(2)}\right)$. We can do it quickly in R. Notice that we are using slightly different notation to type into R. R and we will sometimes use the R notation outside of the R code. For example, you may see yhat in the text instead of ŷ.

```
#We start out by defining the f function that we will use, the sigmoid
function. We will use this repeatedly. Recall that it is defined as
σ(x)=1/(1+e^-x).
sigmoid <- function(z) {
  return(1/(1+exp(-z)))

#Assign values to the variables.
x=0.2
w1=0.3
w2=0.4
y=0.5
#Calculate yhat.
z2=x*w1
a2=sigmoid(z2)
z3=a2*w2
yhat=sigmoid(z3)
yhat
## [1] 0.5513182
```

11.2 Cost Function J

Next, we define an error or cost function. Our task, as it has been throughout this text, is to find a model which can take inputs and make good predictions as to what the correct output (also called the ground truth) should be. As we said above, ŷ is the estimate of the correct output. We use the variable y usually to denote the actual or ground truth rather than its estimate. In the above example, suppose x is the cost of a cup of coffee and y is the satisfaction level. Given the cost, we want to predict the satisfaction. Suppose we have one training example where the cup of coffee costs $0.2 and the satisfaction is 0.5. And suppose the weights are as given above. Then our simple neural network above predicts a satisfaction of 0.5513182. Now we can see that there is a difference between what the network predicts and what the ground truth is. This difference is referred to as the error or the cost. (Don't be confused when we say cost here. It so happens that in this particular example, we happen to be talking about money, but that is just a coincidence. The cost function is not tied to the use of money.) We can well imagine that for each example in our dataset, that is, for each cup of coffee in our dataset, there will be an amount of error between the actual satisfaction and the predicted satisfaction. We could take the average of each of these errors and say that is the average error or the average cost. First let us define cost for just one example in the dataset. Then we will define it for the whole dataset. For just one example, we have

$$J = 1/2\,(y - \hat{y})^2$$

This looks odd since we said that the cost is the difference between y and ŷ. It turns out that squaring that difference has advantages. One of the advantages is that it eliminates the possibility of cancelation of negative and positive errors when we want to add up the costs of a bunch of examples. The factor of ½ also has some advantages. Later we will want to take the derivative of the cost function and when we take the derivative, the square, and the factor of ½ will cancel out when using the chain rule. It is common but not necessary to have the factor of ½ in the cost J.

```
J=0.5*(y-yhat)^2
J
## [1] 0.001316779
```

Next, we encapsulate this in a function. We call the function jCostScalar(). The word "scalar" is included in the name because this calculation results in a scalar (not a matrix).

```
#Now we encapsulate the above in a function.
jCostScalar=function(xValue=x,w1Value=w1,w2Value=w2,yValue=y){
  #sample call: jCostScalar(x,w1,w2,y)
  z2=xValue*w1Value
  a2=sigmoid(z2)
  z3=a2*w2Value
  yhat=sigmoid(z3)
  J=0.5*(yValue-yhat)^2
  return(J)
}
jCostScalar(x,w1,w2,y)
## [1] 0.001316779
```

Note that the output from our data is numeric, and thus this kind of problem is referred to as a regression problem and not a classification problem. Neural networks may also be employed for classification, and in that case the calculation of error would be different, and the error function would be different. Often in a classification problem, a function known as the softmax function is used.

11.3 Two-Input Neural Network – Feedforward

Next, we work on a network with two inputs.

As you can see from Figure 11.4, if there are two inputs, there must also be two weights in the first layer. The calculation for $z^{(2)}$ is no longer $z^{(2)} = xw^{(1)}$ but rather the sum of the products of the inputs and their corresponding weights: $z^{(2)} = x_1w_1^{(1)} + x_2w_2^{(1)}$. After this calculation, all the

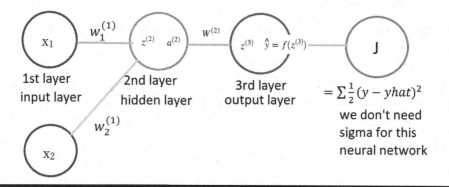

Figure 11.4 **2–1–1 architecture and the cost function J.**

subsequent calculations for this network will be the same as for the 1–1–1 network. If we define two vectors as $\mathbf{x} = \begin{bmatrix} x_1 & x_2 \end{bmatrix}$ and $\mathbf{w}^{(1)} = \begin{bmatrix} w_1^{(1)} w_2^{(1)} \end{bmatrix}$, then the calculation above could be written as the dot product of $\mathbf{x}$ and $\mathbf{w}$.

$$z^{(2)} = \mathbf{x} \cdot \mathbf{w}^{(1)} \tag{11.1}$$

However, it will turn out to be more general if we define these as two matrices rather than two vectors.

We just saw that the dot product works well for the calculation of $z^{(2)}$. Will matrices also work? Now, as always, we have a choice of defining the dimensions of these as 1×2 or 2×1. Since we want to multiply them and desire that the result be the scalar (technically a 1×1 matrix) $z^{(2)}$, either the first should be 1×2 and the second 2×1 or maybe we can use transposes to achieve a 1×1 dimensional result. As long as we get our desired calculation $\left(x_1 w_1^{(1)} + x_2 w_2^{(1)} \right)$, any format will do.

$$X = \begin{bmatrix} x_1 x_2 \end{bmatrix} \text{ dimensions } 1 \times 2$$

$$W^{(1)} = \begin{bmatrix} w_1 \\ w_2 \end{bmatrix} \text{ dimensions } 2 \times 1$$

$$z^{(2)} = XW^{(1)} (1 \times 2) \times (2 \times 1)$$

$a^{(2)} = f\left(z^{(2)} \right)$, where f is either the sigmoid function or some other threshold function

$$z^{(3)} = a^{(2)} w^{(2)}$$

$$\text{prediction} = \text{yhat} = a^{(3)} = f\left(z^{(3)} \right) = f\left(f\left(XW^{(1)} \right) w^{(2)} \right)$$

$$J = 1/2 \left(y - \text{yhat} \right)^2$$

$$J = 1/2 \left(y - f\left(f\left(XW^{(1)} \right) w^{(2)} \right) \right)$$

In R, we have the following.

```
#Start out with both X and W1 defined as vectors. In this case, the dot
product makes sense.
x1=0.2
x2=0.15
X=c(x1,x2) #It is not convenient in RStudio to make a character bold, and
so instead we are using a capital letter to indicate a vector.
w11=0.3
w12=0.25
W1=c(w11,w12)
#One way to achieve the dot product is as follows.
sum(X*W1)
## [1] 0.0975
```

```
#However, it will be convenient later for X and W1 to be defined as matrices.
We will also use capital letters here for matrices.

X=matrix(X,1,2)
W1=matrix(W1,2,1)

#The 2 other quantities we want to set are neither vectors nor matrices
but rather scalars.
w2=0.4
y=0.5

#It will be convenient to define variables for the sizes of the input
layer, hidden layer, and output layer. Then we can use these to define
the dimensions of the needed matrices when the layer sizes change. We can
see that the sizes of X and W both depend on the layer sizes. For
example, one of the dimensions of X is 2. Why is it 2? Because there are
two nodes in the input layer. If the input layer had three nodes, then
one of the dimensions of X would have to be 3. Thus, we will define the
dimensions of the different layers here and then use those variables to
define the dimensions of the matrices.

inputLayerSize=2
hiddenLayerSize=1 #We won't use this yet.
outputLayerSize=1 #We won't use this yet.

X=matrix(X,1,inputLayerSize)
W1=matrix(W1, inputLayerSize,1)

z2=X%*%W1 #Technically z2 should be a matrix, but we are leaving it
non-capitalized to help us remember that it only has one element in it.
The same is true for the following variables.
a2=sigmoid(z2)
z3=a2*w2
yhat=sigmoid(z3)
J=0.5*(y-yhat)^2
J #When we print out J, we see it is actually a matrix.
##                [,1]
## [1,] 0.001364727
```

RStudio tip: To check the value of a quantity in the Source panel, select that quantity with your mouse and then Run.

```
#Here is a version of the cost function for two input variables.
jCost2Inputs=function(xValue=X,w1Value=W1,w2Value=w2,yValue=y){
  #jCost2Inputs(X,W1,w2,y)
  z2=xValue%*%w1Value
  a2=sigmoid(z2)
  z3=a2*w2Value
  yhat=sigmoid(z3)
  J=0.5*(yValue-yhat)^2
  return(J)
}
jCost2Inputs() #Optionally we can leave out the arguments since the
defaults happen to be correct as is
```

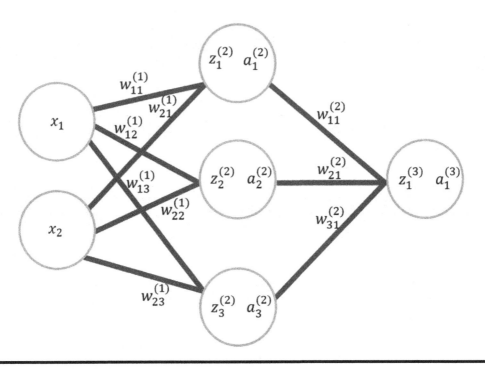

Figure 11.5 2–3–1 architecture.

```
##                 [,1]
## [1,]  0.001364727
```

```
#Does our code generalize to more than two inputs?
#Not yet.
```

11.4 2–3–1 Neural Network

Next, we work on a network with a 2–3–1 architecture. As you can see from the diagram, adding more nodes to the hidden layer seems to add a good bit of complexity to the network. Whereas in the 2–1–1 network, we had just two weights to deal with in layer 1, now we have six ($= 2 \times 3$) weights. You can see that if there were four nodes in the hidden layer, there would be eight ($= 2 \times 4$) weights in this layer, and if there were three nodes in the input layer and four nodes in the hidden layer there would be 12 weights. Furthermore, in Figure 11.5, there are now three weights in the second layer as compared with only one weight in the 2–1–1 network.

11.5 Weight Indices

How do the indices work for the first layer weights? For a weight $w_{i,j}^{(1)}$, the i indicates node number from the layer *to the left of the weight*, and the j indicates the node number from the layer *to the right of the weight*. So, for example, $w_{2,3}^{(1)}$ is the weight between the first layer node 2 and the second layer node 3. Note, some texts use the convention we are using, whereas some texts use the opposite convention.

11.6 Hidden Layer Calculations

How do we calculate the input into the hidden layer's first node? This value is denoted by $z_1^{(2)}$.

$$z_1^{(2)} = x_1 w_{11}^{(1)} + x_2 w_{21}^{(1)} \tag{11.2}$$

In general, for the kth node in layer 2 we have

$$z_k^{(2)} = \sum_i x_i w_{ik}^{(1)} \tag{11.3}$$

Now, in the previous network architecture example (the 2–1–1 architecture), we were able to define the calculation of the second layer value $z^{(2)}$ by using matrices. We had $z^{(2)} = XW^{(1)}$ (with dimensions $(1 \times 2) \times (2 \times 1)$). Let's work on the calculation of the current second layer using matrices as well.

In the previous case, we defined matrices for the inputs X and the weights $W^{(1)}$. We will define both for our current architecture, and now we will add in one more matrix, a matrix to hold all of the z values in the second (the hidden) layer. That is, we want a matrix that will hold the values $z_1^{(2)}, z_2^{(2)}$, and $z_3^{(2)}$. Naturally we will call this matrix $Z^{(2)}$ and define it as $Z^{(2)} = \begin{bmatrix} z_1^{(2)} & z_2^{(2)} & z_3^{(2)} \end{bmatrix}$. Again, we have the option of setting its dimensions to 1×3 or to 3×1. We will decide on that after defining X and $W^{(1)}$.

We are hoping to write a matrix equation like this:

$$XW^{(1)} = Z^{(2)} \tag{11.4}$$

We will allow the use of the transpose operator if we need it.

Somehow we need to end up with the product of our X and $W^{(1)}$ matrices as being either a 3×1 or a 1×3. What options does that leave us for the dimensions of X and $W^{(1)}$? X is going to be either 1×2 or 2×1. $W^{(1)}$ is going to be either 2×3 or 3×2. Actually it could be possible that $W^{(1)}$ be 1×6 or 6×1, but this won't work well for us. If X is 1×2, then $W^{(1)}$ would need to be 2×3 (in order to be able to write $XW^{(1)}$). If X is 2×1, then there is no configuration of $W^{(1)}$ that will give us a $Z^{(2)}$ which is either 1×3 or 3×1. So now we know that X must be 1×2 if we are going to be able to write XW. This means that $W^{(1)}$ must be 2×3. This means that their product $Z^{(2)}$ *must* be 1×3. Be aware that other texts may reverse the order of X and $W^{(1)}$ like this: $W^{(1)}X = Z^{(2)}$, and this may imply different configurations, so please take note.

We now have the dimensions for the required matrices. But does XW actually give the correct values of $Z^{(2)}$? The correct values, remember, are what is given in Equation 11.3.

X is 1×2 and looks like this:

$$X = \begin{bmatrix} x_1 x_2 \end{bmatrix}$$

Because $W^{(1)}$ is 2×3, the best candidate for the placement of the weights in $W^{(1)}$ is

$$W^{(1)} = \begin{bmatrix} w_{1,1}^{(1)} & w_{1,2}^{(1)} & w_{1,3}^{(1)} \\ w_{2,1}^{(1)} & w_{2,2}^{(1)} & w_{2,3}^{(1)} \end{bmatrix} \tag{11.5}$$

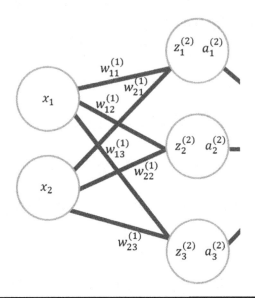

Figure 11.6 First two layers of the 2–3–1 neural network architecture.

So with the above configuration, let us explore what $XW^{(1)}$ looks like and whether it gives the product for the $Z^{(2)}$ we seek.

Let us first confirm what the $Z^{(2)}$ that we are seeking is. It has three elements: $Z^{(2)} = \begin{bmatrix} z_1^{(2)} & z_2^{(2)} & z_3^{(2)} \end{bmatrix}$ (Figure 11.6).

The correct calculations for each of the elements of $Z^{(2)}$ are as follows.

$$z_1^{(2)} = x_1 w_{11}^{(1)} + x_2 w_{21}^{(1)} \tag{11.6}$$

$$z_2^{(2)} = x_1 w_{12}^{(1)} + x_2 w_{22}^{(1)} \tag{11.7}$$

$$z_3^{(2)} = x_1 w_{13}^{(1)} + x_2 w_{23}^{(1)} \tag{11.8}$$

$$Z^{(2)} = \begin{bmatrix} z_1^{(2)} & z_2^{(2)} & z_3^{(2)} \end{bmatrix} = \begin{bmatrix} x_1 w_{11}^{(1)} + x_2 w_{21}^{(1)} & x_1 w_{12}^{(1)} + x_2 w_{22}^{(1)} & x_1 w_{13}^{(1)} + x_2 w_{23}^{(1)} \end{bmatrix} \tag{11.9}$$

Is this what $XW^{(1)}$ provides us with (Figure 11.7)?

$$XW^{(1)} = \begin{bmatrix} x_1 & x_2 \end{bmatrix} \begin{bmatrix} w_{1,1}^{(1)} & w_{1,2}^{(1)} & w_{1,3}^{(1)} \\ w_{2,1}^{(1)} & w_{2,2}^{(1)} & w_{2,3}^{(1)} \end{bmatrix} \tag{11.10}$$

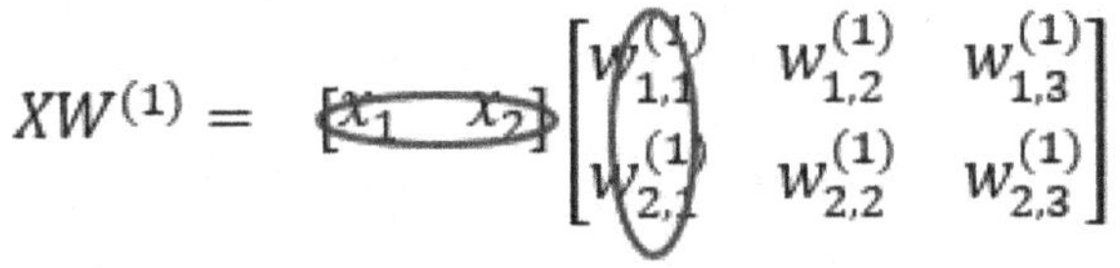

$$XW^{(1)} = \begin{bmatrix} x_1 & x_2 \end{bmatrix} \begin{bmatrix} w_{1,1}^{(1)} & w_{1,2}^{(1)} & w_{1,3}^{(1)} \\ w_{2,1}^{(1)} & w_{2,2}^{(1)} & w_{2,3}^{(1)} \end{bmatrix}$$

Figure 11.7 How to multiply rows and columns.

The ovals suggest how the first multiplication is performed, and we can see that it produces the correct first element of $Z^{(2)}$. The reader may verify that the other two elements are also correct.

Thus, we have established that $XW^{(1)} = Z^{(2)}$ expresses all the multiplications and sums that need to be performed to obtain all the correct z values.

Does this generalize to input and hidden layers that have more nodes?

We have also seen that when the number of nodes in either the input layer or the hidden layer increases, the number of weights increases substantially.

If we have more than two nodes in X, or if we have more than three nodes in $Z^{(2)}$, will the equation still be correct? What does the size (dimensions) of X do to the matrix $W^{(1)}$, and what does the size of $Z^{(2)}$ do to it? The following diagram shows the current situation. We can ignore the network after Z as we have yet to discuss it (Figure 11.8).

If we add a new node to X, we can see that it will need to be connected to each of the three nodes in the hidden layer. This means we will add three new weights to $W^{(1)}$. This will produce a new row in $W^{(1)}$. That however will not affect the number of nodes of $Z^{(2)}$ (of the hidden layer). Each element of $Z^{(2)}$ will involve more computation, but the dimensions of $Z^{(2)}$ will remain the same. Which dimension of $W^{(1)}$ changes? The number of rows, i.e., if the dimension of $W^{(1)}$ is n × m, the n changes.

Now we analyze what is the effect of increasing the number of nodes in the hidden layer. Looking at the network diagram (in its current state), we can see that for each new node in the hidden layer, we will need two more weights, one for each of the nodes in X. You should verify that these two new weights will become a new column according to the rules of matrix multiplication. Thus if $W^{(1)}$ was originally n × m, the m will increase by 1 for each additional node in $Z^{(2)}$.

From this analysis, it should become clear that the dimensions of $W^{(1)}$ are

inputLayerSize × hiddenLayerSize.

If we design $W^{(1)}$ to have these dimensions, then the formula $XW^{(1)} = Z^{(2)}$ will hold generally for any input layer size and any hidden layer size.

Let us see how what we have discussed so far appears as R code.

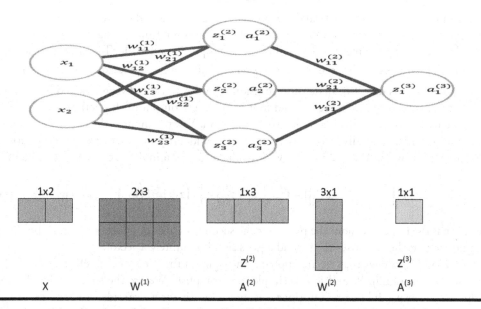

Figure 11.8   Visualization of the dimensions involved in the 2–3–1 architecture.

11.6.1 2–3–1 NetWork.R

```
#So far, we have a calculation for Z2 in terms of X and W1.
#We will define W1 to have small randomly selected numbers initially.
This is typically the way the weights are initially set. The intelligence
of the system then comes into play as training proceeds, and these
weights are adjusted to produce better predictions.
inputLayerSize=2
hiddenLayerSize=3
outputLayerSize=1 #We won't use this yet.
```

```
#runif stands for random uniform distribution. It generates random
numbers. Note: runif(inputLayerSize*nnhiddenLayerSize,-1,1) has three
arguments. The first argument is the number of observations to be
generated. So in our code, we are generating 2x3=6 observations. These
will populate W1.
The second and third arguments are the lower and upper bounds on the
range of random numbers that are selectable. Here we are limiting the
numbers to be between -1 and +1.
```

```
set.seed(3) #Make the code generating random numbers below reproducible.
W1<<-matrix(runif(inputLayerSize*hiddenLayerSize,-1,1),inputLayerSize,hid
denLayerSize)
x1=0.2
x2=0.15
X=c(x1,x2)
X=matrix(X,1,2)
#So far, all we have done is the calculation of Z2.
Z2=X%*%W1
Z2
##                 [,1]         [,2]        [,3]
## [1,] -0.04052847 -0.09770276 0.07215849
```

We continue with the mathematical description of the 2–3–1 neural network. So far, we have $Z^{(2)}$. Just as in the 2–1–1 network, we apply the threshold/activation function sigmoid() to the values of $Z^{(2)}$. We want to apply some sort of threshold to the input of *each* node. This means we apply this function to each node of the second layer *separately*. This can be expressed as $\mathbf{f}\left(Z^{(2)}\right)$. Notice that the **f** is bold. Why is that? Recall in our discussion of multivariate and vector-valued functions that if a function is vector-valued, then a bold font is used. The output of this action is a vector! Also it may be useful to ask if this is a multivariate function. Yes, the input is the *vector* $Z^{(2)}$ which has three components. (Actually, it is a matrix, but we can identify this matrix as a vector with three elements.) Thus, we have a multivariate vector-valued function in **f**. We can write it explicitly as

$$\mathbf{f}\left(\begin{bmatrix} z_1^{(1)} & z_2^{(1)} & z_3^{(1)} \end{bmatrix}\right) = \mathbf{f}\left(z_1^{(1)}, z_2^{(1)}, z_3^{(1)}\right) = \begin{bmatrix} f\left(z_1^{(1)}\right) & f\left(z_2^{(1)}\right) & f\left(z_2^{(1)}\right) \end{bmatrix} \qquad (11.11)$$

Notice that the last expression (the part after the second equals sign) does not use the boldfaced f. Also notice that the part after the second equals sign is definitely a vector.

Equation 11.1 shows that we are applying the sigmoid function to each element of $Z^{(2)}$. This is the de facto action in R, and so it is simple to accomplish. We use the letter "a" for the output of this action, as we did before, but since it is now a matrix (or we can identify it as a matrix), we denote it as $A^{(2)}$. It is a 1×3 matrix.

$$A^{(2)} = \begin{bmatrix} a_1^{(2)} & a_2^{(2)} & a_3^{(2)} \end{bmatrix} = \begin{bmatrix} f\left(z_1^{(1)}\right) & f\left(z_2^{(1)}\right) & f\left(z_2^{(1)}\right) \end{bmatrix} \tag{11.12}$$

```
sigmoid <- function(z) {
  return(1/(1+exp(-z)))
}
A2=sigmoid(Z2)

##              [,1]       [,2]       [,3]
## [1,] 0.4898693 0.4755937 0.5180318
```

$A^{(2)}$ has the same dimensions as $Z^{(2)}$, 1×3.

11.7 Output Layer Calculations and Cost

Our next step is to obtain $Z^{(3)}$. We are denoting this as a matrix, even though it is a 1×1 matrix.

$$Z^{(3)} = a_1^{(2)} w_1^{(2)} + a_2^{(2)} w_2^{(2)} + a_3^{(2)} w_3^{(2)}.$$

Again, this calculation could be accomplished with the dot product of vectors, but in keeping with our matrix representation, we will accomplish it with the product of $A^{(2)}$ and a new matrix which we will call $W^{(2)}$. $W^{(2)}$ holds the three weights in the second layer of weights. Thus, it can either be 1×3 or 3×1. Since $A^{(2)}$ is 1×3, we choose $W^{(2)}$ to be a 3×1 matrix so that the product $A^{(2)} W^{(2)}$ is 1×1.

$$W^{(2)} = \begin{bmatrix} w_1^{(2)} \\ w_2^{(2)} \\ w_3^{(2)} \end{bmatrix}$$

$$A^{(2)} W^{(2)} = Z^{(3)}$$

In general, if hiddenLayerSize stands for the number of nodes in the hidden layer, and outputLayerSize stands for the number of nodes in the output layer, then $A^{(2)}$ will be a $1 \times$ hiddenLayerSize matrix, and $W^{(2)}$ will be a hiddenLayerSize $\times$ outputLayerSize matrix.

Finally, to get our prediction $\hat{y}$ for a given input X and given weight matrices $W^{(1)}$ and $W^{(2)}$, we feed the 1×1 matrix $Z^{(3)}$ into the scalar-valued sigmoid() function, which we denote as f to get

$$f\left(Z^{(3)}\right) = \hat{y}$$

And given ground truth value y we can calculate the error with the same equation as in the 2–1–1 network.

$$J = 1/2\left(y - \hat{y}\right)^2$$

In R, we have the following code.

```
#Next create a 3 x 1 W2 matrix.
#We will use the outputLayerSize setting here.
W2<<-matrix(runif(hidW2<<-matrix(runif(hiddenLayerSize*outputLayerS
ize,-1,1),hiddenLayerSize,outputLayerSize)
W2
##                [,1]
## [1,] -0.7507331
## [2,] -0.4107982
## [3,]  0.1552198
Z3=A2%*%W2
Z3
##                [,1]
## [1,] -0.4827253
yhat=Z3
#If we know the ground truth y label for our input vector X,
#we can also calculate the error.
#Suppose
y= 0.5
#Then
J=0.5*(y-yhat)^2
J
##             [,1]
## [1,]  0.4828745
```

We have accomplished what is referred to as *forward propagation* of the neural network. We have figured out how to express the forward propagation for various network architectures. The next step is to do what is called backward propagation or backpropagation. Backpropagation is the *learning process* by which we hope to improve our predictions.

11.7.1 Why the Sigmoid Function?

Before we go onto how learning occurs, let us address one additional issue. We have seen that the sigmoid function has been a feature of all three of the neural networks we have discussed. What is the purpose of including the sigmoid function, and what limitations would we left with if we did not use it?

Let us go back to our simplest architecture, the 1–1–1 architecture. Without the sigmoid function, what would our calculation be? We would have $w^{(1)}x = z^{(1)}$ and $w^{(2)}z^{(1)} = z^{(2)}$. Substituting $w^{(1)}x$ in the second equation for $z^{(1)}$, we get $w^{(2)} w^{(1)}x = z^{(2)}$. Thinking of x as the input and $z^{(2)}$ as the output, this is a *linear* function of x. That is to say, it's graph is a straight line (and in fact a straight line through the origin) and the slope of the line is simply $m = w^{(2)} w^{(1)}$. But we are trying to model all kinds of relationships between our input and our output. Clearly a straight-line relationship that passes through the origin is severely limited. If our only parameter is the slope of that line, we will not be able to fit the model to the data with sufficient flexibility. Later on, we will consider networks with more layers, and we have already considered layers with more than just a single node. However, if you reflect on these architectures, you will realize that no matter how many layers we include, if we do not include the sigmoid function (or some other non-linear function), then the equation we get, which expresses the relation of the output z to the input x, will always be linear. Including more nodes in a layer also does not alter this fact. For example, if we include two input nodes, denoting them by x_1 and x_2, we will arrive at $z = f(x_1, x_2)$, but it will be a linear function of x_1 and x_2. We discussed this in Chapter 9, and we would identify this as a plane in three dimensions. Again, trying to model an arbitrarily complex relationship between the two inputs x_1 and x_2, and the output z, using a plane sets a severe limitation on our ability to capture non-linear relationships.

On the other hand, there is a theorem referred to as the **universal approximation theorem** which states that *any continuous function* can be approximated by a neural network with a finite number of layers and nodes if we have an activation function like our sigmoid function.[1] Thus, the neural networks we are working with will provide us with tremendous modeling power.

Next, we study how a neural network learns.

---

[1] Balázs Csanád Csáji (2001) Approximation with Artificial Neural Networks; Faculty of Sciences; Eötvös Loránd University, Hungary.

Backpropagation in Neural Networks

As we have mentioned, the learning in the neural network takes place through the process called backpropagation. The goal is to adjust the weights in the neural network in such a way that the predictions yhat of y become better and the prediction error is reduced. This adjustment relies on the calculation of the derivative of the cost function with respect to each of the weights (individually). The derivatives are then used with the hope of finding a set of weights which make the cost as small as possible. Since cost is another word for error in this context, we are seeking the configuration of the neural network weights that will lead to the least error in our predictions.

11.7.2 What Can be Adjusted in the Network to Reduce the Costs?

In the network, the only items we can adjust are the weights. We can't adjust the inputs. Those are given to us. There is really nothing else in the network to adjust except for the weights. Thus, we are seeking a set of weights which lead to the least error. We spent the previous chapter discussing the method of gradient descent, and it is that method which will be applied here. Let us review our reasoning.

For those who have taken a first semester calculus course, the idea of minimizing a quantity may ring a bell. We use the derivative to find a maximum or minimum of a function. In the process of backpropagation, the derivative is also employed and again to search for a minimum.

However, the process is significantly different than in the first semester calculus course. You may recall that in the first semester calculus course, the derivative is set to zero, and then that equation is solved. It is generally assumed that it is possible to solve for zero, and the problems presented in the course are almost always set up to be solvable in this way. However, many equations are not easily solvable for zero. As we mentioned in the last chapter, an example of such a function is $f(x) = x^5 - x + 1$. Even such a seemingly simple function cannot be solved for zero. A neural network is a relatively complicated function, and although it is possible to *find the derivative*, setting it equal to zero and solving that equation may be very difficult or not even possible.

Instead of throwing up our hands and surrendering though, the technique of gradient descent is employed, and this will enable the pursuit of a minimum for the cost function. Thus, we still seek the derivative of the cost function. Then, however, once we calculate the derivative, we use it, by means of the technique of gradient descent, to adjust the weights of the neural network in such a way that the error is reduced. The method is not foolproof and will not always find the values of the weights which would result in the absolute smallest error, but it does produce excellent results, as is in evidence in the spectacular success of image recognition and natural language processing algorithms, among many other applications.

This backpropagation algorithm was developed in the later half of the 20th century – see Chapter 4 of Haykin, S. *Neural Networks – A Comprehensive Foundation*, 2nd ed., p. 43. Before the discovery of the algorithm, *manual* changes to the network weights was used. This means that the scientist just changed the weights manually and tested the prediction to see if it improved. In general, it is not that straightforward to know how to "distribute the error" among all the different weights in a network. By "distributing the error", we mean how much each weight must be changed in the network in order to reduce the overall error of prediction. It will turn out that the contribution that a hidden node will make to the output is dependent on both weights downstream and the activity of the node.

Thus, our job now is to find the derivative of the cost function with respect to the network weights. As before, we start off with the simplest network we have discussed and then proceed to the more complicated ones.

Here we have the 1–1–1 network (Figure 11.9) and have added the cost function J into the diagram. We want to see how the cost changes with respect to a change in either the weight $W^{(2)}$ or $W^{(1)}$. (In this simple network, these matrices only contain a single element.) Then we adjust the weights with that information.

Thus, we seek the derivative of J with respect to $W^{(2)}$ (which since it is 1×1, we may express as $w^{(2)}$). We will also follow the same logic for $W^{(1)}$ (which since it is 1×1, we may express as $w^{(1)}$), and so we will also calculate the derivative of J with respect to $w^{(1)}$. *This is the method of gradient descent which is the essence of backpropagation.*

Our current goal is to find $\dfrac{dJ}{dw^{(1)}}$ and $\dfrac{dJ}{dw^{(2)}}$.

11.7.3 Notation

The following is a table (Table 11.1) for the symbols used in the code and the mathematical symbol along with definitions and dimensions. Although we have not considered X to have

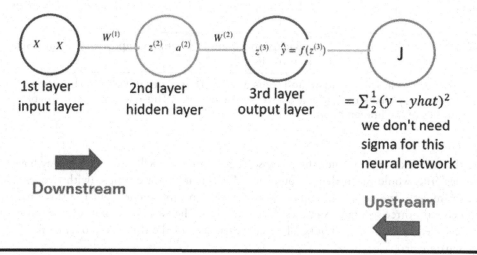

Figure 11.9 Illustration of the meaning of downstream and upstream. The summation sign Σ is not necessary here but is used in more complicated architectures.

Table 11.1 Notation for Neural Networks

Code Symbol	Math Symbol	Definition	Dimensions
X	X	Input data, each row in an example	(numExamples, inputLayerSize)
Y	Y	Target data	(numExamples, outputLayerSize)
W1	$W^{(1)}$	Layer 1 weights	(inputLayerSize, hiddenLayerSize)
W2	$W^{(2)}$	Layer 2 weights	(hiddenLayerSize, outputLayerSize)
Z2	$Z^{(2)}$	Layer 2 activation	(numExamples, hiddenLayerSize)
A2	$A^{(2)}$	Layer 2 activity	(numExamples, hiddenLayerSize)
z3	$z^{(3)}$	Layer 3 activation	(numExamples, outputLayerSize)
jcostScalar, jCost2Inputs, averageJCost, jCost	J	Cost	(1, outputLayerSize)
dJ_dz3	$\dfrac{\partial J}{\partial z^{(3)}}$	Partial derivative of cost with respect to $z^{(3)}$	(numExamples, outputLayerSize)
dJ_dw2	$\dfrac{\partial J}{\partial w_1^{(2)}}$	Partial derivative of cost with respect to $W^{(2)}$	(1, 1)
dJ_dW1	$\dfrac{\partial J}{\partial W^{(1)}}$	Partial derivative of cost with respect to $W^{(1)}$	(inputLayerSize, hiddenLayerSize)
Delta2	$\delta^{(2)}$	Backpropagating error 2	(numExamples, hiddenLayerSize)
Delta3	$\delta^{(3)}$	Backpropagating error 1	(numExamples, outputLayerSize)

Some of these names are standard and some are not. There does not seem to be much consensus, for example, on the use of "activity" versus "activation". These terms most probably derive from studies of the human brain.

more than one example in it, for the purpose of generality, we will allow that X may have many examples. This would mean that X could be a 3 × 2 matrix, for example (with two inputs and three examples). The network diagram would have two input nodes, but the three rows of X would contain three separate examples. For example, if the two inputs into our neural network were "calories_burned" and "hours_of_sleep", then each of the three rows of X could represent three separate people.

Furthermore, note the two terms "activation" and "activity". We have been using the term "activation function" and will continue to use that term (as well as "threshold function").

Sometimes the Z terms are referred to as activation terms, but we will not use that word often. Also, sometimes the word "activity" is used for the A terms. We will not use that word often either. Nevertheless, for compatibility with some other texts, we mention this terminology in this table. Further note that every neural network in this text has only a single node in the output layer. Also note that unless we are doing "batch processing" of data, the numExamples will be 1. (We will explain batch processing later.)

Note in the 1–1–1 network, we sometimes refer to the weights with capital letters (as though they were matrices) and sometimes with lowercase letters. The choice of lowercase or uppercase in a particular section is made to make the explanation easier. Since it is a 1–1–1 network, each matrix of weights only contains a single weight.

11.8 Calculation of $\dfrac{\mathrm{dJ}}{\mathrm{dw}^{(2)}}$

Since $w^{(2)}$ is closer to J in the network diagram we will work on it first. Also, we will find that some of the calculations needed for $\dfrac{\mathrm{dJ}}{\mathrm{dw}^{(2)}}$ will also be needed for $\dfrac{\mathrm{dJ}}{\mathrm{dw}^{(1)}}$, and we can cut down on the work needed for $\dfrac{\mathrm{dJ}}{\mathrm{dw}^{(1)}}$ by keeping a record of the calculation of $\dfrac{\mathrm{dJ}}{\mathrm{dw}^{(2)}}$ in order to avoid repeated calculation of the same quantity. In fact, this is a common practice in computer science and is called memoization.

11.8.1 Memoization to Save Resources

In a few pages, we will have shown both of the following equations are true:

$$\frac{\mathrm{dJ}}{\mathrm{dw}^{(2)}} = \frac{\mathrm{dJ}}{\mathrm{d}\left(y-\mathrm{yhat}\right)^2} \frac{\mathrm{d}\left(y-\mathrm{yhat}\right)^2}{\mathrm{d}\left(y-\mathrm{yhat}\right)} \frac{\mathrm{d}\left(y-\mathrm{yhat}\right)}{\mathrm{dyhat}} \frac{\mathrm{dyhat}}{\mathrm{dz}^{(3)}} \frac{\mathrm{dz}^{(3)}}{\mathrm{dw}^{(2)}}$$

and the longer expression

$$\frac{\mathrm{dJ}}{\mathrm{dw}^{(1)}} = \frac{\mathrm{dJ}}{\mathrm{d}\left(y-\mathrm{yhat}\right)^2} \frac{\mathrm{d}\left(y-\mathrm{yhat}\right)^2}{\mathrm{d}\left(y-\mathrm{yhat}\right)} \frac{\mathrm{d}\left(y-\mathrm{yhat}\right)}{\mathrm{dyhat}} \frac{\mathrm{dyhat}}{\mathrm{dz}^{(3)}} \frac{\mathrm{dz}^{(3)}}{\mathrm{da}^{(2)}} \frac{\mathrm{da}^{(2)}}{\mathrm{dz}^{(2)}} \frac{\mathrm{dz}^{(2)}}{\mathrm{dw}^{(1)}}$$

If you stare at both, you will see that they have several factors in common. In particular, the string of factors

$$\frac{\mathrm{dJ}}{\mathrm{d}\left(y-\mathrm{yhat}\right)^2} \frac{\mathrm{d}\left(y-\mathrm{yhat}\right)^2}{\mathrm{d}\left(y-\mathrm{yhat}\right)} \frac{\mathrm{d}\left(y-\mathrm{yhat}\right)}{\mathrm{dyhat}} \frac{\mathrm{dyhat}}{\mathrm{dz}^{(3)}} \tag{11.13}$$

is common to both. We will define this common set of factors as $\delta^{(3)}$ using the Greek symbol δ (pronounced delta).

$$\delta^{(3)} = \frac{\mathrm{dJ}}{\mathrm{d}\left(y-\mathrm{yhat}\right)^2} \frac{\mathrm{d}\left(y-\mathrm{yhat}\right)^2}{\mathrm{d}\left(y-\mathrm{yhat}\right)} \frac{\mathrm{d}\left(y-\mathrm{yhat}\right)}{\mathrm{dyhat}} \frac{\mathrm{dyhat}}{\mathrm{dz}^{(3)}} \tag{11.14}$$

Once $\delta^{(3)}$ has been calculated for $\dfrac{dJ}{dw^{(2)}}$, then it won't be necessary to calculate it again for $\dfrac{dJ}{dw^{(3)}}$. This is not particularly important here because this network is tiny. But in large neural networks, significant computational expense can be avoided. Further, when we recode our neural network in a few chapters using a modular approach, this will be a critical step.

As mentioned, the process of storing previously computed results is called memoization. The δ s may be matrices or scalars. It will depend on whether there is more than one node in a layer. In this text, we write delta2 or delta3 for scalars and Delta2 or Delta3 for matrices in the code. In the mathematical equations, we use $\delta^{(2)}$ and $\delta^{(3)}$. Note that the Greek letter may represent either a matrix or a scalar and so is a bit less informative than the Roman letter symbol.

It is important to state that defining and using deltas is simply a convenience and is in no way necessary for understanding or running a neural network. We have included it in the text because, up until the present, it has been widely used in the literature.

`11.8.2 Downstream and Upstream

While we are introducing new terminology, we mention the terms *upstream* and *downstream* within the network. (Refer to Figure 11.9.) In the feedforward calculations, it seems natural to say the network is flowing from left to right. On the other hand, in backpropagation, it may seem natural to say the network is flowing from right to left. However, in our discussions, we will always say the network flows from left to right. Therefore, an item which is downstream refers to an item in the network "to the right", and the word "upstream" means some item in the network "to the left".

11.8.3 Back to the Derivatives

Now that we have explained the δ notation, let us refocus on finding the derivatives $\dfrac{dJ}{dw^{(1)}}$ and $\dfrac{dJ}{dw^{(2)}}$.

First, we rewrite the definition of J.

$$J = \tfrac{1}{2}(y - \hat{y})^2$$

At first glance, it does not look as though J has any relationship to $w^{(1)}$ or $w^{(2)}$. It does not seem that J is a function of either of these. But of course, if we write out the full expression for $\hat{y}$ in the equation for J, we will see that $w^{(1)}$ and/or $w^{(2)}$ show up. Reading from our previous Section 11.1,

$$\hat{y} = f\left(f\left(xw^{(1)}\right)w^{(2)}\right)$$

so that

$$J = \frac{1}{2}(y - \hat{y})^2 = \frac{1}{2}\left(y - f\left(f\left(xw^{(1)}\right)w^{(2)}\right)\right)$$

and so J is clearly a function of both $w^{(1)}$ and $w^{(2)}$.

As we said, since $w^{(2)}$ is closer to J, we will work on its derivative $\frac{dJ}{dw^2}$ first, and to do that, it is convenient to rewrite J as

$$J = \frac{1}{2}\left(y - f\left(a^{(2)}w^{(2)}\right)\right)^2$$

Here it is clear that J depends on $w^{(2)}$. We will need the chain rule to calculate $\frac{dJ}{dw^{(2)}}$ since $w^{(2)}$ is embedded in the function f which is embedded in a squaring function and so on. This will require repeated use of the chain rule. Don't be too discouraged though because basically that is the *only* mathematical rule needed to accomplish backpropagation. In fact, it may be better to rename backpropagation as "repeated use of the chain rule".

In the above equation for J, renaming of the quantities may make the use of the chain rule clearer, and we will do this now as an example below, but then we won't repeat this kind of exercise for other similar uses of the chain rule later.

$z^{(3)} = a^{(2)}w^{(2)}$ [z is the product of the input and weight]

$\hat{y} = f\left(z^{(3)}\right)$ [we pass z through the threshold function sigmoid]

$e = y - \hat{y}$ [e is the error: the difference between the actual and predicted output]

$s = e^2$ [s is the square of the error]

$J = \frac{1}{2}s$ [the constant of $\frac{1}{2}$ is just to make the derivative we will take later look nicer]

(11.15)

Now we can write J as any of the following expressions.

$$J = \frac{1}{2}s = \frac{1}{2}e^2 = \frac{1}{2}(y - \hat{y})^2 = \frac{1}{2}\left(y - f\left(z^{(3)}\right)\right)^2 = \frac{1}{2}\left(y - f\left(a^{(2)}w^{(2)}\right)\right)^2$$

Next calculate $\frac{dJ}{dw^2}$ with the use of the chain rule.

$$\frac{dJ}{dw^{(2)}} = \frac{dJ}{ds}\frac{ds}{de}\frac{de}{d\hat{y}}\frac{d\hat{y}}{dz^{(3)}}\frac{dz^{(3)}}{dw^{(2)}}$$

(11.16)

Note that the chain rule tells us that to get to the derivative of J with respect to $w^{(2)}$, we simply compute the derivatives of each step of the process (moving from right to left) and take the product of these derivatives. This will also be the case for the derivative of J with respect to $w^{(1)}$.

Note that this can alternatively be written as

$$\frac{dJ}{dw^{(2)}} = \frac{dJ}{d(y-yhat)^2} \frac{d(y-yhat)^2}{d(y-yhat)} \frac{d(y-yhat)}{dyhat} \frac{dyhat}{dz^{(3)}} \frac{dz^{(3)}}{dw^{(2)}} \tag{11.17}$$

Calculating each of the derivatives above in Equation 11.16 using the renaming in 11.15 leads us to

$$\frac{dJ}{dw^{(2)}} = \delta^{(3)} \frac{dz^{(3)}}{dw^{(2)}} = \left(\frac{1}{2}\right)(2e)(-1)\left(f'\left(z^{(3)}\right)\right)\frac{dz^{(3)}}{dw^{(2)}} = e(-1)f'\left(z^{(3)}\right) = -\left(y-\hat{y}\right)f'\left(z^{(3)}\right)\frac{dz^{(3)}}{dw^{(2)}} \tag{11.18}$$

Next check that, as we said above in expression 11.13, the first four terms here (11.18) are exactly what we decided to call $\delta^{(3)}$ and so only the last term $\frac{dz^{(3)}}{dw^{(2)}}$ is not included in $\delta^{(3)}$. Thus, we have

$$\frac{dJ}{dw^{(2)}} = \delta^{(3)} \frac{dz^{(3)}}{dw^{(2)}} \tag{11.19}$$

Practice 11.8.1

1. Explain why $\dfrac{d(y-yhat)}{dyhat} = -1$.

Noting that

$$\frac{dz^{(3)}}{dw^{(2)}} = a^{(2)}$$

we get

$$\frac{dJ}{dw^{(2)}} = -\left(y-\hat{y}\right)f'\left(z^{(3)}\right)\frac{dz^{(3)}}{dw^{(2)}} = \delta^{(3)} \frac{dz^{(3)}}{dw^{(2)}} = \delta^{(3)}a^{(2)} \tag{11.20}$$

It is sometimes observed that $\dfrac{dJ}{dw^{(2)}}$ is proportional, by a factor of $\delta^{(3)}$, to the input size itself, $a^{(2)}$.

A *note about using the chain rule*: The above Equation 11.17 required the use of the chain rule four times. We could write the derivative with fewer uses of the chain rule, for example, like this: $\dfrac{dJ}{dw^{(2)}} = \dfrac{dJ}{de} \dfrac{de}{d\hat{y}} \dfrac{d\hat{y}}{dw^{(2)}}$. This is correct but would require additional uses of the chain rule within some of these derivatives. (Try it and see.) Equation 11.17, with four uses of the chain rule, breaks the use of the chain rule into its smallest possible steps.

Another note: In our *code*, the threshold/activation function is the sigmoid function; we could replace f with σ and then write out $f'\left(z^{(3)}\right) = \sigma\left(z^{(3)}\right)\left(1-\sigma\left(z^{(3)}\right)\right)$ (we showed this result in the previous math chapter in the proof of Equation 10.8), but we won't need to express this derivative as a function of σ because, *in our code*, the following is used for the derivative of sigmoid.

```
sigmoidPrime<-function(z){
return(exp(-z)/(1+exp(-z))^2)
```

Practice 11.8.2

1. In the expression above, $\dfrac{dJ}{dw^{(2)}} = \delta^{(3)}a^{(2)}$, which is the factor of proportionality? And which is the input?

11.9 Calculation of $\dfrac{dJ}{dw^{(1)}}$

Next, we work on the calculation of $\dfrac{dJ}{dw^{(1)}}$. Just to alert you to the pattern in our results, we mention that $\dfrac{dJ}{dw^{(1)}}$ will look very similar to $\dfrac{dJ}{dw^{(2)}}$. We will define $\delta^{(2)}$ (not $\delta^{(3)}$ which we already defined) so that $\dfrac{dJ}{dw^{(1)}} = \delta^{(2)}\dfrac{dz^{(2)}}{dw^{(1)}}$. You can see the similarity with Equation 11.20. In fact, if we were to add more layers into the neural network architecture, a similar pattern would extend to those layers as well. The point of expressing the derivatives in terms of these deltas is to emphasize that the derivatives are obtained by calculating the derivative of the appropriate z and calculations (the delta) which have been done earlier (downstream) (Figure 11.10).

Proceeding to the calculation of $\dfrac{dJ}{dw^{(1)}}$, first write J explicitly as a function of $w^{(1)}$.

$$J = \frac{1}{2}\left(y - f\left(a^{(2)}w^{(2)}\right)\right)^2 = \frac{1}{2}\left(y - f\left(f\left(xw^{(1)}\right)w^{(2)}\right)\right)^2$$

We will focus on the expression after the second equals sign.

$$J = \frac{1}{2}\left(y - f\left(f\left(xw^{(1)}\right)w^{(2)}\right)\right)^2 \tag{11.21}$$

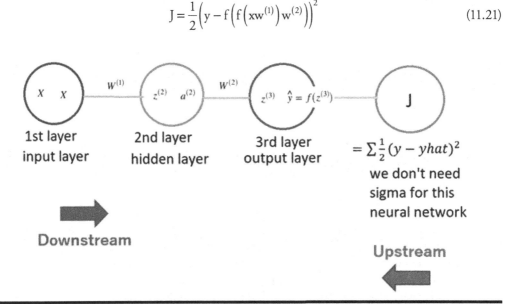

Figure 11.10   Illustration of the meaning of downstream and upstream. The summation sign Σ is not necessary here but is used in more complicated architectures.

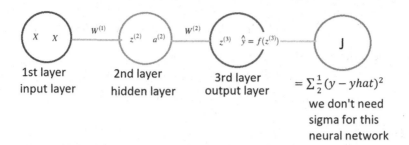

Figure 11.11   1–1–1 architecture including cost J.

Now we see that we will need to repeat the chain rule even more than four times to get to the derivative of J *with respect to* $w^{(1)}$. This is because $w^{(1)}$ lies inside more compositions of functions than did $w^{(2)}$ (Figure 11.11).

$$\frac{dJ}{dw^{(1)}} = \frac{dJ}{d(y-yhat)^2}\frac{d(y-yhat)^2}{d(y-yhat)}\frac{d(y-yhat)}{dyhat}\frac{dyhat}{dz^{(3)}}\frac{dz^{(3)}}{da^{(2)}}\frac{da^{(2)}}{dz^{(2)}}\frac{dz^{(2)}}{dw^{(1)}} \qquad (11.22)$$

We have used the chain rule six times, and this results in seven factors! This is because we have gone back through two more processes of the network.

Actually, the network diagram can help us to see the factors in the chain rule. Starting at J, after the first two factors in the chain rule (the first two factors get us "through" the J node), there is a factor in the chain rule for each quantity in the path to $w^{(1)}$.

Using the definition of $\delta^{(3)}$ from before, this can be written as

$$\frac{dJ}{dw^{(1)}} = \delta^{(3)} \frac{dz^{(3)}}{da^{(2)}}\frac{da^{(2)}}{dz^{(2)}}\frac{dz^{(2)}}{dw^{(1)}}$$

Each of these three derivatives can be calculated as

$$\frac{dz^{(3)}}{da^{(2)}} = \frac{d\left(a^{(2)}*w^{(2)}\right)}{da^{(2)}} = w^{(2)}$$

$$\frac{da^{(2)}}{dz^{(2)}} = \frac{df\left(z^{(2)}\right)}{dz^{(2)}} = f'\left(z^{(2)}\right) = \frac{d\left(sigmoid\left(z^{(2)}\right)\right)}{dz^{(2)}} = sigmoid'\left(z^{(2)}\right) -$$ here for clarity we are writing sigmoid() in addition to writing f():

$$\frac{dz^{(2)}}{dw^{(1)}} = \frac{d\left(x*w^{(1)}\right)}{dw^{(1)}} = x$$

so that

$$\frac{dJ}{dw^{(1)}} = \delta^3 \frac{dz^{(3)}}{da^{(2)}}\frac{da^{(2)}}{dz^{(2)}}\frac{dz^{(2)}}{dw^{(1)}} = \delta^3 w^{(2)} sigmoid'\left(z^{(2)}\right)x \qquad (11.23)$$

Now since each of $\delta^3 \dfrac{dz^{(3)}}{da^{(2)}} \dfrac{da^{(2)}}{dz^{(2)}}$ is obtained downstream of $w^{(1)}$, we define $\delta^{(2)}$ so that it covers all the factors in the above expression except for the last one:

$$\delta^{(2)} = \delta^{(3)} \frac{dz^{(3)}}{da^{(2)}} \frac{da^{(2)}}{dz^{(2)}} = \delta^{(3)} W^{(2)} f'\left(z^{(2)}\right)$$

which gives us

$$\frac{dJ}{dw^{(1)}} = \delta^{(2)} \frac{dz^{(2)}}{dw^{(1)}} = \delta^{(2)} x \tag{11.24}$$

Now a pattern similar to what was seen for $\dfrac{dJ}{dw^{(2)}}$ is evident, and again we can say that the derivative of J with respect to the weight is a constant $(\delta^{(2)})$ times the input (x) that multiplies the weight. Note that in these equations, we can refer to either $\dfrac{dz^{(2)}}{dw^{(1)}}(= x)$ or $\dfrac{dz^{(3)}}{dw^{(2)}}\left(= a^{(2)}\right)$ as the *inputs* into layers 2 and 3, respectively. In Table 11.1, these inputs are also referred to as the activities.

Notice that Equations 11.20 and 11.24 imply that the amount by which the weight is adjusted depends on the size of the input to it where the input would be $a^{(2)}$ for Equation 11.20 since that is the input directly upstream for $w^{(2)}$ and x for Equation 11.24 since that is the input directly upstream for $w^{(1)}$. The inputs are sometimes referred to as the activities, and then we would say that the amount by which a weight is adjusted is proportional to its activity.

11.10 Updating Weights and Searching for the Minimum Cost

Now all the hard work is done. The network can now "learn". This learning is done by updating the weights. The updates to the weights will occur for each training example run through the network. Remember that since these are training examples; each of them comes with a label, that is, a y value, a ground truth value. Therefore, it is possible to measure the error between the prediction yhat and ground truth y value. Then, with the definition of J, we can proceed to obtain the derivatives $\dfrac{dJ}{dw^{(1)}}$ and $\dfrac{dJ}{dw^{(2)}}$. These derivatives are then used in the updating scheme to obtain new, updated values for $w^{(1)}$ and $w^{(2)}$, as follows.

Equations for updating the weights to obtain new weights

$$new\_w^{(1)} = w^{(1)} - \frac{dJ}{dw^{(1)}}$$

$$new\_w^{(2)} = w^{(2)} - \frac{dJ}{dw^{(2)}} \tag{11.25}$$

We run this scheme for each training example, with the hope of a small reduction in the cost J from each iteration. We expect that reduction based on the fact that this is the application of the gradient descent method being applied to the cost function. Note the minus sign appears in the

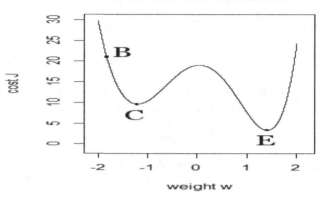

Figure 11.12   Cost J as a function of a single weight w.

above two equations because the derivative tells the direction of *increase* in J, but what is needed is the direction of *decrease*.

Most implementations of this algorithm allow a little more flexibility than what is written above. We may not want to decrease the w's by exactly the amount of the derivative but rather by some fraction (or multiple) of the derivative. Therefore, an additional factor called the learning rate is inserted. It is also referred to as the step size. It may turn out, for example, that if we use the full value of the derivative, it will produce too large of a change in the w's, causing us to overshoot the minimum and moving beyond that which would produce a minimum cost. Figure 11.12 illustrates this situation. In this figure, the x-axis would be the value of a (single) weight, say w, and the y-axis is the cost J. (We visualize just a single weight because it would require more dimensions to visualize more weights.) Movement along the x-axis implies adjustment of the weight w, and as w changes, we obtain different values for J. Of course, we want to find the minimum value of J and seek the value of w which would generate that value of J.

Suppose we are trying to get to the minimum cost E, but we happen to start out with a weight which is to the right of E, say w = 2. The derivative will tell us to move to the left. That is, the derivative and therefore gradient descent will indicate that to reduce J, we need to reduce w. However, if the step size is too large, we may move past E. It is possible that we may move all the way to w = −1/2. In order to avoid this kind of problem, we can adjust the step size. Different step sizes can be played with to find the lowest average cost.[2]

Below, we use the letter "r" to stand for the learning rate or step size. Now our updating scheme will be as follows.

Equations for updating the weights to obtain new weights (learning rate included)

$$\text{new}\_w^{(1)} = w^{(1)} - r\frac{dJ}{dw^{(1)}}$$

$$\text{new}\_w^{(2)} = w^{(2)} - r\frac{dJ}{dw^{(2)}}$$

(11.26)

---

[2] We use the word *average* to mean the average over all the examples in our dataset.

Practice 11.10.3

1. In the expression for $\dfrac{dJ}{dw^{(1)}}$, what is the *superscript* for the delta that is used?

2. In the expression for $\dfrac{dJ}{dw^{(2)}}$, what is the *superscript* for the delta that is used?

3. Suppose we were to design a 1–1–1–1 neural network so that it had two hidden layers and three layers of weights with the most downstream being labeled $w^{(3)}$. What would the superscript for the delta in the formula for $\dfrac{dJ}{dw^{(3)}}$ be?

4. As a mnemonic, is the superscript for the delta n + 1 or n − 1 for $\dfrac{dJ}{dw^{(n)}}$?

11.11 Backpropagation for the 2–1–1 Neural Network

Next, we seek the derivatives for each weight in the 2–1–1 network (Figure 11.13). The difference between the 2–1–1 architecture and the 1–1–1 network is only in the first layer, and so both the calculation of the derivative with respect to $w^{(2)}$ and the formula for $\delta^{(3)}$ will remain the same. The following is the scalar multiplication that we performed for the 1–1–1 network for the second layer.

$$\frac{dJ}{dw^{(2)}} = \frac{dJ}{d\left(y - yhat\right)^2} \frac{d\left(y - yhat\right)^2}{d\left(y - yhat\right)} \frac{d\left(y - yhat\right)}{dyhat} \frac{dyhat}{dz^{(3)}} \frac{dz^{(3)}}{dw^{(2)}}$$

$$\frac{dJ}{dw^{(2)}} = \delta^3 a^{(2)}$$

$$\delta^3 = -\left(y - \hat{y}\right)f'(u)$$

Regarding the first layer, as we saw in the feedforward description for this network, the input layer and first layer weights are now matrices (or vectors).

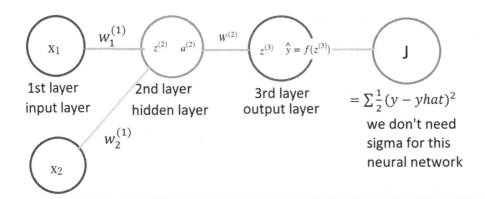

Figure 11.13   2–1–1 architecture including cost J.

For now, however, we ignore the fact that we eventually chose to express them as matrices, and we focus on each weight and input *individually*. Recall that we had this equation:

$$z^{(2)} = x_1 w_1^{(1)} + x_2 w_2^{(1)}$$

We now want to calculate both $\dfrac{\partial J}{\partial w_1^{(1)}}$ and $\dfrac{\partial J}{\partial w_2^{(1)}}$. In the course of completing this task, we will also define $\delta_1^{(1)}$ and $\delta_2^{(1)}$.

After we complete these, we can then store the results in matrices which we can call $\dfrac{\partial J}{d W^{(1)}}$ (notice the capital W) and $\delta^{(1)}$ (a matrix).

Actually, the only difference between the calculation we want to do now $\dfrac{\partial J}{\partial w_1^{(1)}}$ and the first layer derivative calculation in the 1–1–1 neural network is that we need to add a subscript to the previously used $w^{(1)}$ notation. Other than that, the chain rule will give us the same results.

$$\frac{\partial J}{\partial w_1^{(1)}} = \frac{dJ}{d(y-\text{yhat})^2} \frac{d(y-\text{yhat})^2}{d(y-\text{yhat})} \frac{d(y-\text{yhat})}{d\text{yhat}} \frac{d\text{yhat}}{dz^{(3)}} \frac{dz^{(3)}}{da^{(2)}} \frac{da^{(2)}}{dz^{(2)}} \frac{\partial z^{(2)}}{\partial w_1^{(1)}}$$

$$\frac{\partial J}{\partial w_2^{(1)}} = \frac{dJ}{d(y-\text{yhat})^2} \frac{d(y-\text{yhat})^2}{d(y-\text{yhat})} \frac{d(y-\text{yhat})}{d\text{yhat}} \frac{d\text{yhat}}{dz^{(3)}} \frac{dz^{(3)}}{da^{(2)}} \frac{da^{(2)}}{dz^{(2)}} \frac{\partial z^{(2)}}{\partial w_2^{(1)}}$$

Thus, we can define $\delta_1^{(2)}$ (the first element in our delta matrix), with the expression for $\delta^{(2)}$ (the same value we had in our 1–1–1 architecture). Also note that in the 2–1–1 architecture, we see that $\delta_1^{(2)} = \delta_2^{(2)}$.

Recall that we defined $\delta^{(2)}$ so that it would cover everything in the chain rule except for the last factor.

$$\delta_1^{(2)} = \frac{dJ}{d(y-\text{yhat})^2} \frac{d(y-\text{yhat})^2}{d(y-\text{yhat})} \frac{d(y-\text{yhat})}{d\text{yhat}} \frac{d\text{yhat}}{dz^{(3)}} \frac{dz^{(3)}}{da^{(2)}} \frac{da^{(2)}}{dz^{(2)}}$$

$$\delta_2^{(2)} = \frac{dJ}{d(y-\text{yhat})^2} \frac{d(y-\text{yhat})^2}{d(y-\text{yhat})} \frac{d(y-\text{yhat})}{d\text{yhat}} \frac{d\text{yhat}}{dz^{(3)}} \frac{dz^{(3)}}{da^{(2)}} \frac{da^{(2)}}{dz^{(2)}}$$

And for the final term *in the chain rule* we recognize $\dfrac{dz^{(2)}}{dw_1^{(1)}} = a_1^{(1)} = x_1$, and so

$$\frac{dJ}{dw_1^{(1)}} = \delta_1^{(2)} \frac{dz^{(2)}}{dw_1^{(1)}} = \delta_1^{(2)} x_1$$

We can write the following as well.

$$\frac{dJ}{dw_2^{(1)}} = \delta_2^{(2)} \frac{dz^{(2)}}{dw_2^{(1)}} = \delta_2^{(2)} x_2$$

Since $\delta_2^{(2)}$ and $\delta_2^{(2)}$ are equal, the adjustment to weights $w_2^{(1)}$ and $w_2^{(1)}$ will be proportional with the same constant of proportionality to their activities (that is, proportional to their respective inputs x_1 and x_2).

11.12 Define the Matrices for the Derivative and Delta2

Now we can *define* the following two matrices, one to hold the deltas and the other to hold the derivatives.

$$\delta^{(2)} = \begin{bmatrix} \delta_1^{(2)} \\ \delta_2^{(2)} \end{bmatrix} \tag{11.27}$$

$$\frac{dJ}{dW^{(1)}} = \begin{bmatrix} \dfrac{dJ}{dw_1^{(1)}} \\ \dfrac{dJ}{dw_2^{(1)}} \end{bmatrix} \tag{11.28}$$

We also have the matrix for the inputs X.

$$X = \begin{bmatrix} x_1 & x_2 \end{bmatrix} \tag{11.29}$$

If we use *element-by-element multiplication* (not matrix multiplication *or* scalar multiplication), the following will give the expression for $\dfrac{dJ}{dW^{(1)}}$, where element-by-element multiplication is denoted by $\odot$ below. Element-by-element multiplication is also known as Hadamard multiplication.[3]

$$\frac{dJ}{dW^{(1)}} = X^{\mathrm{T}} \odot \delta^{(2)} \tag{11.30}$$

Note that both X^{T} and $\delta^{(2)}$ are 2×1 and that multiplying element-by-element gives a 2×1 result, and that is what we need for this derivative. Note the similarity with the expression for $\dfrac{dJ}{dw^{(1)}}$ (small w) in the 1–1–1 architecture from Equation 11.24:

$$\frac{dJ}{dw^{(1)}} = \delta^{(2)} \frac{dz^{(2)}}{dw^{(1)}} = \delta^{(2)}x = x\delta^{(2)}$$

Side note: In some sense, we may want to say that Equation 11.30 above is more general than 11.24 for the 1–1–1 architecture, especially if we think of the transpose of a scalar as just that scalar itself. That is to say, if we use the transpose in the equation for the 1–1–1 architecture (11.24) with the understanding that the transpose of a scalar is the scalar itself, then we can express both the 1–1–1 and the 2–1–1 architectures with 11.30. Also, make sure to remember that this is element-by-element multiplication and not matrix multiplication.

---

[3] Sometimes we may just use * to denote Hadamard multiplication, and this will be true in our code.

11.13 Writing the Updated Equations with Matrices

Now we are in a position to express the updating of the first layer weights $W^{(1)} = \begin{bmatrix} w_1^{(1)} \\ w_2^{(1)} \end{bmatrix}$

and the second layer weight $w^{(2)}$ using $\dfrac{dJ}{dW^{(1)}}$ and $\dfrac{dJ}{dw^{(2)}}$. (Notice the capital W and small w.)

Equation for updating the weights to obtain new weights with learning rate and matrix
Actually, only one of these is a matrix equation:

$$\text{new}\_w^{(1)} = w^{(2)} - r\frac{dJ}{dw^{(2)}} \quad \left(\text{a scalar equation}\right)$$

$$\text{new}\_W^{(2)} = W^{(1)} - r\frac{dJ}{dW^{(1)}} \quad \left(\text{a matrix equation}\right)$$

As mentioned previously, writing $\dfrac{dJ}{dW^{(1)}}$ could easily look puzzling as it seems to ask, "What is the derivative of the scalar J with respect to a matrix?" However, this is just a *notation* that enables us to store the derivatives of J with respect to $w_1^{(1)}$ and $w_2^{(1)}$ in a single matrix.

Now we can complete the R code for backpropagation!

11.14 1–1–1 Neural Network R Code

```
#We need sigmoid and its derivative.
sigmoid <- function(z) {
  return(1/(1+exp(-z)))
}
sigmoidPrime<-function(z){
  return(exp(-z)/(1+exp(-z))^2)
}
#We first do feedforward with a concrete set of values. Then we
generalize to a function for any given set of values.
#Concrete set of values:
x=0.2
w1=0.3
w2=0.4
y=0.5 #In order to calculate an error, a "ground truth" value for y is
required, and so here we randomly select a value of 0.5 to allow
completion of the calculation of J.
#Feedforward process:
z2=x*w1
a2=sigmoid(z2)
z3=a2*w2
yhat=sigmoid(z3)
yhat
## [1] 0.5513182
J=0.5*(y-yhat)^2
#This is the "error" J. Note that the actual error is just
y-yhat=(0.5-0.5513182), but we are using J as our error measure.
The reasons for this were explained earlier.
```

```
J
## [1] 0.001316779
```
#Now we encapsulate the above calculations in a function. We use the word
"scalar" in the name because it is only the cost for a single row from
our dataset, not for the entire dataset.

```
jCostScalar=function(xValue=x,w1Value=w1,w2Value=w2,yValue=y){
  #Sample call: jCostScalar(x,w1,w2,y)
  z2=xValue*w1Value
  a2=sigmoid(z2)
  z3=a2*w2Value
  yhat=sigmoid(z3)
  J=0.5*(yValue-yhat)^2
  return(J)
}
jCostScalar(x,w1,w2,y)
## [1] 0.001316779
```

#Finding derivatives with respect to w2 and W1
#As explained earlier, we need the derivatives because the "learning
process" consists of updating the weights in the system. Updating weights
consists of multiplying the original weight by a multiple of the
derivative and subtracting that value from the prior weight.

Practice 11.14.4

1. Optional challenge: We just said that we subtract from the prior weight. What if you built
a neural network that used division instead of subtraction? That is, suppose the update process looked like $\text{new}_w = \dfrac{w}{r\frac{dJ}{dw}}$. After reading through our complete code, you can try to

modify the code with this update process and compare the results of training obtained with
this new formula with those obtained with the traditional formula.

#Calculate dJ/dw2 and dJ/dW1 - notice the small "w" and the capital "W".
These lead to the workhorse of neural networks: backpropagation. In some
texts, these are denoted just with dw2 and dW1, but we use a more sugges-
tive notation of dJ _ dw2 and dJ _ dW1.
#Since w2 is closer to J (in the network), we work on that first.
#We saw that repeated application of the chain rule gives us
#dJ _ dw2=(y-yhat)*(-f'(z3))*(a2), where f denotes the sigmoid function.
#All of these quantities have already been calculated or specified above.
```
dJ _ dw2=(y-yhat)*(-sigmoidPrime(z3))*(a2)
dJ _ dw2
## [1] 0.00653756
```
#Next define delta3.
#delta3 = dJ _ d(y-yhat) * (d(y-yhat)) _ dyhat * dyhat _ dz3
```
delta3=(y-yhat)*(-sigmoidPrime(z3))
delta3
## [1] 0.0126944
```
#Unfortunately, the notation is a little bit awkward - the delta has a
3 (delta3), but we are calculating a derivative with respect to a weight
that has a 2 (dJ _ dw2), and we have an "a" with a 2 (a2), so the delta's

number does not match with the other numbers. We could have called this "delta2", but the convention is to call it "delta3". This can be remembered if we note that all the information needed to calculate delta3 is obtained from layer 3 (the output layer). All the information needed to calculate delta2 comes from layer 2 and higher numbered layers. (In our three-layer network, that means layers 2 and 3.)

```
dJ _ dw2=delta3*a2
dJ _ dw2
## [1] 0.00653756
```

#Next we calculate dJ _ dW1 which we saw can be written as
*#dJ _ dw1 = delta3 * dz3 _ da2 * da2 _ dz2 * dz2 _ dw1*

```
dJ _ dw1 = delta3 * w2 * sigmoidPrime(z2)*x
dJ _ dw1
## [1] 0.0001902447
```

#Recall that delta2 was defined in terms of delta3:
*#delta2=delta3 * dz3 _ da2 * da2 _ dz2*

```
delta2=delta3*w2*sigmoidPrime(z2)
delta2
## [1] 0.0009512237
dJ _ dw1=delta2*x
dJ _ dw1
## [1] 0.0001902447
```

#The entire logic of the neural network learning process is
*#new weight = old weight - r*derivative*

```
print("Original weights")
## [1] "Original weights"
print(w1)
## [1] 0.3
print(w2)
## [1] 0.4
```

#Choose an arbitrary learning rate r. Note, researchers will try finding a best r for their particular application of the neural network. For example, in trying to predict patient outcomes, it may turn out that an r = .2 is best. In fraud detection, it may turn out that a different r is better.

```
r=2
w2=w2-r*dJ _ dw2
w1=w1-r*dJ _ dw1

print("updated weights")
## [1] "updated weights"
print(w1)
## [1] 0.2996195
print(w2)
## [1] 0.3869249
```

#The above is the entire learning process. Updating the weights using the derivative is the primary step in a neural network improving its performance.
#Now we encapsulate the above process in a function.
#Construct a function called updateWeights() which will calculate the derivatives for a given set of x,w1,w2, and y and also update the weights

using these derivatives. This will allow the network to learn from its errors (but just for this one data point).
#Then *run updateWeights()through a loop – once for each example in the dataset.*

```
updateWeights<-function(xValue="x",w1Value="w1",w2Value="w2",yValue="y",r=2)
{
```
  #sample call, where weights will be a vector whose elements are accessed through indexing as seen here:
  #weightsList=updateWeights(.5,weights[1],weights[2],   .6,.2)
  #updateWeights() will be constructed to return a list.

  #Note, we will need an initial setting of the weights[] vector, and that should be done outside this function. It will look like this: weights = runif(2,-1,1). This creates a vector of length 2 of random numbers between -1 and 1.

  #After running updateWeights(), its output is assigned to a list named weightsList[] which can be used to update the weights vector like this:
  #weights=c(weightsList[[1]], weightsList[[2]]).

  #Start with the generation of yhat using the parameters from this current function updateWeights()
```
  z2=xValue*w1Value
  a2=sigmoid(z2)
  z3=a2*w2Value
  yhat=sigmoid(z3)
```

#Calculate deltas and derivatives
```
  delta3=(yValue-yhat)*(-sigmoidPrime(z3))
  dJ _ dw2=delta3*a2
  delta2=delta3*w2Value*sigmoidPrime(z2)
  dJ _ dw1=delta2*xValue
```
#Update the weights
```
  w2Value =w2Value-r*dJ _ dw2
  w1Value =w1Value-r*dJ _ dw1
```
#Return the update values of the weights as a list
```
  returnedList=list(w1Value,w2Value)
  returnedList<-setNames(returnedList, c("w1","w2"))
  return(returnedList)
```


  #end of updateWeights()
```
}
```

```
x=0.2
w1=0.3
w2=0.4
y=0.5
weights=c(w1,w2)
print("weights original")
## [1] "weights original"
weights
```

```
## [1] 0.3 0.4
#As we said, updateWeights() returns a named list. We can therefore assign
it to a variable which we call weightsList. We access the elements of that
list (which will be the updated weights) using the familiar double bracket
subset function.
weightsList=updateWeights(.5,weights[1],weights[2],   .6,.2)
weights=c(weightsList[[1]],weightsList[[2]])
print("weights updated")
## [1] "weights updated"
weights
## [1] 0.3001142 0.4012342
#Note, we can also see the weights by  checking the value of weightsList
```

Practice 11.14.5

1. Why is there a subtraction sign in w2=w2Value-r*dJ _ dw2 above?
2. Why do we choose to use the double brackets [[]] instead of single brackets [] to access the elements of weightsList?
3. If single brackets were used, what additional adjustment would be required?

11.14.1 Read In the Entire Data Set

Next, we try passing an entire dataset through the network, but one row at a time, updating the weights each time a row is read in. This means the network will learn from each element in our dataset. We will use a dataset about wine prices and rating. The original data is available at https://www.kaggle.com/zynicide/wine-reviews/version/2. We are using version 2 from that website and the first 150 k option. To keep the dataset small, we will only use Chardonnay data from NZ and Australia.

```
wine <- read.csv("winemag-data_first150k.csv")
#In the next line, we use the logical OR operator, which is the symbol |.
wine <- wine[wine["variety"]=="Chardonnay",]
wine <- wine[wine["country"]=="Australia"| wine["country"]=="New Zealand",]
```

Practice 11.14.6

1. From the entire set of wine data from Kaggle, write a single expression to filter the variety to Chardonnay and the countries to only New Zealand and Australia.
2. Remove all the columns of the wine dataset except for "points" and "price" columns.

```
colnames(wine)
##  [1] "X1"        "country"      "description" "designation" "points"
##  [6] "price"     "province"     "region _ 1"  "region _ 2"  "variety"
## [11] "winery"
#We will only work with points and price.
wine <- wine[,c('points','price')]
colnames(wine)
## [1] "points" "price"
nrow(wine)
## [1] 1123
#Remove any cases that have NA
```

```
wine<-wine[complete.cases(wine),]
nrow(wine)
## [1] 1092
#Split data into train and test sets.
#floor() rounds a number down.
```

Practice 11.14.7

1. What does floor() do? Test it on floor(2), floor(1.9), and floor(1.3).

```
#smp_size will be the number of elements in our training set. Here
we are grabbing about 75% of the data for training and the rest for
testing.

smp_size <- floor(0.75 * nrow(wine))
set.seed(123)
train_ind <- sample(seq_len(nrow(wine)), size = smp_size)

#Create a training set and testing set.
#Although we split the data into training and testing sets, we do this
just as an example. We won't actually use the test set.
train <- wine[train_ind, ]
test <- wine[-train_ind, ]
#In this modeling task, we will attempt to predict the price of the
wine from the points the wine received in its rating.
#Create vectors for score and price, and normalize both of them. We
define a normalizing function that takes the entire set of values of
a variable and maps them to the interval [-0.5,0.5]. We will call it
normal.5(). It is often true that normalizing data before running it
through a neural network gives better results.
normal.5 <- function(x){
    xNew <- ((x- min(x))/(max(x)-min(x)))-0.5
    return(xNew)
}
```

Practice 11.14.8

1. Suppose x = c(0, 3, 10). Without running code, what will the function normal.5() without the "−0.5" term do to 0? What will it do to 10? What will it do to 3? That is, what will

```
((x- min(x))/(max(x)-min(x)))
```

do to each of these three values?

```
points=train$points
points=normal.5(points)

price=train$price
price=normal.5(price)
#First, we train our model (the neural network) on the entire training
set. Then we use that model to make a prediction on a single value.
xValue is the parameter name for the single value on which we will
make a prediction and is set to .90 by default. The parameter for the
learning rate will be called learnR.
```

```r
predNNSingleValue<-function(inputX=points, outputY=price, xValue=.90,
learnR=1){
    #Sample call: predNNSingle(inputX=points,outputY=price,xValue=.90,
    learnR=1)

#This will be the looping variable.
count=0
#The initial values of w1 and w2 need to be set prior to running
predNNSingle().
#Note that this function updates the weights each time a new example
from the training data is passed forward through the network. In a
future version of our algorithm, we create what is called a batch func-
tion which feeds the entire training set through the network before
updating the weights. Then this batch function will sum up the gra-
dient (partial derivative) effects for all the data and do a single
update. We will see precisely what this means later.
#Note that inputX is the parameter used for the training dataset,
whereas xValue is the parameter to hold a new, single test value for
which the network will make a prediction.

#Set the two weights to random numbers between -1 and 1 initially.

  weights= runif(2,-1,1)

  for (input in inputX){
    count=count+1
    currentPrice=outputY[count]

    weightsList=updateWeights(input,weights[1],weights[2],
currentPrice, learnR)
    weights=c(weightsList[[1]],weightsList[[2]])
  }
  #Generate the yhat: the prediction.

  z2=xValue*weights[1]
  a2=sigmoid(z2)
  z3=a2*weights[2]
  yhat=sigmoid(z3)
#Generate some textual output.
  print(paste0("number of rows: ",count))
  print(paste0("Given the input: ", xValue))
  print("the predicted output would be")
  return(yhat)
  #end of predNNSingle
}
#Remember that points and price contain the entire dataset for these
two columns.
#We will run predNNSingleValue a few times with different arguments.
predNNSingleValue(inputX=points,outputY=price,xValue=.2, learnR=1)
## [1] "number of rows: 819"
## [1] "Given the input: 0.2 with learning rate: 1"
## [1] "the predicted output would be"
## [1] 0.1803434
```

```
predNNSingle(inputX=points,outputY=price,xValue=.9, learnR=1)
## [1] "number of rows: 819"
## [1] "Given the input: 0.9 with learning rate: 1"
## [1] "the predicted output would be"
## [1] 0.2674109
predNNSingle(inputX=points,outputY=price,xValue=.2, learnR=25)
## [1] "number of rows: 819"
## [1] "Given the input: 0.2 with learning rate: 25"
## [1] "the predicted output would be"
## [1] 0.04608745
predNNSingle(inputX=points,outputY=price,xValue=.9, learnR=25)
## [1] "number of rows: 819"
## [1] "Given the input: 0.9 with learning rate: 25"
## [1] "the predicted output would be"
## [1] 0.3495848
```

It would be amazing if this simplest of all possible neural networks could make accurate predictions, but we don't expect it to. Furthermore, note that we have trained it on a small dataset of just 819 instances. Also note that predNNSingleValue() has been constructed to only test with a single new value denoted by xValue. You may want to revise this so that you test on the entire test data set. You can rename this to predNNTestData().

11.14.2 Epochs

At first glance it may seem odd, but we can actually train the weights again with the *same set of training data*. Each repetition of the training with the entire dataset is called an epoch, and typically there is another parameter in the function signature, which we can call epoch and which may be set to a number like 500 or more (meaning we would run the same training set through the network, 500 or more times). This will generally improve the performance on the test dataset! However, our network is very primitive at this point, and we need to develop it further. Most neural networks have more nodes in the hidden layer. We will build our next network with a 2–3–1 architecture.

Practice 11.14.9

1. Write a loop to check predictions of **predNNSingle()** for all learning rates from 0.5 to 50 at increments of 0.1. The loop should print out the difference, i.e., what **predNN-ingle()** predicts for an xValue of .9 minus what it predicts for the xValue of .2. Perhaps a good learning value would be one that gives a large difference between the predictions of these two xValues.
2. Add the **jCostScalar()** function into **predNNSingle()**, and as part of the output of **predNNSingle()**, print out what it determines to be the cost.
3. Optional challenge: Rewrite **predNNSingle()** to have a signature as follows.
4. **predNN**(data="wine", percentSplit=0.75, learnR=1). It should read in the entire dataset, split it into a training set and test set (using percentSplit). Let dataTrain be the dataframe that contains the training data and dataTest be the dataframe that contains the test data. You can assume that the data only contains two columns, with the first being the input and the second being the output. Then get the input (it was called 'points' in our last example) from dataTrain[[1]] and the output from dataTrain[[2]], and use

that to update the weights. Then with the updated weights, calculate the cost (error) associated with each instance in the test set (presumably with a loop), calculate the average error over all the test data, and print out the results.

5. Optional challenge: If you did the previous optional challenge, try adding in another parameter called epoch that will cause the updating to be run through a loop so that you can train the weights many times with the same training data (as described above). Compare the error after the network has gone through 500 epochs with how it performed after just 1 epoch.

6. How would you change the initialization of the weights to be random values of −10 to 10? Try it. Does it produce any change in the performance?

11.15 Backpropagation for the 2–3–1 Neural Network in R

See Figures 11.14 and 11.15.

11.15.1 Coding the Feedforward Process for the 2 × 3 × 1 Architecture

```
#We will need both of these functions.

sigmoid <- function(z) {
  return(1/(1+exp(-z)))
}
```

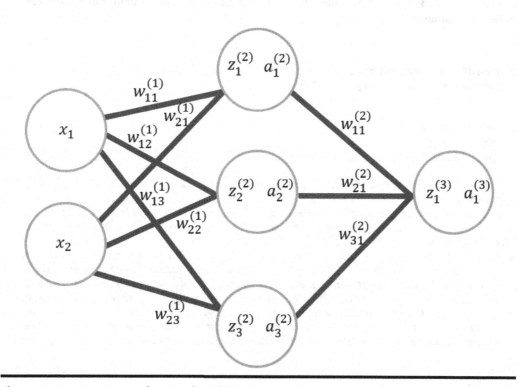

Figure 11.14 2–3–1 neural network architecture.

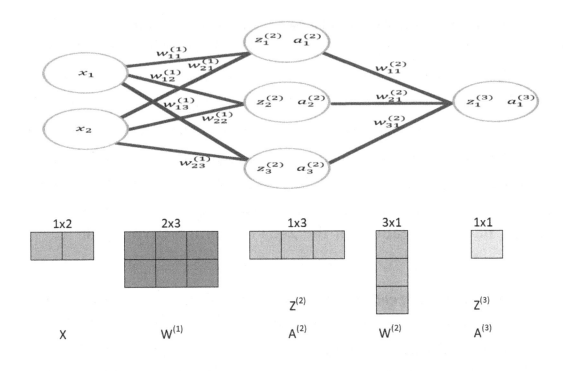

Figure 11.15 **2–3–1 neural network architecture with visual representation of the dimensions of each component.**

```
sigmoidPrime<-function(z){
  return(exp(-z)/(1+exp(-z))^2)
}

inputLayerSize=2
hiddenLayerSize=3
outputLayerSize=1

#We represent the feedforward process for this 2-3-1 network as a matrix
expression.
#In the following, w1sub23 refers to a weight in W1 with subscripts 2,3.
Note that with regard to the matrix W1, w1sub23 refers to the weight in
the second row and third column; that is,
#w1sub23 is W1[2,3]. Here we have used the fact that W1 is a matrix and
we can refer to elements of a matrix with the square bracket notation.
#With regard to the network diagram Figure 11.14, w1sub23 means that it
originates from node 2 in the left-hand (upstream) layer and terminates
in node 3 in the right-hand (downstream) layer.
#As mentioned earlier, note that other texts may use the reverse indexing
for the weights of the network diagram Figure 11.14.

x1=0.2
x2=0.15
X=c(x1,x2)
```

#In order to allow for possible changes in the network architecture, we will let the dimensions of X be determined by variables like inputLayerSize.

Note that numExamples (from Table 11.1 earlier in this chapter), is 1 in this next matrix.

X=**matrix**(X,1, inputLayerSize)

#Next set values of W1 to random values between −1 and 1 and pass that into the matrix() function where we set the number of rows to inputLayerSize and the number of columns to hiddenLayerSize.

$$W^{(1)} = \begin{bmatrix} w_{1,1}^{(1)} & w_{1,2}^{(1)} & w_{1,3}^{(1)} \\ w_{2,1}^{(1)} & w_{2,2}^{(1)} & w_{2,3}^{(1)} \end{bmatrix} \tag{11.31}$$

set.seed(3)
#Note that the first argument to the matrix function below is runif(input LayerSize*hiddenLayerSize,-1,1).
W1=**matrix**(**runif**(inputLayerSize*hiddenLayerSize,-1,1),inputLayerSize,hiddenLayerSize)
dim(W1)
[1] 2 3
Z2=X%*%W1
#Z2 is a matrix
Z2
[,1]   [,2]   [,3]
[1,] -0.04052847 -0.09770276 0.07215849
#Z2 is supposed to hold the three input values of the three nodes in the hidden layer (the second layer). We can see from the fact that Z2=X%*%W1 that the number of columns of W1 is the same as the number of nodes in Z2.
#For example, Z2sub1 (also written as Z2[1,1]) should contain x1*w1sub11 + x2*w1sub21
where the weights are those going to node 1 in the second layer and originating from nodes 1 and 2 in the first layer.
#Reading from the subscripts of these two weights in the above sum, we also take note that these are from the first column of the matrix W1. Thus, we can surmise that the weights in the second column of W1 will appear in the calculation of the input into the second node of the second (the hidden) layer.
#Checking W1
W1
[,1]   [,2]   [,3]
[1,] -0.6639169 -0.2301153 0.2042013
[2,] 0.6150328 -0.3445314 0.2087881

Practice 11.15.10

1. Given the matrix W1 above, what would W1 [2, 1] be?

#We want to confirm that the first entry of Z2 (=X%*%W1) is x1*w1sub11 + x2*w1sub21
#Another way to express this is to say we want Z2[1] to be X[1,1]*W1[1,1]+X[1,2]*W1[2,1].
#We use R's double equal sign operator to test for equality.

```
Z2[1]==X[1,1]*W1[1,1]+X[1,2]*W1[2,1]
## [1] TRUE
```
#We can also check the same thing by checking if Z2[1] is the dot product of the first row of X and the first column of W1.

```
X[1,]%*%W1[,1]
##                  [,1]
## [1,] -0.04052847
Z2[1]==X[1,]%*%W1[,1]
##          [,1]
## [1,] TRUE
```
#Similarly, the reader should confirm that the third entry of Z2 is being correctly calculated.
#Next, the sigmoid function is applied to each value of Z2 individually to obtain A2. R is perfectly suited for this operation because a function f applied to a vector applies f element by element to the vector. This is exactly what is needed here.

```
A2=sigmoid(Z2)
A2
##          [,1]        [,2]        [,3]
## [1,] 0.4898693 0.4755937 0.5180318
```
#So far in the feedforward process, we have

#A2=sigmoid(X%*%W1)
#and thus a single matrix equation has represented the entire process!

#A2 is a 1 by 3 matrix. W2 should contain the weights between layers 2 and 3. The dimensions may be 3 × 1 or 1 × 3.
#If W2 were designed to be 1 × 3, the calculation A2%*%W2 is not possible as this would be a 1 × 3 times a 1 × 3 matrix.[4] Note that it is possible to consider reversing the factors, for example W2%*A2, but we will always put A2 to the left of W2. We are holding to our rule that left-hand factors should be upstream of the right-hand factors. Again, other texts may reverse this.

#First show our 3 × 1 W2 matrix, and again initially populate it with random values.

$$\mathrm{W}^{(2)} = \begin{bmatrix} w_1^{(2)} \\ w_2^{(2)} \\ w_3^{(2)} \end{bmatrix} \tag{11.32}$$

```
set.seed(3)
W2=matrix(runif(hiddenLayerSize*outputLayerSize,-1,1),hiddenLayerSize,outputLayerSize)
Z3=A2%*%W2
```

#z3 is currently a matrix, albeit a 1 × 1 matrix.

---

[4] Note that A2%*%t(W2) works dimensionally but is the same calculation as if W2 were designed to be 3×1 and the calculation A2%*%W2 were performed.

#This will cause some confusion later, and so we choose to make it a scalar.

```
z3=as.vector(Z3)
#again apply sigmoid
yhat=sigmoid(z3)
```

#In order to calculate a cost J, we need a ground truth value y against which to calculate an error. For purposes of illustration, we arbitrarily choose a value of 0.5.

```
y=0.5
J=0.5*(y-yhat)^2
J
## [1] 0.0007186051
```
#Now the feedforward process of the entire 2 × 3 × 1 network can be represented by a single matrix equation.
#We could have written out the process without matrices, and it is left as an exercise for the reader to write this out explicitly.

#Test the following just to confirm everything is ok.

```
J==0.5*(y-sigmoid(sigmoid(X%*%W1)%*%W2))^2
##         [,1]
## [1,]  TRUE
```

11.15.2 Coding the Backpropagation Process for the 2 × 3 × 1 Architecture

11.15.2.1 Derivatives for the 2 × 3 × 1 Network

Now we focus on determining the derivatives of J with respect to each of the weights in the network. We focus first on the three weights in $W^{(2)}$ (Figure 11.16).

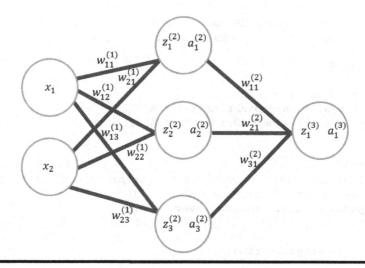

Figure 11.16   2–3–1 neural network architecture.

11.16 Derivatives for $\mathbf{W}^{(2)}$

#There should be three derivatives: dJ_dw2sub1, dJ_dw2sub2, and dJ_dw2sub3.
#Note that it may be more general to use notation like dJ_dw2sub11, dJ_dw2sub21, and dJ_dw2sub31, since these are entries of a matrix, but for now we will use dJ_dw2sub1, dJ_dw2sub2,and dJ_dw2sub3.

$$\frac{\partial J}{\partial \mathbf{W}^{(2)}} = \begin{bmatrix} \dfrac{\partial J}{\partial w_1^{(2)}} \\ \dfrac{\partial J}{\partial w_2^{(2)}} \\ \dfrac{\partial J}{\partial w_3^{(2)}} \end{bmatrix} \tag{11.33}$$

#Note that these are partial derivatives although we do not use partial derivative notation in the R coding. We will not use any partial derivative notation in the R coding for the weights in W1 as well. We mentioned earlier in the math discussion that we can write the chain rule with five factors or fewer. Here, to keep things a bit tidy, we will choose fewer terms. The reader should note, however, that some of these factors may have multiple factors embedded in them.

#Repeated application of the chain rule gives
#dJ_dw2sub1 = dJ_(d(y-yhat))*(d(y-yhat))_dyhat*dyhat_dz3*dz3_dw2sub1
#Calculating the derivatives gives
#dJ_dw2sub1=(y-yhat)*(-f'(z3))*(a2sub1), where as usual f denotes the sigmoid function.
#We have calculated all of these derivatives, and so the first entry of the matrix of partial derivatives is obtained here:

```
dJ_dw2sub1=(y-yhat)*(-sigmoidPrime(z3))*(A2[1]) #Notice the w is not
capitalized since w is the element, not the matrix.
dJ_dw2sub1
## [1] -0.004616113
```

#The two other derivatives from W2 are
```
dJ_dw2sub2=(y-yhat)*(-sigmoidPrime(z3))*(A2[2])
dJ_dw2sub3=(y-yhat)*(-sigmoidPrime(z3))*(A2[3])
```

#Define delta3
*#We see that delta3 does not change from our prior network architecture because the 2-3-1 architecture and the 1-1-1 architecture are the same from the **beginning of the output layer** onward.*
#delta3 = dJ_(d(y-yhat)) * (d(y-yhat))_dyhat * dyhat_dz3

```
delta3=(y-yhat)*(-sigmoidPrime(z3))
delta3
## [1] -0.009423153
```

```
#Using delta3, we can rewrite the derivatives as
dJ_dw2sub1=delta3*(A2[1])
dJ_dw2sub2=delta3*(A2[2])
dJ_dw2sub3=delta3*(A2[3])
```

#We can write the above three equations as a single matrix equation if we store these three partial derivatives in a single matrix. Notice we use a capital "W" below. This indicates that dJ_dW2 is a matrix. We could consider the two possibilities depending on whether we want dJ_dW2 to be 1 × 3 or 3 × 1:
```
#dJ_dW2=delta3*A2
#or
#dJ_dW2=delta3*t(A2)
#We will choose 3 × 1 for reasons that will be clear later.
```

```
dJ_dW2=delta3*t(A2)
dJ_dW2
##                    [,1]
## [1,] -0.004616113
## [2,] -0.004481593
## [3,] -0.004881493
```
#The above uses scalar multiplication by delta3. (This could be considered Hadamard multiplication if we reformulate delta3 as a matrix Delta3 with three elements each equal to delta3.) This works since there is only one delta3 value. Since delta3 is a scalar, we use the uncapitalized "d". If it were a matrix, we would call it Delta3.
#There is only one delta3 value because the outer layer only has one node. If there were more nodes, we would need to treat it as a matrix, and we would use Hadamard multiplication.

11.17 Derivatives for $\mathbf{W}^{(1)}$

#Next, we use the notation dJ_dW1 to store the derivatives of J with respect to each of the weights in W1. Since it will store one derivative for each weight in W1, it is natural to consider dim(dJ_dW1) to be the same as dim(W1). Just as with W1, there will be one column for each node in the hidden layer. (Notice that each column has the same second subscript and recall that we have chosen our notation so that the second subscript indicates the downstream node.)

$$\frac{\partial J}{\partial W^{(1)}} = \begin{bmatrix} \dfrac{\partial J}{\partial w_{1,1}^{(1)}} & \dfrac{\partial J}{\partial w_{1,2}^{(1)}} & \dfrac{\partial J}{\partial w_{1,3}^{(1)}} \\ \dfrac{\partial J}{\partial w_{2,1}^{(1)}} & \dfrac{\partial J}{\partial w_{2,2}^{(1)}} & \dfrac{\partial J}{\partial w_{2,3}^{(1)}} \end{bmatrix} \tag{11.34}$$

#First, we will look at dJ_dw1sub11.
#dJ_dw1sub11 is the derivative of J with respect to the weight W1[1,1].
```
W1[1,1]
## [1] -0.6639169
```
#The repeated use of the chain rule again gives us

```
#dJ_dw1sub11 = dJ_(d(y-yhat)) * (d(y-yhat))_dyhat * dyhat_dz3 * dz3_
da2sub1 * da2sub1_dz2sub1 * dz2sub1_dw1sub11

#Recalling that delta3 = dJ_(d(y-yhat)) * (d(y-yhat))_dyhat * dyhat_dz3,
we can write
#dJ_dw1sub11 = delta3 * dz3_da2sub1 * da2sub1_dz2sub1 * dz2sub1_dw1sub11
#dJ_dw1sub11 =  delta3  *  w2Sub1  *  sigmoidPrime(z2sub1) * x1

dJ_dw1sub11 =  delta3  *  W2[1]  *  sigmoidPrime(Z2[1]) * X[1,1]
#We still need five more derivatives. Next find the derivative with
respect to W1[2,1], dJ_dw1sub21.
#Note that it may be confusing that in the network diagram, we use double
subscripts for the weights in the second layer W2, even though W2 is only
a 3 × 1 matrix. The double subscripts are used to so that a
generalization to more nodes in the output layer is smoother. We could
have more than one node in the output layer, and then W2 would have more
columns. However, in the code, as mentioned earlier, there is a single
subscript for weights in the W2 matrix.

dJ_dw1sub21  =  delta3  *  W2[1]  *  sigmoidPrime(Z2[1]) * X[1,2]
#Next dJ_dw1sub12 and dJ_dw1sub22
#Note that in the network diagram, the path to J of both of dJ_dw1sub12
and dJ_dw1sub22 leads through z2[2] and W[2].
dJ_dw1sub12 =  delta3  *  W2[2]  *  sigmoidPrime(Z2[2]) * X[1,1]
dJ_dw1sub22 =  delta3  *  W2[2]  *  sigmoidPrime(Z2[2]) * X[1,2]
#Finally the last two derivatives:
dJ_dw1sub13 =  delta3  *  W2[3]  *  sigmoidPrime(Z2[3]) * X[1,1]
dJ_dw1sub23 =  delta3  *  W2[3]  *  sigmoidPrime(Z2[3]) * X[1,2]

#Is it possible to express all six of these as some matrix equation using
matrices for X, W2, Z2, and of course dJ_dW1? It will turn out that the
following expression will be what is needed.
t(X)%*%((delta3*t(W2))*sigmoidPrime(Z2))  #Note that there is a Hadamard
multiplication (the last asterisk). Additionally, pay attention to the
parentheses. delta3 is a scalar and thus results in a.
##                  [,1]            [,2]            [,3]
## [1,]  0.0003126811 -0.0002890870 1.082796e-04
## [2,]  0.0002345109 -0.0002168152 8.120968e-05
```

Practice 11.17.11

1. How many entries are there in the matrix dJ_dW1?
2. How many entries are there in the matrix dJ_dW2?
3. If there were four nodes in layer 2, what would be the dimensions of dJ_dW1?
4. In regard to memoization, how much work or what work does it save in the calculation of dJ_dW1 to define and use delta3 instead of recalculating it for each derivative?
5. What would your answer be to the previous question if there were four nodes in layer 2?
6. In each of the six calculations dJ _ dw1sub11, dJ _ dw1sub21, ..., there is an "*" symbol, which denotes multiplication. Is this scalar, vector, matrix, or Hadamard multiplication? This is not referring to the matrix equation but rather the six individual entries.

```
#Returning to the proposed expression for dJ _ dW1:
```

`t(X)%*%((delta3*t(W2))*sigmoidPrime(Z2))`

We consider the dimensions of each of the factors.

```
X
##        [,1]  [,2]
## [1,]   0.2  0.15
W2
##                [,1]
## [1,]  -0.6639169
## [2,]   0.6150328
## [3,]  -0.2301153
Z2
##                 [,1]            [,2]           [,3]
## [1,]  -0.04052847  -0.09770276  0.07215849
```
`#X is 1x2`
`#W2 is 3x1`
`#Z2 is 1x3`
`#And as noted earlier, dJ _ dW1 will be the same dimensions as W1: 2 × 3.`
`# t(X) %*% ((delta3*t(W2)) * sigmoidPrime(Z2))`
`# 2 × 1            1 × 3            1 × 3`

Notice that the last multiplication is the Hadamard element-by-element multiplication! If not, 1×3 by 1×3 multiplication does not work. Some readers may ask why this should be Hadamard. The answer is that we are trying to construct a matrix expression which gives the correct calculations to store in the partial derivatives matrix dJ _ dW1 and Hadamard will give this result. This is the only reason for the use of Hadamard multiplication.

`#We can see that the dimensions of the above expression are what we` *were aiming for. That is, we are expecting dJ _ dW1 to be 2×3, and the above expression results in a 2×3 matrix.*
`#What about the values of the individual entries? Are they being cal-`*culated correctly?*

`#t(X) gives a column matrix of x1 and x2.`

$$\begin{bmatrix} x_1 \\ x_2 \end{bmatrix}$$

`t(X)`
```
##         [,1]
## [1,]  0.20
## [2,]  0.15
```
`#Recall W2 is $3 \times 1$ (or more generally hiddenLayerSize × outputLayerSize).`
`#delta3*t(W2) gives a row matrix of`

$$\begin{bmatrix} delta3 * w_1^2 & delta3 * w_2^2 & delta3 * w_3^2 \end{bmatrix}$$

`delta3*t(W2)`
```
##                 [,1]            [,2]           [,3]
## [1,]  0.006256191  -0.005795548  0.002168412
```
`#Now examine the Hadamard product of delta3*t(W2) and sigmoidPrime(Z2)`
`and remember that sigmoidPrime(Z2) is $1 \times 3$ because Z2 is $1 \times 3$.`

$$\left[\text{delta3w}_1^2 \quad \text{delta3w}_2^2 \quad \text{delta3w}_3^2 \right] \odot \left[\text{sigmoidPrime}\left(z_1^2\right) \quad \text{sigmoidPrime}\left(z_2^2\right) \quad \text{sigmoidPrime}\left(z_3^2\right) \right]$$

$$= \left[\text{delta3w}_1^2\text{sigmoidPrime}\left(z_1^2\right) \quad \text{delta3w}_2^2\text{sigmoidPrime}\left(z_2^2\right) \quad \text{delta3w}_3^2\text{sigmoidPrime}\left(z_3^2\right) \right]$$

(11.35)

```
#Next, the product of the 2 × 1 column matrix t(X) and the 1 × 3 row
matrix [delta3*t(W2) * sigmoidPrime(Z2)] will end up combining each ele-
ment of the first matrix with each element of the second resulting in
the 2 × 3 matrix below.
```

$$\begin{bmatrix} x_1 \\ x_2 \end{bmatrix} \left[\text{delta3w}_1^2\text{sigmoidPrime}\left(z_1^2\right) \quad \text{delta3w}_2^2\text{sigmoidPrime}\left(z_2^2\right) \quad \text{delta3w}_3^2\text{sigmoidPrime}\left(z_3^2\right) \right]$$

$$= \begin{bmatrix} x_1\text{delta3w}_1^2\text{sigmoidPrime}\left(z_1^2\right) & x_1\text{delta3w}_2^2\text{sigmoidPrime}\left(z_2^2\right) & x_1\text{delta3w}_3^2\text{sigmoidPrime}\left(z_3^2\right) \\ \\ x_2\text{delta3w}_1^2\text{sigmoidPrime}\left(z_1^2\right) & x_2\text{delta3w}_2^2\text{sigmoidPrime}\left(z_2^2\right) & x_2\text{delta3w}_3^2\text{sigmoidPrime}\left(z_3^2\right) \end{bmatrix}$$

(11.36)

```
#We saw earlier that
#dJ _ dw1sub11 = delta3 *  W2[1]   * sigmoidPrime(Z2[1]) * x1
#Thus, at least for the first element of the partial derivative matrix,
we have the correct calculation. (Note that we don't need any trans-
poses in the calculation of dJ _ dw1sub11 since we are only calculating
dJ _ dw1sub11, which is just one element in the matrix dJ _ dW1. The
W2[1] and x1 are scalars, and so transpose has no meaning.
#The reader should confirm the other entries. Now we can write the
matrix equation for the derivative of J with respect to the matrix W1.
```

$$\frac{dJ}{dW_1} = X^T \left(\delta^{(3)}\left(W^{(2)}\right)^T \odot \sigma'\left(Z^{(2)}\right) \right)$$

(11.37)

where the ⊙ is the Hadamard product.

```
dJ _ dW1=t(X) %*% ((delta3*t(W2)) * sigmoidPrime(Z2)) #Note the parentheses.
 #The delta3*t(W2) operation is not general and will not work if delta
is not a scalar.
```

Again, for purposes of memoization, we can also define the *matrix*, Delta2. It will contain the Hadamard product.

$$\text{Delta2} = \delta^{(2)} = \delta^{(3)}(W^{(2)})^T \odot \sigma'\left(Z^{(2)}\right)$$

(11.38)

```
Delta2 <- (delta3*t(W2))*sigmoidPrime(Z2)
Delta2
##              [,1]          [,2]            [,3]
## [1,]  0.001563406  -0.001445435  0.0005413979
```

```
dim(Delta2)
## [1] 1 3
dim(X)
## [1] 1 2
t(X)%*%Delta2
##                   [,1]          [,2]          [,3]
## [1,]  0.0003126811 -0.0002890870 1.082796e-04
## [2,]  0.0002345109 -0.0002168152 8.120968e-05

#Of course, using Delta2 gives the same result for dJ _ dW1.
dJ _ dW1== t(X) %*%Delta2
##         [,1] [,2] [,3]
## [1,] TRUE TRUE TRUE
## [2,] TRUE TRUE TRUE
```

Now we have matrix expressions for both $\dfrac{dJ}{dW^{(2)}}$ and $\dfrac{dJ}{dW^{(1)}}$!

```
#Derivatives for the 2 × 3 × 1 network:
#delta3=(y-yhat) *(-sigmoidPrime(z3))
dJ _ dW2=delta3*t(A2) #which, since delta is a scalar, can also be cal-
culated as t(A2)*delta3.
#Delta2 = (delta3*t(W2)) * sigmoidPrime(Z2)
dJ _ dW1= t(X) %*%Delta2
```

11.18 Updating the Weights

We will use our matrix expressions to update matrices of our weights, $W^{(1)}$ and $W^{(2)}$!

```
W2 = W2Value-r*dJ_dW2
W1 = W1Value-r*dJ_dW1
```

We now construct the **updateWeights**() function for the 2-3-1 architecture.
```
updateWeights<-function(XValue=X,W1Value=W1,W2Value=W2,yValue=y,r=2){
  #Sample call:
  #weightsList=updateWeights(X,W1,W2,3,4) #The parameters are specified.
(Note learning rate is r and r = 4.)
  #Or use the defaults:
  #weightsList=updateWeights()
  #Note that the output of the function is a list of the updated weights.

  sigmoid <- function(z) {
    return(1/(1+exp(-z)))
  }
  sigmoidPrime<-function(z){
    return(exp(-z)/(1+exp(-z))^2)
  }

Z2=XValue%*%W1Value
A2=sigmoid(Z2)
z3=A2%*%W2Value
z3=as.vector(z3)
```

```
yhat=sigmoid(z3)
J=0.5*(yValue-yhat)^2
print("the current cost is")
print(J)
#Here is a one-line version of the calculation of J.
#J=0.5*(y-sigmoid(sigmoid(XValue%*%W1Value)%*%W2Value))^2 #However, we
will need the (intermediate) variables Z2 and A2 for the calculations of
the derivatives below, and this one-line version does not create them.

#Derivatives for the 2 × 3 × 1 network:
delta3=(yValue-yhat)*(-sigmoidPrime(z3))
dJ_dW2=delta3*t(A2)
delta2 = (delta3*t(W2Value)) * sigmoidPrime(Z2)
dJ_dW1= t(XValue) %*%Delta2

#Update in matrix form:

W2=W2Value-r*dJ_dW2
W1=W1Value-r*dJ_dW1

#After weights are updated, calculate predicted value of y.
Z2=XValue%*%W1
A2=sigmoid(Z2)
Z3=A2%*%W2 #We use uppercase "Z" because this is a (1 × 1) matrix.
z3=as.vector(Z3)
yhat=sigmoid(z3)

print(paste0("target value y : ",yValue))
print(paste0("predicted value: ",yhat))

returnedList=list(W1,W2)
returnedList<-setNames(returnedList, c("W1","W2"))
return(returnedList)


  #end of updateWeights()
}
```

Below we run **updateWeights**() repeatedly and check what happens to the cost after each iteration. We are using just a single instance of X in this test. And we are using a single y-value for the ground truth. If the cost decreases after each call of **updateWeights**(), it would mean that the weights are getting better at predicting this one value of y. This is not such a difficult task, but nevertheless, it is good to see that the cost does decrease. On the other hand, we are using the same data for training and testing which is not of course a good practice.

In the next chapter, we will have the network run over an entire dataset and at the same time will employ an entirely new programming paradigm: object-oriented programming. First let us confirm that the costs are decreasing and that the prediction is getting closer to the target.

```
weightsList=updateWeights()
## [1] "the current cost is"
## [1] 0.0007186051
```

```
## [1] "target value y : 0.5"
## [1] "predicted value: 0.465547918490719"
W1=weightsList[["W1"]]
W2=weightsList[["W2"]]
weightsList=updateWeights()
## [1] "the current cost is"
## [1] 0.000593473
## [1] "target value y : 0.5"
## [1] "predicted value: 0.468696758632693"
W1=weightsList[["W1"]]
W2=weightsList[["W2"]]
weightsList=updateWeights()
## [1] "the current cost is"
## [1] 0.0004899465
## [1] "target value y : 0.5"
## [1] "predicted value: 0.471562220396749"
```

To sum up, we need to obtain derivatives of the error with respect to each weight. The chain rule tells us that the derivatives with respect to upstream weights can be calculated by means of derivatives with respect to weights further downstream. As a result of this, we see that we will sometimes calculate a derivative of a product (like x times w_{11}), and sometimes we will need to calculate a derivative of the sigmoid function.[5]

Practice 11.18.12

1. Test the **updateWeights**() with a larger input vector X. For example, try an X which contains five inputs instead of just two. Also, change the size of the hidden layer to have ten nodes. This will be in effect testing out our code on a 5–10–1 network architecture. Does it run? Do the costs still decrease? Don't forget that you will need to adjust the sizes of the weight matrices as well.

11.19 Running an Entire Dataset through the 2–3–1 Network

In the last example, we ran one example at a time. This is not realistic. We want to train and test the network on an entire dataset, and we present that next. We will work with the exercise–mood dataset at Kaggle.com which explores the relationship between exercise and mood. We will test to see how well a person's mood can be predicted based on the number of calories they burn and the number of hours they sleep. The original data is available at https://www.kaggle.com/aroojanwarkhan/fitness-data-trends. To get some understanding of the data, we will look at a three-dimensional (3D) graph of the input and output data and look at how well *linear regression* works with this data.

We are interested in predicting a person's mood from the amount of exercise they do and the number of hours they sleep. Therefore, we place mood on the z-axis (the vertical axis). We have also run a regression model on the data and plotted the regression surface. The regression surface is the model and would be used to make predictions. We are not going to discuss regression in this text in detail and only present this here to orient ourselves with the data before proceeding with

---

[5] Or some other threshold function. We will see another threshold function later.

our neural network coding. We will however include the code to generate this graph, and within this code is the code to run the regression model.

One fact that can be observed from analyzing the graph is that the mood variable is limited to just three possible values. Thus, the heights of the dots are only in three possible levels.

In the code below, we have normalized the calories burned and hours slept but not the mood. We have also used two different colors for the dots. The color depends on another variable called `bool _ of _ active` which categorizes each of the individuals as either active or inactive. Blue dots represent the inactive individuals, and orange dots represent the active individuals. We won't use this variable in our neural network code. Although the code will generate different colored balls, in Figure 11.17 we use different markers instead of different colors as the graph is shown in black and white.

We can see from Figure 11.17 that the regression model has only a rough fit to the data. The regression equation turns out to be

$$\textbf{mood} = 75.12 * \textbf{hours\_of\_sleep} + 62.90 * \textbf{calories\_burned} + 221.74$$

This can be used to predict mood from the two input variables. The graph of this 3D equation is the plane shown in Figure 11.17. We will also see in the code for the regression that both coefficients pass their respective p-tests and thus are usable. However, we will also see that the so-called "multiple R-square" value is extremely low, meaning that the model is not useful. You can also see that using the regression plane (the plane in the graph in Figure 11.17) will not be very accurate in making predictions. This is because of the "linear" nature of the regression model we are using. Suffice to say that neural networks are more flexible than linear regression. Again, we won't discuss

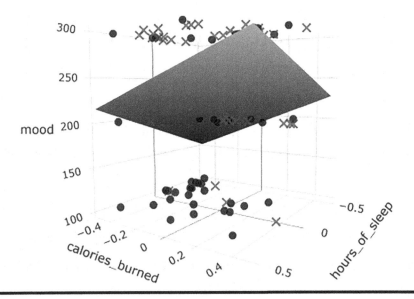

Figure 11.17 Mood as a function of calories burned and hours slept including regression plane. The marker symbol depends on another variable called bool_of_active.

these results any further. Again, we have only presented this graph to orient ourselves with the data before proceeding with our neural network development.

11.19.1 R Code for Figure 11.17

```
#This code, and in particular the plot_ly() function, generates an
interactive graph in RStudio.
#We download the data from Kaggle as exercise_mood.csv.
normal.5 <- function(x){
  xNew <- ((x-min(x))/(max(x)-min(x)))-.5
  return(xNew)
}
install.packages(plotly)
install.packages(reshape2)
library(plotly)
library("reshape2")
mooddf <- read.csv("exercise_mood.csv")
mooddf<-mooddf[complete.cases(mooddf),]
my_df=mooddf
hours_of_sleep=my_df$hours_of_sleep
calories_burned=my_df$calories_burned
mood=my_df$mood
hours_of_sleep=normal.5(hours_of_sleep)
calories_burned=normal.5(calories_burned)
bool_of_active=my_df$bool_of_active
active_factor=factor(bool_of_active,labels = c("inactive", "active"))

my_df=as.data.frame(cbind(hours_of_sleep,calories_burned,mood,
active_factor))
mooddf_plot <- plot_ly(my_df,
                       x = hours_of_sleep,
                       y = calories_burned,
                       z = mood,
                       type = "scatter3d",
                       mode = "markers")

mood_lm <- lm(mood ~  hours_of_sleep + calories_burned,
              data = my_df)


#Graph resolution (more important for more complex shapes)
graph_reso <- 0.05

#Setup axis
axis_x <- seq(min(my_df$hours_of_sleep), max(my_df$hours_of_sleep),
by = graph_reso)
axis_y <- seq(min(my_df$calories_burned), max(my_df$calories_burned),
by = graph_reso)
#Sample points
mood_lm_surface <- expand.grid(hours_of_sleep = axis_x,calories_burned =
axis_y,KEEP.OUT.ATTRS = F)

mood_lm_surface$mood <- predict.lm(mood_lm, newdata = mood_lm_surface)
```

```
mood_lm_surface <- acast(mood_lm_surface, hours_of_sleep ~ calories_
burned, value.var = "mood") #y ~ x

hcolors=c("blue","orange")[active_factor]
mood_plot <- plot_ly(my_df,
                     x = ~hours_of_sleep,
                     y = ~calories_burned,
                     z = ~mood,
                     text = "active/inactive",
                     type = "scatter3d",
                     mode = "markers",
                     marker = list(color = hcolors))

mood_plot <- add_trace(p = mood_plot,
                       z = mood_lm_surface,
                       x = axis_x,
                       y = axis_y,
                       type = "surface")

mood_plot
mood_lm
##
## Call:
## lm(formula = mood ~ hours_of_sleep + calories_burned, data = my_df)
##
## Coefficients:
##    (Intercept)   hours_of_sleep   calories_burned
##         221.74            75.12             62.90
summary(mood_lm)
##
## Call:
## lm(formula = mood ~ hours_of_sleep + calories_burned, data = my_df)
##
## Residuals:
##     Min      1Q  Median      3Q     Max
## -168.11  -71.35   11.57   77.80  120.89
##
## Coefficients:
##                 Estimate Std. Error t value Pr(>|t|)
## (Intercept)      221.738      9.013  24.603   <2e-16 ***
## hours_of_sleep    75.122     38.643   1.944   0.0549 .
## calories_burned   62.900     28.407   2.214   0.0293 *
## ---
## Signif. codes:  0 '***' 0.001 '**' 0.01 '*' 0.05 '.' 0.1 ' ' 1
##
## Residual standard error: 81.32 on 93 degrees of freedom
## Multiple R-squared:  0.09214,    Adjusted R-squared:  0.07261
## F-statistic: 4.719 on 2 and 93 DF,  p-value: 0.01117
```

Practice 11.19.13

1. Check the correlations between the two input variables. Check them before they were normalized and then after. Is there a substantial change in the correlations?

11.19.2 On to Neural Networks

```
#Set Network Dimensions.
inputLayerSize=2
hiddenLayerSize=3
outputLayerSize=1
set.seed(3)
W1=matrix(runif(inputLayerSize*hiddenLayerSize,-1,1),inputLayerSize,hidde
nLayerSize)
W2=matrix(runif(hiddenLayerSize*outputLayerSize,-1,1),hiddenLayerSize,out
putLayerSize)
normal.5 <- function(x){
  xNew <- ((x-min(x))/(max(x)-min(x)))-.5
  return(xNew)
}
#Read in dataset. It is called exercise_mood.csv.
mood <- read.csv("exercise_mood.csv")
#Remove any cases that have NA.
mood<-mood[complete.cases(mood),]
colnames(mood)
## [1] "date"              "step_count"      "mood"
"calories_burned"
## [5] "hours_of_sleep"   "bool_of_active"   "weight_kg"
mood=mood[,c("mood","calories_burned","hours_of_sleep")]

#Split data into "train" and "test" sets.
smp_size <- floor(0.75 * nrow(mood))
set.seed(123)
train_ind <- sample(seq_len(nrow(mood)), size = smp_size)

train <- mood[train_ind, ]
test <- mood[-train_ind, ]
colnames(mood)
## [1] "mood"              "calories_burned" "hours_of_sleep"
#Choose input variables and output variables.
moodInputs=train[,c("calories_burned","hours_of_sleep")]
moodInputs=normal.5(moodInputs)
moodOutput=train[,"mood"]
moodOutput=normal.5(moodOutput)
countS=0

#Define a function to loop through every row of the dataset.
fullUpdateWeights<-function(inputX=moodInputs,outputY=moodOutput, W1Val=
W1,W2Val=W2){
  #sample call:
  #fullUpdateWeights(inputX=moodInputs,outputY=moodOutput,W1,W2)

  weights=list(W1Val,W2Val) #We need to change parameters in the "for"
loop from weightsList=updateWeights(X,weights[1],weights[2],
currentMoodOutput,.2) to weightsList=updateWeights(X,weights[[1]],weig
hts[[2]], currentMoodOutput,.2)

  sigmoid <- function(z) {
    return(1/(1+exp(-z)))
  }
```

```r
sigmoidPrime<-function(z){
  return(exp(-z)/(1+exp(-z))^2)
}


for (predictor in rownames(inputX)){
  #We will iterate through each row, collecting each set of input
  values from inputX and storing it in a matrix called predictorMat and
  simultaneously storing the output value in currentMoodOutput. These
  values are then used to update the weights using updateWeights. Then the
  next set of inputs and outputs are employed to update the weights, until
  we have run through the entire data set.
  predictorMat=unlist(inputX[predictor,])
  predictorMat=matrix(predictorMat,1,2)
  countS=countS+1
  outputY= unlist(outputY)
  currentMoodOutput=outputY[countS]
```

Practice 11.19.14

1. Explain the above currentMoodOutput=outputY[countS] statement.

```r
      weightsList=updateWeights(predictorMat,weights[[1]],weights[[2]],
  yValue=currentMoodOutput,.2)

      weights=list(weightsList[[1]],weightsList[[2]])

      if(countS==nrow(inputX)){#this will be used in the next section
  called Repeated Training: Epochs.

        countS=0
      }



    } #We have iterated through the entire data set and with each
  iteration we updated the weights. Next we measure the cost.

    print(weights)

    inputsMat=as.matrix(moodInputs)
    y=as.matrix(moodOutput,ncol=1)
    Z2=rowSums(inputsMat%*%weights[[1]])
    A2=sigmoid(Z2)
    Z3=rowSums(A2%*%t(weights[[2]]))
    yHat=sigmoid(Z3)
  #We want to sum up all the
    J=(1/nrow(inputsMat))*(0.5*sum((y-yHat)^2))

    print("the cost, J, for this epoch is")
    print(J)

    returnedList<-setNames(weights, c("W1","W2"))
    return(returnedList)
```

```
    #end of fullUpdateWeights()
}
```

Practice 11.19.15

1. What would have been wrong with doing if(countS==length(inputX)) instead of **if**(countS==**nrow**(inputX)) as done above?
2. If m=**matrix**(1:12,nrow=4,ncol=3), what does **rowSums**(m) do? Explain in words.
3. What is the output of **rowSums**(), and what is the type of the output?
4. What are the possible types of inputs that **rowSums**() can accept in general?

```
JCost<-function(moodInputsVal=moodInputs,moodOutputVal=moodOutput,
W1Val=W1,W2Val=W2) {#We encapsulate the cost calculation above which
calculated the average cost over all the instances.

    inputsMat=as.matrix(moodInputsVal)
    y=as.matrix(moodOutputVal,ncol=1)

    Z2=rowSums(inputsMat%*%W1Val)
    A2=sigmoid(Z2)
    Z3=rowSums(A2%*%t(W2Val))
    yHat=sigmoid(Z3)
    J=(1/nrow(inputsMat))*(0.5*sum((y-yHat)^2))

    print("the cost, J, for this epoch is")
    print(J)

}


#First find the error on training set.
moodInputs=train[,c("calories _ burned","hours _ of _ sleep")]
moodOutput=train[,"mood"]

#Then run fullUpdateWeights repeatedly, and then check error on test
set.

fullUpdateWeights(inputX=moodInputs,outputY=moodOutput,W1,W2)
## [[1]]
##                [,1]        [,2]       [,3]
## [1,]  -0.7025095 -0.2546609 0.2037947
## [2,]   0.5319202 -0.3997879 0.2077013
##
## [[2]]
##                [,1]
## [1,]  -1.1078438
## [2,]  -0.8357552
## [3,]  -0.1986204
##
## [1] "the cost, J, for this epoch is"
## [1] 0.7395155
#We update the weight matrices W1 and W2 before running fullUpdate-
Weights() again
W1=weightsList[["W1"]]
W2=weightsList[["W2"]]
```

```
weightsList=fullUpdateWeights(inputX=moodInputs,outputY=moodOutput,
W1,W2)
## [[1]]
##              [,1]       [,2]      [,3]
## [1,] -0.7363406 -0.2801577 0.1959591
## [2,]  0.4740215 -0.4447504 0.1940089
##
## [[2]]
##              [,1]
## [1,] -1.3061192
## [2,] -1.0662849
## [3,] -0.3860218
##
## [1] "the cost, J, for this epoch is"
## [1] 0.3696064
W1=weightsList[["W1"]]
W2=weightsList[["W2"]]

weightsList=fullUpdateWeights(inputX=moodInputs,outputY=moodOutput,
W1,W2)
## [[1]]
##              [,1]       [,2]      [,3]
## [1,] -0.7657613 -0.3036134 0.1866735
## [2,]  0.4329453 -0.4781514 0.1809098
##
## [[2]]
##              [,1]
## [1,] -1.4344280
## [2,] -1.2123725
## [3,] -0.5022757
##
## [1] "the cost, J, for this epoch is"
## [1] 0.2144073

#Test set: We can see how well the algorithm performs on the test
data as well.
moodInputs=test[,c("calories_burned","hours_of_sleep")]
moodInputs=normal.5(moodInputs)

moodOutput=test[,"mood"]
moodOutput=unlist(moodOutput)
moodOutput=normal.5(moodOutput)
countS=0

JCost(moodInputs,moodOutput,W1,W2)
## [1] "the cost, J, for this epoch is"
## [1] 0.01907332
```

11.20 Repeated Training: Epochs

We can run the **fullUpdateWeights**()through a loop. We will call the function that runs the loop, **predNNEpoch**(). With its current definition, the loop will print out all the print statements for each iteration of the loop; thus, the reader may wish to comment out the print statements first. However, we would like to know what the cost, J, is after all the iterations (and maybe other quantities as well). Unfortunately, the *scope* of all the variables used in **fullUpdateWeights**() is limited to within the **fullUpdateWeights**() function. This means that if we try to make reference to the cost, J, inside our **predNNEpoch**(), but outside the **fullUpdateWeights**() function, R won't be able to find J and will therefore give an error. There is a solution to this. If you use the "<<-" instead of the "<-" for the assignment operator, then R makes the variable available to the calling function's environment. This "double arrow" is called the superassignment operator. One way to describe its meaning is that it makes the variable available in more parts of the code. There is often a warning regarding the use of "<<-". It is said that this can give unintended consequences. One such unintended consequence is that we may not want variables outside our function to be altered by what is happening inside of the function. Another point made about using the superassignment operator is that is may conflict with the spirit of functional programming. Nevertheless, we will create a global value of J here, naming it globalJ

```
globalJ <<- J
```

just after the line

```
J=0.5*(yValue-yhat)^2
```

in the **fullUpdateWeights**() function. Then globalJ will be available outside of **fullUpdateWeights**(), and after the loops have completed, we can print out globalJ to see the final cost. With this change to **fullUpdateWeights**(), we run **predNNEpoch**().

```
#Even though we call this function predNNEpoch, suggesting that it will
output a prediction, we will leave it to the reader to make predictions
with it. One way would be to make some global values for the weights and
then use those values to run through a forward() method.
predNNEpoch <- function(inputX=moodInputs,outputY=moodOutputs,W1Value,
W2Value,epochs=n,rValue=1){
  #Sample call:

  #predNNEpoch(inputX=moodinputs,outputY=moodOutput,W1Value=W1,W2Valu
e=W2,epochs=5,rValue=.1)
  for(k in 1:epochs){

    weightsList <<- fullUpdateWeights(inputX,outputY,W1Value,W2Value,
rValue=1)
    W1Value <- weightsList[["W1"]]
    W2Value <- weightsList[["W2"]]
    print(paste0("Epoch number: ", k, "  globalJ: ", globalJ))
  }
  #print(paste0("globalJ: ", globalJ))

}
#We should reset the weights first.
W1=matrix(runif(inputLayerSize*hiddenLayerSize,-1,1),inputLayerSize,
hiddenLayerSize)
W2=matrix(runif(hiddenLayerSize*outputLayerSize,-1,1),hiddenLayerSize,
outputLayerSize)
predNNEpoch(inputX=moodinputs,outputY=moodOutput,W1Value=W1,W2Value=W2,ep
ochs=5,rValue=.1)
## [1] "Epoch number: 1  globalJ: 0.0890687689497513"
```

```
## [1] "Epoch number: 2  globalJ: 0.0215483095576332"
## [1] "Epoch number: 3  globalJ: 0.00863264698924389"
## [1] "Epoch number: 4  globalJ: 0.00487937576235561"
## [1] "Epoch number: 5  globalJ: 0.00368296253087151"

}
```

We can see that the cost is being reduced.

Practice 11.20.16

1. List 2 variables that are "local" to **updateWeights**().
2. Check to see if the two variables you found above are listed in the RStudio panel titled Environment.
3. If a variable is created only within a function, it will not appear in the Environment panel. It will only appear in the Environment panel if somewhere else in your code, at some time or another, you created a variable with that name, outside of the function. On the other hand, if you followed the advice above and put globalJ <<- J into **updateWeights**(), do you see globalJ in the Environment panel?

11.21 Hyperparameters – Learning Rates, set.seed() Number of Nodes and Layers, and Epochs

By experimentation, you will find that learning rates, set.seed(), and epochs all have large roles in improving the performance of the net.

One explanation for this is that there are many local traps to get caught in, that is, many local minimums , which are not the absolute minimum, of the cost function to get stuck in. Changing the set.seed() changes the original (random) settings for the weights. The effect of this is to start us out at a different location on the cost surface. (We say surface and not curve because we have multiple dimensions and in fact it may be better to say hypersurface). From this random starting point, we may discover a point with a the lowest possible cost (this is what we hope for), or on the other hand, we may discover just a local minimum. As was suggested earlier in the text, we might liken this to the genetics with which different children are born. Given a particular starting point (a particular set of genes) may have a significant effect on future accomplishments (Figure 11.18).

```
"Epoch number: 94   globalJ: 0.000119592814568133"
"Epoch number: 95   globalJ: 0.000113939748705093"
"Epoch number: 96   globalJ: 0.000108294449265562"
"Epoch number: 97   globalJ: 0.000102667164656141"
"Epoch number: 98   globalJ: 9.70683723703841e-05"
"Epoch number: 99   globalJ: 9.15087733964453e-05"
"Epoch number: 100  globalJ: 8.59992860604487e-05"
```

Figure 11.18 The error after 100 epochs.

11.22 Conclusion

We have created a neural network with three layers. In the next chapter, we will use classes to make our code more elegant.

Practice 11.22.17

1. Can you make changes to the statement `inputLayerSize=2` and to the statement `pre dictorMat=`**`matrix`**`(predictorMat,1,2)` so that we can include another variable from the original mood dataset into our set of predictor variables? Try to include the individual's weight (named weight_kg) into the set of predictor variables. You will have to add "weight_kg" at several locations in the code.

Chapter 12

Programming a Neural Network Using OOP in R

The object-oriented programming (OOP) paradigm provides elegant solutions to programming problems. We will present such a solution for our neural network algorithm. The subject of OOP is vast, and one could spend a semester or more just studying the OOP design concepts. Here we will try to explain the most basic idea in just a few words.

Functions Coded in This Chapter
trainTestSplit
sScore
prepNormalize

12.1 Object-Oriented Programming Notation with R

In many programming languages (for example, Python, Java, C++), we sometimes see code that uses the dot notation. For example in Python, you may see math.sqrt(). Generally, (not always), this is a result of the fact that OOP is being employed. Note however that R does not use the dot notation in this way. Where a dot may be employed in other languages, R will usually use the dollar sign "$". Next we will see that OOP is based on the idea of *classes*.

12.2 Classes as Blueprints

A class is said to be like a blueprint. In the same way that a car manufacturer makes a blueprint for a particular model of car and then uses the blueprint to create many examples or "instances" of cars, in OOP, a class is a blueprint, and we can use it to create any number of instances of that class. We may sometimes use the word "object" instead of "instance" in the following.

Note: Don't confuse the word instance here with the way we have used the word instance with regard to data sets.

285

12.3 Example of a Class

Typically, when introducing the concept of classes, some textbooks give the example of a Student class. This would be a *blueprint* for what a student would be. Of course, a student is an infinitely complicated entity, but usually a programmer has a specific task in mind; for example, if the programmer is working for the school administration, they may need to keep a record of students' grades, the courses they are taking, their transcripts, and so on. They don't really care about the infinite complexity of what it is to be a student. They may just need to define a few variables, like *major, zip code, GPA*, just to keep it simple. Then they also will define some functions that may be convenient. For example, we may define a function to figure out if the student qualifies for a scholarship, which we could call scholarOK().The idea in OOP is to put these 3 variables and this function *together* into the so-called blueprint of Student. The blueprint is called a class. Once we write this blueprint (as code), then we can create what is called an *instance* of the class and in fact make an instance for *each* student in the school. If this is not clear, please keep reading.

12.4 Creating an Instance of the Class

The syntax for creating an *instance* of a student (once the blueprint for student has been written) in OOP languages looks something like

JohnSmith=**Student**("mathematics, 178845, 3.8, "John Smith")[1]

where

mathematics is John Smith's major
178845 is his zip code
3.8 is his GPA

Once we have created this instance, *JohnSmith*, of the class, we can use our function on him like this

JohnSmith.scholarOK()

That is where we see the dot notation popping up. Often, in OOP languages, the part before the dot is the instance (object), and the part after the dot is a function defined in the class. If we run JohnSmith.scholarOK(), we should get (if the programmer has done their job) a result that tells us whether John Smith is eligible for a scholarship. For example, the output of this could be "yes". If we had created another student like this

NaomiOsaka=Student("physics", 178558, 3.9, "Naomi Osaka")

---

[1] You may wonder why we have the name John Smith written twice. The John Smith in quotation marks would be the name of the student. The JohnSmith part, without quotes, is the name of the object. They don't have to be the same, but if there is no other convention for naming the object, we may as well give it the name of the student.

then we could write

NaomiOsaka.scholarOK()

to calculate her eligibility for a scholarship.[2]

Practice 12.4.1
1. Create an instance of the Student class with your name and information using the above described syntax.
2. What may be another useful field that the Student class may contain?
3. What may be another useful function that the Student class may contain?

12.5 A Neural Network Class

In the discussion below, we will create a neural network class. It will have functions like `backProp()`, `forward()`, `Jcost()`, and so on. Once we write the neural network class (the blueprint), we create an instance of it something like this:

```
nnExample1= Neural_Network ("inputs",4,"outputs")
```

where "`inputs`" would hold the inputs to the neural network (what we have been denoting with X in previous chapters), 4 would be the number of nodes in the hidden layer, and "`outputs`" would be the output variable data (the labels). Actually, the syntax in R is slightly different. It looks like this.

```
nnExample1<-Neural_Network$new(inputs, 4, outputs)
```

Once we have created our example, `nnExample1`, we can run the `backProp`() function with something like

```
nnExample1.backProp(inputs, 4,outputs)
```

which would presumably cause the network to train itself with the input and output variables supplied. Actually, as we mentioned, the syntax in R does not use the dot but rather the dollar sign, and so it will look like this

```
nnExample1$backProp(inputs, 4,outputs)
```

The other functions can be called similarly.

12.5.1 Methods

One piece of terminology. When a function is defined inside a class, it is not usually called a function, but rather it is called a *method*. You may object to having to learn a new term, but it can

---

[2] The dot notation is not restricted only to functions appearing on the right-hand side. We can also have variables there. We won't use that feature in our class, and so we are leaving that topic out of the discussion.

be useful to say something is a method and not just a function. Immediately, it would be clear that this function has been defined within a class.

Practice 12.5.2

1. Suppose we want to call the **JCost**() method on the nnExample1 instance of our Neural_Network class. What would we type to call this method?

12.6 Why Use Classes for a Neural Network?

One question that the reader may have is, Why make a class out of this? We don't have need for multiple instances of our neural network. We just need one example, like nnExample1. Then we can use it repeatedly. This is true. However we can suggest 4 possible reasons for writing a neural network class. The first reason is the elegance of the solution. Hopefully, after reading this chapter, the reader will recognize this solution as elegant. Second, this is often the way the solutions are presented in the literature. Additionally, this will give the reader a chance to learn about classes and in particular about how to create classes in R. Finally, two chapters from now, we will develop a much more flexible design for neural networks that can easily be adapted to deep learning structures like convolutional neural networks. In that presentation, class design is essential.

12.7 Classes in R

How is a class created in R? We will need to include the necessary variables and the necessary functions, and we need to know the *syntax* for including these. For our neural network class, the necessary variables are the *input variables*, the *output variables*, and the *number of nodes in the hidden layer*. (We will allow for more than 3 nodes in the hidden layer.) We will also include the *learning rate r* as a variable and one more variable which will be explained later. In R, these variables, when designing a class, are referred to as *fields*. The functions, as we said above, are referred to as *methods*. How is all this put together?

There are several ways to work with classes in R. We will use the S5 system[3] to construct a class, and this is achieved with the use of the **setRefClass()** function. (We have not discussed the different systems in R, but this topic has to do with the historical development of the R language.) Using the **setRefClass()** function, we will have to place the fields *in a list* and place the methods (functions) *in another list*. The construction of a class called Neural_Network using **setRefClass()** looks like this:

```
Neural_Network <- setRefClass("Neural_Network",

fields = list(
#Variables that are listed here are referred to as either, fields, member
variables, or class member variables, although we may not always use this
terminology.

#The list of fields began with an open parenthesis. This is the end of
the list of fields, and it ends with a closing parenthesis
),
```

---

[3] This is one of the most recent techniques for creating classes. This occurs within the S5 R system. There are other techniques within the S3 and S4 R systems.

```
methods = list(
#Next we have to fill in the methods (functions). We will have a
backProp() method, a forward() method, and a JCost() method. They are all
defined here. There is also a special method called initialize() that
generally has to be created. Once we fill in the code for these methods,
we are done.
            initialize = function() {#fill in the code here

    },

            forward = function(nnX,nny) { #fill in the code here
    },
            backProp = function(nnX,nny) { #fill in the code here
    },
            JCost = function(nnX,nny) {    #fill in the code here


    }

#List of methods started with an open parenthesis. This is the end of the
list of methods, and it ends with a closing parenthesis.
)
# setRefClass is the function in R that creates our class. It started
with an open parenthesis, as do all functions in R, and here it ends with
the closing parenthesis which comes as the end of the Neural_Network
class definition.
)
```

12.8 Fields

In our code, nnX stands for the input variables, and we will require it to be a matrix. nny stands for the output field and will also be a matrix. We will also have a numeric field called nnhiddenLayerSize. There is also a numeric field r for the learning rate. Finally, we throw in one more field named "suppress" which will be either yes, "y", or no, "n", and is a flag for whether to suppress the output of some **print**() statements in our code. All these variables are written into the class definition here. Technically they should be referred to as fields, but we will frequently revert to using the term "variable".

```
fields = list(nnX="matrix", nnhiddenLayerSize = "numeric", nny =
"matrix", r="numeric",suppress="character")
```

We are specifying the class of each field above[4]. For example, we are specifying that nnX should be a matrix. It is also possible to not specify which class nnX is by writing nnX="Any", but this could lead to errors when running the code if the user inputs something other than a matrix so, if possible, it may be best to specify the class now. However in a later chapter, we will allow more flexibility.

Practice 12.8.3
   1. Name two *class member variables* in our class.

---

[4] You can check the class of an object with the class() function.

12.9 Methods

The methods will also be stored in a list. For our neural network class, we will define a **back-Prop()**, **forward()**, **JCost()**, and the special, **initialize**() method. The **initialize**() method is used in the S5 system and the **setRefClass**() function. The arguments for the **initialize**() method will determine the arguments needed to generate an instance of our class. A few paragraphs above, we gave a sample of how an instance *might* be generated. However, for our particular code, an instance will *actually* be generated with the following.

```
nn1<-Neural_Network$new(inputs, 3, outputs,4,"y")
```

You can see that to create a new instance, we supply 5 arguments. It is in the **initialize**() method that we specify that for a new instance to be created, 5 arguments are necessary. The following is the beginning of the **initialize**() method.

```
initialize = function(a=matrix(), b=c(),c=matrix(),d=c(),e=c())
```

Because there are 5 arguments here: a, b, c, d, and e, this will mean that to instantiate (create) an instance of our class, 5 arguments must be input. You can also see that the type of argument is also specified here so that for example, the first argument "a" must be a matrix.

Next, the arguments are assigned to the elements of the fields list. For example,

```
nnX<<-a
```

Note that all assignments use the superassignment operator <<-. This is generally true for all methods defined in the class; many (if not most) variables defined inside methods will be needed outside the method and thus we use the superassignment operator to assign values to them. Recall that assigning them to be non-local variables accomplishes this. Local variables may be created inside the **initialize**() method if their purpose is only to facilitate calculations within the **initialize**() method. We have a few of these in our code such as inputLayerSize and outputLayerSize.

12.10 Batch Updating

In this implementation of a neural network, we will also learn about batch updating. In the past, we have updated the weights for each example in the dataset one at a time. That is to say, the first example is fed into the network, the error is calculated for that example, and the weights are adjusted. Then the next example is fed into the network and the process is repeated with each example in the data set. In batch updating, we feed the entire dataset into the network *before* we update the weights. Through some algebraic tricks, we sum up the gradients due to each example. We call this *sum either* dJ_dW2 or dJ_dW1 depending on which layer we are working on and then proceed as normal to update the weights.

Practice 12.10.4

1. Find the code in the last neural network from the previous chapter, that allowed for all the examples to be read into the network.

12.11 Preparation for Using the Neural Network

```r
#Use exercise-mood data.
#The original data is available at
#https://www.kaggle.com/aroojanwarkhan/fitness-data-trends
mood <- read.csv("exercise_mood.csv") #added underscore to name
#Remove any cases that have NA
mood<-mood[complete.cases(mood),]
#We will limit the number of variables to work with.
mood=mood[,c("mood","calories_burned","hours_of_sleep")]
#Split data into train and test sets and store both in a list.
trainTestSplit<-function(dataset="mood"){
  #Sample call:
  #trainAndTest=trainTestSplit(mood)
  #train =trainAndTest[["train"]]
  #test  =trainAndTest[["test"]]
  smp_size <- floor(0.75 * nrow(dataset))
  set.seed(123)
  train_ind <- sample(seq_len(nrow(dataset)), size = smp_size)

  train <- dataset[train_ind, ]
  test <- dataset[-train_ind, ]
  returnedList=list(train,test)
  returnedList<-setNames(returnedList, c("train","test"))
  return(returnedList)
}

sScore <- function(x){
  xNew=(x-mean(x))/sd(x)
  return(xNew)
}

sigmoid <- function(z) {
  return(1/(1+exp(-z)))
}
sigmoidPrime<-function(z){
  return(exp(-z)/(1+exp(-z))^2)
}
```

12.12 Neural Network Class

```r
Neural_Network <- setRefClass("Neural_Network",

#Sample construction:
#nn1<-Neural_Network$new(inputs, 3, outputs,5,'y'). The fourth argument is
the learning rate r, and the fifth argument is for suppressing print
statements.

#"fields" is a list of attributes for the class.
#We also need to indicate that nnX is a matrix, nnhiddenLayerSize is a
matrix, r is numeric, and so on.
fields = list(nnX="matrix", nnhiddenLayerSize = "numeric", nny =
"matrix", r="numeric",suppress="character",W1="matrix", W2="matrix"),
methods = list(
```

```
                                        initialize = function(a=matrix(),
b=c(),c=matrix(),d=c(),e=c()) {

                                nnX <<- a
                                nnhiddenLayerSize <<- b
                                nny <<- c
                                r <<- d
                                suppress <<- e #This is just used to
suppress output when running the backpropagation method in a loop. You
will see what this does in a little while.
                                inputLayerSize <- dim(nnX)[2]
                                outputLayerSize <- dim(nny)[2]
                                set.seed(3)
                                W1 <<- matrix(runif(inputLayerSize
*nnhiddenLayerSize,-1,1),inputLayerSize,nnhiddenLayerSize)
                                W2 <<- matrix(runif(nnhiddenLayerSize
*outputLayerSize,-1,1),nnhiddenLayerSize,outputLayerSize)

                                        },

#We will define a forward() method.
 forward = function(nnX,nny) {
   #First normalize the input data. nnX and nnY are renamed as nnx_local,
nnY_local to avoid ambiguity and because the inputs and outputs should
not change.
     nnX_local <- sScore(nnX)
     nny_local <- sScore(nny)

 #Recall that the initial weights were randomly generated and that the
dimensions of the weight matrices W1 an0d W2 were determined by the layer
sizes.
     Z2 <- nnX_local%*%W1 #Remember that we are running this in batch
-meaning that nnX_local will contain not just one example but rather the
entire set of data (or the first batch). Thus Z2 will not be a row matrix
but rather it will have many rows -one for each example in the data set.
Note this also means that each row in Z2 will have an entry for each node
of the second layer.
     A2 <- sigmoid(Z2)
     Z3 <- A2%*%W2
     yHat <- sigmoid(Z3)
     return(yHat)

#the end of forward() method
},
```

Practice 12.12.5

1. Which fields in the forward() method are local? Why did we choose to make them local?

    #Define the backpropagation method.

The most important method is the backProp() method. It will take care of updating the weights. The weight matrices W1 and W2 are not local to the backprop() method and therefore, once the backProp() method is run, the non-local variables W1 and W2 will be updated. We can then run the forward method on either the test data or entirely new examples with (hopefully) improved predictions.

```
  backProp = function(nnX,nny) {
#Sample call: nn1$backProp(inputs, outputs)
  We will want to run backProp in a loop through many iterations.
#The following print() statements print out the current weights. If we
run the loop 500 times, we won't want to see the weights each time. We
can set the suppress argument to "y" in the initial instantiation of our
instance like this:
  nn1<-Neural_Network$new(inputs, 3, outputs,.05,"y")
  This will avoid printing the output of the following print statements.
    if(suppress=="n"){
print("Original W")
print(W1)
print(W2)
}

local_nnX <- sScore(nnX)
local_nny <- sScore(nny)
Z2<-nnX%*%W1
A2<-sigmoid(Z2)
Z3<-A2%*%W2
yHat<-sigmoid(Z3)
```

Next we calculate Delta3.

Note that Delta3 is not one dimensional. This is because we are pushing through the entire dataset at once, and so for each instance there is a delta. However, in our previous implementation of the neural network, where we pushed one instance at a time, there was *also* a separate delta3 for each instance, but since we handled just one instance at a time, the delta3 for each instance was a one-dimensional scalar. Now, however, Delta3 will have dimension

```
numberOfExamples x outputLayerSize (=numberOfExamples x 1)
```

```
#Note the matrices local_nny-yHat and -sigmoidPrime(Z3) are of dimension
numberOfExamples x 1, and the * multiplication is element by element
(Hadamard).
Delta3=(local_nny-yHat) * (-sigmoidPrime(Z3))
```

Next, we deal with dJ_dW2. When we only were dealing with one instance at a time, dJ_dW2 was of dimension `hiddenLayerSize x 1`. One way to deal with the fact that the entire dataset is being sent into the network at once is to have dJ_dW2 be of dimension `hiddenLayerSize x numberOfExamples`. This would mean that each row would contain partial derivatives of J with respect to a particular weight, and the difference between the entries of a particular row would be that they were calculated for each particular instance. For example, if there were just 3 examples in our dataset (and as before 3 nodes in the hidden layer), dJ_dW2 would look like this:

$$
\begin{bmatrix}
\dfrac{\partial J}{\partial w_1^{(2)}}\text{(for 1st example)} & \dfrac{\partial J}{\partial w_1^{(2)}}\text{(for 2nd example)} & \dfrac{\partial J}{\partial w_1^{(2)}}\text{(for 3rd example)} \\[2ex]
\dfrac{\partial J}{\partial w_2^{(2)}}\text{(for 1st example)} & \dfrac{\partial J}{\partial w_2^{(2)}}\text{(for 2nd example)} & \dfrac{\partial J}{\partial w_2^{(2)}}\text{(for 3rd example)} \\[2ex]
\dfrac{\partial J}{\partial w_3^{(2)}}\text{(for 1st example)} & \dfrac{\partial J}{\partial w_3^{(2)}}\text{(for 2nd example)} & \dfrac{\partial J}{\partial w_3^{(2)}}\text{(for 3rd example)}
\end{bmatrix}
$$

This *could be* a candidate for $\dfrac{\partial J}{\partial W^{(2)}}$.

Practice 12.12.6

1. If this were $\dfrac{\partial J}{\partial W^{(2)}}$, what would its dimensions be if there were 50 examples?

2. If this were $\dfrac{\partial J}{\partial W^{(2)}}$, what would its dimensions be if there were 50 examples and if the hidden layer had 2 weights?

If the matrix above were $\dfrac{\partial J}{\partial W^{(2)}}$, how would we use this to update the W2 weights? We have just 3 weights in W2 (in this example). But we have 3 sets of derivatives for each weight in this matrix. The simplest idea would be to update the weights using the first column (these would be from the first example), then update the weights with the next column, and so on.

Practice 12.12.7

1. What are the dimensions of A2 for the current dataset?

The above plan for updating, however, is not what is meant by batch updating, and we will handle the process differently. We use the equation

```
#dJ_dW2=t(A2)%*%Delta3
Note that t(A2) has dimensions hiddenLayerSize x numberOfExamples, and
Delta3 has dimensions numberOfExamples x outputLayerSize.
Therefore, this multiplication is permitted and results in dJ_dW2 having
dimensions hiddenLayerSize x outputLayerSize (which would be 3 × 1 in our
example above). Note that this is not the same as the candidate for
dJ_dW2 posed above.
```

Why can we switch from a matrix of size `hiddenLayerSize x numberOfExamples` to one of size `hiddenLayerSize x outputLayerSize`? For example, if we had 100 examples, why would we switch from 3×100 to 3×1? What is the implication of going from a matrix of dimension `hiddenLayerSize x numberOfExamples` to `hiddenLayerSize x outputLayerSize`? In other words, what are we doing when we calculate t(A2)%*%Delta3? Let us examine t(A2) and Delta3.

$$\left(A^{(2)}\right)^{\mathrm{T}} = \begin{bmatrix} a_1^{(2)}(\text{for 1st example}) & a_1^{(2)}(\text{for 2nd example}) & a_1^{(2)}(\text{for 3rd example}) \\ a_2^{(2)}(\text{for 1st example}) & a_2^{(2)}(\text{for 2nd example}) & a_2^{(2)}(\text{for 3rd example}) \\ a_3^{(2)}(\text{for 1st example}) & a_3^{(2)}(\text{for 2nd example}) & a_3^{(2)}(\text{for 3rd example}) \end{bmatrix} \tag{12.1}$$

$$\delta^{(3)} = Delta3 = \begin{bmatrix} \text{delta3}\left(\text{for 1st example}\right) \\ \text{delta3}\left(\text{for 2nd example}\right) \\ \text{delta3}\left(\text{for 3rd example}\right) \end{bmatrix} \tag{12.2}$$

$(A^{(2)})^{\mathrm{T}}\delta^3$

$$= \begin{bmatrix} a_1^{(2)} \text{ delta3 from 1st example} & a_1^{(2)} \text{ delta3 from 2nd example} & a_1^{(2)} \text{ delta3 from 3rd example} \\ a_2^{(2)} \text{delta3 from 1st example} & a_2^{(2)} \text{ delta3 from 2nd example} & a_2^{(2)} \text{ delta3 from 3rd example} \\ a_3^{(2)} \text{delta3 from 1st example} & a_3^{(2)} \text{ delta3 from 2nd example} & a_3^{(2)} \text{ delta3 from 3rd example} \end{bmatrix}$$

$$(12.3)$$

This will be our choice for calculating the derivative matrix for the batch update process.

$$\frac{\partial J}{\partial W^{(2)}} = \left(A^{(2)}\right)^{\mathrm{T}}\delta^{(3)} - \frac{\partial J}{\partial W^{(2)}} \tag{12.4}$$

is a matrix, a 3×1 matrix, and is in fact the matrix just above in Equation (12.3).

Let us investigate this a bit further.

Note that each of the terms in each of the sums in the above matrix in Equation (12.3) is a partial derivative that we have seen before. For example,

$$a_1^{(2)} \text{ delta3 from 1st example is } \frac{\partial J}{\partial w_1^{(2)}}$$

also written as dJ _ dw2sub1. However, it is *just for the first example*. Also note the uncapital-ized "w", so it is for an individual weight. Note we have not developed any convenient notation to indicate "for the first example", and so we are writing it out by hand. Some textbooks use the superscript with parentheses around it, but we are already using this notation for layer levels.

Thus, the first element of the above 3×1 matrix is the sum of the contributions of the derivatives $\frac{\partial J}{\partial w_1^{(2)}}$ *over each example*:

$$\sum_{\text{over all examples}} \frac{\partial J}{\partial w_1^{(2)}}$$

The second element of the above 3×1 matrix is $\frac{\partial J}{\partial w_2^{(2)}}$ *over each example*:

$$\sum_{\text{over all examples}} \frac{\partial J}{\partial w_2^{(2)}}$$

Thus, $\frac{\partial J}{\partial W^{(2)}}$ being a 3×1 matrix has each its 3 elements as a sum of derivatives, *one term for each example in our dataset.*

Alternatively, we can say that the batch update $\dfrac{\partial J}{\partial W^{(2)}}$ is the matrix sum of

$$\dfrac{\partial J}{\partial W^{(2)}}_{\text{for the 1st example}} + \dfrac{\partial J}{\partial W^{(2)}}_{\text{for the 2nd example}} + \dfrac{\partial J}{\partial W^{(2)}}_{\text{for the 3rd example}}$$

where these are the following 3×1 matrices.

$$\dfrac{\partial J}{\partial W^{(2)}}_{\text{for the 1st example}} = \begin{bmatrix} a_1^{(2)} \text{ delta3 from 1st example} \\ a_2^{(2)} \text{ delta3 from 1st example} \\ a_3^{(2)} \text{ delta3 from 1st example} \end{bmatrix} = \begin{bmatrix} \dfrac{\partial J}{\partial w_1^{(2)}} \\ \dfrac{\partial J}{\partial w_2^{(2)}} \\ \dfrac{\partial J}{\partial w_2^{(2)}} \end{bmatrix}_{\text{for 1st example}} \quad (12.5)$$

$$\dfrac{\partial J}{\partial W^{(2)}}_{\text{for the 2nd example}} = \begin{bmatrix} a_1^{(2)} \text{ delta3 from 2nd example} \\ a_2^{(2)} \text{ delta3 from 2nd example} \\ a_3^{(2)} \text{ delta3 from 2nd example} \end{bmatrix} = \begin{bmatrix} \dfrac{\partial J}{\partial w_1^{(2)}} \\ \dfrac{\partial J}{\partial w_2^{(2)}} \\ \dfrac{\partial J}{\partial w_2^{(2)}} \end{bmatrix}_{\text{for 2nd example}} \quad (12.6)$$

$$\dfrac{\partial J}{\partial W^{(2)}}_{\text{for the 3rd example}} = \begin{bmatrix} a_1^{(2)} \text{ delta3 from 3rd example} \\ a_2^{(2)} \text{ delta3 from 3rd example} \\ a_3^{(2)} \text{ delta3 from 3rd example} \end{bmatrix} = \begin{bmatrix} \dfrac{\partial J}{\partial w_1^{(2)}} \\ \dfrac{\partial J}{\partial w_2^{(2)}} \\ \dfrac{\partial J}{\partial w_2^{(2)}} \end{bmatrix}_{\text{for 3rd example}} \quad (12.7)$$

Practice 12.12.8

1. Suppose we had 4 examples in our dataset. Write the equation for $\dfrac{\partial J}{\partial w_1^{(2)}}$. (Notice the small w.) You can write it in mathematical notation or code notation.

That is, it is as though we are giving each *example* a "vote" in what the derivative of J with respect to a particular weight should be and then summing up these votes.

Figure 12.1 illustrates this. It shows 3 vectors, each one representing a separate *example's* gradient dJ_dW2: v(0,1,1), t(2,2,0), and u(2,1,0). If our dataset contains only 3 examples, then the vector *sum* for all three examples would be the total (batch) gradient and is represented by s(4,4,1), the black vector, as it is the vector sum of the 3 vectors. Note that the axes for this diagram are NOT the same as those for Figure 10.10 or Figure 11.13. For example, in the 2D diagram in

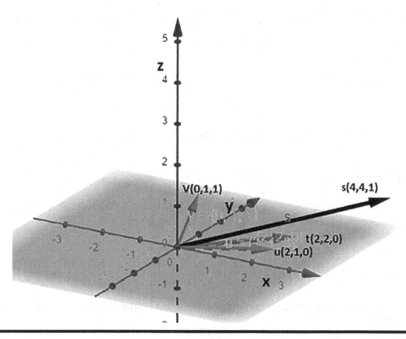

Figure 12.1   3 vectors representing 3 separate examples. The dimensions (x, y, and z axes) are partial derivatives with respect to three weights.

Figure 11.13, the x-axis represented a *weight* and the y-axis represented the error or the cost J. Here, first of all, note that there is no cost axis. *Each **axis** is a derivative of the cost function with respect to a weight.* Since we are limited to 3 dimensions, for purposes of visualization, we are *assuming* there are only 3 weights. The *axes are the partial derivatives with respect to each of the weights,* i.e., dJ_dw1, dJ_dw2, and dJ_dw3. Next, what are the vectors? Each vector represents a gradient *for a particular example,* and so we have the 3 colored vectors. Thus, it should be clear that each vector has a component in this dJ_dw1dJ_dw2dJ_dw3-space (as opposed to w1w2J-space). The black vector represents the sum of the 3 colored vectors and would tell us by how much to adjust the weight matrix W2 *for the batch processing of all 3 examples.* Of course in reality, we will have more than 3 weights and more than 3 examples. We only assume 3 examples and 3 weights for the purpose of visualizing the situation.

Practice 12.12.9

1. How many weights are we assuming layer W2 has?
2. What would our diagram look like if we had only 2 weights in W2?
3. What would our diagram look like if we had 2 examples and 2 weights?

Don't be confused by the above explanation. The fact that the number of weights is equal to the number of examples is just a coincidence. We could discuss a situation with more examples. This would mean more arrows in the above diagram.

We could not conveniently discuss more weights since that would require more than 3 dimensions which would be difficult to picture. But in terms of the *equations* above, it would only mean that the dimension of the batch update derivative matrix $\frac{\partial J}{\partial W^{(2)}}$ would have more than 3 rows.

Note that if there is just one example in our dataset, then the situation reduces to what we did in the previous chapter on neural networks.

Thus, the expression

$$\frac{\partial J}{\partial W^{(2)}} = \left(A^{(2)}\right)^T \delta^{(3)} \qquad (12.8)$$

will imply this batch processing of all the examples in one fell swoop.

```
dJ_dW2=t(A2)%*%Delta3

# Next we deal with dJ_dW1 using batch updating. Now, since Delta3 is a
matrix, the formula for delta2 from last chapter
delta2 = (delta3*t(W2)) * sigmoidPrime(Z2)
will not work.
We cannot use the scalar multiplication operator * to the right of
delta3.

#However the Hadamard multiplication is still applicable to the left of
sigmoidPrime(Z2).
```

Delta3 has dimensions

```
numberOfExamples x outputLayerSize
```

t(W2) has dimensions

```
outputLayerSize x hiddenLayerSize
```

sigmoidPrime(Z2) has dimensions

```
numberOfExamples x hiddenLayerSize
```

And so, the following definition of Delta2 implies its dimensions are

```
numberOfExamples x hiddenLayerSize
  Delta2 = (Delta3%*%t(W2)) * sigmoidPrime(Z2)
```

$$\text{Delta2} = \delta^{(2)} = \delta^{(3)} \left(W^{(2)}\right)^T \odot \sigma'\left(Z^{(2)}\right) \qquad (12.9)$$

Now on to $\frac{\partial J}{\partial W^{(1)}}$. We note that t(local_nnX) has dimensions

```
inputLayerSize x numberOfExamples
```

And so, the following implies the dimensions of dJ_dW1 would be

```
inputLayerSize x hiddenLayerSize
  dJ_dW1= t(local_nnX) %*%Delta2
```

Now with our batch calculations for the derivatives, we update the weight matrices.

```
With the use of the superassignment operator, the weight matrices will
be available outside of the backprop() method and thus can be used in
calculating the cost J.
  W2<<-W2-r*dJ_dW2
  W1<<-W1-r*dJ_dW1

  if(suppress=="n"){
  print("New W")
  print(W1)
  print(W2)
  }

  #the end of the backProp method


},
```

Practice 12.12.10

1. Note the size of the sum of the 3 vectors in Figure 12.1. It is considerably larger than that of any of the vectors v, t, and u. This will mean that the size of the gradient (not the direction, just the size) will be significantly different if we do non-batch updating. This can be compensated for by choosing a different (smaller) learning rate r when using batch processing. But nonetheless, the gradient will be larger and will depend on the batch size (the size of the dataset[5]). This would mean that if we had a large dataset, we would have to think about the appropriate size to set for r. Instead of this situation, we could balance the size of the sum by dividing it by the size of the dataset. Can you implement this change?

```
JCost = function(nnX,nny) {
#sample call: nn1$JCost(X,y)

  inputLayerSize<-dim(nnX)[2]
  outputLayerSize<-dim(nny)[2]

  local_nnX<-as.matrix(local_nnX)
  local_nny<-as.matrix(local_nny)

  Z2<-nnX%*%W1
  A2<-sigmoid(z2)
  Z3<-A2%*%W2
  yHat<-sigmoid(Z3)
  #We calculate the average error.
  J <- 0.5*sum((nny-yHat)**2)/nrow(nny)
  #J <- 0.5*sum((nny-yHat)**2)
  return(J)


}
#end of Neural_Network class definition
))
```

---

[5] We have not considered using a batch size less than then entire dataset, but this is often tested, for example, a batch size of 100. Also, note a batch size of 1 means updating the weights after each example in the dataset is pushed through the network (as we did in the previous chapter).

Practice 12.12.11

1. Another option for a threshold function is the tanh() function. It is part of your basic R installation. Make a plot of it, and then discuss the similarities and dissimilarities with the sigmoid() function.
2. Note that you do not need to apply the same threshold function to Z2 as to Z3. Suppose you wanted to change the threshold function on just Z2. Which parts of the code would need to be reconsidered and recalculated?
3. Suppose you wanted to change the threshold function on just Z3. Which parts of the code would need to be reconsidered and recalculated?

Steps for running Neural_Network class

```
#1. Split data to training and testing sets.
trainAndTest=trainTestSplit(mood)
#2. Create train set.
train =trainAndTest[["train"]]

#3. Separate training dataframe into inputs and outputs.
#Here we use "inputs" for input and "outputs" for output.
inputs=train[,c("calories_burned","hours_of_sleep")]

outputs=train[,"mood"]

prepNormalize <- function(inp=inputs,outp=outputs){
#Arguments 1 and 3 to Neural_Network need to be matrices.
inputs <- as.matrix(inp)
outputs<-as.matrix(outp)
#Normalize the data.
inputs<<-sScore(inputs )
outputs<<-sScore(outputs)
}
```

Practice 12.12.12

1. Explain the use of the "<-" and the "" in the definition of prepNormalize().
2. In prepNormalize(), using <<- could be considered poor programming practice. It could create problems because we might run prepNormalize() multiple times and that would mean running sScore multiple times on the inputs and outputs. In this particular case, that would not make any difference because centering data that is centered at 0 will still be centered at 0 and dividing by the standard deviation when the standard deviation is 1 will not change the data either. Nevertheless, it could be considered poor programming practice. How could you change prepNormalize() so that it does not have to use superassignment (<<-) Once you made this change, how would you have to change our next line of code below (which is prepNormalize(inputs,outputs))?

```
prepNormalize(inputs,outputs)
```

Practice 12.12.13

1. Which part of our Neural_Network() code implies the necessisty for inputs and outputs to be matrices?

```
#4. Create Neural_Network instance.
nn1<-Neural_Network$new(inputs, 5, outputs,4,"y")
```

```
#5. What is the measure of the error prior to backpropagation in the
training set?
nn1$JCost(inputs, outputs)
## [1] 0.6794433
#6. To find the error prior to backpropagation on test set, read inputs
and outputs from testing data.
test =trainAndTest[["test"]]
inputs=test[,c("calories_burned","hours_of_sleep")]

outputs=test[,"mood"]

prepNormalize(inputs,outputs)
```

```
#7. What is the measure of the error prior to
#backpropagation in the test set?
nn1$JCost(inputs,  outputs)
## [1] 0.665922
#8. To do backpropagation on training set, reset
#everything to the training data.
train =trainAndTest[["train"]]
inputs=train[,c("calories_burned","hours_of_sleep")]

outputs=train[,"mood"]
prepNormalize(inputs,outputs)
#Arguments 1 and 3 to Neural_Network need to be matrices.

#9. Run backProp many times (many epochs).
```

```
for(i in 1:40){
  nn1$backProp(inputs,  outputs)
}
#10. Has the performance improved on the training?
nn1$JCost(inputs,  outputs)
## [1] 0.4930556
#To find out how it has done on the
#the test data, reset inputs and outputs to the testing data.
test =trainAndTest[["test"]]
inputs=test[,c("calories_burned","hours_of_sleep")]

outputs=test[,"mood"]
prepNormalize(inputs,outputs)

#11. What is the measure of the error after backpropagation in the test set?
nn1$JCost(inputs,  outputs)
## [1] 0.4791667
```

Practice 12.12.14

A common replacement for the sigmoid function is the ReLU function (rectified linear unit), a fancy name for a simple function. The function simply compares its input to zero and chooses the larger of the input or zero. Thus, if the input is less than zero, then zero is output. If the input is greater than zero, then the input is output. It looks like Figure 12.2 (where the input of course is the x-axis).

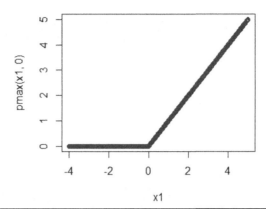

Figure 12.2   Graph of ReLU activation function.

Recall that we use the sigmoid function as an *activation function*, and it is modeling the way a real neuron in the human brain might behave. The ReLU is an alternative choice for the activation function and is also supposed to model a real human neuron. In this model, it is suggesting that the output of the neuron is "unbounded", whereas a sigmoid activation suggests a bounded output.

Tip: To write a ReLU function in R, you can use the pmax() function.

The derivative of ReLU is so simple it may appear confusing. We attack the derivative by asking what it is when x < 0 and then *as a separate question*, what it is when x > 0. Recalling that derivative gives slope, it is obvious that when x < 0, the graph is flat, and so the derivative is 0. When x > 0, the graph is a 45° angle, and thus the derivative is 1.

Tip: One way to write the derivative of ReLU in R is to use ifelse().

1. Write the ReLU function in R using pmax().
2. Recall that the sigmoid function is always bounded. Specifically, it is bounded "from below" by 0 and bounded "from above" by 1. Is the ReLU bounded either from above or below?
3. Optional challenge: Try writing these functions in R and then replacing the sigmoid function with ReLU in our code to see if the results are better or worse.
4. Using the setrefclass() function create a Creditcard class that has fields ccNumber, expire-Date, and creditLimit and a method that increments the credit limit by 100 dollars called incrementCreditLimit100. An example of creating and instance of this class called account1 would be: account1<-Creditcard(1088558,November2028,1500) for an account number 1088558, which expires on November 2028 and with a credit limit of $1500.

Note that other possible replacements for the sigmoid function as an activation function are tanh (the trig function), Leaky Relu, and Softmax.

12.13 Conclusion

In this chapter, we have completed our coding of an n–m–1 neural network with batch updating. We have learned how to implement this using the S5 system class structure. In the next chapter, we add in what is called the bias node to our neural network.

Chapter 13

Adding in a Bias Term

13.1 The Bias Term and Forward Propagation

Now we will introduce another feature of a typical neural network into our code. We include an extra node in each layer called the <u>bias node</u>. Thus, whereas before, when we had two input variables, we used a 2–3–1 architecture, now we will add a special node into all layers except the outer layer. Thus, even though we only have two inputs, the architecture will be 3–4–1. But these extra nodes are not exactly the same as the nodes we have used. They will be *set* to output[1] fixed values of 1. That is, no matter what the data is, these nodes will always output the value 1. That is not true of the other nodes in our network. Their outputs always depend on the inputs and thus on the data. What is the point of adding in these special bias nodes? Let us illustrate this with the following (Figure 13.1).

Suppose we only had two layers and one node in each layer.

The input, x, is in the first layer. The output, y, is the second layer. There is just the one connection labeled w.

Question: What kind of function does this represent?

Answer: y = wx.

Remember every neural network represents a function. In this case it is a very simple function.

Now, suppose we have the following data.

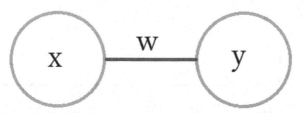

Figure 13.1   Network with just 2 nodes and 1 weight and no threshold function (or we could say the threshold function is the identity function). This simple network represents the simple function y=wx.

---

[1] The word "output" is being used as a verb here.

x	y
0	2
1	3
2	4
3	5

If we graph this, we get (Figure 13.2)

```
x=0:3
y=2:5
plot(x,y, type = "p",col="blue", xlim=c(0,4), ylim = c(0,6), pch = 19)
```

Our objective, as always, is to take the inputs and build a model to predict the outputs. In this simple, xy-plane example, this means we want to fit a curve to this data. Once we have the curve, we can use its equation as the model. It is fairly easy to see what the model *should* be: $y = f(x) = x + 2$. This model fits our data perfectly, and if we use it (on this data), we get perfect predictions. For example, if $x = 2$, then our model gives us $y = 4$, and this matches our data exactly. So too with the rest of the data. Graphically it is clear that the best model is a straight line with slope of 1 and y-intercept of 2.

As a quick digression, actually there are plenty of other models that will fit this data perfectly. Any polynomial of degree greater than or equal to 3 can fit this data. However,

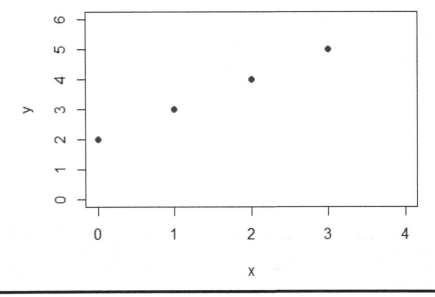

Figure 13.2 Example data to which we may try to fit a model. This data is clearly linear however it would not be best represented by a line that must pass through the origin.

it is typical to say that if there are several models that do equally well in predicting the data, then we will choose the simpler one. This is known as the concept of Ocam's Razor or the concept of parsimony. The idea was similarly expressed by Ptolemy in around 100 AD as "We consider it a good principle to explain the phenomena by the simplest hypothesis possible".

Returning to our data, we said that the model $y = x + 2$ will fit our data perfectly. This is of course the equation of a straight line and is called a linear model with a constant term. The constant term is 2. Now, returning to our network of just 2 nodes, we saw that the function this 2-node network expresses is $y = wx$. Is this network capable of fitting the data perfectly? That is, can we fit the data we have with $y = wx$? The only parameter we can adjust in this function is the w. Can we find a w so that $y = wx$ will fit the data we have? Graphically, $y = wx$ is a straight line *that passes through the origin* and has slope w. Is there such a line that will fit the data? It is clear visually that it is impossible. That is to say, a linear model that does not have a constant term cannot fit the data as well as a model with a constant term.

The general expression for a linear function with a constant term is

$$y = a_0 + a_1 x \tag{13.1}$$

where a_0 is the constant term and a_1 is the slope.

We have identified a limitation in our two-node network. It may do a good job of modeling linear data that goes through the origin, but it doesn't do as good a job of modeling data which is best represented by a model that does not pass through the origin. If we could modify our *network* so that the function it represents includes a constant term, then this limitation would be eliminated. This is the motivation for including a bias node. We will explore what happens when we add a bias node to the input layer. Remember that the bias node is set to output a "1". The diagram in Figure 13.3 represents the system now.

What function does this network generate?

$y = w_1 x + w_b * 1$, which can be written as

$$y = w_1 x + w_b \tag{13.2}$$

This is clearly a linear model in x and y with w_1 and w_b replacing a_1 and a_0 respectively. The parameters here are w_1 and w_b, and with this model, we can represent data whose model does not

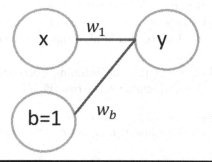

Figure 13.3 Simple network function but with one bias node added in. This network can represent a linear function with a non-zero y-intercept.

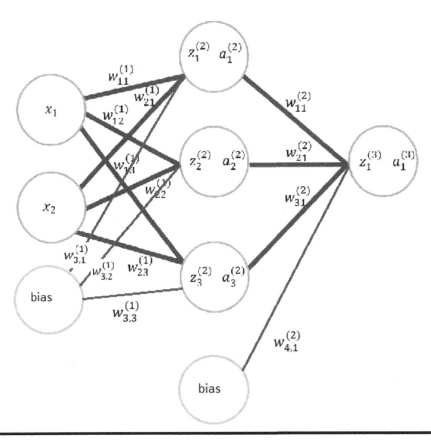

Figure 13.4 The 3–2–1 architecture with a bias node added in for both the input and hidden layers. Note that the bias node in the input layer has 3 associated weights (not just 1).

pass through the origin. It can handle data that is translated[2] either upward or downward from the origin which does not necessarily pass through the origin. As a practical example, suppose we are exploring the relationship between people's mood and the amount of exercise they do at the gym. Suppose that because of the scale with which the researchers choose to measure mood, it is always between 1 and 5. Thus, even if someone does not go to the gym and thus does zero exercise, their mood will never be less than 1. In this case, it would not be a good idea to model the data with a line that goes through the origin. We are more likely to get a good model if we allow for a y-intercept of something other than zero. In the diagram above, this is what the bias term b does, and in general, a bias term will allow for this kind of translation in the model. This can greatly improve the accuracy of the model.

We have now established the motivation for including a bias term. In the following code, we will work with an architecture which includes bias terms (Figure 13.4).

```
#Use exercise-mood data. The original data is available at
#https://www.kaggle.com/aroojanwarkhan/fitness-data-trends.
```

---

[2] In mathematics, the translation of the graph of a function means to move it either horizontally or vertically while maintaining its shape.

```
#We will keep a record of both the weights and the costs as the model is
trained over many epochs, and we will plot both the weights and the costs
at the end of the training.
weightList=list()
costHistory=vector() #We will store the costs here in order to plot the
cost over the epochs.
set.seed(123)
#Remove any cases that have NA
mood<-mood[complete.cases(mood),]
mood=mood[,c("mood","calories_burned","hours_of_sleep")]
#Split data into train and test sets and store both in a list.
trainTestSplit<-function(dataset="mood"){
#sample call
#trainAndTest=trainTestSplit(mood)
#train =trainAndTest[["train"]]
#test  =trainAndTest[["test"]]
  smp_size <- floor(0.75 * nrow(dataset))
  train_ind <- sample(seq_len(nrow(dataset)), size = smp_size)
  train <- dataset[train_ind, ]
  test <- dataset[-train_ind, ]
  returnedList=list(train,test)
  returnedList<-setNames(returnedList, c("train","test"))
  return(returnedList)
}

#Normalize the data.
sScore <- function(x){
  xNew=(x-mean(x))/sd(x)
  return(xNew)
}

#Define the neural network class including bias.
Neural_Network <- setRefClass("Neural_Network",
 fields = list(nnX="matrix", nnhiddenLayerSize = "numeric", nnY =
"matrix", r="numeric",suppress="character", W1="matrix", W2="matrix",
weightList="ANY", BiasWeights1="matrix",BiasWeights2="matrix"),
 methods = list(
    initialize = function(a=matrix(), b=c(),c=matrix(),d=c(),e=c())  {

    nnX<<-a
```

We will begin to keep a record of the dimensions of objects so that the calculations are easier to follow.

```
#We assume 72 examples in our dataset.
```

Item	dim
nnX	72 x 2

```
#We have inserted a browser() expression into the backProp() method to
explore the various objects in our class. The results are presented in
the following format. If there are many rows, we only look at the first
three by inserting a "3" into the head() function.
```

```
Browse[2]> head(nnX,3)
     calories_burned hours_of_sleep
[1,]       -0.2719561      -0.6596955
[2,]        0.9807404      -0.6746086
[3,]       -0.6447825      -0.6746086
```

Practice 13.1.1

1. What are the input variables in the mood data?
2. What is the output variable in the mood data?

```
nnhiddenLayerSize<<-b #Remember that this is part of the class
definition process where b (and c next) is currently just a placeholder.
    nnY<<-c
```

Item	dim
nnY	72 x 1

```
Browse[2]> head(nnY,3)
            mood
[1,]  1.0723637
[2,] -0.1154853
[3,] -1.3033344
```

```
r<<-d
suppress<<-e
inputLayerSize<-dim(nnX)[2]

outputLayerSize<-dim(nnY)[2]
#set.seed(3)
W1<<-matrix(runif(inputLayerSize*nnhiddenLayerSize,
-1,1),inputLayerSize,nnhiddenLayerSize)
```

Item	dim
W1	2 × 3

Practice 13.1.2

1. Referring to the 2–3–1 neural network diagram in Figure 13.4 that includes bias nodes, how many extra weights will need to be added into the first layer when a bias node is added into the first layer?
2. Write down an equation for what comes into each of the 3 nodes in the hidden layer. That is, write 3 equations in total, one for each node.

```
#To add bias for the input layer, create a new matrix of size 1 x
nnhiddenLayerSize that contains only ones. We attach it to W1 as an
additional row at the bottom of W1
    BiasWeights1<<-matrix(runif(1*nnhiddenLayerSize,1,1),1,nnhiddenLayer
Size)
```

Item	dim
BiasWeights1	1 x 3

#We attach this at the bottom of the of W1. The weight matrices are written to the global environment using `<<-`
    W1 <<- **rbind**(W1,BiasWeights1)

Item	dim
W1	3 × 3

    W2<<-**matrix**(**runif**(nnhiddenLayerSize*outputLayerSize,1,1),nnhiddenLayerSize,outputLayerSize)

Item	dim
W2	3 × 1

Practice 13.1.3

1. Referring to 2–3–1 neural network diagram in Figure 13.4 that includes bias nodes, how many extra weights will need to be added into the second layer when a bias node is added into the second layer?

#To add bias for the hidden layer, create a 1 × outputLayerSize matrix of 1s that we attach to W1 as an additional row at the bottom of W1.
    BiasWeights2<-**matrix**(**runif**(1*outputLayerSize,-1,1),1,outputLayerSize)

Item	dim
BiasWeights2	1 x 1

    W2 <<- **rbind**(W2,BiasWeights2)

Item	dim
W2	4 × 1

#We could add in the bias node to nnX, but we will do it in the methods below after the application of the normalization with sScore.
    },
 #We will define a forward method.
   forward = **function**() {
#First normalize the inputs
     local_nnX<-**sScore**(nnX)

Item	dim
nnX	72 × 2

Practice 13.1.4

1. How many examples are there in our dataset?
2. Are the number of examples expressed by the number of columns or rows?
3. If we add a bias term, do we add a new column or row?
4. What is a reason to add the bias node to nnX after the application of the normalization with sScore? What would happen if we did it before applying sScore?

```
local_nnY<-sScore(nnY)
```

Item	dim
nnY	72 × 1

```
#Add a column of ones to the input matrix. Recall that we are working
with batch processing, and so the set of inputs will be a matrix with a
row for each example.
    nnX <- cbind(local_nnX,1) #Remember that because of what is called
recycling in R (similar to broadcasting in Python), this operation
allocates a "1" for each example (each row) of nnX.
```

Item	dim
nnX	72 × 3

```
Browse[2]> head(nnX,3)
      calories_burned hours_of_sleep
[1,]       -0.2719561     -0.6596955 1
[2,]        0.9807404     -0.6746086 1
[3,]       -0.6447825     -0.6746086 1

    Z2<-local_nnX%*%W1
```

Item	dim =	dim(local_nnX)	%*%	dim(W1)
Z2	72 × 3 =	72 × 3	X	3 × 3

```
Browse[2]> head(Z2,3)
            [,1]         [,2]           [,3]
[1,] -0.9759112 -0.12093109 -0.03805055
[2,] -1.8167697 -0.40405772  0.21463811
[3,] -0.7375575 -0.03000003 -0.11729586

    A2<-sigmoid(Z2)
```

Item	Dim
A2	72 × 3

```
Browse[2]> head(A2,3)
          [,1]        [,2]        [,3]
[1,]  0.2737038  0.4698040  0.4904885
[2,]  0.1398219  0.4003378  0.5534545
[3,]  0.3235385  0.4925006  0.4707096
```

Practice 13.1.5

1. The number of columns of A2 is equal to the number of examples: true or false?
2. To add a new bias node to A2, should we increase the number of columns or the number of rows?

```
#Add the bias term for the second layer. We keep the convention of adding
it to the end of the matrix and not the beginning
    A2<- cbind(A2,1)
```

Item	dim
A2	72 × 4

```
Browse[2]> head(A2,3)
          [,1]        [,2]        [,3] [,4]
[1,]  0.2737038  0.4698040  0.4904885    1
[2,]  0.1398219  0.4003378  0.5534545    1
[3,]  0.3235385  0.4925006  0.4707096    1
```

Practice 13.1.6

1. If we were to add the 1 at the beginning of A2, how would the previous line of code have to be modified?
2. Normally we expect the dimensions of Z2 and A3 to be the same since A2 is just the sigmoid function applied to Z2 element by element. However, what are the dimensions of Z2, and what are the dimensions of A2 now?
3. We don't add a bias node into the final layer. How many nodes are in the final layer?
4. What will the dimensions of the final layer be?

```
    Z3<-A2%*%W2
```

Item	dim	dim(A2)	%*%	dim(W2)
Z3	72 × 1 =	72 × 4	X	4 × 1

```
Browse[2]> head(Z3,3)
          [,1]
[1,]  0.1559883
[2,]  0.1198801
[3,]  0.1693897
```

```
    yHat<-sigmoid(Z3)
```

Item	dim
yHat	72 × 1

```
Browse[2]> head(yHat,3)
           [,1]
[1,]  0.5389182
[2,]  0.5299342
[3,]  0.5422464
```

```
#return yHat
     return(yHat)

#the end of forward method
    },
```

13.2 Backpropagation Method Begins Here

```
#Define the backpropagation method.
   backProp = function(nnX="inputs",nnY="outputs") {
#Sample call: nn1$backProp(inputs, outputs)
     if(suppress=="n"){
       print("Original W")
       print(W1)
       print(W2)
     }
```

Practice 13.2.7

1. So far in our code, which variables have been global and why?

```
     local_nnX<-sScore(nnX)
     local_nnY<-sScore(nnY)
```

Item	dim
nnX	72 × 2

Item	dim
nnY	72 × 1

```
#Add the bias to nnX
     local_nnX <- cbind(local_nnX,1)
```

Item	dim
nnX	72 × 3

```
Z2<- local_nnX%*%W1
```

Item	dim	dim(local_nnX)	%*%	dim(W1)
Z2	72 × 3 =	72 × 3	X	3 × 3

```
A2<-sigmoid(Z2)
```

Item	dim
A2	72 × 3

```
#Add the bias term for the second layer.
    A2<- cbind(A2,1)
```

Item	dim
A2	72 × 4

```
Z3<-A2%*%W2
```

Item	dim	dim(A2)	%*%	dim(W2)
Z3	72 × 1 =	72 × 4	X	4 × 1

```
yHat<-sigmoid(Z3)
```

Item	dim
yHat	72 × 1

#Recall our definition of delta3 in 11.14 was written as

$$\delta^{(3)} = \frac{dJ}{d(y-\text{yhat})^2} \frac{d(y-\text{yhat})^2}{d(y-\text{yhat})} \frac{d(y-\text{yhat})}{d\text{yhat}} \frac{d\text{yhat}}{dz^{(3)}}$$

And from equation 11.15 we see that it can also be written as

$$\delta^{(3)} = \frac{dJ}{ds} \frac{ds}{e} \frac{de}{d\hat{y}} \frac{d\hat{y}}{dz^{(3)}}$$

It can be seen that[3]

$$\delta^{(3)} = -(y - \hat{y}) f'(z^{(3)})$$

Sometimes this is written as

$$\delta^{(3)} = -(y - \hat{y}) f'(u)$$

Where we have defined u= $z^{(3)}$

Practice 13.2.8

1. Do any of the factors in delta3 have terms from either layer 1 or layer 2?

```
#Delta3 should not change with a bias term in our 3-layer network.
#Delta3 needs to be a matrix because we are doing batch processing here.

    Delta3=(local_nnY-yHat)*(-sigmoidPrime(Z3))
```

Item	dim =	dim(nnY-yHat)	*	dim(-sigmoidPrime(Z3))
Delta3	72 × 1 =	72 × 1		72 × 1

```
Browse[2]> head(Delta3,3)
          mood
[1,]  -0.1325534
[2,]   0.1607765
[3,]   0.4581013
```

```
#The matrix of derivatives, dJ_dW2, should include an entry for the
derivative of J with respect to the weight of the bias term.
#Since we have a bias node in the hidden layer (and therefore in A2),
there are weights from that node to each node in the next downstream
layer. The next downstream layer is the output layer and has one node,
and therefore there is only 1 extra weight in W2. Therefore dJ_dW2 will
have to have an entry for that weight. (Remember that although the output
of the bias node is fixed, always equal to 1, the weights that connect
the node to any downstream node are  trainable.)

    dJ_dW2=t(A2)%*%Delta3 /dim(t(A2))[2]
```

Item	dim	dim(t(A2))	%*%	dim(Delta3)
dJ_dW2	4 × 1 =	4 × 72	X	72 × 1

---

[3] since $\delta^{(3)} = \dfrac{dJ}{ds} \dfrac{ds}{e} \dfrac{de}{d\hat{y}} - (y - \hat{y})$

Recall that dJ_dW2, when *not* done in batch, should be the input t(A2) times delta3 and will therefore have dimension t(A2). Now that we have introduced a bias term, A2 will have an additional element $b^{(2)}$ (=1). Thus, dJ_dW2 will have an extra element as well, $b^{(2)}$*delta3=delta3. When we work in batch, the additional calculation due to the bias term looks like the following (Figure 13.5). (Instead of 72 examples, for the illustration, we assume only 7.)

$$\begin{bmatrix} b^{(2)}_{ex1}, & b^{(2)}_{ex2}, & \cdots & b^{(2)}_{ex7} \end{bmatrix} * \begin{bmatrix} delta3_{ex1} \\ delta3_{ex2} \\ \vdots \\ delta3_{ex7} \end{bmatrix} = \sum_{i=1}^{7} delta3_i \qquad (13.3)$$

Next, we show A2 not t(A2).

```
Browse[2]> head(A2,3)
          [,1]      [,2]      [,3] [,4]
[1,] 0.2737038 0.4698040 0.4904885    1
[2,] 0.1398219 0.4003378 0.5534545    1
[3,] 0.3235385 0.4925006 0.4707096    1


Browse[2]> head(t(A2) %*% Delta3,3)
          mood
[1,] 2.286138
[2,] 4.298448
[3,] 4.853502
```

```
#Next, we work on dJ_dW1 and therefore Delta2.
#We are hoping that we can use an expression similar to the Delta2
expression we have used before which was
# Delta2 = (Delta3*t(W2)) * sigmoidPrime(Z2)

#W2 currently has a weight for the bias term in layer 2. But for
calculations of dJ_dW1, the chain rule would never involve this bias
term weight because this weight connects to the bias term in layer 2,
which is NOT connected to anything in layer 1. Thus, we will remove
these weights.
```

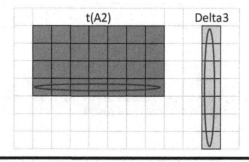

Figure 13.5 Illustration of working with both batch processing and biases. An additional row will be introduced into t(A2) as a result of adding in the bias node. The highlighted ovals illustrates equation 13.3: the additional dot product will need to be calculated.

```
#W2 is 4 × 1 currently, and the last weight is for the bias term. To
remove that weight we can do
#W2WithoutBias<-W2[-dim(W2)[1],]
#where dim(W2)[1] is the number of rows of W2, and with the bias weight,
this is equal to 4, and therefore we are running W2[-4,], which will
remove the 4th row from W2.
#It may seem necessary to adjust Z2 as well because we have a bias term
in the hidden layer. However, although we adjusted the size of A2 to
include the bias term, we did not adjust Z2, so we don't need to readjust
it.
        W2WithoutBias<-W2[-dim(W2)[1],]
```

Item	dim
W2WithoutBias	3 × 1

```
Browse[2]> W2WithoutBias
[1] 0.26195855 0.02403180 0.01004783

        Delta2 <- (Delta3%*%t(W2WithoutBias)) * sigmoidPrime(Z2)
```

Item	dim	Delta3	%*%	dim(t(W2WithoutBias))	*	dim(sigmoidPrime(Z2))
Delta2	72 × 3 =	72 × 1	X	1 × 3		72 × 3

```
Browse[2]> head(Delta2,3)
             [,1]          [,2]          [,3]
[1,] -0.006902686 -0.0007934696 -0.0003328480
[2,]  0.005065461  0.0009275604  0.0003992478
[3,]  0.026264136  0.0027516299  0.0011467818
```

```
#We added in an extra column of ones to nnX, so our calculation below
will generate a derivative for each extra weight (the bias weights for
layer 1).
        dJ_dW1= t(local_nnX)%*%Delta2/dim(t(local_nnX))[2]
```

Item	dim	dim(t(nnX))	%*%	dim(Delta2)
dJ_dW1	3 × 3 =	3 × 72	X	72 × 3

```
Browse[2]> dJ_dW1
                       [,1]          [,2]          [,3]
calories_burned -0.0008209762  6.262604e-05  3.152621e-05
hours_of_sleep  -0.0041177689 -5.288786e-04 -2.236287e-04
                 0.0060667716  7.810747e-04  3.303330e-04
```

Practice 13.2.9

1. How many weights are there that connect to the bias node in layer 1?
2. What are the value of those weights currently?

```
Browse[2]> W2
              [,1]
[1,]  0.26195855
[2,]  0.02403180
[3,]  0.01004783
[4,]  0.06807071

      W2<<-W2-r*dJ_dW2
Browse[2]> W2
              mood
[1,]   0.1031989
[2,]  -0.2744715
[3,]  -0.3270009
[4,]  -0.5946361

Browse[1]> W1
              [,1]        [,2]       [,3]
[1,]  -0.6639169 -0.2301153 0.2042013
[2,]   0.6150328 -0.3445314 0.2087881
[3,]  -0.7507331 -0.4107982 0.1552198

      W1<<-W1-r*dJ_dW1

Browse[2]> W1
                         [,1]        [,2]       [,3]
calories_burned -0.6598121 -0.2304284 0.2040437
hours_of_sleep   0.6356216 -0.3418870 0.2099063
                -0.7810670 -0.4147035 0.1535682
```

```
#We will keep a list of the weights over the training epochs and plot
them at the end of the training. To keep things simple, we will not look
at all the weights. We just track W2[1,1]. We make this variable global.
weightList<<-c(weightList,W2[1,1])
#If we run backProp in a loop with many iterations, we don't want to
print out the weights W1 and W2 in every iteration. This can be
controlled by the "suppress" argument.
      if(suppress=="n"){
        print("New W")
        print(W1)
        print(W2)
      }

# end of the backProp method
```

13.3 JCost Method Begins Here

```
      },
    JCost = function(nnX="inputs",nnY="outputs") {
#Sample call: nn1$JCost(X,y)
      inputLayerSize<-dim(nnX)[2]
      outputLayerSize<-dim(nnY)[2]
```

```
#We are being extra careful to make sure the data are matrices.
    local_nnX<-as.matrix(nnX)
    local_nnY<-as.matrix(nnY)
    local_nnX<-sScore(local_nnX)
    local_nnY<-sScore(local_nnY)
    local_nnX <- cbind(local_nnX,1)
    Z2<- local_nnX%*%W1
    A2<-sigmoid(Z2)
#Add the bias term for the second layer.
    A2<- cbind(1,A2)
    Z3<-A2%*%W2
    yHat<-sigmoid(Z3)


#Return the average cost.
    J <- 0.5*sum((local_nnY-yHat)**2)/nrow(local_nnY)
    return(J)


  }

 ))
```

13.4 Steps for Running the Neural Network

```
#Steps for running Neural_Network class
#1. Split data to training and testing sets.
trainAndTest=trainTestSplit(mood)
#2. Create train set
train =trainAndTest[["train"]]

#3. To separate model inputs and outputs here, we use "inputs" for input
and "outputs" for output.
inputs=train[,c("calories_burned","hours_of_sleep")]

outputs=train[,"mood"]

prepNormalize <- function(inp=inputs,outp=outputs){
#Arguments 1 and 3 to Neural_Network need to be matrices
  inputs <- as.matrix(inp)
  outputs<-as.matrix(outp)
#Normalize the data.
  inputs<<-sScore(inputs )
  outputs<<-sScore(outputs)
}

prepNormalize(inputs,outputs)

#4. create Neural_Network instance
nn1<-Neural_Network$new(inputs, 10, outputs,5,"y")

#5. What is the measure of the error prior to backpropagation in the
training set?
nn1$JCost(inputs,outputs)
```

```
## [1] 0.5445422
#6. To find the error prior to backpropagation on test set, set inputs
and outputs to testing data.
test =trainAndTest[["test"]]
inputs=test[,c("calories_burned","hours_of_sleep")]

outputs=test[,"mood"]

prepNormalize(inputs,outputs)

#7. What is the measure of the error prior to backpropagation in the test
set?
nn1$JCost(inputs, outputs)
## [1] 0.539927
#8. To do backpropagation on training set, reset everything to the
training data.
train =trainAndTest[["train"]]
inputs=train[,c("calories_burned","hours_of_sleep")]

outputs=train[,"mood"]
prepNormalize(inputs,outputs)

#9. Run backProp many times (many epochs).

for(i in 1:50){
  nn1$backProp(inputs,outputs)
}
#10. Has the performance improved on the training?
nn1$JCost(inputs,outputs)
## [1] 0.4930556
#To find out how the network has done on the test data, reset inputs and
outputs to the test data.
test =trainAndTest[["test"]]
inputs=test[,c("calories_burned","hours_of_sleep")]
```

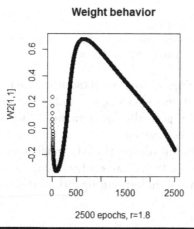

Figure 13.6   Illustration of how the weights change as the network trains. This particular graph shows the weight W2[1,1]. We could examine graphs for any other weight as well.

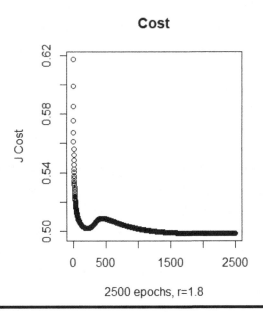

Figure 13.7 Plot of the prediction error of the network (JCost) as the number of epochs increase.

```
outputs=test[,"mood"]
prepNormalize(inputs,outputs)

#11. What is the measure of the error after backpropagation in the
nn1$JCost(inputs,outputs)?
## [1] 0.4791667
```

We can see that there has been improvement in both the training data and the test data after training the neural network. We may want to look at the cost over time (as we increase the number of epochs). As the weights change, we expect that the cost will decrease. We kept a record of one of the weights, W2[1,1]. Below we will visualize the change in this weight over 2500 epochs and then visualize the cost over the same 2500 epochs (Figure 13.6).

```
wl=as.vector(unlist(weightList))
plot(1:2500,wl, main="Weight behavior", xlab="epoch", ylab="W2[1,1]")
plot(1:2500,costHistory, main="Cost", xlab = "epoch" ,ylab="J Cost")
```

We see that the weight is changing. The pattern of the change in this weight cannot be understood in isolation of the changes in all the other weights, and in fact the challenge of understanding a complicated system of weights is generally not attempted. These changes, however, do lead to a decrease in the cost or error of the network.

In the next chapter, we take full advantage of the modularity available when OOP programming is used to develop flexible code that can easily expand the types of neural networks we can code to include what is known as deep learning algorithms (Figure 13.7).

Chapter 14

Modular Version of Neural Networks for Deep Learning

Our final version of neural network code will take a somewhat different perspective on the structure of neural networks. Up until now, *the hidden layer* nodes have consisted of two separate processes:

- the calculation of Z (the inputs X times the weights $W^{(1)}$)
- the calculation of A (the activation process f(Z)).

We treated both of these *together* as a *single layer*. Now, however, it will be convenient to think of these two processes as two separate layers. In fact, the reader may agree that this seems more natural.

The motivation here is to assist us in the coding. Our fundamental object in this new design will be the layer, whereas the fundamental object previously was the entire neural network. Object-oriented programming (OOP) *design* is an important study. There we learn how to think about how to divide our programming task into appropriate classes. With our focus on layers as the fundamental object, it will be easy to create new layers and connect them. In OOP terminology, the term "message" is important. For us, a message is just the calling of a method defined within the class. We will define both a forward-propagation method and a backpropagation method for the layer class. Each layer object will be thought of as accepting information, processing it, and sending information out. This is like what we may envision in a human neural network as well. The forward-propagation method will follow this design. It will accept information, process it, and pass it forward (downstream). We can think of the intake of information as taking in the results of a message that was generated upstream. We can think of output information as sending a message downstream. This seems to align very nicely with the way we may envision nodes working in the human brain. However, our backpropagation method will also have this same kind of design: accepting information, processing it, and passing it out (downstream). Perhaps human neurons also have this ability in the sense that they must have some capacity for learning. The analogy may or may not be that clear, but for our artificial neural network, this is how we will design the layer class. That is, we will design the layer class's backpropagation method to accept

Functions and Methods Coded in This Chapter
tanh_prime
mse
ms_prime
initialize
forward_propagation
backProp_propagation
use
predict
fit

information, process it, and pass it out downstream. You will see that we will change our notation to suit this new approach. For each layer's forward-propagation process, we will refer to its input as X and its output as Y. We will make this clearer shortly.

The results will be rewarding and will facilitate the easy addition of new layers to our network and the creation of new types of layers, for example, convolutional layers for image processing.

14.1 Backpropagation

We will begin the modular approach with a focus on backpropagation and we will start that with a review of our previous approach to backpropagation.

For the backpropagation process, recall that we saw calculations like the following.

Calculation for $w^{(2)}$

$$\frac{dJ}{dw^{(2)}} = \frac{dJ}{ds} \frac{ds}{e} \frac{de}{d\hat{y}} \frac{d\hat{y}}{du} \frac{du}{dw^{(2)}} \tag{14.1}$$

which also can be written as

$$\frac{dJ}{dw^{(2)}} = \frac{dJ}{d(y-yhat)^2} \frac{d(y-yhat)^2}{d(y-yhat)} \frac{d(y-yhat)}{dyhat} \frac{dyhat}{dz^{(3)}} \frac{dz^{(3)}}{dw^{(2)}} \tag{14.2}$$

Calculation for $w^{(1)}$

$$\frac{dJ}{dw^{(1)}} = \frac{dJ}{d(y-yhat)^2} \frac{d(y-yhat)^2}{d(y-yhat)} \frac{d(y-yhat)}{dyhat} \frac{dyhat}{dz^{(3)}} \frac{dz^{(3)}}{da^{(2)}} \frac{da^{(2)}}{dz^{(2)}} \frac{dz^{(2)}}{dw^{(1)}} \tag{14.3}$$

We mentioned that there were two additional terms in the calculations of the derivative of the (further upstream) weight $W^{(1)}$ as compared to the calculations for the derivative of $W^{(2)}$. We saw that this was due to the fact that there were two additional processes for which the chain rule must account (as well as the change in the last term in 14.2). These were the additional calculations of derivatives for

a. $A^{(2)}$ as the output of the activation function in the first layer
b. $Z^{(2)}$: the input to the first layer.

14.1.1 Beginning with a 1–1–1 Architecture

For the time being, will work with the 1–1–1 architecture so that we can avoid matrices (Figure 14.1).

We observed that once dJ_dw2 is calculated, almost all of its calculations can also be used for the calculation of dJ_dw1. (The final term in dJ_dw2 will not be useful as you can see it does not occur in the calculation of dJ_dw1.) All but the last factor can be reused. In the digital version of this text this is highlighted in green and we will refer to it as the green factors.

$$\frac{dJ}{dw^{(2)}} = \frac{dJ}{d\left(y-yhat\right)^2} \frac{d\left(y-yhat\right)^2}{d\left(y-yhat\right)} \frac{d\left(y-yhat\right)}{dyhat} \frac{dyhat}{dz^{(3)}} \frac{dz^{(3)}}{dw^{(2)}} \tag{14.4}$$

We can see that when doing the backpropagation process for layer 1, if we were to have access to the green factors, our calculation will be all that much easier.

In our new modular approach to writing the code, we will write the code for layer 1 (and generally for any layer) to accept inputs from the previous (downstream) layer and give outputs to the upstream layer – remember we do the calculation for the downstream layer $w^{(2)}$ before we do the calculation for the further upstream $w^{(1)}$, and so we have available any calculations that were done for layer $w^{(2)}$. The four green factors calculated for layer 2 will be treated as input to the *backpropagation calculation for layer 1*. That is, we can think of

$$\frac{dJ}{d\left(y-yhat\right)^2} \frac{d\left(y-yhat\right)^2}{d\left(y-yhat\right)} \frac{d\left(y-yhat\right)}{dyhat} \frac{dyhat}{dz^{(3)}} \tag{14.5}$$

as input to the layer 1 backpropagation process.

Note that this entire calculation, Equation 14.5, can be written as $\dfrac{dJ}{dz^{(3)}}$.

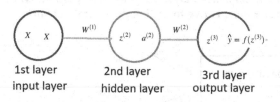

Figure 14.1 **1–1–1 architecture. Note that the first layer has two X's. The first is the input, and the second is the output. Of course, in the first node, the input and output are the same, and so we repeat X twice.**

Practice 14.1.1

1. What is the justification for saying Equation 14.5 can be written as $\dfrac{dJ}{dz^{(3)}}$? (Figure 14.2).

Once given that part, what more is left to calculate in order to get $\dfrac{dJ}{dw^{(1)}}$?

$$\frac{dJ}{dw^{(1)}} = \frac{dJ}{d(y - yhat)^2} \frac{d(y - yhat)^2}{d(y - yhat)} \frac{d(y - yhat)}{dyhat} \frac{dyhat}{dz^{(3)}} \frac{dz^{(3)}}{da^{(2)}} \frac{da^{(2)}}{dz^{(2)}} \frac{dz^{(2)}}{dw^{(1)}} \tag{14.6}$$

The answer is, we still need the last 3 factors in the above equation (14.6).

$$\frac{dz^{(3)}}{da^{(2)}} \frac{da^{(2)}}{dz^{(2)}} \frac{dz^{(2)}}{dw^{(1)}}$$

The term to the far left, $\dfrac{dz^{(3)}}{da^{(2)}}$, is just the downstream weight in the layer 2, $w^{(2)}$. The other two factors, $\dfrac{dz^{(3)}}{da^{(2)}} \dfrac{da^{(2)}}{dz^{(2)}}$, are completely independent of any layer other than the current layer (layer 1), and so we won't view them as inputs to the backpropagation for layer 1 but rather as inputs *within* layer 1 (Figure 14.3).

We will say that to calculate the backpropagation term for layer 1, $\dfrac{dJ}{dw^{(1)}}$, we need factors that are "local to" layer 1 and also the inputs $\dfrac{dJ}{dz^{(3)}}$ and $w^{(2)}$.

Summarizing, what we need is

1. what was already calculated for the next downstream backpropagation calculation $\left(\dfrac{dJ}{dz^{(3)}} \right)$

Back Propagation Code for Layer 1

Figure 14.2 **Some calculations from layer 2 are used as an input when doing the calculations for layer 1 in this modular perspective to coding the neural network.**

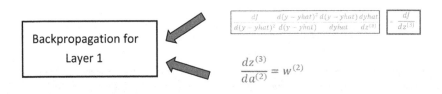

Figure 14.3 **Information that will be provided to the code for layer 1.**

2. $w^{(2)} \left(= \dfrac{\partial z^{(3)}}{\partial a^{(2)}} \right)$, the weight originating from the layer 1 node

3. information that can be obtained from layer 1 itself, $\dfrac{da^{(2)}}{dz^{(2)}} \dfrac{dz^{(2)}}{dw^{(1)}}$. We refer to it as local information.

We can also divide up the calculation of $\dfrac{dJ}{dw^{(1)}}$ into downstream and local calculations like this:

$$\frac{dJ}{dw^{(1)}} = \frac{dJ}{da^{(2)}} \frac{da^{(2)}}{dw^{(1)}} \qquad (14.7)$$

where the blue (this is highlighted in blue in the digital version of this text) $\dfrac{dJ}{da^{(2)}}$ comes from downstream *code* or the downstream weight and the gold (this is highlighted in gold in the digital version of this text) $\dfrac{da^{(2)}}{dw^{(1)}}$ is local.

Note that, as we have said, the layer 2 calculations will already have generated $\dfrac{dJ}{dz^{(3)}}$, and so if we write our code for layer 2 so that it "spits out" this $\dfrac{dJ}{dz^{(3)}}$ information, then we can use that output for our calculations for layer 1. This will become clearer shortly.

14.2 Generalized Layer Notation

Now we begin to refer to the *output of a layer in the forward-propagation process* as Y and the *input to a layer* as X. We do this to make our notation uniform over all layers. With this notation, it will not be necessary to refer to the outputs of a layer as $a^{(1)}$, $a^{(2)}$, and so on but rather just as Y. Using Y (or y), we can write Equation 14.7 as

$$\frac{dJ}{dw^{(1)}} = \frac{dJ}{dy} \frac{dy}{dw^{(1)}} \qquad (14.8)$$

or dJ_dw1 = dJ_dy * dy_dw1.

Now we have achieved one of our goals: making the backpropagation calculation of layer 1 independent of prior layer calculations (where the downstream layer calculations are treated as an input to the process). The diagram of our backpropagation modularization effort is shown in Figure 14.4.

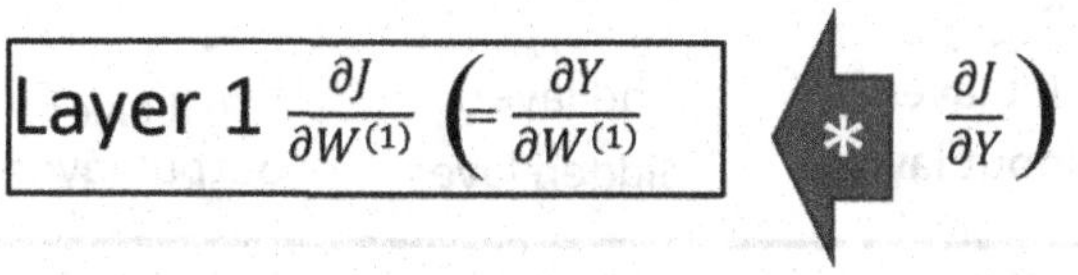

Figure 14.4 Derivative calculation of $\dfrac{\partial J}{\partial W^{(1)}}$ as local information $\dfrac{\partial Y}{\partial W^{(1)}}$ times downstream components $\dfrac{\partial J}{\partial Y}$. Note the multiplication sign in the arrow. Y is the output of this layer in the feedforward process.

We recognize this as the chain rule:

$$\frac{\partial J}{\partial W_1^{(1)}} = \frac{\partial J}{\partial y} \frac{\partial y}{\partial W_1^{(1)}} \tag{14.8}$$

This articulation of the chain rule nicely expresses the fact that the calculation comes partly from what is available in layer 1 and partly from what comes from downstream.

We have discussed the use of Y for the output. Now what about the symbol X for the input. We have been using X as the input when discussing the first layer. Now, regardless of the layer, we will let X denote the input to that layer. The following diagram illustrates our new perspective.

$$X \Rightarrow \boxed{\text{layer}} \Rightarrow Y$$

14.3 $\dfrac{\partial J}{\partial X} = \dfrac{\partial J}{\partial Y}$?

We want to make the following observation.

$\frac{\partial J}{\partial X} = \frac{\partial J}{\partial Y}$, but this does not seem correct. In fact, it is not correct unless we clarify which X and which Y we are referring to.

Recall our 1–1–1 example (Figure 14.5).

From the standpoint of the third layer, what is the *input* that must be multiplied by the weight $w^{(2)}$ to get $z^{(3)}$? It is $a^{(2)}$. Since $a^{(2)}$ is the input to layer 3, we will write[1]

$$X = a^{(2)}$$

and we will also write

$$\frac{\partial J}{\partial X} = \frac{\partial J}{\partial a^{(2)}}$$

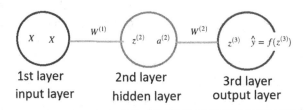

Figure 14.5 A 1–1–1 network. Now we will be viewing $a^{(2)}$ as the input to layer 3 and thus with our new paradigm we may label it with X.

---

[1] We are being sloppy here. For this illustration, the partial derivative should be expressed as a normal derivative, but when we are using multiple inputs and outputs, this will be correct.

$$\frac{\partial J}{\partial X} \Longleftarrow \boxed{\text{Layer } n} \Longleftarrow \frac{\partial J}{\partial Y} = \frac{\partial J}{\partial X} \Longleftarrow \boxed{\text{Layer } n+1} \Longleftarrow \frac{\partial J}{\partial Y}$$

Figure 14.6   Modular approach to backpropagation process. We see inputs and outputs of layers here.

On the other hand, *from the standpoint of **the second layer***, we can ask, what is the output? It is also $a^{(2)}$. Thus, if by Y we mean the output of the *second* node, we can write $\dfrac{\partial J}{\partial Y} = \dfrac{\partial J}{\partial a^{(2)}}$. Therefore, we can write

$$\frac{\partial J}{\partial Y} = \frac{\partial J}{\partial X}, \text{ as long as it is clear that X and Y are associated with different nodes} \quad (14.10)$$

with X being the input to layer 3 and Y being the output of layer 2. We are planning to include many layers in our neural network, and we will expect these relationships to hold for each layer. The diagram in Figure 14.6 shows the relationship between one layer and the next in the context of backpropagation. We have just established the center equation of this diagram: $\dfrac{\partial J}{\partial Y} = \dfrac{\partial J}{\partial X}$.

The key point so far is that from the standpoint of layer $n + 1$, the partial derivative with respect to its input X is the same as the partial derivative of the output Y of layer n.

14.4 Splitting Layers So They Represent Single Processes

Now we will take one more step toward achieving flexibility in our code through modularization.

Because we would like to add additional layers with varying types of activation, it will be useful to separate the calculation of Z from the calculation of A and speak of them as different steps or different layers. The diagram in Figure 14.7 illustrates each process as a new layer. Note that the labels on the edges no longer necessarily indicate a multiplication operation. In the case of edges labeled with a w, the operation is multiplication. However, when the edge is labeled with an f, the operation is the application of f to the output of the upstream layer.

Practice 14.4.2
1. How many activation layers are pictured, and how many matrix multiplication layers are pictured? (Note the last node is for J, and we won't refer to it as either an activation layer or a multiplication layer.)

In Figure 14.8, it should be clear that however many layers we add, each layer will receive an input and then generate an output.

Figure 14.9 illustrates that *in the forward-propagation process*, the output of one layer will be the input of the next layer.

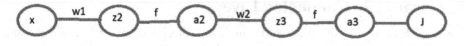

Figure 14.7   Each process is represented as a separate layer.

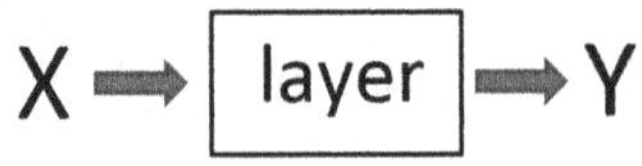

Figure 14.8 General layer behavior.

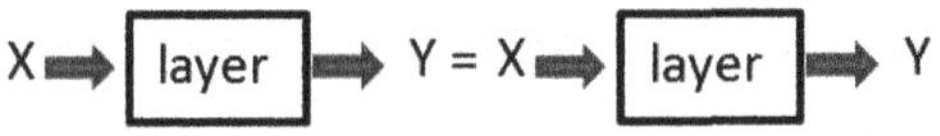

Figure 14.9 Forward propagation.

14.5 Linear versus Non-Linear Layers

We have seen that the calculation of z_2 for a 1–1–1 architecture with a bias term looks like

$$z_2 = x_1 w_1 + \text{bias}$$

This is a linear function of w_1. (It is also a linear function of x_1, but that won't be relevant here.) If we have a 2–1–1 architecture, then $z_2 = x_1 w_1 + x_2 w_2 + \text{bias}$. This is *also* referred to as linear in w_1 and w_2. If we have a 2–3–1 architecture, then the result Z2 is a vector, but each component is calculated with a linear function. For example, $z_1^{(2)} = x_1 w_{11} + x_2 w_{21} + \text{bias}_1$.

We can express each component $z_j^{(2)}$ with the following:

$$z_j^{(2)} = b_j + \sum_i x_i w_{i,j} \tag{14.11}$$

where b_j is the weight from the bias node to $z_j^{(2)}$. Each component is derived from a linear calculation.

Practice 14.5.3
1. In Equation 14.11, what quantity does the letter "i" index?
2. In Equation 14.11, what quantity does the letter "j" index?

On the other hand, the activation function in our network should not be linear. We have used the sigmoid function for the activation function in prior chapters but have mentioned other possibilities. We need non-linear functions in the design of a neural network. If the entire neural network consisted of (the composition of) linear functions, its capacity to learn would be severely limited as it would enforce a linear model on any and all data.

Practice 14.5.4
1. Give two other activation functions that we have mentioned earlier in the text.

14.6 Linear Fully Connected Layer

Now that we have separated the network into a sequence of linear and non-linear processes, we begin with the analysis of the linear layers. We will suppose that we have any number of x input nodes and any number of y output nodes in a layer. For example, recalling our mood dataset,

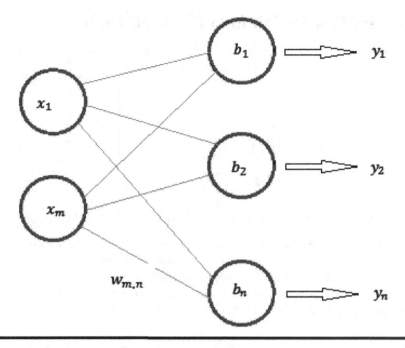

Figure 14.10 Single process FC *linear* layer.

if we want to have *calories_burned* and *hours_of_sleep* as inputs to our model, then the first layer would have two input nodes. It can also have any number of output nodes. We have used diagrams where the first layer connects to three output nodes. We now draw our layers in a new way as shown in Figure 14.10.

Recall that given any output y_i (previously referred to as z_i), we calculate it as $y_i = b_j + \sum_i x_i w_{i,j}$.

Thus, we read the b_j nodes in the above diagram as indicating that the b_j node is *added* to the incoming sum.

Also note that each output is connected to all the x input nodes. Such a layer is referred to as a *fully connected (FC) layer*. In deep learning, other types of connection architectures are used as well as the FC architecture,[2] and we will see an example of this in the next chapter.

The picture in Figure 14.10 looks a bit different from past diagrams; however, it represents the same process we have dealt with in earlier chapters, and in fact it is less complicated because it only has the linear calculation in it. It does not contain the threshold function. This is exactly what we want. *We want to break the steps into less complicated and therefore more easily modularized portions.*

We have m nodes in the first column of circles. There are n outputs. Since we are switching to X and Y notation, we say each output y_i is obtained by

$$y_j = b_j + \sum_i x_i w_{i,j} \tag{14.12}$$

---

[2] We will use some of these in the deep learning convolutional neural network in the next chapter.

14.7 Forward Propagation for a Linear FC Layer

We can represent the calculations for all the y_j given in Equation 14.12 with matrices as follows. Let m be the number of x inputs and n the number of y outputs.

$$X = \begin{bmatrix} x_1 & \cdots & x_m \end{bmatrix} \quad W = \begin{bmatrix} w_{1,1} & \cdots & w_{1,n} \\ \vdots & \ddots & \vdots \\ w_{m,1} & \cdots & w_{m,n} \end{bmatrix} \quad B = \begin{bmatrix} b_1 & \cdots & b_n \end{bmatrix}$$

$$Y = \begin{bmatrix} y_1 & \cdots & y_n \end{bmatrix} = XW + B \tag{14.13}$$

This is the complete calculation of the forward propagation through this FC layer.

> Recalling our mathematics discussion in an earlier chapter, note that this expression of Y as a function of X is a multivariate vector-valued function. The inputs are X, and the outputs are Y. If we care to give a name to the function, say g, we could say that our FC layer is a vector-valued multivariate function. In fact, we could say it is a *linear* vector-valued multivariate function.

$$g: \mathbf{R}^m \to \mathbf{R}^n$$

> It will turn out that activation layers are also vector-valued multivariate functions, and we can also observe for activation layers that the input size and output size are equal.
> Pushing data successively through these layers is equivalent to taking the composition of these functions. The composition of such functions will also be vector-valued and multivariate.

Next, we consider what backpropagation looks like for this layer.

14.8 Backpropagation for a Linear FC Layer – Calculation of $\dfrac{\partial J}{\partial W}, \dfrac{\partial J}{\partial B}, \dfrac{\partial J}{\partial Y}, \dfrac{\partial J}{\partial X}$

We now concern ourselves with backpropagation and the calculations for $\dfrac{\partial J}{\partial W}, \dfrac{\partial J}{\partial B}, \dfrac{\partial J}{\partial Y}$, and $\dfrac{\partial J}{\partial X}$. The need to calculate $\dfrac{\partial J}{\partial W}$ and $\dfrac{\partial J}{\partial B}$ is clear from previous chapters, but one may ask why we need $\dfrac{\partial J}{\partial Y}$. Remember, however, from Equation 14.9 that this is a piece in the chain rule, and more importantly, it is the piece that holds the downstream calculations. Finally, the reason we need to calculate $\dfrac{\partial J}{\partial X}$ is to be able to pass it to the next upstream layer's calculation because as we pointed out above in Equation 14.10, $\dfrac{\partial J}{\partial Y} = \dfrac{\partial J}{\partial X}$.

Practice 14.8.6

1. As a review question, why do we want to calculate $\dfrac{\partial J}{\partial W}$?

We start with the calculation of $\dfrac{\partial J}{\partial W}$ (capital W). We use the abbreviation FC for "fully connected". Consider $\dfrac{\partial J}{\partial w}$ (lowercase "w") for an arbitrary weight w in the FC layer. By the multivariate chain rule,

$$\frac{\partial J}{\partial w} = \sum_{j=1}^{n} \frac{\partial J}{\partial y_j} \frac{\partial y_j}{\partial w} \tag{14.14}$$

Caution: The n *here and the layer number* n *have nothing to do with each other.*

Which, if any, of these factors is "local" to the layer, and which of them are given from downstream calculations? We see that $\dfrac{\partial J}{\partial y_j}$ is given from downstream calculations, and the calculation $\dfrac{\partial y_j}{\partial w}$ is local. The calculation which is local will depend on what kind of layer we are using, either a FC linear layer, a non-linear activation layer, or some other type of layer.

Practice 14.8.6

1. What does n stand for in Equation 14.14 above?
2. How many *terms* are there in the right-hand side of 14.14?
3. Suppose we have a variable z which is a function, f, of x and y, and then suppose that x is a function g of t and y is a function h of t. We write this as $z = f(x, y)$ and $x = g(t)$ and $y = h(t)$. Write the expression for $\dfrac{dz}{dt}$.
4. As an example of the above question, suppose $z = f(x, y) = 2x + y^2$ and $\mathbf{x}(t) = [6t, t + 2]$. (Remember that $\mathbf{x}(t) = [6t, t + 2]$ is shorthand for $x = 6t$ and $y = t + 2$.) Find $\dfrac{dz}{dt}$.
5. Why in the above example did we write $\dfrac{dz}{dt}$ instead of $\dfrac{\partial z}{\partial t}$?
6. Why in Equation 14.14 above did we write $\dfrac{\partial J}{\partial w}$ instead of $\dfrac{dJ}{dw}$?
7. Find $\dfrac{dz}{dt}$ in #4 above without using the chain rule.

Equation 14.14 gives a calculation for each of the entries $\dfrac{\partial J}{\partial w_{i,j}}$, and if we write it more explicitly, we have

$$\frac{\partial J}{\partial w_{i,j}} = \frac{\partial J}{\partial y_1} \frac{\partial y_1}{\partial w_{i,j}} + \cdots + \frac{\partial J}{\partial y_n} \frac{\partial y_n}{\partial w_{i,j}} \tag{14.15}$$

As stated above, this is simply a statement of the chain rule. The second factor of each term asks for a derivative of a y_i with respect to each of the w's in the given FC. However, in our neural network, y_i may not be a function of every w. If you view Figure 14.10 or the diagrams of the 2–3–1 networks from previous chapter, it is evident that a particular $w_{i,j}$ is only connected to a single y. Specifically $w_{i,j}$ will only be connected to y_j. Thus, if $i \neq j$, then $\dfrac{\partial y_i}{\partial w_{i,j}} = 0$! This is an important observation and significantly reduces the complexity of the equation above. We can simplify it as

$$\frac{\partial J}{\partial w_{i,j}} = \frac{\partial J}{\partial y_j} \frac{\partial y_j}{\partial w_{i,j}} = \frac{\partial J}{\partial y_j} x_i \tag{14.16}$$

Equation 14.16 above applies to all elements $w_{i,j}$ in the matrix W. Thus, we can now obtain a compact expression for $\dfrac{\partial J}{\partial W}$ (capital "W").

First however, by definition

$$\frac{\partial J}{\partial W} = \begin{bmatrix} \dfrac{\partial J}{\partial w_{1,1}} & \cdots & \dfrac{\partial J}{\partial w_{1,n}} \\ \vdots & \ddots & \vdots \\ \dfrac{\partial J}{\partial w_{m,1}} & \cdots & \dfrac{\partial J}{\partial w_{m,n}} \end{bmatrix} \tag{14.17}$$

But as a result of Equation 14.16, we get

$$\frac{\partial J}{\partial W} = \begin{bmatrix} \dfrac{\partial J}{\partial y_1} x_1 & \cdots & \dfrac{\partial J}{\partial y_n} x_i \\ \vdots & \ddots & \vdots \\ \dfrac{\partial J}{\partial y_1} x_m & \cdots & \dfrac{\partial J}{\partial y_n} x_m \end{bmatrix} \tag{14.18}$$

We can "factor" the right-hand side and rewrite it as

$$\frac{\partial J}{\partial W} = \begin{bmatrix} x_1 \\ \vdots \\ x_m \end{bmatrix} \begin{bmatrix} \dfrac{\partial J}{\partial y_1} & \cdots & \dfrac{\partial J}{\partial y_n} \end{bmatrix} \tag{14.19}$$

$$= X^T \frac{\partial J}{\partial Y} \tag{14.20}$$

Practice 14.8.7

1. What are the dimensions of the two matrices in Equation 14.19, and what are the dimensions of their product?
2. What is the first term of the result of the product of the matrices in Equation 14.19?

Now we have our first update formula for the weights for an FC linear layer! Note that it does depend on being supplied with $\frac{\partial J}{\partial Y}$, and we will be sure to output it (with a return() statement) in our code from the downstream layer calculations.

Practice 14.8.8

1. In our previous neural networks from the previous chapter, find the "equivalent" expression for $\frac{\partial J}{\partial W}$.

14.9 Calculating $\frac{\partial J}{\partial B}$

Next, we find the formula for updating the bias B. Recall that in a previous chapter, the bias was added to the input layer and hidden layer matrices by adding an extra column, and we did not write out an explicit formula for $\frac{\partial J}{\partial B}$ there. This is a new approach that takes advantage of the modular design of the code.

Again, by definition we write

$$\frac{\partial J}{\partial B} = \left[\begin{array}{ccc} \frac{\partial J}{\partial b_1} & \cdots & \frac{\partial J}{\partial b_n} \end{array} \right] \tag{14.21}$$

The chain rule gives us

$$\frac{\partial J}{\partial b_j} = \frac{\partial J}{\partial y_1}\frac{\partial y_1}{\partial b_j} + \cdots + \frac{\partial J}{\partial y_n}\frac{\partial y_n}{\partial b_j} \tag{14.22}$$

Practice 14.9.9

1. What does n stand for in Equation 14.22 above?
2. How many terms are there in the right-hand side of 14.22?
3. If $y_1 = b_1 + x_1 w_{1,1} + x_2 w_{2,1}$, find $\frac{\partial y}{\partial b_1}$.
4. If $y_j = b_j + \sum_i x_i w_{i,j}$, find $\frac{\partial y_j}{\partial b_j}$.

Refer to Figure 14.10.

Note that b_j is connected to only one of the y_i, and that is when $i = j$. Thus, in Equation 14.22 above, all terms will be zero except where the subscript for b and y are the same.

$$\frac{\partial J}{\partial b_j} = \frac{\partial J}{\partial y_j}\frac{\partial y_j}{\partial b_j} \tag{14.23}$$

Recalling Equation 14.12

$$y_j = b_j + \sum_{i=1}^{m} x_i w_{i,j}$$

we note there are no b's in the second term, and so

$$\frac{\partial y_j}{\partial b_j} = \frac{\partial b_j}{\partial b_j} + 0 = 1 \tag{14.24}$$

Thus,

$$\frac{\partial J}{\partial b_j} = \frac{\partial J}{\partial y_j} \tag{14.25}$$

We have found derivatives with respect to b_j for all j, and so we get

$$\frac{\partial J}{\partial B} = \left[\begin{array}{ccc} \frac{\partial J}{\partial y_1} & \cdots & \frac{\partial J}{\partial y_n} \end{array} \right] = \frac{\partial J}{\partial Y}$$

$$\frac{\partial J}{\partial B} = \frac{\partial J}{\partial Y} \tag{14.26}$$

This is our second formula and will used to update the bias weights. As stated above, in the last chapter, the bias term was embedded in the weights matrices, and so we did not do a "separate" update of the bias weight. Now, however, we will use $\dfrac{\partial J}{\partial B}$ to update B, in a way similar to the way we have been updating $W^{(1)}$ and $W^{(2)}$ with code like

```
W1 <- W1-r*dJ_dW1
W2 <- W2-r*dJ_dW2.
```

14.10 Calculating $\dfrac{\partial J}{\partial X}$

Finally, we said that we want our code to output $\dfrac{\partial J}{\partial X}$ so that it can be used in the next upstream layer (where it will be referred to as $\dfrac{\partial J}{\partial Y}$). Now we derive its formula. By definition,

$$\frac{\partial J}{\partial X} = \left[\begin{array}{ccc} \frac{\partial J}{\partial x_1} & \cdots & \frac{\partial J}{\partial x_m} \end{array} \right] \tag{14.27}$$

Again, we employ the chain rule to an arbitrary element in the above matrix. Note that in this equation, X is the input to our layer and Y is the output of this *same* layer. Just to make sure you caught that, we repeat Y is the output for the same layer as X here.

$$\frac{\partial J}{\partial x_i} = \frac{\partial J}{\partial y_1}\frac{\partial y_1}{\partial x_i} + \cdots + \frac{\partial J}{\partial y_n}\frac{\partial y_n}{\partial x_i} \tag{14.28}$$

Again, referring to Figure 14.10 or Equation 14.12, we see there is exactly one connection from input x_i to output y_j, and that will be the connection labeled with weight $w_{i,j}$. Thus, we arrive at

$$\frac{\partial J}{\partial x_i} = \frac{\partial J}{\partial y_1}w_{i,1} + \cdots + \frac{\partial J}{\partial y_n}w_{i,n} \tag{14.29}$$

Combining Equations 14.28 and 14.29, we have

$$\frac{\partial J}{\partial X} = \left[\begin{array}{ccc} \frac{\partial J}{\partial y_1}w_{1,1} + \cdots + \frac{\partial J}{\partial y_n}w_{1,n} & \cdots & \frac{\partial J}{\partial y_1}w_{m,1} + \cdots + \frac{\partial J}{\partial y_n}w_{m,n} \end{array} \right] \tag{14.30}$$

$$\frac{\partial J}{\partial X} = \left[\begin{array}{ccc} \frac{\partial J}{\partial y_1} & \cdots & \frac{\partial J}{\partial y_n} \end{array} \right] \left[\begin{array}{ccc} w_{1,1} & \cdots & w_{m,1} \\ \vdots & \ddots & \vdots \\ w_{1,n} & \cdots & w_{m,n} \end{array} \right] \tag{14.31}$$

$$\frac{\partial J}{\partial X} = \frac{\partial J}{\partial Y}W^t \tag{14.32}$$

Now we have all the necessary equations for the FC linear layer.

$$\frac{\partial J}{\partial W} = X^T \frac{\partial J}{\partial Y} \tag{14.33}$$

$$\frac{\partial J}{\partial B} = \frac{\partial J}{\partial Y} \tag{14.34}$$

$$\frac{\partial J}{\partial X} = \frac{\partial J}{\partial Y}W^t \tag{14.35}$$

We can now proceed to code the FC layer.

14.11 Coding an FC Layer

We will assume the reader has some understanding of OOP design style in our code. Briefly, we are using the principle of **inheritance**.

> Inheritance is a mechanism in which one class acquires the property of another class. For example, a child inherits the traits of his/her parents. With inheritance, we can

reuse the fields and methods of the existing class. Hence, inheritance facilitates reusability and is an important concept of OOP.[3]

In our code, we first create a general or "grandparent" class called Layer. It will have some basic properties (fields) and methods that we want all our layers to possess. We can then allow the FC layer to inherit that structure (and then build off that structure).

> When we say inherit, we mean that any methods or fields that we write for the grandparent class will be inherited by the "child" class. We can use them as they are (as they have been written in the grandparent class) or we can overwrite them within the child class.

When we write the code for the activation layer, we will allow it too to inherit structure from our Layer class (and then build off that structure) as well. This is very standard program design in OOP.

In the following code, we will change the terminology a little. Instead of dJ_dW, dJ_dX, and dJ_dY, we will use some other common terminology: *weight_error*, *input_error*, and *output_error*, respectively. We will also use the word "slice" to refer to taking a subsection or part of a matrix, dataframe, list, or vector.

```
Layer <- setRefClass("Layer", fields = list(input="ANY",  output =
"matrix"),
             methods = list(initialize = function(a,c) {
                       input <<- a
                       output <<- c
                     },
#Define a forward-propagation method.
forward_propagation = function(input) {
#In the "grandfather" class, we just create a "placeholder" method and
don't fill in any details. Each "child" class will "fill-out" the
specifics for its particular version of the method.
                     },
#Define the backpropagation method.
backProp_propagation = function(output_error, learning_rate) {
                     }

                   )
#end of Layer class definition
                 )
```

Now we proceed to define the FC layer which will inherit from the Layer class. The fact that it inherits from the Layer class is specified in R with the code contains = "Layer".

```
# 1. weights_error is the name we are using for dJ_dW in this code.
# 2. output_error is the name we are using for dJ_dY in this code.
# 3. input_error is the name we are using for dJ_dX in this code.
```

[3] https://www.guru99.com/java-class-inheritance.html.

Practice 14.11.10

1. With the above notation, write Equation 14.33 as code.
2. With the above notation, write Equation 14.34 as code.
3. With the above notation, write Equation 14.35 as code.

```
FCLayer <- setRefClass("FCLayer", contains = "Layer",
              fields = list(
                         input_size = "numeric",
                         output_size = "numeric",
                         weights = "matrix",
                         bias = "matrix"
                         ),
              methods = list(
                      initialize = function(input_size, output_size){
                        weights <<- matrix(runif(input_size*output_
size, -1, 1), input_size, output_size)
                        bias <<- matrix(runif(output_size, -1, 1),
1, output_size)
                      },
                      forward_propagation = function(input_data){
                        input <<- input_data
                        output <<- (input %*% weights) + bias
                        return(output)
                      },
#Recall that the backpropagation code will accept dJ_dY from the
previous layer as one factor of the calculation of dJ_dW. This was
referred to this as the downstream calculation. Here, this is the
output_error.
                      backProp_propagation = function(output_error,
learning_rate){
#Next is the code for equation 14.35. input_error is dJ_dX.

input_error <<- output_error %*% t(weights)
#We use matrix() to convert train_x to a matrix.
weights_error <<-matrix(input) %*% output_error
weights <<- weights - (learning_rate * weights_error) # dJ_dW is
weights_error.
bias <<- bias - (learning_rate * output_error) # dJ_dY is output_error.
We said that we need to spit out dJ_dX so the next upstream layer will
have this calculation available to use. In our code, dJ_dX is called
the input error.
  return (input_error)
                      }
              )
#end of Layer class definition
              )
```

14.12 Activation Layer

The activation layer is non-linear and takes inputs that in previous chapters were labled Z (Z2 or Z3) and processes them with an activation function which we have denoted as f. The diagram looks like Figure 14.11.

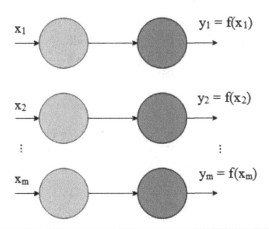

Figure 14.11 Activation layer.

The inputs can originate from any type of layer. In all our previous networks, this was the FC linear layer, but later we will explore a deep learning structure where this is not the case.

14.13 Forward Propagation for the Activation Layer

Forward propagation is just a matter of applying the activation function to the each of the inputs. That is, for each i,

$$y_i = f(x_i)$$

Or in matrix form,

$$Y = \begin{bmatrix} f(x_1) & \cdots & f(x_m) \end{bmatrix} = f(X) \tag{14.36}$$

That is it! This is our forward-propagation formula for the activation layer.

14.14 Backpropagation for the Activation Layer

First note that *there are no weights to update* in this layer because there are no weights in the layer! Therefore, we won't have to calculate a derivative with respect to weights for the activation layer backpropagation process. That is, whereas for the FC layer we needed all three derivatives $\frac{\partial J}{\partial W}, \frac{\partial J}{\partial Y}$, and $\frac{\partial J}{\partial X}$, for the activation layer we will only need to calculate $\frac{\partial J}{\partial X}$, and the only reason we have to calculate it is to be able to pass it on to the next upstream backpropagation process. We will suppose, as before, that we are given $\frac{\partial J}{\partial Y}$ (from the code for the downstream layer). Whereas in the FC layer, the size of the inputs and the size of the outputs could be different, here they are the same, and we use m to denote this size.

$$\frac{\partial J}{\partial X} = \left[\begin{array}{ccc} \frac{\partial J}{\partial x_1} & \cdots & \frac{\partial J}{\partial x_m} \end{array} \right] \qquad (14.37)$$

As before, we focus on an individual element in the above matrix, and by a similar use of the chain rule, we have

$$\frac{\partial J}{\partial x_i} = \frac{\partial J}{\partial y_1}\frac{\partial y_1}{\partial x_i} + \cdots + \frac{\partial J}{\partial y_n}\frac{\partial y_n}{\partial x_i} \qquad (14.38)$$

In the activation layer as well, with reasoning like previous chain rule equations, we have that if $i \neq j$, then

$$\frac{\partial y_j}{\partial x_i} = 0 \qquad (14.39)$$

Thus,

$$\frac{\partial J}{\partial x_i} = \frac{\partial J}{\partial y_i}\frac{\partial y_i}{\partial x_i} \qquad (14.40)$$

and

$$\frac{\partial J}{\partial X} = \left[\begin{array}{ccc} \frac{\partial J}{\partial y_1}\frac{\partial y_1}{\partial x_1} & \cdots & \frac{\partial J}{\partial y_m}\frac{\partial y_m}{\partial x_m} \end{array} \right] \qquad (14.41)$$

Practice 14.14.11

1. Show that if $i \neq j$, then $\frac{\partial y_j}{\partial x_i} = 0$.

Now recall that for each of the m applications of f to the m inputs x_i (for i in $\{1, \ldots, m\}$), we are applying the same activation function f. This means that $y_i = f(x_i)$ no matter which x_i, and so we can use $f'(x_i)$ to denote $\frac{\partial y_i}{\partial x_i}$. Therefore

$$\frac{\partial J}{\partial X} = \left[\begin{array}{ccc} \frac{\partial J}{\partial y_1}f'(x_1) & \cdots & \frac{\partial J}{\partial y_m}f'(x_m) \end{array} \right] \qquad (14.42)$$

Here we can use the Hadamard product (element-by-element multiplication) to write this as

$$\frac{\partial J}{\partial X} = \frac{\partial J}{\partial Y} \odot f'(x_1) \qquad (14.43)$$

That is all we need for the backpropagation calculations for the activation layer. Now we are ready to write the activation layer code.

Practice 14.14.12

  1. Write Equation 14.43 in code.

14.15 Coding an Activation Layer

We will leave the type of activation function to be used unspecified, and therefore in our code at this point, we will just refer to it as `activation` (and `activation_prime`). These will be options that will be decided after an actual instance of the class is created. We will create an `add()` method and will use it to add layers of various types. When an activation *layer* is added, it is at that point that the user chooses an activation *function* (sigmoid, ReLU, tanh, or some other).

```
ActivationLayer <- setRefClass("ActivationLayer", contains = "Layer",
                     fields = list(
                        activation = "function",
                        activation_prime = "function"
                     ),
#The type of activation function is not specified, and here it is just
referred to as activation in the initialize method. This allows the user
to specify their own activation function.
methods = list(initialize = function(a, c){
                        activation <<- a
                        activation_prime <<- c
                     },
            forward_propagation = function(input_data){
                        input <<- input_data
                        output <<- activation(input_data)
                        return(output)
                     },
            backProp_propagation = function(output_error,learning_
rate){
            return(activation_prime(input) * output_error)
                     }
                  )
               )
```

14.16 Coding the Neural Network Class, Creating an Instance, and Running It

Now we build the neural network class. It will have an **initialize**() method, an **add**() method, a use() method, a **predict**() method, and a **fit**() method. The **add**() method is new for us. It will allow us to add as many layers as we want to the network and will allow us to add them in any order – meaning we can add a flatten layer wherever we want, we can add a FC layer wherever we want, and so on. The use() method will allow use to choose which error measure is used. Typically, this is *mse* (mean squared error), but other measures can be designed and utilized. The **predict**() method will take input data and report back the predicted output. It can be used on either the training or testing data. The **fit**() method is where the training of the model takes place.

First, we define a few functions that are needed.

```r
#tanh() is already part of the base R installation. We can use tan() as
an activation function.
tanh_prime <- function(x){
  return(1 - tanh(x)^2)
}


#Loss function and its derivative
#In the previous chapters, we used the name JCost. Here we use another
standard name, mse. It should not be difficult to see why it is called
mean squared error. It is the same function as JCost.
mse <- function(y_true, yHat){
  return(0.5*mean(y_true - yHat)^2)
}


mse_prime <- function(y_true, yHat){
  return((yHat - y_true) / length(y_true))
}


#Define our class. It is called Network.
Network <- setRefClass("Network", fields = list(layers = "list",
                                                 loss = "ANY",
                                                 loss_prime = "ANY",
                                                 err = "numeric",
                                                 error = "ANY"),
            methods = list(initialize = function(){
            #layers as list and loss and loss_prime as zero.
            #We reassign their values in the backpropagation.
                           layers <<- list()
                           loss <<- 0
                           loss_prime <<- 0
                           },
               #allows the addition new layers to the list.
#Assign list indices.
               add = function(lay){
               layers[[length(layers)+1]] <<- lay
                           },
#We define a function which will allow the user to choose which loss
function to use. In other words, if the user wants to create a different
loss function and use it, this will be easily accomplished.
        use = function(loss, loss_prime){
                           loss <<- loss
                           loss_prime <<- loss_prime
                           },
#A function which will take input data and use the trained network to
make predictions on that input data.
        predict = function(input_data){
                   #Create a list for predictions.
                   #Later we convert it to a dataframe.
                   samples <- nrow(input_data)
                   result <- list()
                     for (i in 1:samples){
                       output <- t(matrix(input_data[i,]))
                         for (layer in layers){
                          output <-layer$forward_propagation(output)
                         }
```

```
#Let's round our predictions to a decimal notation.
        result[[i]] <- round(output, 5)
                }
        result <- as.data.frame(matrix(unlist(result),
nrow=length(unlist(result[1])))))
            return(t(result))
                },
#The next method is where the training takes place.
    fit = function(x_train, y_train, epochs, learning_rate){
        #number of samples == number of rows for training
        samples <- nrow(x_train)
        #loop through number of epochs
        for (i in 1:epochs){
        #assign global variable to 0
        err <<- 0
        #loop through number of samples
            for (j in 1:samples){
            #t(matrix(slice)) - we use this motation to enable vector
calculations, as after slicing and converting a slice to matrix, R
automatically transposes it.
            output = t(matrix(x_train[j,]))
                for (layer in layers){
                output = layer$forward_propagation(output)
                    }
            #update errors
            err <<- err + loss(y_train[j,], output)
            error <<- loss_prime(y_train[j,], output)
            #loop through layers for backpropagation
                for(layer in rev(layers)){
                error <<- layer$backProp_propagation(error,
learning_rate)
                }
            }
            #Calculate average error.
            err <<- err / samples
            #Print string to track model training.
            print(paste("Epoch num", i, "/", epochs, "; Error:",
round(err, 6)))
            }
        }
        )
#end of Network class
        )
```

14.16.1 Testing the Network with XOR

The XOR logical operator has an important role in the history of neural networks. In the late 1950s, a psychologist, Rosenblatt, conceived of the Perceptron as a simplified mathematical model of how the neurons in our brains operate: it takes a set of binary inputs (nearby neurons), multiplies each input by a continuous valued weight (the synapse strength to each nearby neuron), and thresholds the sum of these weighted inputs to output a 1 if the sum is big enough and otherwise a 0. (In the same way, neurons in the brain either fire or do not.) In the late 1960s, Marvin Minsky, founder of the MIT AI Lab, and Seymour Papert, director of the lab at the time, were two of the researchers who were skeptical of the hype about neural networks and in 1969 published their skepticism in the form of rigorous analysis of the limitations of Perceptrons in a seminal book aptly named *Perceptrons*. They showed that the state-of-the-art neural networks that Rosenblatt had developed were unable to model a relatively simple function, the XOR operator. In fact, Minsky's book convinced most of the world that neural networks were a discredited dead-end.[4]

In Chapter 2 of this text, we studied logic, and there we learned about the 4 operators: AND, OR, NOT, and IF THEN. There is one more operator that is often discussed. It is called the *exclusive* OR or just XOR. As a quick intro to XOR, suppose you tell your child, "You may go to the movies or you may go to the beach", and then suppose your child goes to both the movies and the beach, would you be able to scold your child saying they disobeyed you? In English, this "or" is not clear. You could have meant you could go to one or the other but not both, or you could have meant that you can go to just one or the other or both. The ambiguity in English is not something computer scientists or logicians want in their analysis. Thus, they use OR to mean one or the other or both and XOR to mean one or the other but not both. The truth table for XOR is

P	Q	P XOR Q
T	T	F
T	F	T
F	T	T
F	F	F

This is non-linear and "not separable". We will not discuss this, but the interested reader can investigate this issue elsewhere. Minsky pointed out that neural networks at that time could not model this common function. If you are confused with the use of the word function for a truth table or logical operator, we can (and will) replace T with 1 and F with 0, and then we have a function with two inputs and one output. That is, the input data is

1	1
1	0
0	1
0	0

And the corresponding outputs are

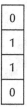

[4] https://www.andreykurenkov.com/writing/ai/a-brief-history-of-neural-nets-and-deep-learning/.

Meaning, if we call this function f (instead of XOR), then we can say

$$f(1,1) = 0$$

$$f(1,0) = 1$$

$$f(0,1) = 1$$

$$f(0,0) = 0$$

And this is the complete definition of this function f (no other inputs to deal with). Now we may wish to take this two-input data and see if we can train our neural network to predict the outputs. In olden days (in the 1960s), they could not do this. That is to say, the models could not give good predictions. What about *our* neural network? The answer, as you will see, is that it works well with this data and the error will decrease as we continue to train it.

```
#Now let's check if the network is working.
#x_train - ind. variable
x_train = rbind(c(0, 0), c(0, 1), c(1, 0), c(1, 1))

#y_train - target variable
y_train = rbind(c(0), c(1), c(1), c(0))
```

We have defined a bunch of possible layers, but we haven't put them all together to form a neural network. If you are familiar with Legos, we have a bunch of building blocks, but now we will build something (Figure 14.12).

As mentioned earlier, we coded an **add**() method which is used to add new layers to the class. In the previous chapter, once the instance was created, it had all the layers in it. However, with our new design, we add layers as we wish and in whatever order we want.

Figure 14.12 From layers to a network.

```
#Now we define our network.
net <- new("Network")
#Here is where we add layers with the add() method.
net$add(FCLayer(2, 3))
net$add(ActivationLayer(tanh, tanh_prime))
net$add(FCLayer(3, 1))
net$add(ActivationLayer(tanh, tanh_prime))
#Choose a loss function and it's prime.
net$use(mse, mse_prime)
#Now train the network for 100 epochs.
net$fit(x_train, y_train, epochs=100, learning_rate=0.5)
## [1] "Epoch num 1 / 100 ; Error: 0.567677"
## [1] "Epoch num 2 / 100 ; Error: 0.476398"
## [1] "Epoch num 3 / 100 ; Error: 0.468664"
## [1] "Epoch num 4 / 100 ; Error: 0.456908"
## [1] "Epoch num 5 / 100 ; Error: 0.441044"
## [1] "Epoch num 6 / 100 ; Error: 0.433835"
## [1] "Epoch num 7 / 100 ; Error: 0.436079"
## [1] "Epoch num 8 / 100 ; Error: 0.430549"
## [1] "Epoch num 9 / 100 ; Error: 0.428423"
## [1] "Epoch num 10 / 100 ; Error: 0.424426"
                              ⋮
## [1] "Epoch num 99 / 100 ; Error: 0.151977"
## [1] "Epoch num 100 / 100 ; Error: 0.078189"
```

We can see that the network trains well on the XOR. This breakthrough was achieved with the use of multilayer perceptrons and the backpropagation algorithm, something that Minsky thought would not be feasible.

Next, we will use our modular structure to develop a type of *deep learning algorithm* known as a *convolutional neural network*. We will train it on a well-known dataset, the MNIST dataset consisting of 50,000 or more handwritten digits and ask the network to classify them as one of the 10 digits from 0 to 9. The dataset itself was collected by the distinguished data scientist Yan LeCunn.

Chapter 15

Deep Learning with Convolutional Neural Networks

Now that we have modularized our code, we can add in new types of layers. We will add in a convolutional layer and two other types of layers that are generally included in a convolutional neural network (CNN). CNNs have proved extremely successful with image recognition. They are also used for numerous other applications. We present the CNN here to show that our coding skills have brought us to a remarkable place. However, it is not required that the reader explore every detail in this chapter. Nevertheless, we will find that the modular approach explained in the previous chapter affords a great deal of flexibility in the design of neural networks. We will end this chapter with the analysis of the MNIST data and we will see that we are able to classify handwritten digits with suprising accuracy.

Whereas up until this point we have learned about two types of layers in neural networks: fully connected (FC) layers and activation layers, in this chapter, we will learn about new types of layers. The new layer types we study are the convolutional layer, the max pooling layer, and the flatten layer. We will see that we can add these in whatever order (architecture) we desire. Data scientists have experimented with different architectures looking for best predictions and classifications. At the end of the chapter, we build a CNN with the following architecture.

Architecture	
1	Convolutional layer
2	Max pooling layer
3	Convolutional layer
4	Max pooling layer
5	Flatten layer
6	FC layer
7	Activation layer
8	FC layer
9	Activation layer

Functions and Methods Coded in This Chapter
corr2d
relu_prime
initialize
forward_propagation
backProp_propagation
use
predict
fit

Here are the functions we build in this chapter.

15.1 Dataset – Handwritten Repository of Digits from 0 to 9

Our data will come from the MNIST (Modified National Institute of Standards and Technology) database. It is a large database of handwritten digits that is commonly used for training various image processing algorithms. The database is also widely used for training and testing in the field of machine learning. The black and white images fit into a 28×28 pixel bounding box and are grayscale. (Figure 15.1).

The MNIST database contains 60,000 training images and 10,000 testing images. Half of the training set and half of the test set were taken from NIST's training dataset, while the other half of the training set and the other half of the test set were taken from NIST's testing dataset. There have been a number of scientific papers on attempts to achieve the lowest error rate; one paper, using a hierarchical system of CNNs, manages to get an error rate on the MNIST database of 0.23%. The original creators of the database keep a list of some of the methods tested on it. In their original

Figure 15.1   Sample images from MNIST test dataset.

paper, they use a support-vector machine to get an error rate of 0.8%. An extended dataset similar to MNIST called EMNIST has been published in 2017, which contains 240,000 training images and 40,000 testing images of handwritten digits and characters.[1]

15.2 Converting Images into Inputs

How are images fed into a neural network? We hinted at this back in Chapter 4, when we tried to represent the red, blue, and yellow squares in order to explore conditional independence. There we created an array with 3 layers. (Do not expect the layers we have been discussing with neural networks have anything to do with those layers – same word, completely different use.)

Images can be represented as arrays. If the image is grayscale, then we can construct an array with the same dimensions as the image has pixels (pixels comes from the phrase "picture elements"). Each element of the array will consist of a number from 0 to 255. Usually, the larger the number, the lighter the pixel with 0 indicating black. If the image is 8 pixels by 8 pixels, it may look like Figure 15.2.

Each pixel is a shade of gray.

We could then "unravel" this array (matrix) into a vector of length 8 × 8 = 64. That would result in an input vector with 64 elements. Then we would proceed as before to construct the rest of our neural network.

Early attempts at image recognition proceeded along these lines. However, we may spot a weakness with this approach. The kind of neural networks we have built so far do not give any importance to relationships that may exist between adjacent inputs. That is, it may be true that elements x_{26} and element x_{27} may be related, but the neural network has no way to take advantage of this. In fact, in our neural networks so far, there is no reason why we cannot rearrange our input vector and move around the different elements. We would not expect there to be any change in our predictions and any change in the accuracy. However, image data certainly seems to have some

---

[1] https://en.wikipedia.org/wiki/MNIST_database.

Figure 15.2 8 × 8 array of grayscale pixels (picture elements). Each pixel is a shade of gray on a scale of 0–255.

kind of internal relationships. If a pixel in one location is very dark, it may be correct to expect that adjacent pixels will also be dark. But our current neural network design cannot take advantage of these relationships to improve the results. This is the kind of issue that researchers were faced with. The question is, how can we take advantage of local relationships in the input data?

The idea behind CNNs is to try to harness the fact that neighboring inputs are related instead of simply throwing out this information. Somehow, we want to take groups of neighboring pixels together at the same time and process them. Someone came up with the following clever idea.

We create what is called a filter. For example, given the 8 × 8 grayscale image in Figure 15.2, we may create a 4 × 4 filter. That filter is dragged across the image, sort of like what you may do if you use a smart phone to scan a large image. You start at one corner of the image, placing your phone there and then drag it across the entire image. What is done with the "interfacing" data as you drag the filter across the image? The idea is to drag the filter to one position, take a "snapshot", then move the filter one pixel down (or across), take a second snapshot, and then continue until you have covered every pixel at least once. This is referred to as convolving the filter over the image. Each *region of the image* of which a snapshot is taken is referred to as a *receptive field*. What are these snapshots? Remember that each pixel in our image contains a number (between 0 and 255). The filter has dimensions 4 × 4. Each cell in the filter will also contain numbers. We calculate the multiplicative product of each pixel in the receptive field with the "corresponding" pixel in the filter. By corresponding pixel is meant the pixel in the filter that is currently over a given receptive field pixel. Since we have 16 elements in the filter, we are doing 16 multiplications with each "snapshot". For that snapshot, sum up all those products, and that becomes an input into the next layer. Note that this is an example of the dot product we studied in Chapter 10.[2] In terms of what we have done in past chapters, that sum would become an element in the Z vector in the next layer. Then we move the filter. This gives another set of products and their sum. That sum becomes another element in the Z vector. We continue, as we said, until all the pixels have been covered at least once. This process is designed to take groups of pixels together and somehow to "pick up" the relationships between neighboring pixels. In some way, each of these snapshots is a summary of the current receptive field portion of the image. In fact, we can say that it is a kind of weighted summary of the receptive field with the weights being the values in the filter.

---

[2] In the field of signal processing, this is a form of what is called a sliding dot product.

15.2.1 Example of Image and Filter

Suppose we have an image of an X and part of our strategy for classifying the image is to see where there are diagonal lines in the 8 × 8 image. For this example, instead of a grayscale image of an X, we will keep things simple by only using black and white. A pixel that is black will have a value of +1, and a pixel which is white will have a value of −1 as in the following image.

We use a filter that resembles a diagonal line. The filter is a 2 × 2 matrix that resembles a diagonal line moving from top left to bottom right.

In Figure 15.3, notice in the upper left-hand side of the image, we identify a 2 × 2 section of the X image that contains a diagonal line with a dashed border. We also identify a section of the X image that does not contain any diagonal line. It is identified with a bold border and is at the top center of the X image. If the filter is placed over the dashed line portion of the X image and corresponding pixels are multiplied together and then those results are summed up, we get

$$(1 \times 1) + (-1 \times -1) + (1 \times 1) + (-1 \times -1) = 4$$

On the other hand, if we do this for the area where there is no diagonal (the bold bordered area), we get something smaller.

$$(-1 \times 1) + (-1 \times -1) + (1 \times 1) + (1 \times -1) = 0$$

This process will identify where a pattern in the image is similar to the pattern in the filter. The larger the resulting calculation, the more likely it is that the pattern in the image is similar to the pattern in the filter. Note that the calculations we performed in the two equations above are actually dot products. If we repeat this as we drag the filter over the entire image, it is referred to as a sliding dot product (Figure 15.4).

1	-1	-1	-1	-1	-1	-1	1
-1	1	-1	-1	-1	-1	1	-1
-1	-1	1	-1	-1	1	-1	-1
-1	-1	-1	1	1	-1	-1	-1
-1	-1	-1	1	1	-1	-1	-1
-1	-1	1	-1	-1	1	-1	-1
-1	1	-1	-1	-1	-1	1	-1
1	-1	-1	-1	-1	-1	-1	1

Figure 15.3   8 × 8 image of X.

Figure 15.4   Filter for identifying diagonal line.

15.2.2 Image Matrix, Filter Matrix (Kernel), and Convoluted Feature

Generally, however, the outputs that are generated as we slide the filter over the image are not stored in a vector, (like the vector Z from previous chapters). Rather they are stored in a matrix. In fact, this matrix could be thought of as an image. This output matrix can be thought of as transformation of the input matrix. Each pixel in the output image is a weighted sum of the pixels in some neighborhood of the input image. Thus, the output image's entries are a sort of blending of a neighborhood of input pixels. We will call the image data the *image matrix*; the filter is called the *filter matrix* or the *kernel*. As we said, the Z output will be set up as a matrix instead of a vector and the elements of the matrix are computed as just described. This matrix is called the *convoluted feature*. It turns out that different types of filters (meaning particular patterns of numbers in the filter) may detect edges, diagonals, and so on. Other filters can perform transformations of the image such as blurring, sharpening, and so on. As another example, the following matrix will facilitate edge detection.

$$\begin{bmatrix} 1 & 0 & -1 \\ 0 & 0 & 0 \\ -1 & 0 & 1 \end{bmatrix}$$

It should be noted that the theory behind filters does not originate strictly from the idea of summarizing input data. It also derives from studies of the neurology of visual perception. In the 1950s and 1960s, scientists, notably, David Hubel and Torsten Wiesel, realized that there are parts of the brain (sets of neurons) that can detect various simple structures like variously oriented edges, vertical lines, horizontal lines, borders, and so on.[3]

As another example, suppose we are trying to find L-shaped edges. A good candidate for a filter for this shape would be a matrix that also looks like an L. In other words, it is a matrix that has 0's everywhere except for in an L shape. For example,

$$\begin{bmatrix} 0 & 50 & 0 \\ 0 & 50 & 0 \\ 0 & 50 & 50 \end{bmatrix}$$

When this matrix is centered directly over an L-shaped edge, the dot product of the receptive field at that location and this matrix will give a relatively large value (as compared to the dot product when the matrix is not directly centered at an edge). Again, getting a large value will indicate that an L shape has been found.

15.2.3 Adjustments to Improve the Network

You may imagine that there are many tweaks that we can use to try to improve accuracy. Accuracy may mean, how accurately the CNN can predict when an image of a human face shows a smile or a frown or neither, how accurately we can identify cancer in a CT scan, or how accurately we can read human written numbers or letters. In terms of tweaks to the CNN, we may ask what filter size should be applied, how many pixels to slide the filter between snapshots, what to do when we

---

[3] https://hackernoon.com/a-brief-history-of-computer-vision-and-convolutional-neural-networks-8fe8aacc79f3.

reach the end of the image, and so on. All these would become hyperparameters in the model. We may also ask what type of activation function works best, how many layers should be used, should FC layers be used in between these so-called convolutional layers and at what positions in the network.

15.2.4 Convolutional Layers Are Not FC Layers

Next, we note that the convolutional layer described above is not a FC layer. Each element in the *convoluted feature matrix* is calculated from just a single snapshot and thus from just a single receptive field. Remember that a receptive field is usually a small neighborhood of the entire input image. Thus, each element in the convoluted feature matrix is only connected to a neighborhood of inputs and not the whole input matrix. Thus, this layer is not FC. This is sometimes referred to as *local connectivity* since each neural network is connected to only to a subset of the input image.

15.2.5 Additional Characteristics of the Convolutional Layer

We have not mentioned it yet, but the weights in the filter *remain the same for all the snapshots*. Sometimes this is referred to as *parameter sharing* because of the sharing of these weights. Furthermore, the architecture is a bit more complicated than we have described so far. We don't employ just one filter in a convolutional layer. We employ several filters. For example, we could have a filter for edges oriented at 45°, a filter for horizontal edges, a filter for vertical edges, and so on. Each one of these filters results in a convoluted feature matrix, and then we bunch these convoluted feature matrices all together as a 3D array with each filter generating its own layer in this 3D array.

15.2.6 Color Images

What happens when we want to work with color images? Instead of storing the pixel values (from 0 to 255) in a matrix as we did for the grayscale image, we store it in an array with 3 layers. One layer of the array will give the strengths of the amount of red in the pixel, one layer for the amount of green, and one layer for the amount of blue. That is where the abbreviation RGB comes from (Figure 15.5).

Figure 15.5 Low-resolution color image where the pixel nature is evident.

15.3 Convolution as an Operation

Recall that in mathematics, we talk about addition (+), subtraction (−), multiplication (×), and division (/) as binary operators or operations. A binary operation takes two arguments; typically we put one on the left and one on the right (like 3 + 5), and then it outputs a result (8). We can describe a convolutional layer as an operation that takes two inputs: the image matrix and the filter (kernel). It then outputs a feature map. If we are dealing with a grayscale image, the image matrix will have two dimensions which we can call height and width (h × w), and the filter will also have two dimensions which can be denoted as (f_h, f_w), where we have used f to remind us that these are dimensions of the filter. Then if we use $\bowtie$ to denote this convolution operator we can write

$$(h, w) \bowtie (f_h, f_w) \mapsto \text{feature map}$$

which is just a way of writing that when we combine the input matrix (representing the image) and the filter, we get a feature map. We could also express it as a function with two inputs like this:

$$\big((h, w), (f_h, f_w)\big) \mapsto \text{feature map}$$

but we will stick with the operator notation.

In the case of a color image, the input matrix gets an extra dimension (so there are the 3 layers for R, G, and B), and it is referred to as an image volume (or array). The filter also gets an extra dimension (so there are the 3 layers for R, G, and B), but it is still called the filter or kernel. You may wonder how the multiplication is done in this case between the image volume and the kernel. It is done layer by layer so that the red input layer only gets multiplied by a "red" filter layer, the green input layer only gets multiplied by a "green" filter, and so on.

The filter plays the role that weights played in our neural networks of previous chapters. That is to say, the numbers in the filter are trainable (using backpropagation).

15.4 Forward Propagation for the Convolutional Layer

As an example, we consider a 3 × 3 input matrix and a 2 × 2 filter as shown in Figures 15.6 and 15.7.

We will actually define 3 related operations: correlation, convolution, and full convolution. Before attempting to define convolution, we will first define an operation between the input

x_{11}	x_{12}	x_{13}
x_{21}	x_{22}	x_{23}
x_{31}	x_{32}	x_{33}

Figure 15.6 Input matrix.

$$\begin{array}{|c|c|}
\hline
F_{11} & F_{12} \\
\hline
F_{21} & F_{22} \\
\hline
\end{array}$$

Figure 15.7   Filter matrix.

matrix and the filter matrix called correlation. The correlation operation is slightly simpler than convolution. The convolution of two matrices will just be the correlation of the input matrix and the transpose of the filter matrix.

15.4.1 Correlation of Input and Filter Matrices

We will use the symbol $\bowtie_c$ to denote the correlation of two matrices (Figures 15.8 and 15.9).

As we can see, the correlation of the 3×3 image matrix and the 2×2 filter matrix results in a 2×2 matrix. The O stands for output. (We have used Y more generally for the output, and we could have called this Y.) How are the O's calculated? As we said earlier, the filter is dragged across the input matrix. To obtain the first O calculation, O_{11}, we place the filter at the upper left-hand corner of the input matrix and then do element-by-element calculations as follows:

$$O_{1,1} = F_{1,1}x_{1,1} + F_{1,2}x_{1,2} + F_{2,1}x_{2,1} + F_{2,2}x_{2,2} \tag{15.1}$$

To get the O_{12} calculation, we move the filter so that the upper left-hand cell of the filter is at the $x_{1,2}$ position and again do element-by-element calculations as follows:

$$O_{1,2} = F_{1,1}x_{1,2} + F_{1,2}x_{1,3} + F_{2,1}x_{2,2} + F_{2,2}x_{2,3} \tag{15.2}$$

The remaining two entries of the correlation matrix are calculated similarly as

$$O_{2,1} = F_{1,1}x_{2,1} + F_{1,2}x_{2,2} + F_{2,1}x_{3,1} + F_{2,2}x_{3,2} \tag{15.3}$$

$$O_{2,2} = F_{1,1}x_{2,2} + F_{1,2}x_{2,3} + F_{2,1}x_{3,2} + F_{2,2}x_{3,3} \tag{15.4}$$

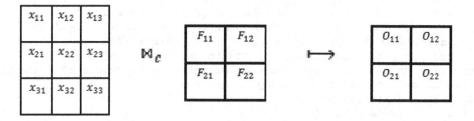

Figure 15.8   Correlation of image matrix and filter matrix to output the correlation feature matrix.

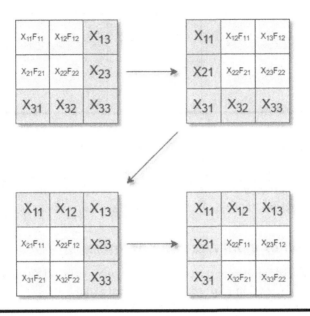

Figure 15.9 This shows the *correlation* calculation. The snapshots are shown in light shading and show the element-by-element matching that generates the output. The lightly shaded matrix is dragged from left to right and down and right to left again.

Practice 15.5.1

1. Where should the upper left-hand cell of the filter matrix be located to generate the equation $O_{2,1} = F_{1,1}x_{2,1} + F_{1,2}x_{2,2} + F_{2,1}x_{3,1} + F_{2,2}x_{3,2}$?
2. If the input matrix X is 5×5 and the feature matrix F is 2×2, what will the dimensions of the output matrix O be? Remember that we drag F across X and we do not go beyond the edges of X.
3. If the input matrix X is 5×5 and the feature matrix F is 3×3, what will the dimensions of the output matrix O be? Remember that we drag F across X and we do not go beyond the edges of X.
4. If X is of dimensions $a \times b$ and F is of dimensions $m \times n$, what would the dimensions of O be?

```
#Correlation function for two 2D matrices
corr2d <- function(x, f){#x holds the image matrix and f the filter matrix
  h <- dim(f)[1] # height of filter
  w <- dim(f)[2] # width of filter
#y will be the output of the correlation of matrices x and f.
#If X is 5 × 5 and F is 3 × 3, then O will be (5-3+1) × (5-3+1)=3 × 3.
  y <- array(data=0, dim=c(dim(x)[1] - h + 1, dim(x)[2] - w + 1))
#Each cell in y must be generated, and to do this, loop through each
column of each row. The inner loop below takes us through each column,
and the outer loop takes us through every row.
  for(i in 1:dim(y)[1]){
    for(j in 1:dim(y)[2]){
#What goes into each cell y[i, j]? As we said earlier, it is essentially
a dot product. That is, we take each element of F and multiply it by the
corresponding element in X and then sum the results. We just have to
```

specify exactly which elements we want to multiply in X and in F, but actually we are using all of F so we only need to specify which elements of X to multiply with the corresponding elements of F. We do have to make sure that the elements are properly aligned so that the right elements of X and F are multiplied.

```
#We use the "*" operator here which is element-by-element multiplication.
If we start with x[1,1], then we need to cover the cells in the square-
shaped range x[1,1],  x[1,w], x[h,1], x[h,w]
#where h is the number of rows of F and w is the number columns of F.
When i=1, i:(i+h-1) is exactly the range of rows of x that is needed.
When j=1, j:(j+w-1) is exactly the range of columns that is needed. Thus,
x[i:(i+h-1), j:(j+w-1)] is the range of cells we want to multiply by F
to get the first element of the output feature. Taking the sum of
element-by-element multiplication gives a scalar which can be assigned to
y[i, j]. As we loop over i and j, we generate all the elements y[i, j]
for the output matrix.
      y[i, j] <- sum(x[i:(i+h-1), j:(j+w-1)] * f)#Multiply the slice of x
(the submatrix of x) by the filter f, element by element.
    }
  }
  return(y)
}
```

In our calculation of the forward-propagation equations, we will use correlation, and so we use the above Equations (15.1)–(15.4) as the calculations, and these equations can be written succinctly as

$$O = X \bowtie_c F \tag{15.5}$$

Later on, in our code for forward propagation, this will appear inside a loop as

```
output[,,k] <<- output[,,k] + corr2d(input[,,d], weights[,,d,k]) + bias[k]
```

15.5 Convolution of Input and Filter Matrices

Now that we have defined correlation, we will mention the convolution of two matrices. We won't actually be using convolution in our code, but we present it for completeness.

The convolution of the input matrix with the filter matrix is defined as the correlation of the input matrix with the transpose of the filter matrix (or the rotation of the filter matrix by 180°). That is, we perform the following correlation.

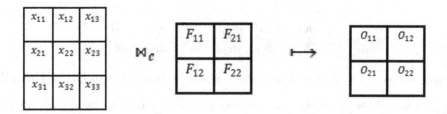

If we use the convolution symbol ⋈, then we don't need to show the transpose since this symbol implies taking the transpose of F before performing correlation (Figure 15.10).

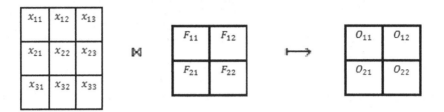

Figure 15.10   Convolution of input matrix and filter matrix.

Practice 15.5.2

1. Suppose we have an R function for the above operator called convo(). What parameters might you expect it to have?

Naturally, the elements of the output of convolution will be different than the elements of the output of correlation. It is left to the reader to check this.

15.5.1 *Calculations of the Gradient of J with Respect to F,* $\dfrac{\partial J}{\partial F}$

It was mentioned above that the trainable parameters in the convolutional layer are the elements of the filter matrix F. Thus, we seek $\dfrac{\partial J}{\partial \mathbf{F}}$. This is akin to $\dfrac{\partial J}{\partial \mathbf{W}}$ for the FC layer from last chapter since F is where the weights are located in a convolutional layer. As usual, the size of the gradient matrix is the same size as the matrix of weights. In our current example, $\dfrac{\partial J}{\partial \mathbf{F}}$ will be 2×2, and we will want a partial derivative with respect to each of the weights F_{ij}. The *chain rule* leads us to the following 4 expressions.

$$\frac{\partial J}{\partial F_{11}} = \frac{\partial J}{\partial O_{11}}\frac{\partial O_{11}}{\partial F_{11}} + \frac{\partial J}{\partial O_{12}}\frac{\partial O_{12}}{\partial F_{11}} + \frac{\partial J}{\partial O_{21}}\frac{\partial O_{21}}{\partial F_{11}} + \frac{\partial J}{\partial O_{22}}\frac{\partial O_{22}}{\partial F_{11}} \tag{15.6}$$

$$\frac{\partial J}{\partial F_{12}} = \frac{\partial J}{\partial O_{11}}\frac{\partial O_{11}}{\partial F_{12}} + \frac{\partial J}{\partial O_{12}}\frac{\partial O_{12}}{\partial F_{12}} + \frac{\partial J}{\partial O_{21}}\frac{\partial O_{21}}{\partial F_{12}} + \frac{\partial J}{\partial O_{22}}\frac{\partial O_{22}}{\partial F_{12}} \tag{15.7}$$

$$\frac{\partial J}{\partial F_{21}} = \frac{\partial J}{\partial O_{11}}\frac{\partial O_{11}}{\partial F_{21}} + \frac{\partial J}{\partial O_{12}}\frac{\partial O_{12}}{\partial F_{21}} + \frac{\partial J}{\partial O_{21}}\frac{\partial O_{21}}{\partial F_{21}} + \frac{\partial J}{\partial O_{22}}\frac{\partial O_{22}}{\partial F_{21}} \tag{15.8}$$

$$\frac{\partial J}{\partial F_{22}} = \frac{\partial J}{\partial O_{11}}\frac{\partial O_{11}}{\partial F_{22}} + \frac{\partial J}{\partial O_{12}}\frac{\partial O_{12}}{\partial F_{22}} + \frac{\partial J}{\partial O_{21}}\frac{\partial O_{21}}{\partial F_{22}} + \frac{\partial J}{\partial O_{22}}\frac{\partial O_{22}}{\partial F_{22}} \tag{15.9}$$

Focusing on the second *factor* in each *term* above, although there are 16 such factors, note they all are of the form $\dfrac{\partial O_{ij}}{\partial F_{kl}}$. What can be said about these? Referring to Equations (15.1)–(15.4) above, which give expressions for the 4 elements of the O matrix, we see, for example, that

$$O_{1,1} = F_{1,1}x_{1,1} + F_{1,2}x_{1,2} + F_{2,1}x_{2,1} + F_{2,2}x_{2,2}$$

and so in the first of the above four equations (Equation 15.6), we see that the second factor of the first term gives

$$\frac{\partial O_{11}}{\partial F_{11}} = x_{1,1}$$

Let us try the next term, which contains $\frac{\partial O_{12}}{\partial F_{11}}$. Here we need the expression for O_{12}.

$$O_{1,2} = F_{1,1}x_{1,2} + F_{1,2}x_{1,3} + F_{2,1}x_{2,2} + F_{2,2}x_{2,3}$$

From here, we can see that

$$\frac{\partial O_{12}}{\partial F_{11}} = x_{12}$$

Continuing with the 2 remaining terms in Equation (15.6), we find that

$$\frac{\partial O_{21}}{\partial F_{11}} = x_{2,1} \text{ and } \frac{\partial O_{22}}{\partial F_{11}} = x_{2,2}$$

Thus, we can rewrite Equation (15.6) as

$$\frac{\partial J}{\partial F_{11}} = \frac{\partial J}{\partial O_{11}}x_{11} + \frac{\partial J}{\partial O_{12}}x_{12} + \frac{\partial J}{\partial O_{21}}x_{21} + \frac{\partial J}{\partial O_{22}}x_{22} \tag{15.10}$$

It is left to the reader to confirm the remaining partial derivatives of J with respect to each of the weight matrices F_{ij}.

$$\frac{\partial J}{\partial F_{12}} = \frac{\partial J}{\partial O_{11}}x_{12} + \frac{\partial J}{\partial O_{12}}x_{13} + \frac{\partial J}{\partial O_{21}}x_{22} + \frac{\partial J}{\partial O_{22}}x_{13} \tag{15.11}$$

$$\frac{\partial J}{\partial F_{21}} = \frac{\partial J}{\partial O_{11}}x_{21} + \frac{\partial J}{\partial O_{12}}x_{22} + \frac{\partial J}{\partial O_{21}}x_{31} + \frac{\partial J}{\partial O_{22}}x_{32} \tag{15.12}$$

$$\frac{\partial J}{\partial F_{22}} = \frac{\partial J}{\partial O_{11}}x_{22} + \frac{\partial J}{\partial O_{12}}x_{23} + \frac{\partial J}{\partial O_{21}}x_{32} + \frac{\partial J}{\partial O_{22}}x_{33} \tag{15.13}$$

Recall that in our initial work on backpropagation in an earlier chapter, we were able to express a group of equations as a single matrix equation using matrix multiplication. We saw this again in this chapter in Equation (15.5) which expressed O as the correlation of X and F. It turns out that the above equations can also be expressed as a single matrix equation. Again the operation is correlation! You may check that the above 4 equations can be written as the following correlation.

x_{11}	x_{12}	x_{13}
x_{21}	x_{22}	x_{23}
x_{31}	x_{32}	x_{33}

$\bowtie_c$

$\dfrac{\partial J}{\partial O_{11}}$	$\dfrac{\partial J}{\partial O_{12}}$
$\dfrac{\partial J}{\partial O_{21}}$	$\dfrac{\partial J}{\partial O_{22}}$

$\rightarrow$

$\dfrac{\partial J}{\partial F_{11}}$	$\dfrac{\partial J}{\partial F_{12}}$
$\dfrac{\partial J}{\partial F_{21}}$	$\dfrac{\partial J}{\partial F_{22}}$

This can be written as

$$\frac{\partial J}{\partial F} = X \bowtie_c \frac{\partial J}{\partial O} \tag{15.14}$$

In our code below, this will be written inside a loop like this:

```
weights[,,d,k] <<- corr2d(input[,,d], output_error[,,k])
```

Practice 15.5.3

1. Where should the upper left-hand cell of the partial derivative of E with respect to O matrix be placed to generate this equation $\dfrac{\partial J}{\partial F_{21}} = \dfrac{\partial J}{\partial O_{11}} x_{21} + \dfrac{\partial J}{\partial O_{12}} x_{22} + \dfrac{\partial J}{\partial O_{21}} x_{31} + \dfrac{\partial J}{\partial O_{22}} x_{32}$?

15.5.2 Calculations of the Gradient of E with Respect to X, $\dfrac{\partial J}{\partial X}$

As was the case for the FC layer and the activation layer, $\dfrac{\partial J}{\partial X}$ is necessary for the convolutional layer as well. Recall it is needed to pass on to the next upstream layer (as was done in the previous chapter). Thus, it is necessary to calculate the gradient of J with respect to every input x_{ij}. Starting with $\dfrac{\partial J}{\partial x_{11}}$, we see that

$$\frac{\partial J}{\partial x_{11}} = \frac{\partial J}{\partial O_{11}} \frac{\partial O_{11}}{\partial x_{11}} + \frac{\partial J}{\partial O_{12}} \frac{\partial O_{12}}{\partial x_{11}} + \frac{\partial J}{\partial O_{21}} \frac{\partial O_{21}}{\partial x_{11}} + \frac{\partial J}{\partial O_{22}} \frac{\partial O_{22}}{\partial x_{11}} \tag{15.15}$$

Regarding the *second factor* in each of the *terms* above and recalling that O_{ij} is an element in the convoluted feature matrix (the output matrix), we note that not every element in the input matrix is connected to every element in the output matrix. In our simple example of the 3×3 input matrix, only 4 inputs connect to a particular O_{ij}. (That is to say, only 4 inputs are involved in the calculation of a particular O_{ij}.) For the above equation, check the diagrams in Figures 15.8 and 15.9 to see that x_{11} is only connected to O_{11}. Thus, we get

$$\frac{\partial J}{\partial x_{11}} = \frac{\partial J}{\partial O_{11}} F_{11} + \frac{\partial J}{\partial O_{12}} 0 + \frac{\partial J}{\partial O_{21}} 0 + \frac{\partial J}{\partial O_{22}} 0 \tag{15.16}$$

Using similar reasoning, we arrive at the following equations for the derivatives of J with respect to each of our 9 inputs to the convolutional layer.

$$\frac{\partial J}{\partial X_{12}} = \frac{\partial J}{\partial O_{11}}F_{12} + \frac{\partial J}{\partial O_{12}}F_{11} + \frac{\partial J}{\partial O_{21}}0 + \frac{\partial J}{\partial O_{22}}0 \tag{15.17}$$

$$\frac{\partial J}{\partial X_{13}} = \frac{\partial J}{\partial O_{11}}0 + \frac{\partial J}{\partial O_{12}}F_{12} + \frac{\partial J}{\partial O_{21}}0 + \frac{\partial J}{\partial O_{22}}0 \tag{15.18}$$

$$\frac{\partial J}{\partial X_{21}} = \frac{\partial J}{\partial O_{11}}F_{12} + \frac{\partial J}{\partial O_{12}}0 + \frac{\partial J}{\partial O_{21}}F_{11} + \frac{\partial J}{\partial O_{22}}0 \tag{15.19}$$

$$\frac{\partial J}{\partial X_{22}} = \frac{\partial J}{\partial O_{11}}F_{22} + \frac{\partial J}{\partial O_{12}}F_{21} + \frac{\partial J}{\partial O_{21}}F_{12} + \frac{\partial J}{\partial O_{22}}F_{11} \tag{15.20}$$

$$\frac{\partial J}{\partial X_{23}} = \frac{\partial J}{\partial O_{11}}0 + \frac{\partial J}{\partial O_{12}}F_{22} + \frac{\partial J}{\partial O_{21}}0 + \frac{\partial J}{\partial O_{22}}F_{11} \tag{15.21}$$

$$\frac{\partial J}{\partial X_{31}} = \frac{\partial J}{\partial O_{11}}0 + \frac{\partial J}{\partial O_{12}}0 + \frac{\partial J}{\partial O_{21}}F_{21} + \frac{\partial J}{\partial O_{22}}0 \tag{15.22}$$

$$\frac{\partial J}{\partial X_{32}} = \frac{\partial J}{\partial O_{11}}0 + \frac{\partial J}{\partial O_{12}}0 + \frac{\partial J}{\partial O_{21}}F_{22} + \frac{\partial J}{\partial O_{22}}F_{21} \tag{15.23}$$

$$\frac{\partial J}{\partial X_{33}} = \frac{\partial J}{\partial O_{11}}0 + \frac{\partial J}{\partial O_{12}}0 + \frac{\partial J}{\partial O_{21}}0 + \frac{\partial J}{\partial O_{22}}F_{22} \tag{15.24}$$

Is there a matrix representation of these equations? Yes, these 9 equations can be represented as a single matrix equation. However, the operation is not correlation or convolution but is a variation of convolution known as *full convolution* which we denote with $\bowtie_f$.

$$\frac{\partial J}{\partial X} = \frac{\partial J}{\partial O} \bowtie_f F \tag{15.25}$$

Practice 15.5.4

1. Suppose we have a convolution function called **convo**() that takes 2 arguments. Suppose that $\frac{\partial J}{\partial O}$ is called *output_error*, and suppose the matrix F is referred to as *weights* in your code. How would you express the above Equation (15.25) in your code?

Full convolution is illustrated in Figure 15.11. It differs from convolution as it begins by placing the filter matrix F *partially outside* the boundaries of the matrix dJ/dO. The full convolution operation will generate Equations (15.16)–(15.24).

Figure 15.11 **This shows the process of "full convolution". The filter matrix slides across the partial derivative matrix from left to right. Next, F would then be dropped down one row and begin in the far left position, and then F would be slid from left to right again and again dropped and slid from left to right.** *Only three positions for F are shown, but if the movments continue, there are 9 positions, generating the 9 equations.*

The visual for the first equation, (15.16), appears as the left set of cells in the Figure 15.11.

The first set of cells in Figure 15.11 is the visual representation of the fact that the only non-zero term in Equation (15.16) is $\dfrac{\partial J}{\partial O_{12}} F_{11}$. It is seen that there is only a single cell of intersection of filter matrix F with the $\dfrac{\partial J}{\partial O}$ matrix. Wherever there is no intersection, we get a 0 for the corresponding term in (15.16).

Next, we slide the matrix F to the right and obtain the second set of cells. There we see that the intersection produces $\dfrac{\partial J}{\partial O_{11}} F_{12}$ and $\dfrac{\partial J}{\partial O_{12}} F_{11}$. These are the two non-zero terms in Equation (15.17).

Next, to get the third equation above, Equation (15.18), we again slide F to the right one unit. This time there is one intersection in the diagram and one non-zero term in the equation. Next, F would then be dropped down one row and begin in the far left position and then would be slid from left to right again and again dropped and slid from left to right. Only three positions for F are shown in Figure 15.11, but if the movements continue, there are 9 possible positions for F, each generating one of the nine equations.

In our code, this is a rare time when we utilize a pre-built function from an R package. For full convolution, we use the **convolution**() function from the OpenImageR package. It will appear in our code, again inside a loop, like this:

```
in_error[,,d]  <<- in_error[,,d] +  convolution(output_
error[,,k],weights[,,d,k], "full")
```

We have now seen that both forward propagation and backpropagation of $\dfrac{\partial J}{\partial F}$ and $\dfrac{\partial J}{\partial X}$ can be expressed as a convolution of the appropriate matrices.

$$O = X \bowtie_C F \tag{15.26}$$

$$\frac{\partial J}{\partial F} = X \bowtie_C \frac{\partial J}{\partial O} \tag{15.27}$$

$$\frac{\partial J}{\partial X} = \frac{\partial J}{\partial O} \bowtie_f F \tag{15.28}$$

15.6 Further Details in Setting Up a CNN

We are not going to cover all the details for setting up a CNN. Our main point here is to point out that now that the neural network code has been coded in a modular OOP design, adding new types of layers can be done in a clean and efficient manner. Below, however, we will briefly mention some of the other concepts for a CNN.

15.6.1 Kernel

Kernel (also called filter) is a matrix that is used to find the feature of an image. Often a 4×4 or 3×3 matrix is used.

15.6.2 Depth

Depth corresponds to the number of filters we use for the convolution operation. We mentioned that we may employ a filter for detecting horizontal edges, another filter for detecting vertical edges, another for detecting $45°$ edges, and so on. If three filters are used, we say the depth is 3. This will also generate 3 separate feature maps. The feature maps are stacked next to each other to form an array. For example, if there are 3 filters, then the depth of the array would be 3. Each of the feature maps is 2D, but there would be 3 of them.

15.6.3 Stride

Stride controls how the filter convolves (slides) around the input volume (matrix). The amount by which the filter shifts between each snapshot is the stride. We have assumed so far that the stride is 1, but we could play with that number and perhaps the network would perform better. Additionally, the stride affects the size of the feature matrix. For example, imagine an 8×8 input matrix, a 2×2 filter, and a stride of 1. The size of the feature matrix will be 7×7. What happens if we increase the stride to 2? That means the first position of the upper left-hand side of the filter on the input matrix will be at the 1,1 position, but after the first stride (sliding of the filter), the filter will be at position 1,3; next at 1,5; and so on, and it will reach the right-hand side of the input matrix with just 4 snapshots. Thus, we will have fewer snapshots and therefore a smaller feature matrix and in this case, with a stride of 2, the size of the feature matrix will be 4×4.

15.6.4 Padding

Suppose we have an input matrix of size 6×6, a filter matrix of size 4×4, and a stride of 4. We would start at the 1,1 position and next move to the 1,5 position. At this point, the right-hand side of the filter matrix would be at 1,8 (if there were such a position), and so it would extend beyond the border of the input matrix. This would cause inconsistencies in the calculations. To avoid such inconsistencies we would have to stop taking snapshots before the left-hand side of the filter reached the right-hand side of the input matrix[4]. In such a case, extra cells, called padding, are added to the input matrix so that the dimensions are properly divisible (without a remainder, i.e., without extending beyond the border of the (padded) matrix). Usually, the extra cells have zeros in them. (Figure 15.12).

---

[4] A similar issue would arise when reaching the bottom of the input matrix.

0	0	0	0	0	0	0	0
0	0	1	1	0	0	0	0
0	0	0	1	1	1	0	0
0	0	0	0	1	1	1	0
0	0	0	0	1	1	0	0
0	0	0	1	0	0	0	0
0	0	1	1	0	0	0	0
0	0	0	0	0	0	0	0

Figure 15.12   Padding with 0s.

15.7 Code for CNN

We will stray from our policy of building almost all our functions and will use a few pre-built functions that can be found in R packages. We use the **convolution**() function from the OpenImageR package. The function will be used to perform the operation ⋈ we described above of the convolution of two matrices. We have written our own function, **corr2d**(), for the correlation of two matrices. Additionally we use the function **load.mnist**() from the deepnet R package, and we use **dummyVars**() function from the caret R package. In our discussion, we will need to refer to the layers of the network and also remember that the input matrix or output matrix or filter matrix may not be a matrix at all but actually a 3D array. We also use the word "layer" for the layers of the array. To avoid confusion, we will try to use the phrase "depth layer" for the layers of the array. Furthermore, our code includes the concept of channels. We are using the MNIST data in this chapter. These are grayscale images and not color. We mentioned that for color, the input volume (array) has 3 depth layers, RGB: red, green, and blue. We say that each depth layer is a separate channel. In our code below, we include the channel parameter (often denoted as "ch"), and so although we are not going to test it, the code should also work on the classification of color images as well.

```
#The packages listed below need to be installed.
library(OpenImageR)
library(deepnet)
library(caret)
library(sigmoid)
# Correlation function for two 2D matrices
corr2d <- function(x, f){
  h <- dim(f)[1]
  w <- dim(f)[2]
  y <- array(data=0, dim=c(dim(x)[1] - h + 1, dim(x)[2] - w + 1))
  for(i in 1:dim(y)[1]){
    for(j in 1:dim(y)[2]){
```

```
        y[i, j] <- sum(x[i:(i+h-1), j:(j+w-1)] * f)
    }
  }
  return(y)}
```

15.7.1 Base Class for Each Layer of CNN Structure

```
## Member variables
#input: input of a layer
#output: output of a layer

Layer <- setRefClass("Layer", fields = list(input="ANY",  output = "ANY"),
  methods = list(initialize = function(a,c) {
                            },
```
#Forward-propagation function: Notice the body of this function will be
left blank now but will be written in for derived classes. This is
standard OOP coding design. (ConvLayer, MaxPoolLayer, FCLayer,
ActivationLayer, FlattenLayer).
```
  forward_propagation = function(input) {
                            },
```
#Backpropagation function: Notice the body of this function will be left
blank now but will be written in for derived classes. This is standard
OOP coding design. (ConvLayer, MaxPoolLayer, FCLayer, ActivationLayer,
FlattenLayer).
```
  backProp_propagation = function(output_error, learning_rate) {
                            }
                            #We keep these 2 methods just for inheritance.
                            )
                        )
```

#Convolution layer class of CNN inherits base class layer.
For each block of image shape, the convolutional filter is applied.
The filter dimension is determined by kernel size.
#We now define the convolutional layer. Once defined, it can be added to
our network with net$add(ConvLayer(c(28, 28, 1), c(5, 5), c(5))). We see
that it expects 3 parameters, which as always will be found in the
"initialize" method.
#We can see, in the "initialize" method, that these are input_shape,
kernel_shape, and layer_depth. The value for input_shape is c(28, 28,
1).This means that our input data is a 28 × 28 × 1 array (also called
volume when talking about convolutional networks). These are the
dimensions of the images in pixels. Since they are grayscale and not
color, the last dimension is 1. If they were color, we would have a layer
for red, a layer for green, and a layer for blue, RGB.
#In the following code, we will have filters that are 3D. In our
explanation above, we mostly talked about flat filters of just two
dimensions. However, we also mentioned that multiple filters should be
used so as to capture different features (horizontal edges, vertical
edges, etc.). In the first convolutional layer, we use 5 filters
(=1 filter with layer depth of 5).
We are using dWeights and dBias to indicate the derivative of J with
respect to the weights and the bias, respectively.

15.7.2 *Convolutional Layer*

```
#Below we find the following parameters:
# input_shape: Generally speaking, shape means dimensions, and so this is
a vector which shows the dimensions of the input.
# input_depth: This will be the depth of the incoming input. If we are
talking about the first layer and the images are grayscale, then this
depth will be 1. If the images are color, then it would be 3 (1 for each
of the RGB layers).
# kernel_shape: kernel and filter are synonymous, and so this is a vector
that represents the dimensions of the filter.
# output_shape: A vector used in forward propagation that determines the
dimensions of the output of the convolutional layer. Remember that the
output volume will generally have fewer rows and columns than the input
but will have as many layers as does the filter.
# in_error: This is the error that our backpropagation method returns so
that it can be passed to the previous upstream layer for the previous
upstream layer's backpropagation calculation.
# dWeights: In our previous notation, this is dJ_dW, or we could also
call it dJ_dFilter.
# dBias: This is dJ_dBias.


ConvLayer <- setRefClass("ConvLayer", contains = "Layer",
                    fields = list(
                        input_shape = "ANY",
                  input_depth = "ANY",
                        kernel_shape =  "ANY",
                        layer_depth =  "ANY",
                        output_shape = "ANY",
                        weights = "ANY",
                        bias = "ANY",
                        in_error = "ANY",
                        dWeights = "ANY",
                        dBias = "ANY"
                        ),
                    methods = list(
                        initialize = function(input_shape, kernel_shape,
layer_depth){
#Initialize member variables.
#The dimensions of all member variables must be matched.
            input_shape <<- input_shape #Shape is the dimensions of
the input.
            input_depth <<- input_shape[3] # This is the depth of
the incoming array.
            kernel_shape <<- kernel_shape #Remember kernel and
filter are synonymous, and so this is the filter dimension.
            layer_depth <<- layer_depth[1]
#The output number of columns (NOC) will be the input NOC - the kernel
NOC + 1. #The output number of rows (NOR) will be input NOR - kernel
NOR + 1.
            output_shape <<- c(input_shape[1]-kernel_shape[1]+1,
            input_shape[2]-kernel_shape[2]+1, layer_depth[1])
#We are storing all the weights in one array. For example, if we
construct a layer with ConvLayer(input_shape =c(28, 28, 1), kernel_shape
=c(5, 5), and layer_depth =c(5))), then the weights array will have
```

dimensions 5 × 5 × 1 × 5. We start out with random weights. The data
parameter is filled with random values. The dimensions of the weight
array are assigned to the "dim" parameter of the array function.

```
                weights <<- array(data = runif(kernel_shape[1]*kernel_
shape[2]*input_shape[3]*layer_depth[1]), dim = c(kernel_shape[1], kernel_
shape[2], input_shape[3], layer_depth[1])) - 0.5
```

Practice 15.7.5

1. Why is bias 5 × 1 below? What is the 5 for and what is the 1 for?

```
                bias <<- array(data = runif(layer_depth[1]), dim =
c(layer_depth[1], 1)) - 0.5
                    },
```

#Forward-propagation method for convolutional layer

```
forward_propagation = function(input_data){
                    input <<- array(data = input_data, dim =
input_shape)
                    output <<- array(data = 0, dim = output_shape)
```

#Convolutional operations are performed for each image shape and region.
#layer_depth is 5 and input_depth is 1. Since the layer depth is 5, it
means we have five 2D filters. We also say that it is a five-layer array
or five-layer volume.

```
                for(k in 1:layer_depth){
                    for(d in 1:input_depth){
```

#The output array has 5 layers just as the filter layer had 5 layers. We
run the corr2d function on each layer separately and add that result to
the previous state of the output layer. We also add in the bias.

```
                    output[,,k] <<- output[,,k] +
corr2d(input[,,d], weights[,,d,k]) + bias[k]
                        }
                    }
```

#The output array is returned by this forward_propagation method.

```
                    return(output)
                },
```

#In the language of object-oriented programming (OOP), if one class
(convolutional layer in our case) inherits from another class (the
"grandfather" Layer class in our case) and if in the child class, we
rewrite a method that was in the grandfather class, that method is said
to be overridden. Thus, we are overriding the backward_propagation
function. We have done this many times in this chapter (without using the
word "overriding").

15.7.3 Backpropagation Method for Convolutional Layer

```
backProp_propagation = function(output_error, learning_rate){
                    in_error <<- array(data = 0, dim = input_shape)
#dWeights and dBias are set to 0
                    dWeights <<- array(data = 0, dim = c(kernel_
shape[1], kernel_shape[2], input_depth, layer_depth))
                    dBias <<- array(data = 0, dim = c(layer_depth,
1))
```

```
#Convolutional operations are performed for input_error for each layer of
the filter.
                              for(k in 1:layer_depth){
                                for(d in 1:input_depth){
#Next is where dJ_dX, from equation (15.28), is calculated. (Here it is
called in_error.)
#It is the convolution of dJ_dO and the filter. This means doing the
correlation of
in_error[,,d] <<- in_error[,,d] + convolution(output_error[,,k],
weights[,,d,k], "full")
dWeights[,,d,k] <<- corr2d(input[,,d], output_error[,,k])
                                }
dBias[k] <<- layer_depth * sum(output_error[,,k])
                                }
#Updating weights and bias
                weights <<- weights - learning_rate * dWeights
                bias <<- bias - learning_rate * dBias
                return(in_error)
                    }
                  )
)
```

15.8 Max Pooling Layer

Max pooling is an additional process (layer) that is performed in CNN. Here is an example. Suppose the input is a 4 × 4 matrix and that we have a 2 × 2 filter that we'll run over our input and suppose we use a stride of 2 (meaning that we move the filter 2 units before taking a new "snapshot" so that we won't overlap regions).

For each of the regions represented by the filter, we will take the **max** of that region and create a new, output matrix where each element is the max of a region in the original input.

Here is an example of max pooling. From each snapshot, we select the maximum of that group of cells (Figure 15.13).

We also want to record from which locations the maximum values were obtained. This is information is held in what is called the **mask** (Figure 15.14).

Max pooling is typically applied after a convolutional layer, and it is applied to the output of the convolutional layer. That is, it is applied to the feature map. Also remember that the output of a convolutional layer can be, and usually is, an array with multiple depth layers (multiple feature maps). Thus, we will need to run max pooling on each of the depth layers, and its output will have the same number of depth layers.

Figure 15.13   2 × 2 max pooling. The underlined values are the largest in their blocks. Thus, they are the ones that appear in the new layer. Note that in this diagram, the filter itself is not shown. However, the filter is of the same size as the output.

Figure 15.14   This shows the mask based on the figure 15.13. The ones show the location of the maximum values for each snapshot.

The introduction of a pooling layer is used to reduce the size of data. It also has other benefits such as reduction of what is called *overfitting* of the model.

What is overfitting? Generally, in modeling, we say that although there is a relationship between the inputs and outputs of our data, there is also some noise in the data which can distort our ability to see that relationship and distort our ability to extract that relationship. Overfitting means learning the random noise in the data and thereby missing the "true" relationship between inputs and outputs. Max pooling can help to reduce this.

There are three types of pooling methods – they are max pooling, average pooling, and min pooling. Max pooling takes the input data and outputs the maximum value from the input data. Average pooling takes the average of the input data, and min pooling takes the minimum.

It is said that max pooling is a type of sampling, and thus, with large datasets and large networks, max pooling can reduce computational cost by reducing the number of weights to be learned. It is usually applied to non-overlapping regions (as we did here). If the pooling is being applied to a multi-channel image, the pooling for each channel should be done separately.

Practice 15.8.6

1. What parameter can be increased to reduce the size of the output of the pooling layer?

15.8.1 Coding the Max Pooling Layer

```
#Max pooling layer class inherits from the base class we called Layer.
# For each block of image shape the max pixel value is obtained.
# The filter dimension is determined by an initial parameter. Since the
filter is a square, we only need to specify one value.

# The member variables
##kernel_sh: the size of one of the dimensions of the filter. Since it is
a square we only need one dimension.
## stride: the number of pixels by which we slide our filter matrix over
the input matrix
MaxPoolLayer <- setRefClass("MaxPoolLayer", contains = "Layer",
  fields = list(kernel_sh = "numeric", stride = "numeric", mask = 'ANY'),
  methods = list(initialize = function(kernel_sh, stride){
  kernel_sh <<- kernel_sh # Initialize kernel (filter) size. This will be
a scalar. In our example below, it is 4. This means the kernel is 4 × 4.
  stride <<- stride     # initialize stride
                },
```

Practice 15.8.7

    1. We will create two max pooling layers both with the same type of call: **MaxPoolLayer**(4, 2)). What does the 4 stand for, and what does the 2 stand for?

```
#Overridden forward-propagation function
#Notice output, input, and mask are global, while ch, f, s, h_old,
w_old, h_new, and w_new are local.
 #Output values and mask values should be saved and modified through
iterations, and that is how training works.
 #ch, f, s, h_old, w_old, h_new, and w_new don't need to be saved.
That's why they are local.
forward_propagation = function(input_data){
 input <<- input_data # Put input data into input. In Figure 15.13, it
was the 4 × 4 matrix.
 ch <- dim(input)[3]    # Put image channel size into channel size.
 f <- kernel_sh         # Put kernel_sh into local variable f.
 s <- stride            # Put stride into local variable s.

# Input dimension of this layer. We use "_old" to indicate that these
are the dimensions we are starting with, but part of the point of max
pooling is to reduce the size of the data, and so the old dimensions
will be converted to new dimensions (and we will use "_new" to store
those).
 h_old <- dim(input)[1] # put input image height into h_old
 w_old <- dim(input)[2] # put input image width into h_old

#Output dimension of this layer. If h_old=8 and stride=2, then h_new=4.
Ceiling is used to round off the result.
h_new <- ceiling((h_old) / s)        # Calculate output height.
w_new <- ceiling((w_old) / s)        # Calculate output width.

output <<- array(data=0, dim=c(h_new, w_new, ch)) #Initialize output
variable with all zeros.
#mask will be the same size as the original input data. It will be used
to record which elements of the input volume (array) contained the
maximum value for that snapshot.
mask <<- array(data=0, dim=c(h_old, w_old, ch))    #Initialize mask
variable with all zeros.

# get max value for each slice(block)
#We first need to focus on an individual snapshot area (call it subarea),
and then we will get the max value from within the cells of that area.
Slices are used to get subareas of the input image from which you are
going to get max value.
 for(k in 1:ch){ # Iterate through channels.
    for(i in 1:h_new){ # Iterate through the image height.
       for(j in 1:w_new){ # Iterate through the image height.
          #i1 and i2 are the upper row number and lower row number for the
subarea.
j1 and j2 are the upper and lower column numbers for the subarea.
          i1 <- (i - 1) * s + 1    #For example, when i=1 (the first
iteration of the loop) and suppose the stride, s, is 2, then we get
# (1-1)*2 +1 =1 as the first row of the subarea.
```

```
        i2 <- i1 + s - 1 #Given the example values above, this is 2.
        if( i2 > h_old ) i2 <- h_old #If we have moved beyond the last
value of the input volume's greatest column number, then just set the
last column to the greatest column number. This is our (slightly
imperfect) way of dealing with what to do when we get to the border and
actually slide off the border.
        j1 <- (j - 1) * s + 1
        j2 <- j1 + s - 1
        if( j2 > w_old ) j2 <- w_old
        slice <- input[i1:i2, j1:j2, k] # Now we have the boundaries
of the subarea. Use them to subset (also called slice) the input
(volume). The k is the channel number - meaning the depth layer. Remember
that we have allowed input to have more than one depth layer, and this
shows up in the fact that input has 3 dimensions - input[ , , ].
#We are currently in a nested set of loops, and the values for each
loop index are i, j, and k. We fill in this position of the output
matrix.
        output[i, j, k] <<- max(slice) # Put max value into output.
#Remember that which() returns an index.
# which(slice == max(slice) returns the index (in the form of i, j, and k
) if the maximum value of our slice (subarea).
        max_coord <- which(slice == max(slice), arr.ind = TRUE)
# Calculate the coordinate of the max value.
#The expression below looks like it is some sort of multiplication, but
that is not correct. Multiplication needs some operation symbol (like *).
This is subsetting. It is taking a matrix, and
#before looking at this line, let us quickly review this with an example.
```

15.8.2 Quick Review of Arrays

```
arraySample <- array(1:24,dim = c(4,3,2))
arraySample
## , , 1
##
##      [,1] [,2] [,3]
## [1,]    1    5    9
## [2,]    2    6   10
## [3,]    3    7   11
## [4,]    4    8   12
##
## , , 2
##
##      [,1] [,2] [,3]
## [1,]   13   17   21
## [2,]   14   18   22
## [3,]   15   19   23
## [4,]   16   20   24
arraySample[1:2,2:3,1]
##      [,1] [,2]
## [1,]    5    9
## [2,]    6   10
arraySample[1:2,2:3,1][2,1] #This is not multiplication.
## [1] 6
```

15.8.3 Now Returning to the Code

```
mask[i1:i2, j1:j2, k][max_coord[1], max_coord[2]] <<- 1
# Put 1 into mask's max coordinate.
                }
            }
        }
return(output)
```

15.8.4 Backpropagation for Max Pooling

What will backpropagation look like? We are seeking dJ_dX. The input matrix is larger than the output matrix. The chain rule, dJ_dX = dJ_dY * dY_dX, although not exactly correct for matrices, gives us a roadmap for how to think about dJ_dX. We are given dJ_dY (output_error), and so we only need to work out dY_dX where Y is the output volume of our max pooling layer and X is the input volume of our max pooling layer. Remember that Y consists of a bunch of maximums from subareas of X. Let's focus on X. Some of the x's from X are the maximums of their subareas and some (most) are not. Suppose x_{cd} is a max of its subregion and y_{mn} is the corresponding (equal) value in the output volume. Then $dy_{mn}\_dx_{cd}$ will be 1 since the input and output are the same. To understand this, recall that in a *linear* layer, the derivative dy_dx is the weight that multiplies x to get y. That is dy_dx=w when y=wx. But is max pooling a linear layer? Yes. Each output value can be obtained from the dot product of the x's from the subarea and weights which are either 1 or 0 depending on whether the corresponding x is the max or not of that subarea. Thus, $dy_{mn}\_dx_{cd}$ will be 1, and $dy_{mn}\_dx_{ij}$ for any other x_{ij} in the subarea will be 0. In fact, we have shown that dY_dX is actually the mask. Now what about dJ_dX? dJ_dX will be the mask times dJ_dY, and dJ_dY is given to us.

```
#Our backProp_propagation function will take the output_error (dJ_dY from
upstream) and the learning rate as its arguments. It will return the
input_error (dJ_dX) to be passed on to the next (downstream) layer.
#In our code, the MaxPoolLayer will be place after a ConvLayer. The first
ConvLayer has layer_depth of 5, and the second ConvLayer has a depth of
10. These will be the channel sizes in the MaxPoolLayers.
    backProp_propagation = function(output_error, learning_rate){
        ch <- dim(output)[3] # Put output channel size into ch.
        s <- stride # Put stride into local variable s.
        #Output dimensions of this layer.
        h_old <- dim(output)[1]                  # height of output
        w_old <- dim(output)[2]                  # width of output

#Input dimensions of this layer
        h_new <- dim(input)[1] # height of input
        w_new <- dim(input)[2] # width of input

        in_error <- array(data = 0, dim = dim(mask)) # Initialize in_error
with 0.
# Reverse pooling operation.
            for(k in 1:ch){# iterate through channels
#We iterate through the output rows and columns.
                for(i in 1:h_old){
                    for(j in 1:w_old){
```

```
#i1 and i2 form the (row-based) boundaries of the current subarea of the
input matrix. j1 and j2 form the (column-based) boundaries of the current
subarea of the input matrix.
                          i1 <- (i - 1) * s + 1
                          i2 <- i1 + s - 1
#If we go beyond the lowest row of the input matrix, then adjust i2 to be
the lowest row number.
                          if( i2 > h_new ) i2 <- h_new
                          j1 <- (j - 1) * s + 1
                          j2 <- j1 + s - 1
#If we go beyond the highest column of the input matrix, then adjust j2
to be the highest column number.
                          if( j2 > w_new ) j2 <- w_new
                          slice <- mask[i1:i2, j1:j2, k] # get slice
                          max_coord <- which(slice == max(slice), arr.ind =
TRUE) # Calculate the coordinate of the max value.
#Remember that in_error was set to all zeros a few lines above. Now we
will replace some of those zeros with output_error, but for most of the
zeros, we will leave them as zero. This accords with our statement above:
dJ_dX will be the mask times dJ_dY, and dJ_dY is given to us.
                          in_error[i1:i2, j1:j2, k][max_coord[1], max_
coord[2]] <- output_error[i, j, k]    # Replace in_error's max coordinate
values with output_error's corresponding values.
                                    }
                                }
                            }
#Now we return dJ_dX.
                                return(in_error)
                            }
                        )
)
```

15.8.5 Coding the FC Layer

```
FCLayer <- setRefClass("FCLayer", contains = "Layer",
                        fields = list(
                            input_size = "numeric",
                            output_size = "numeric",
                            weights = "matrix",
                            bias = "matrix",
                            input_error = "ANY",
                            weights_error = "ANY"
                            ),
            methods = list(initialize = function(input_size, output_size)
{weights <<- matrix(runif(input_size*output_size, -1, 1), input_size,
output_size)bias <<- matrix(runif(output_size, -1, 1), 1, output_size)
                            },

forward_propagation = function(input_data){
                            input <<- input_data
                            output <<- (input %*% weights) + bias
                            return(output)
                        },
```

```
backProp_propagation = function(output_error, learning_rate){
                        input_error <<- output_error %*% t(weights)
    #We use matrix() to convert train_x slice to vector format.
    weights_error <<-matrix(input) %*% output_error
#Here you had a mistake also. We need to subtract learning_rate*error
from the original weights.
    weights <<- weights - (learning_rate * weights_error)
  #same for the bias
    bias <<- bias - (learning_rate * output_error)
                        return (input_error)
                    }
                  )
                  )
#Activation layer
#member variables
#  activation: name of the activation function
#  activation_prime: name of the derivative function of the activation
function
ActivationLayer <- setRefClass("ActivationLayer", contains = "Layer",
                    fields = list(
                        activation = "function",
                        activation_prime = "function"
                    ),
  methods = list(initialize = function(a, c){
                        activation <<- a
                        activation_prime <<- c
                    },
  forward_propagation = function(input_data){
                        input <<- input_data
                        output <<- activation(input_data)
                        return(output)
                    },
  backProp_propagation = function(output_error, learning_rate){

    return(activation_prime(input) * output_error)
                    }
                  )
                  )
```

15.9 Flatten Layer

There are points in the network where we want to have a vector as input. This is required when the layer that follows is an FC Layer. Often, a FC layer will follow a pooled layer. Thus, we need to take the output of the pooled layer and transform it to a vector. This is a simple operation. It is called flattening because we take the pooled feature map and "unravel" it into a "flat" vector as shown below. Notice that the matrix on the left and the vector on the right contain exactly the same elements. There is no modification to, or reduction of, the elements themselves. Only the shape is changed (from matrix or array to vector) (Figure 15.15).

Even when the previous layer contains an array with more than one layer as below, we can still apply a flattening process. The picture below is *illustrative only*, as the number of entries on the right does not appear to be the same as the number of entries on the left, but in fact, the process of flattening does not reduce the number of elements (Figure 15.16).

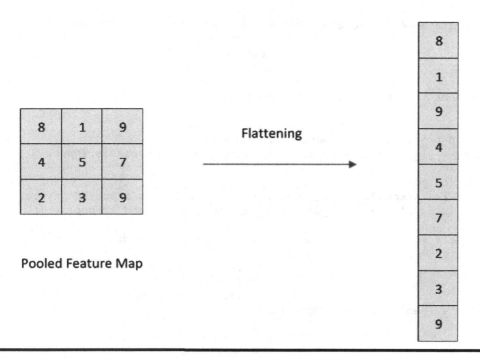

Figure 15.15 **The process of flattening as applied to a single matrix. The output of the flattening layer can be fed into a standard neural network layer since the output is a vector.**

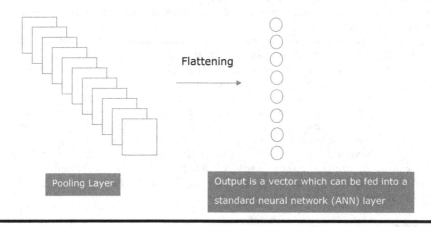

Figure 15.16 **The process of flattening when applied to a volume consisting of more than one matrix.**

As seen in Figure 15.16, we have multiple pooled feature maps from the previous step which are then transformed into a single vector or one-column matrix.

```
#FlattenLayer of CNN - structure inherits from the base class
Layer.#Dimension transformation function. We transform the input matrix
into a n × 1 column-like matrix
```

```r
FlattenLayer <- setRefClass("FlattenLayer", contains = "Layer",
                            fields = list(
                                output = "ANY",
                                input = "ANY"
                            ),
  methods = list(initialize = function(){
                            },

forward_propagation = function(input_data){
input <<- input_data #Put input_data into member variable input.

return(output)
output <<- array(data = t(input[,,1]), dim = length(input))#Convert the
first layer of the input_data into array of n × 1 and transpose it.

#If there are more layers in the input volume, concatenate all of them into
one large vector. Use dep as an index for the depth of the input volume.
                            if(dim(input)[3]>1){
                                for (dep in 2:dim(input)[3]){
                                    output <<- c(output,array(data =
t(input[,,dep]), dim = length(input)))
                                }
                            }

                            return(output)
                            },
```

#Next, we code the backpropagation method for this flatten layer.
#Backpropagation will accept the output_error (= dJ_dY) and return input_
error (= dJ_dX). The learning_rate is not used here because there are no
"learnable" parameters.
#What is dJ_dX? As usual we recall the chain rule as a roadmap for what
is needed: dJ_dX = dJ_dY * dY_dX. (Our usual caution is that the "*" here
needs to be the appropriate type of multiplication and thus depends on
whether we are talking about matrices or scalars, and it could be matrix
multiplication or Hadamard multiplication.) As usual again, since we are
given dJ_dY, we only need to calculate dY_dX. Again, when we write dY_dX,
both Y and X are **matrices**, but we focus on their elements and consider
dy_dx. Now in the flatten layer, all we are doing is taking each element
from the input volume and copying it to an element in the output vector.
Thus y = x and dy_dx is 1 for each x. With this line of reasoning, it
should be clear that dY_dX is a matrix of 1s and that therefore (from the
chain rule above) dJ_dX equals dJ_dY.

Practice 15.9.8

1. Why do we need to take the transpose of the output_error? What is the shape of output_error?

```r
#Convert the output error into array and transpose it.
backProp_propagation = function(output_error, learning_rate){
input_error <<- array(data = t(output_error), dim = dim(input))
                return(input_error)
                }
            )
#end of backpropagation for the flatten layer
```

```
tanh_prime <- function(x){
  return(1 - tanh(x)^2)
}
sigmoid_prime <- function(x){
  return (sigmoid(x)*(1-sigmoid(x)))
}
```

Practice 15.9.9

1. Why don't we use the plus operator, +, instead of the concatenate operator, c(), to join together all the layers of the input in the forward-propagation method of the flatten layer?

```
#We won't use relu or it's derivative in this CNN, but we define it here
for the possible use to construct alternative network architectures.
relu_prime <- function(x){
  len <- length(x)
  result <- array()
  for (i in 1:len) {
    if(x[i]>0)
      result[i] <- 1
    else result[i] <- 0

  }
  return (result)
}
#Mean square error function (mse) as the Loss function
mse <- function(y_true, y_pred){
  return(mean(y_true - y_pred)^2)
}

#Derivative of mse function used for backpropagation

mse_prime <- function(y_true, y_pred){
  return(2*(y_pred - y_true) / length(y_true))
}
```

15.10 Network Class

Almost done! Finally, we create a Network class!

15.10.1 Coding the Network Class in R

```
Network <- setRefClass("Network", fields = list (layers = "list",
                                                  loss = "ANY",
                                                  loss_prime = "ANY",
                                                  err = "numeric",
                                                  error = "ANY",
                                                  errPredict="ANY"),
                        methods = list(
                          initialize = function(){
```

```
#layers as list: This means that whatever architecture we choose for our
CNN, the choice of our layers will be stored in this list called layers.
We initialize it here with just an empty list, but then we define an
add() method which will simply add new layers to this list.
                        layers <<- list()
#loss and loss_prime are set to 0s here, but these will be updated in the
backpropagation method.
                        loss <<- 0
                        loss_prime <<- 0
                    },
#add() function gives the ability to add new layers to the layers list.
  add = function(lay){
layers[[length(layers)+1]] <<- lay
                    },
#Next define the use() method.
#The use() method allows us to set the loss function we want to use. We
have not discussed other possible loss functions, but there are several
candidates. We have been using the mse loss function in previous
chapters. (We called it JCost.) mse stands for mean squared error and is
the most common loss function in statistics. It goes by other names as
well such as quadratic loss or L2 loss. Another possible candidate for
the loss function is the mean absolute error (MAE). Another called the
hinge loss (also called the multiclass SVM loss) is used for
classification of losses. Yet another loss function for classification is
the cross-entropy loss - lots of fancy names for mostly simple concepts.
("Cross-entropy" is a bit complicated.)
By defining this use() method, we make it easy to substitute a different
loss function. The use of a different loss function would affect the
performance of the network, possibly improving performance, and so it is
advisable to test various loss functions.
#Here is how we call the use() method:
# net$use(mse, mse_prime)
#Define the use() method by simply assigning the arguments to their
global counterparts.
                        use = function(loss, loss_prime){
                          loss <<- loss
                          loss_prime <<- loss_prime
                        },
```

Practice 15.10.10

1. Above, we defined an object called layers. (This is not the Layer class defined earlier.) What type of object is it?
2. After layers is defined, the add() function (defined just above here) manipulates it. In a few pages, we will see lines of code like net$add(ConvLayer(c(28, 28, 1), c(5, 5), c(5))). After this line is run, will layers still be an empty list or how will it have changed?
3. What does a single example look like for the MNIST data? What is it an example of? What are its dimensions?
4. Below, you will see a line like this: for (layer in layers){ . What is the index of this loop?
5. Add a browser() statement after this statement: for (i in 1:samples){ . Run the entire code. Rstudio should stop at the browser statement. As you hit the enter key, RStudio will, step by step, proceed through the code. The first time you hit the enter key it will run

the browser() statement itself (because it actually stops just before the browser() statement), and the next time you hit the enter key it will run the next line, and so on. Before hitting the enter key the second time, you can put the statement dim(input_data[[i]]) into the console, and you will get the answer to part (i) below. What are the dimensions of the following?

   i. input_data[[i]]
   ii. matrix(input_data[[i]])
   iii. t(matrix(input_data[[i]]))

6. In the function predict(), is the data being pushed through in a batch or example by example?

15.10.2 *Predict Method*

```
#This method will be called with test rather than training data. We call
it after our network is trained. We use the predict method on the test
data to measure how the network is performing on the training data. To
see how the network is performing on the first 100 elements of our test
data, we would call it like this:
# net$predict(x_test[1:100])
                    predict = function(input_data){

#We need to know how many elements we will be testing in the test set
because this will determine the number of iterations needed in the loop
below. This number will be denoted as samples.
                    samples <- length(input_data)
#Create a list to hold the predicted values.
#Later we convert it to a dataframe.
                    result <- list()
#We will need a variable to store our error.
                    errPredict <<- 0
#Loop through samples.
                    for (i in 1:samples){
                    output = t(matrix(input_data[[i]]))
#With each sample, we send it through the network, and thus we have to
loop through layers as well. (This loop is nested within the loop above.)
The sample is referred to as "output" and was defined just above.
                    for (layer in layers){
# It's a little bit clumsy here, but we call the input to this forward
propagation "output", and we also call the output of the forward
propagation "output".
                    output = layer$forward_propagation(output)
                    }
#We will round our predictions to 5 decimal places.
    result[[i]] <- round(output, 5)
#result[[i]] is more or less the yield of the forward propagation and
is thus the prediction (what we have called yhat in past chapters).
We want to compare this with the ground truth label y_test. We use
the selected loss function to do this calculation and then update
errPredict.
    errPredict <<- errPredict + loss(result[[i]], y_test[[i]])
                    }
#Calculate average error.
    errPredict <<- errPredict / samples
    print(paste("The prediction error is: ", (errPredict)))
```

```
result <-
as.data.frame(matrix(unlist(result),nrow=length(unlist(result[1])))))

return(t(result))
            },
```

15.10.3 Training the Network – the fit() Method

```
#We call this method "fit" which refers to the task of fitting the model
to the data.
  fit = function(x_train, y_train, epochs, learning_rate){
#The number of samples is the number of rows for training.
  samples <- length(x_train)
#Loop through the number of epochs.
    for (i in 1:epochs){
#Assign the global variable err to 0.
        err <<- 0
#Loop through the number of samples.
          for (j in 1:samples){
```

```
#t(matrix(slice)) - we use t() because after slicing and converting a
slice to matrix, R automatically transposes the result, and so we have to
take the transpose again to get it back to its original shape.
              output = t(matrix(x_train[[j]]))
              for (layer in layers){
```

```
#This next statement is one of the most powerful results of our choice to
use OOP and modularization of the code. What is forward_propagation here?
We have defined so many different forward-propagation methods; which one
is it? Is it forward_propagation for the FCLayer, for the ConvLayer, for
the ActivationLayer, or for MaxPoolLayer? It is all of these! In the
current loop, we are looping through the list of layers. Above we used
the add() function to add layers to the list layers. Now layers is the
list of the layers in our neural network. Thus, in the statement below,
layer$forward_propagation accesses the forward_propagation method for the
current layer in our loop!
              output = layer$forward_propagation(output)
              }
```

```
#update errors
#Here we are updating the error. The error is measured using the loss
function.
```

Practice 15.10.11

1. Suppose y_train[[500]] = c(1,0,0,0,0,0,0,0,0,0). What is the digit being drawn in the 500th example?
2. Suppose output = c(.2, .3 , .4, .1, .2, .2, .3, .1, .1, .2). What digit is implied by this output?
3. Assuming we are using mse for the loss function, what will be the measure of the loss if the output for the j = 500th sample is as in question number 2 above?

```
        err <<- err + loss(y_train[[j]], output)
        error <<- loss_prime(y_train[[j]], output)
```

```
#Loop through the layers in reverse order for backpropagation, with each
iteration performing the necessary procedures. For example, in layers
```

where there are weights, the weights will be updated. In all the layers,
dJ_dX will be calculated.

```
                            for(layer in rev(layers)){
                                error <<-layer$backProp_propagation
(error, learning_rate)
                                }
                            }
#Calculate average error.
err <<- err / samples
#Print a string to track model training.
 print(paste("Epoch num", i, "/", epochs, "; Error:", (err)))
                                }
                            }
                        )
                        )
```

15.11 Getting the Data Ready

The MNIST database of handwritten digits, currently available from the page http://yann.lecun.com/exdb/mnist/, has a training set of 60,000 examples and a test set of 10,000 examples. It is a subset of a larger set available from NIST. The digits have been size-normalized and centered in a fixed-size image. MNIST dataset consists of images of digits from 0 to 9, each of size $28 \times 28 \times 1$.

It is a good database for testing learning techniques and pattern recognition methods on real-world data while spending minimal efforts on preprocessing and formatting.

We use MNIST database to train and test our network.

15.11.1 Loading MNIST Data with R

The following code loads the MNIST data and puts it into local variables (Figures 15.17 and 15.18).

```
#Load mnist data.
#The files are obtained from http://yann.lecun.com/exdb/mnist/.
The files there are zipped using the .gz format (not the more familiar
.zip format). You can still unzip them in the normal way, and they must
be unzipped. There are 4 files. When they are unzipped, they appear like
those in Figure 15.17.
However, the names need to be changed in order for our code to work. The
dot needs to be changed to a hyphen so that they look like those in
Figure 15.18.
```

Figure 15.17   MNIST files after unzipping but before changing the name.

Figure 15.18   MNIST files after unzipping after changing the name.

```
Otherwise you will get an error message like this:
Error in file(filename, "rb") : cannot open the connection
In addition: Warning message:
```

```
#The directory for the location of the mnist data should be set
correctly.
#Assuming the data is in the working directory
dir = getwd()
mnist <- load.mnist(dir)
x_train <- mnist$train$x      #Put training image into x_train variable.
y_train <- mnist$train$y      #Put training label into y_train variable.
x_test <- mnist$test$x        #Put test image into y_train variable.
y_test <- mnist$test$y        #Put test label into y_train variable.
```

We are trying to put the data into a format which we can use in our predict() and fit() methods. As we mentioned above, y_train (and y_test) needs to be a list that contains the labels for each of the examples in the training (and testing) dataset. Initially, when we load the data with the function above, load.mnist() y_train will look like

```
str(y_train)
 int [1:60000] 5 0 4 1 9 2 1 3 1 4 ...
```

This means that the *label* for the first example in the training set is 5, the label for the second example in the training set is 0, and so on. However, as we mentioned above, we want to get it into the format of a list containing 10-element vectors like 0 0 0 1 0 0 0 0 0 0. The next few pages show how this is done.

```
# Normalization of image values
x_train <- x_train / 255
x_train <- array(data = x_train,
                 dim = c(dim(x_train)[1], 28, 28, 1))
#We have yet to cover the use of anonymous functions, but the following
code makes use of them.
```

15.11.2 Anonymous Functions

An anonymous function is a function which is defined *and* used at the same time. Normally, we define a function with a name and then insert the behavior like this: myFunctionName<-function(){write behavior here}. Then we use (call) the function later with myFunctionName(). When an anonymous function is used, we just write the following.

function() write behavior here

There is no name for the function, and there are no brackets used to encase the behavior. The function does not have a name and so is called an anonymous function.

Our intention is to use it immediately and not at some other point in the code, and so it does not need a name to refer to it at some future point in the code.

Recall that the lapply() function typically "applies" a function to some object with syntax like apply("some object", function). We use lapply(), below but the function is not some pre-existing function but rather an anonymous function we define directly within the lapply() function.

Practice 15.11.12

1. What type of object is returned by lapply()? A vector, a matrix, a dataframe, or something else?
2. Suppose p is the 4×6 matrix, matrix(1:24, nrow=4). What is p[2,]?
3. What type of object is p[2,]?
4. Suppose p is a 4D array with dimensions $2 \times 3 \times 4 \times 2$. What type of object is p[2, , ,]?

```
#Note: below we use the seq() function. seq(m) gives the same result as
the R code:  1:m
#x_train has been obtained directly from minst$train$x. This is a 4D
array. Checking str(x_train) shows this since the result is num [1:60000,
1:28, 1:28, 1].
#Recall that lapply will output a list.
#Thus, the following statement will output a list with 6000 elements, and
each element will be a 3D array.
x_train <- lapply(seq(dim(x_train)[1]), function(x) array(data =
x_train[x, , , ], dim = c(28, 28, 1)))
x_test <- x_test / 255
x_test <- array(data = x_test,
                dim = c(dim(x_test)[1], 28, 28, 1))
x_test <- lapply(seq(dim(x_test)[1]), function(x) array(data =
x_test[x, , , ], dim = c(28, 28, 1)))


y_train <- as.factor(y_train)           ### Encode data as a factor.
y_train <- data.frame(y_train)          ### Create dataframes.
```

15.11.3 Dummy Variables

The subject of dummy variables is a topic in statistics, and it may be good to spend some time with a statistics text to understand it fully. But we will cover it briefly here.

The y values, for both y_train and y_test, are the elements of the set {0, 1, 2, ..., 9}. Although they appear to be numeric variables, really they are just 10 different categories that are the 10 different classes of our class variable. They do not function as numeric variables, meaning we don't apply numeric operations like addition, subtraction, multiplication, and so forth on them. They are in fact categorical variables. Therefore, we have transformed y_train and y_test to factors.

Here is a view of the first 5 elements of y_train (Figure 15.19).

Next, we create a set of new variables based on the elements of y_train. We mentioned earlier that we would like each label to be in the form of a 10-element vector like 0 0 0 1 0 0 0 0 0 0. That is, for example, instead of the label "3", we want the label to look like 0 0 0 1 0 0 0 0 0 0. For the label "0", we will use 1 0 0 0 0 0 0 0 0 0. Thus, we have some work to do. The typical way to handle

Figure 15.19 y_train contains the labels for the elements of x_train.

original variable	newVar1	newVar2	newVar3	newVar4	newVar5	newVar6	newVar7	newVar8	newVar9	newVar10
5	0	0	0	0	0	1	0	0	0	0
0	1	0	0	0	0	0	0	0	0	0
4	0	0	0	0	1	0	0	0	0	0
1	0	1	0	0	0	0	0	0	0	0
9	0	0	0	0	0	0	0	0	0	1

Figure 15.20 Transform the representation of a variable which originally had 10 levels to 10 new binary variables. This is called "one-hot encoding" or "creating dummy variables". For example, the first row shows that the original value of 5 is now expressed in terms of the 10 new "dummy" variables as 0000010000 and 4 is expressed as 0000100000.

this is to create a new variable for each possible value of the original variable. (The original variable is shown in Figure 15.19.) We have 10 different possible values for the original variable. Therefore, we will create 10 new binary (0/1) variables. The picture looks like Figure 15.20.

To represent the first value, 5, we use 0s and 1s in the 10 newly constructed variables. This is typically done in the context of modeling and represents a technique for handling categorical variables. As mentioned above, we will not go into the topic in detail especially because here, we are only considering performing this to reformat our data. We are using a function in the R caret package called dummyVar() which is designed for the purpose of modeling, but as we said, we are actually just using it to reformat our data and so not in the way it is typically used. But since dummyVar() makes it easy to get this 0/1 representation of the labels, we use it and hope that the designers of caret will not be angry. This technique goes by the name "one-hot encoding" or "creating dummy variables".[5]

Below we use the dummyVars() function to create the list of new variables and then use a second line of code to convert our original y_test data to the new representation. This involves a caret function called predict() which is *not* related to our predict() method. We won't go into the details here, but the interested reader can review the caret package to arrive at a fuller understanding of these 2 lines of code.

```
dm <- dummyVars(" ~ .", data=data.frame(y_train))
#Create full set of dummy variables.
```

---

[5] In the traditional dummy variable method, if there are n levels in the categorical variable, then there would be n − 1 new variables created rather than n new variables created.

```
y_train <- data.matrix(predict(dm, newdata = y_train))# Obtain matrix by
converting all the variables in a dataframe to numeric mode.
y_train <-  lapply(seq(nrow(y_train)), function(x) array(data =
y_train[x, ], dim = c(1, 10)))  #Apply functions over y_train.

y_test <- as.factor(y_test)  #Encode data as a factor.
y_test <- data.frame(y_test) #Create dataframes.
dm <- dummyVars(" ~ .", data=data.frame(y_test)) #Create full set of
dummy variables.
y_test <- data.matrix(predict(dm, newdata = y_test)) #Obtain matrix by
converting all the variables in a dataframe to numeric mode.
y_test <-  lapply(seq(nrow(y_test)), function(x) array(data =
y_test[x, ], dim = c(1, 10))) #Apply functions over y_test.
```

15.12 Building Neural Networks

Finally! Now we have the tools to flexibly design CNN architectures.

In this experiment, we built our network with the following architecture.

List of layers we will use. Note that the reader may try experimenting with other architectures by adding additional layers or removing some layers.

Layer 1	Convolutional layer
Layer 2	Max pooling layer
Layer 3	Convolutional layer
Layer 4	Max pooling layer
Layer 5	Flatten layer
Layer 6	FC layer
Layer 7	Activation layer
Layer 8	FC layer
Layer 9	Activation layer

```
#Run a CNN.
net <- new("Network")
net$add(ConvLayer(c(28, 28, 1), c(5, 5), c(5)))
#We won't add an Activation layer yet.
net$add(MaxPoolLayer(4, 2))
net$add(ConvLayer(c(12, 12, 5), c(5, 5), c(10)))
net$add(MaxPoolLayer(4, 2))
net$add(FlattenLayer())
net$add(FCLayer(4*4*10, 80))
net$add(ActivationLayer(sigmoid, sigmoid_prime))
net$add(FCLayer(80, 10))
net$add(ActivationLayer(sigmoid, sigmoid_prime))
net$use(mse, mse_prime) # Set loss function as minimum square error.
net$fit(x_train[1:1000], y_train[1:1000], epochs=10, learning_rate=0.02)
## [1] "Epoch num 1 / 10 ; Error: 0.0422055078025024"
## [1] "Epoch num 2 / 10 ; Error: 0.00830806778482087"
## [1] "Epoch num 3 / 10 ; Error: 0.00735704870922104"
## [1] "Epoch num 4 / 10 ; Error: 0.00851585327934148"
## [1] "Epoch num 5 / 10 ; Error: 0.00130752358489207"
```

```
## [1] "Epoch num 6 / 10 ; Error: 0.000496195020275294"
## [1] "Epoch num 7 / 10 ; Error: 0.000508413273418541"
## [1] "Epoch num 8 / 10 ; Error: 0.000478143950713281"
## [1] "Epoch num 9 / 10 ; Error: 0.000457436194834232"
## [1] "Epoch num 10 / 10 ; Error: 0.000408494945447802"
```

The mse can roughly be used to indicate the percentage error, and so we can see that the CNN is incorrectly classifying about 4 out of 10,000 handwritten digits. However, this is on the training data. To properly evaluate the algorithm, we apply it to test data. We will do that shortly.

Practice 15.12.13

1. In each of the add() statements above, we are adding a layer. What in our class definition determines how many arguments are needed to construct a particular layer? For example, what in the class definition of max pooling determines that we need 2 arguments in **MaxPoolLayer**(4, 2) when we add the max pooling layer?
2. What are the parameters (not arguments) in the following construction of the convolutional layer?

```
add(ConvLayer(c(12, 12, 5), c(5, 5), c(10)))
```

Note: In writing this code, it is important to realize that the code may run even though there are errors in it. In fact, it may even perform well with the errors. This would easily lead the coder to accept the code as correct. However, by meticulous review of the code, you may find that errors may still exist, and this will lead to far better results. In fact, this situation occurred in the author's writing of the text. The above results were obtained when the FlattenLayer code looked like this:

```
FlattenLayer <- setRefClass("FlattenLayer", contains = "Layer",
                            fields = list(
                                ou = "ANY" ),
```

In other words, there was a typo where "ou" was supposed to be *output*, and additionally the parameter *input* was not declared in the fields list. It was only with careful review that the code was updated since it already appeared to run well. However, with this update, the results significantly improved as did the speed of execution.

```
[1] "Epoch num 1 / 2 ; Error: 0.00668546288761649"
[1] "Epoch num 2 / 2 ; Error: 0.000123137465943509"
[1] "Epoch num 3 / 10 ; Error: 0.000101427268278542"
[1] "Epoch num 4 / 10 ; Error: 9.0226086896785e-05"
[1] "Epoch num 5 / 10 ; Error: 7.90758048840167e-05"
[1] "Epoch num 6 / 10 ; Error: 5.88974346822353e-05"
[1] "Epoch num 7 / 10 ; Error: 2.51778874290376e-05"
[1] "Epoch num 8 / 10 ; Error: 7.5288551691289e-06"
[1] "Epoch num 9 / 10 ; Error: 3.57684291855527e-06"
[1] "Epoch num 10 / 10 ; Error: 2.42716374108034e-06"
```

And this higher accuracy continued beyond what is shown here.

15.12.1 Test on the Test Data

However, we have not tried the trained network on the test data yet. To see how the network performs on the test data, we use our predict method. We will place the statement

```
net$predict(x_test[1:100])
```

inside the definition of the **fit**() method, just after this line:

```
print(paste("Epoch num", i, "/", epochs, "; Error:", (err)))
```

Now if we rerun **fit**() method with something like this

```
net$fit(x_train[1:1000], y_train[1:1000], epochs=5, learning_rate=0.05)
```

we will see that the model performs well on the test data as well. The statements about prediction refer to the test data here.

```
## [1] "started"
## [1] "Epoch num 1 / 5 ; Error: 0.00180209922856268"
## [1] "The prediction error is:  0.000522716769"
## [1] "Epoch num 2 / 5 ; Error: 0.0003367772855047"
## [1] "The prediction error is:  0.000282139208999999"
## [1] "Epoch num 3 / 5 ; Error: 0.000162616202981466"
## [1] "The prediction error is:  0.000111830625"
## [1] "Epoch num 4 / 5 ; Error: 0.000111693151333251"
## [1] "The prediction error is:  9.34702240000001e-05"
## [1] "Epoch num 5 / 5 ; Error: 0.000105619567691381"
## [1] "The prediction error is:  8.9984196e-05"
```

Practice 15.12.14

1. We have come to a remarkable place in our understanding and coding skills. We have used the powerful OOP programming paradigm and we have also learned how to code a powerful neural network algorithm.
2. Can you find a way to reconstruct the MNIST data from x_train so that you can see the original handwritten image of a digit? You can use any functions that you find in R or on the web.

Chapter 16

R Packages for Neural Networks, Deep Learning, and Naïve Bayes

R Naïve Bayes packages: e1071 and naivebayes

R Neural Network package: neuralnet

Almost every machine learning algorithm used in practice is available as a package in R. One package called caret includes many different algorithms all under one unified set of commands, and so once you learn how to make predictions with one of the algorithms within caret, the interfaces (calls to set up the classifier, to predict, etc.) are all similar within caret.

Practice 16.0.1

1. Look up caret, and list at least 4 algorithms that it makes available.

We will look into Naïve Bayes and neural network packages in this chapter.

16.1 Naïve Bayes

The Naïve Bayes algorithm we implemented falls under the category of multinomial Naïve Bayes algorithms. The term "multinomial" is employed because we have developed an algorithm for a nominal (categorical) class variable and because we have not limited ourselves to class variables with just 2 levels. If the class variable is binary (having exactly 2 levels), then the Bayes algorithm would be referred to as a Bernoulli Naïve Bayes algorithm.

We will explore two Naïve Bayes algorithm packages. One comes from a package with the somewhat off-putting name of *e1071*. The other package we will explore is called *naivebayes*. Both of these can easily be installed into RStudio using either the install packages option under the tools menu in RStudio or by using the function install.packages() like this:

install.packages("e1071")
install.packages("naivebayes")

389

Both algorithms use a similar set of commands to run them.

1. First you tell them what the variables you are using are. You say which is the class variable and which are the predictor variables. You also say on which data you want to run this. In this step, you create the model, and so in general you would want to use the training data for this first step.
2. The second step is to take the model that you create in the first step and use it to make predictions. Generally, again, we would like to make predictions on the test data, and so we use the test data in this second step.

The first step is accomplished with a function called **naiveBayes**() in the *e1071* package and using **naive_bayes**() in the *naivebayes* package. For the second step, both packages use a function called **predict**(). (Maybe we should have called our function **predict** as well.)

The format for entering the arguments when creating the model (this is in the first step since that is where we create the model) is fairly standard in R. We, of course, as we said, need to identify the input variables and also the output variable. For example, in our Arthritis data, we used "Treatment" as the output variable and "Sex" and "Improved" as the input variables. For many packages, this would be written like this:

Treatment ~ Sex + Improved

And this would be entered into the two first-step functions like this:

naiveBayes(Treatment ~ Sex + Improved, …)
naive_bayes(Treatment ~ Sex + Improved, …)

We also have to say which data we are using, and that is entered after the comma. If it is called *train*, we would write

naiveBayes(Treatment ~ Sex + Improved, train)
naive_bayes(Treatment ~ Sex + Improved, train)

In general, if there are input variables V1, V1, V3, …, Vn and if the output variable is Y, we would write

naiveBayes(Y ~ V1 + V2 + V3 + … + Vn, … train)
naive_bayes(Y ~ V1 + V2 + V3 + … + Vn, … train)

Most probably, this notation comes from the first modeling algorithm (historically speaking), linear regression, where we try to find a linear function that relates the input variables to the output variable. Some R packages use other syntax for entering the variables, and in fact the *naivebayes* package allows for other syntax, but we will stick with this. It would be a good exercise to rewrite our Naïve Bayes algorithm to accept this syntax.

The syntax for the predict function is the same for both packages and will give the predicted class for each individual in the test set. (The naivebayes package has an additional option for generating probabilities of each level of the class variable for each individual of the test set.) For example, if we use step 1 to assign the model to a variable nb like this:

nb = **naiveBayes**(Treatment ~ Sex + Improved, train) #for *e1071*
nb = **naive_bayes**(Treatment ~ Sex + Improved, train) #for *naivebayes*

then for *either* package, we can write

predict(nb, test, type = "class")

For the *naivebayes* package, we can also do

predict(nb, test, type = "prob")

to get the probabilities.

We now show the code to run these and also to compare the results with the code for Naïve Bayes that we constructed in earlier chapters. We will use a modification of the model described above for the *naivebayes* package. Instead of the **naive_bayes**() function, we will build our model with an alternative function from this package, **multinomial_naive_bayes**(), since this is closer to the algorithm we created.

16.1.1 R Code for Running Naïve Bayes Packages

We will list the code for our algorithm from Chapter 8 first as it is necessary to have it in order to do a comparison with the package algorithms.

```
#install.packages("mlbench","mice")
library(mlbench)
library(mice)
library(naivebayes)
library(e1071)
intersect_event=function(a,b,df=df){
  return(df[intersect(a$names,b$names),])}

union_event=function(E,F){
  if(!is.data.frame(E)|!is.data.frame(F)){
    stop("arguments must be a dataframe")
  }
  return(unique(rbind(E,F)))}
multi_union_event=function(E,F,...){return(unique(rbind(E,F,...)))}
complement=function(a,df){
  df[!a,]
}
probBxconditional_prob= function(a,b,s){
  return(prob(intersect_event(a,b,s),s))}
prob<-function( e,  s) {
  return(nrow(e)/nrow(s))}
probAdj<-function( e,  s) {
  if (nrow(e)==0){
    return(nrow(e)+1/nrow(s))
  } else {
    return(nrow(e)/nrow(s))}
}
```

```
bool2event<-function(E_bool,df){return(df[E_bool,])}

conditional_prob=function(a,b,s){
  return(prob(intersect_event(a,b,s),s)/prob(b,s))
}
conditional_prob_bool <- function(varPrior, varPriorLevel, varCondition,
varConditionLevel, df){
  prior_bool <- df[,varPrior] == varPriorLevel
  prior_event <- df[prior_bool,]
  condition_bool <- df[,varCondition] == varConditionLevel
  condition_event=df[condition_bool,]
  return(prob(intersect_event(prior_event,condition_event,df),df)
/prob(condition_event,df))
}
prob_from_params <- function(inputVarName, inputVarLevel, className,
classLevel){
  condMatrix=paste("cond_params",inputVarName,sep="_")
  return(eval(parse(text=paste(condMatrix,'[classLevel,inputVarLevel]',
sep = "")))))
}
library(vcd)
data("Arthritis")
imputeddf=mice(Arthritis,m=1,maxit=50,meth='pmm',seed=500)
completedData <- complete(imputeddf,1)
df=completedData
df$names<-rownames(df
NaiveBayes_singleClassEllipsis=function(className="Class",classValue="dem
ocrat",dfparam=df, ...){
  dfparam=as.data.frame(dfparam)
  dfparam$names<-rownames(dfparam)
  args<-list(...)
  count <- length(args)
  class_bool=dfparam[,className]==classValue
  classE=dfparam[class_bool,]
  numerator=probAdj(classE,dfparam)
  for(i in 1:count){

    numerator=numerator*prob_from_params(names(args)[i],args[[i]],classNa
me,classValue)
  }
  denominator=0
  classLevels=levels(dfparam[,className])
  countOfClassLevels=length(classLevels)
  for(j in 1:countOfClassLevels){
    class_bool=dfparam[,className]==classLevels[j]
    classE=dfparam[class_bool,]
    denominatorFactor=prob(classE,dfparam)
    for(i in 1:count){
denominatorFactor=denominatorFactor*prob_from_params(names(args)[i],args[
[i]],className,classValue)
    }
    denominator=denominator+denominatorFactor
  }
  return(numerator/denominator)
```

```
}
dfparam=df
predNaiveBayes=function(class="Class",dfparam=df,percentSplit=0.7, ...){
  smp_size <- floor(percentSplit * nrow(dfparam))
  train_ind <- sample(seq_len(nrow(dfparam)), size = smp_size)
  train <- dfparam[train_ind, ]
  test <- dfparam[-train_ind, ]
  dfparam=train
dim1 <- list()
  dimnames1 <- list()
  colname <- colnames(dfparam)
  colname <- colname[!is.element(colname, c(class,"names"))]
  for (i in 1:length(colname)) {
    dim1 <- list()
    dimnames1 <- list()
    dim1 <- length(levels(as.factor(dfparam[, class     dim1 <-
append(dim1, length(levels(as.factor(dfparam[, colname[i]])))))
    dimnames1[length(dimnames1) + 1] <-
      list(c(levels(as.factor(dfparam[, class]))))
    dimnames1[length(dimnames1) + 1] <-
      list(c(levels(as.factor(dfparam[, colname[i]]))))
    classnames <- c(levels(as.factor(dfparam[, class])))
    varnames <- c(levels(as.factor(dfparam[, colname[i]])))
    x <- array(1:prod(dim1),
                dim = c(dim1),
                dimnames = dimnames1)
    for (j in 1:length(classnames)) {
      for (k in 1:length(varnames)) {

        x[classnames[j],varnames[k]] <- conditional_prob_bool(colname[i],
arnames[k],class,classnames[j],df)
      }

    }

    assign(paste('cond_params', colname[i], sep = "_"), x, pos =
".GlobalEnv")
  }
  dfparam=test

  forecast=list()
  argsPred=list(...)
    lev=levels(dfparam[,class])
  classprob=0
  predictedclass=lev[1]
  for(i in lev){
    p=NaiveBayes_singleClassEllipsis(class,i,dfparam,...)
    if(classprob<p){
      classprob=p
      predictedclass=i
      forecast[["Instance"]]=argsPred
      forecast[["predicted class"]]=predictedclass
      forecast[["probability of predicted class (if independence
assumption is true)"]]=classprob
```

```
    }
  }
  return(forecast)
}
predNaiveBayes("Treatment",Arthritis, Sex='Female',Improved='Some')
## $Instance
## $Instance$Sex
## [1] "Female"
##
## $Instance$Improved
## [1] "Some"
##
##
## $`predicted class`
## [1] "Placebo"
##
## $`probability of predicted class (if independence assumption is true)`
## [1] 0.6538462

library(vcd)
library(mice)
data("Arthritis")
dfparam=Arthritis
imputeddf=mice(Arthritis,m=1,maxit=50,meth='pmm',seed=500)
completedData <- complete(imputeddf,1)
dfparam=completedData
dfparam=as.data.frame(dfparam)
The new code follows.
```

Begin testing new packages here.

```
#Begin the testing.
compare_Bayes_packages <- function(seed=8, percentToSplit=0.7){
  resultList<-list()
  set.seed(seed)
  percentSplit<-percentToSplit
  smp_size <- floor(percentSplit * nrow(dfparam))
  train_ind <- sample(seq_len(nrow(dfparam)), size = smp_size)
  train <- dfparam[train_ind, ]
  test <- dfparam[-train_ind, ]
  nrow(test)
  nrow(train)
  vectorOfTestPredictions<-NULL
  vectorOfTestActual<-NULL #As an exercise, try making this a list
instead of a vector and redoing the rest of this function
correspondingly.

  #Using our home-built algorithm,
  #loop through all of test data.
  for(i in 1:nrow(test)){
    vectorOfTestActual[i]<-test$Treatment[i]

    vectorOfTestPredictions[i] <- predNaiveBayes("Treatment",test, Sex=
test[i,3],Improved=test[i,5])$`predicted class`
```

```
}
#Note that 2 stands for treatment.
table(test[,2])
accuracy_our_algorithm<-sum(test[,2]==vectorOfTestPredictions)/
nrow(test)


#e1071 package

NBclassfier<-naiveBayes(Treatment~Sex+Improved, data=train)
testPrede1071<-predict(NBclassfier, newdata = test, type = "class")
accuracy_e1071_package<-sum(test[,2]==testPrede1071)/nrow(test)


#naivebayes package with multinomial version of Naïve Bayes
#This requires a different syntax for the inputs to the model building
step.
#You can check the help file for this. We need a matrix for the input
variables.
inputMatrixTrain<-matrix(cbind(Sex=train$Sex,Improved=train$Improved),
ncol = 2)
colnames(inputMatrixTrain)=c("Sex","Improved")
inputMatrixTest<-matrix(cbind(Sex=test$Sex,Improved=test$Improved),ncol
= 2)
colnames(inputMatrixTest)=c("Sex","Improved")
nb <- multinomial_naive_bayes(inputMatrixTrain, train$Treatment)
testPrednaivebayes<-predict(nb, inputMatrixTest, type = "class")
accuracy_naivebayes_package<-sum(test[,2]==testPrednaivebayes)/
nrow(test)

resultList<-list(accuracy_our_algorithm,accuracy_e1071_package,
accuracy_naivebayes_package)
names(resultList)=c("our algorithm","e107 package", "multinomial
naivebayes package")
return(resultList)
}
compare_Bayes_packages(6,.7) #Note that the results change with the value
of the seed.

## $`our algorithm`
## [1] 0.6153846
##
## $`e107 package`
## [1] 0.5384615
##
## $`multinomial naivebayes package`
## [1] 0.3461538
```

Practice 16.2.2

1. Try to get the same printout of vectorOfTestActual, but make it a list instead of the way it is currently defined as a vector.
2. Explain why it is important to use the same set.seed value for the data split when testing using our code and when testing using the Naïve Bayes packages.
3. If you change the set.seed value, is there any similarity in the values of vectorOfTestActual? Explain why there is some similarity.

4. Why does 2 stand for "Treated" and not for "Placebo"? How did this happen?

5. As you see, vectorOfTestActual is showing the vector of the test data of the "Treatment" in each individual of our test data. Can you coerce the output of test$Treatment[i] so that vectorOfTestActual is a vector of the labels so it looks something like

```
vectorOfTestActual
##  [1] "Treated" "Treated" "Treated" "Treated" "Treated" "Treated" "Treated"
##  [8] "Treated" "Treated" "Treated" "Treated" "Treated" "Placebo" "Placebo"
## [15] "Placebo" "Placebo" "Placebo" "Placebo" "Placebo" "Placebo" "Placebo"
## [22] "Placebo" "Placebo" "Placebo" "Placebo" "Placebo"
```

instead of the following?

```
vectorOfTestActual
##  [1] 2 2 2 2 2 2 2 2 2 2 2 2 1 1 1 1 1 1 1 1 1 1 1 1 1 1
```

6. Add in the additional variable age into the analysis, and test how much of an increase (or decrease) there is in the accuracy of each of the algorithms.

7. Explain each line of the code in **compare_Bayes_packages**()

16.2 R Package: neuralnet

Next we explore the neural network package called *neuralnet*.

You can read more about the neuralnet by searching for the R package neuralnet. The pdf located here is useful: https://cran.r-project.org/web/packages/neuralnet/neuralnet.pdf.

To build the network model, we will go through the following two steps. First a function called **as.formula**() is used. Again, it requires that we tell it what the output variable is and what the input variables are. It asks us to provide this in the same format as was done in the previous section. Again, the output variable is separated from the input variables with the tilde symbol "~", and the names of the input variables are separated by a plus "+" sign. Using our mood data, this looks like

```
f <- as.formula(mood ~calories_burned + hours_of_sleep)
```

After this step, we put f into the **neuralnet()** function.

```
nn<-neuralnet(f,data=train,hidden=c(3,5),linear.output=T)
```

The **neuralnet**() function has quite a number of possible arguments. Here is the full version.

```
neuralnet(formula, data, hidden = 1, threshold = 0.01, stepmax = 1e+05,
rep = 1, startweights = NULL, learningrate.limit = NULL, learningrate.
factor = list(minus = 0.5, plus = 1.2), learningrate = NULL, lifesign =
"none", lifesign.step = 1000, algorithm = "rprop+", err.fct = "sse", act.
fct = "logistic", linear.output = TRUE, exclude = NULL, constant.weights
= NULL, likelihood = FALSE)
```

The url to the pdf above describes them all, but let us consider a few of them here. All of the arguments represent various options that researchers have experimented with in order to possibly improve the performance of the neural network.

formula: A symbolic description of the model to be fitted. We saw an example above as f.

hidden: A vector of integers specifying the number of hidden neurons (vertices) in each layer. In the example above with hidden = c(3,5), we would have two hidden layers with 3 and 5 nodes, respectively.

threshold: A numeric value specifying the threshold for the partial derivatives of the error function as stopping criteria. In our networks, we specified how many epochs to run. An alternative approach is to let the network continue training until the derivative gets small enough. We can define what "small enough" is with a threshold value.

algorithm: In our neural networks, we employed the backpropagation algorithm for training the weights. There are other possibilities. The following types are possible: "backprop", "rprop+", "rprop-", "sag", or "slr". "backprop" refers to backpropagation, and "rprop+" and "rprop-" refer to the resilient backpropagation with and without weight backtracking, while "sag" and "slr" induce the usage of the modified globally convergent algorithm (grprop). See details for more information.

err.fct: This is the error function. We used sse (sum of squared error). Another option here is ce (cross-entropy).

act.fct: The activation function used. We can see that the default value is "logistic" which is our sigmoid curve.

Notes

Note the neuralnet() function is actually creating an instance of the neuralnet class. In our code below, this instance is called "nn". Thus, we may expect to see calls to the methods of this class like nn$backprop() (assuming there is a method called backprop()). However, a slightly different style is used here. If there were a backprop(), then we may see something like backprop(nn,).

As we saw just above, the neuralnet() function, which is creating the instance nn of the neuralnet class, takes various arguments. The data argument is the name of the dataframe. Here we are using "train". The hidden() argument allows us to define the architecture of the hidden layers. In the above example, we have indicated two hidden layers, the first one with 3 nodes and the next with 5. The argument linear.output is used to indicate whether we want to do regression linear.output =TRUE or classification linear.output =FALSE. Note that all the neural networks we have constructed in earlier chapters were regression models, and the mood data we are using has a numeric output variable and therefore will also require a regression model.

16.2.1 R Code for neuralnet Package

As before, we split the data for training and testing sets with 75% for the training set as before. The training set and testing set are stored together as two elements of a list, and after a few more steps, we store both in trainAndTest=**trainTestSplit()** .

```
trainTestSplit<-function(dataset="mood"){
  #Sample call:
  #trainAndTest=trainTestSplit(mood)
  #train =trainAndTest[["train"]]
  #test  =trainAndTest[["test"]]
  smp_size <- floor(0.75 * nrow(dataset))
  #set.seed(315)
  train_ind <- sample(seq_len(nrow(dataset)), size = smp_size)

  train <- dataset[train_ind, ]
```

```
    test <- dataset[-train_ind, ]
    returnedList=list(train,test)
    returnedList<-setNames(returnedList, c("train","test"))
    return(returnedList)
}
```

Mood data is used in this example.

```
mood <- read.csv("exercise_mood.csv")
```

On checking the names of the columns, we see that one of them is a date.

```
colnames(mood)
## [1] "date"            "step_count"      "mood"            "calories_burned"

## [5] "hours_of_sleep"  "bool_of_active"  "weight_kg"
```

As we are using packages in this example, we also use a pre-built R function to normalize our data. The function used is **scale**(). According to the help section,

> Scale is generic function whose default method centers and/or scales the columns of a numeric matrix.

It would not be surprising if **scale**() did not work well with date data, and in fact, if we use it on date data, we get an error like this:

Error in scale.default(mood, center = mins, scale = maxs - mins): length of 'center' must equal the number of columns of 'x'

Therefore, first remove the date field.

```
mood <- mood[,-1]
colnames(mood)
## [1] "step_count"      "mood"            "calories_burned"  "hours_of_sleep"
## [5] "bool_of_active"  "weight_kg"
```

Scaling is often performed to map the entire range of data for a particular attribute to either of the intervals [−1,1] or [0,1]. Both of these intervals seem to improve the performance of neural networks as compared with leaving the data unscaled. We will map to [0,1] for this example. This means we want to take the minimum of the set of values of the attribute and map it to 0 and the maximum number of the set of values of the attribute and map it to 1. All the other values are mapped proportionately between 0 and 1. Scale has a *center* parameter and a *scale* parameter (a bit awkward to have a parameter with the same name as the function itself).

To better understand this function, we will experiment with a simple matrix.

```
x <- matrix(1:10, ncol = 2)
x
##       [,1] [,2]
## [1,]    1    6
## [2,]    2    7
## [3,]    3    8
```

```
## [4,]    4    9
## [5,]    5   10
Xmaxs <- apply(x, 2, max) #Use the apply function. The 2 as the second
argument means applying across the second dimension (the columns) to get
the max of each column.
Xmins <- apply(x, 2, min)
Xmaxs
## [1]  5 10
Xmins
## [1] 1 6
#Note: Below is an R shortcut for printing. Placing everything inside
parentheses causes R to print out whatever is in the parentheses.
#In the first example, with no parameters set except the scale parameter
(which is set to false), the default action is to center around 0. With
the scale = FALSE, there is no reduction in the length of the range
of the values of the attribute. (The range was originally from 1 to 5
for the first column and ends up from -2 to 2.)
(centered.x <- scale(x, scale = FALSE))
##        [,1] [,2]
## [1,]   -2   -2
## [2,]   -1   -1
## [3,]    0    0
## [4,]    1    1
## [5,]    2    2
## attr(,"scaled:center")
## [1] 3 8
#In this next example, each column of x has the corresponding value from
center subtracted from it. For the scale parameter, each column of x is
divided by the corresponding value from scale. To find out more about the
scale() function, see the "Details" section of its help file. Remember,
to see the help file, type "?scale" at the console prompt.
(center.half <-scale(x, center = Xmins, scale = Xmaxs - Xmins))
##        [,1] [,2]
## [1,] 0.00 0.00
## [2,] 0.25 0.25
## [3,] 0.50 0.50
## [4,] 0.75 0.75
## [5,] 1.00 1.00
## attr(,"scaled:center")
## [1] 1 6
## attr(,"scaled:scale")
## [1] 4 4
```

Now we return to our mood data. If we set the center attribute to the minimum, this will subtract the minimum from each column, and this will cause the smallest value of the result to be zero (Figure 16.1).

```
maxs <- apply(mood, 2, max)
mins <- apply(mood, 2, min)
maxs
##      step_count              mood calories_burned  hours_of_sleep
##            7422               300             243               9
##   bool_of_active        weight_kg
##             500                66
```

```
mins
##       step_count              mood calories_burned  hours_of_sleep
##               25               100               0               2
##  bool_of_active        weight_kg
##                0               64

scaled <- as.data.frame(scale(mood, center = mins, scale = maxs - mins))
#We can see the maximums and minimums have been scaled to 0 and 1,
respectively.
max(scaled["calories_burned"])
## [1] 1
min(scaled["calories_burned"])
## [1] 0
max(scaled["hours_of_sleep"])
## [1] 1
min(scaled["hours_of_sleep"])
## [1] 0
max(scaled["mood"])
## [1] 1
min(scaled["mood"])
## [1] 0


trainAndTest=trainTestSplit(scaled)
train =trainAndTest[["train"]]
inputs=train[,c("calories_burned","hours_of_sleep")]

outputs=train[,"mood"]
library(neuralnet)

f <- as.formula(mood~calories_burned+hours_of_sleep)
nn<-neuralnet(f,data=train,hidden=c(3),linear.output=T)
plot(nn)
#Printout from plot(nn)
#Note that there is one bias node in each layer with a weight for each
node in the next layer.

test =trainAndTest[["test"]]
colnames(test)
## [1] "step_count"      "mood"            "calories_burned"  "hours_of_sleep"
## [5] "bool_of_active"  "weight_kg"
#We apply compute to the test set.
#Compute returns a list containing the following components.
#neurons: A list of the neurons' output for each layer of the neural
network
#net.result: A matrix containing the overall result of the neural network
pr.nn <- compute(nn,test[,3:4]) #We could use predict((nn,test[,3:4]).
head(pr.nn) #Only some of the printout is shown below. Most of it has
been removed to save space.
## $neurons
## $neurons[[1]]
##      calories_burned hours_of_sleep
## 7  1       0.57613169      0.5714286
## 10 1       0.16460905      0.5714286
## 92 1       0.01646091      0.0000000
```

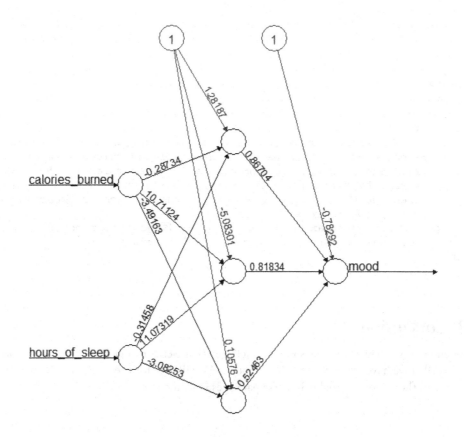

Error: 5.249257 Steps: 636

Figure 16.1   The neural network as depicted in the neuralnet package.

```
##
## $neurons[[2]]
##      [,1]        [,2]        [,3]        [,4]
## 7      1 0.03970419 0.14525599 0.9929803

## 92     1 0.43428650 0.55350759 0.3472065
##
```

#The $net.result element contains the output of the neural network. We
have called this yHat in our previous work. We can see that the result is
based on the normalized input data and thus is in some sense normalized.
We want to denormalize it so that we can interpret the values as mood
scores.

```
## $net.result.
##          [,1]
## 7    0.6550576
```

#We are leaving out most of the printout here.

```
## 92 -0.2310684
```

#With the following denormalization, we can see the predicted mood
scores.

```
pr.nn.denormalized <- pr.nn$net.result*(max(mood$mood)-min(mood$mood))
+min(mood$mood)
```

```
head(pr.nn.denormalized)
##        [,1]
## 7   231.0115
## 10  222.4276
## 14  228.6496
## 15  216.0941
## 23  202.1477
## 24  217.1497
#Take the mood attribute from the test set and denormalize it. Then find
the difference between the actual and the predicted values (test.r -
pr.nn.denormalized), square it, sum over all the examples in the test
set, and average by dividing by the number of elements in the test set.
This is called the MSE (mean squared error) and is a common measure of
accuracy (error) for regression data.
test.r <- (test$mood)*(max(mood$mood)-min(mood$mood))+min(mood$mood)
MSE.nn <- sum((test.r - pr.nn.denormalized)^2)/nrow(test)
MSE.nn
## [1] 6696.39
```

16.3 Conclusion

In this chapter, we have explored some R packages that perform machine learning algorithms similar to what we have covered in earlier chapters. A challenge for the reader would be to implement some of the options available in these packages within our code.

Index

Printed in the United States
By Bookmasters